Postcolonial Theory

Postcolonial Theory

Contexts, Practices, Politics

———————◆———————

BART MOORE-GILBERT

VERSO

London · New York

First published by Verso 1997
© Bart Moore-Gilbert 1997
All rights reserved

Verso
UK: 6 Meard Street, London W1V 3HR
USA: 180 Varick Street, New York NY 10014–4606

Verso is the imprint of New Left Books

ISBN 1–85984–909–1
ISBN 1–85984–034–5 (pbk)

British Library Cataloguing in Publication Data
A catalogue record for this book is available from the British Library

Library of Congress Cataloging-in-Publication Data
A catalog record for this book is available from the Library of Congress

Typeset by CentraCet Ltd, Cambridge
Printed by Biddles Ltd, Guildford and King's Lynn

This book is for my mother Marise, my brothers Patrick, Ames and Lindsay, and in memory of my father, S. M. (Bill) Moore-Gilbert, Game Warden in Tanganyika/Tanzania 1949–1965:
Mwanangwa ni fiya hufa kwa bidiya akenda akiya huyo si mwanangwa.

Contents

Acknowledgements

This book has benefited from the help and support of a number of people. I'd particularly like to thank Peter Hulme for a sympathetic but searching analysis of a first (and unsolicited) draft of the book as a whole; I must also thank Conor Carville, Stephen Slemon, Gareth Stanton, Willy Maley, Helen Carr, Susheila Nasta, Mark Roper, Sam Smithson and Aleks Sierz for reading draft chapters; Jane Desmarais and Andrew Teverson for much appreciated help with the notes; Maria MacDonald for taking some administrative burdens off my shoulders so I could get the book finished on time; Kate Teltscher and Steve Barfield for other help; and my editor, Malcolm Imrie, for knowing when to be patient and when not to be. I'd like also to thank the various groups of MA students who have been in my 'Postcolonial Fiction: Theory and Practice' option since 1993, all of whom have encouraged and challenged me, and ignored my complaints that what I really liked was reading novels. I remember with gratitude discussions on exile and belonging (and copious beer) in KK with Alan MacLachlan (thanks so much for your hospitality) and friends, especially Ayesha and he who obeyed her, Ghulam.

4 July 1996

In the sky there is no east nor west.
We make these distinctions in the mind, then believe them to be true.

The Buddha, *Lankavatara Sutra*

Oh, East is East, and West is West, and never the twain shall meet,
Till Earth and Sky stand presently at God's great Judgement Seat.

Kipling, 'The Ballad of East and West'

The notions of 'East' and 'West' . . . do not cease to be 'objectively real' even though analysis shows them to be no more than a conventional, that is a 'historico-cultural', construction.

Gramsci, *Prison Notebooks*

Preface

Despite the manifold successes of postcolonial studies in reshaping traditional disciplinary configurations and modes of cultural analysis in recent years, they are currently beset by a number of problems which are reflected in a growing number of attacks from outside the field and increasing dissension within. This text is particularly concerned with recent controversies about postcolonial theory, which have led to what seems to some observers to be a growing divide between postcolonial theory on the one hand and the rest of postcolonial criticism on the other. My text defines postcolonial theory as work which is shaped primarily, or to a significant degree, by methodological affiliations to French 'high' theory – notably Jacques Derrida, Jacques Lacan and Michel Foucault. In practice, this will mean the work of Edward Said, Gayatri Spivak and Homi Bhabha. It is the 'intrusion' of French 'high' theory into postcolonial analysis that has perhaps generated the most heated of the many current critical debates, provoking extremes of both approval and disapproval. Representative of the former attitude is Robert Young's *White Mythologies* (1990), which announces 'a new logics of historical writing'[1] in the work of what his later text *Colonial Desire* (1995) calls the 'Holy Trinity' of postcolonial theorists. Young argues that Said, Spivak and Bhabha have enabled a radical reconceptualization of the relationship between nation, culture and ethnicity which has major cultural/political significance. By contrast, the Nobel laureate Derek Walcott damns French theory in an apoplectic tone which is not untypical of many more traditional kinds of postcolonial critic. Complaining of the 'stink' and 'rot' of 'the dead fish of French criticism', Walcott concludes: 'It convinces one that Onan was a Frenchman.'[2]

In the first four chapters, and for purely determinate and strategic purposes, I shall accept the more or less explicit divisions which have been constructed between postcolonial theory on the one hand and the

1

wider field of postcolonial criticism on the other. I must emphasize even at this stage, however, that I do not wish to essentialize the distinction between the two kinds of analysis. Indeed, it is a conviction that the distinctions between them cannot be made absolute that organizes the attempted negotiation in the later parts of my text between the equally avid supporters and detractors of postcolonial theory and, in consequence, between postcolonial theory and postcolonial criticism more broadly understood. The trajectory of Said's career, for instance, is one of progressive disillusionment with some of the 'high theory' which underpins *Orientalism*, as I will show in more detail in chapter 2. From almost immediately after the publication of this seminal text, Said begins to develop in such a way that a decade later he is exploring an accommodation between his own work and some recent versions of 'Commonwealth' literary studies.

I do not want to suggest that postcolonial criticism, meanwhile, is naively positivist or purely empiricist in its assumptions and procedures. While it is generally mediated in a different and more accessible rhetoric, and consequently rarely presents the reader with the same order of immediate difficulty as postcolonial theory, it is often highly theorized, implicitly or explicitly (as is particularly evident in the many Marxist and *marxisant* inflections of postcolonial criticism). In any case, as Barbara Christian argues, 'theory' is not necessarily to be understood in the same way by the West and the non-West (or dominant and subordinate constituencies within the West).[3] Nor do I wish to suggest that there is some absolute divide between theory on the one hand and applied criticism on the other. Said, Spivak and Bhabha all participate in the 'practical' analysis of texts and discourses in a manner comparable with a lot of other postcolonial critics. Finally, I do not wish to homogenize either postcolonial theory or postcolonial criticism as two separate but internally unified kinds of activity. As will be seen, both sub-fields of analysis must be understood as plural in assumption, orientation and procedure, and are at times internally as well as mutually contradictory.

The single instance of the debate over the place of Marxism in postcolonial modes of cultural analysis amply illustrates the truth of this proposition. Within the fields of postcolonial theory, Spivak argues powerfully for the relevance and usefulness of Marxist methods of analysis, including their 'economist' strands, while Bhabha is generally hostile to such work. Said, by comparison, is divided. As will be seen, he places Marx himself squarely within the Orientalist formation, while at the same time relying heavily – if never uncritically – on 'culturalist' strands of Marxism throughout his career. Postcolonial critics and others interested in the connections between culture and imperialism, meanwhile, are equally varied in their attitude. Aijaz Ahmad, like Arif Dirlik, Benita Parry, Chinweizu, Ngugi Wa Thiongo and Neil Lazarus, argue powerfully for the recuperation of Marxism as the best means to conceptualize many of the problems often discussed under the rubric of postcolonial analysis, and Marxism plays an important, if at times ambivalent, part in the thinking of earlier critics as diverse as C. L. R. James, Aimé Césaire and Frantz Fanon.[4] By contrast, figures as diverse as Wole Soyinka, Christopher Miller, Paul Gilroy and Robert Young all see Marxism to some degree as replicating the earlier attempt of Western humanism to impose 'universal' narratives of social development and modes of cultural analysis, which fail to do justice to – or, at times, even to take account of – the particularities and differences of non-Western contexts.

In my first chapter, I will provide an account of the successes of postcolonial studies and some of the general problems it currently faces. I will focus, however, on the attacks on postcolonial theory from both outside and within the field, the most substantial of which are often organized by the argument that it is politically complicit with the dominant neo-colonial regimes of knowledge. Such attacks typically assert that the institutional location of postcolonial theory in the Western academy necessarily and automatically precludes it from being able to perform radical and liberatory kinds of cultural analysis. In order to address such arguments, I will contextualize the emergence of postcolonial theory in terms of the formerly dominant institutional modes of analysis of the complex relations between culture and (neo-)colonialism.

This is followed by three chapters, on Said, Spivak and Bhabha, which attempt to provide detailed and patient critical readings of their work in order to address further the objections outlined in chapter 1. Since Robert Young's ground-breaking comparative study of these three figures in *White Mythologies* (1990), all have produced a substantial volume of new work, which includes, most notably, Said's *Culture and Imperialism* (1993), Spivak's *The Post-Colonial Critic* (1990) and *Outside in the Teaching Machine* (1993), and Bhabha's *Nation and Narration* (1990) and *The Location of Culture* (1994). As these major new texts have appeared, so the debate about the identity, politics, purpose and status of postcolonial theory has grown in scale (and heat) proportionally. A principal aim of my text, then, is to provide a clear analytic account of both the new material which the critics have produced, contextualizing this within a reconsideration of their earlier work, and the controversies which have grown up around both in the intervening period.

In these three longer chapters, I have used the method of 'close reading' which is (perhaps ironically) equally associated with Derridean deconstruction[5] and traditional modes of literary criticism alike. My primary reason for this approach is dissatisfaction with the often airily generalized accounts of the difficulty, perniciousness or irrelevance of postcolonial theory. However, I also feel that some of the enthusiasm for postcolonial theory could be usefully grounded and tested in more detailed analysis of the critics in question. I want, then, to engage as closely as possible with the texts of postcolonial theory (especially those which have appeared since 1990), both to establish what seem to me their major premises, arguments and interrelations and – equally importantly – to put these to as rigorous a scrutiny as I can.

In chapter 5, I will reconsider the general objections to postcolonial theory elaborated in chapter 1 in the light of these critiques of Said, Spivak and Bhabha, suggesting ways in which some of them, at least, need to be modified. I will go on to begin a reassessment of the division which has recently emerged between postcolonial theory and the rest of the field of postcolonial criticism. I will be arguing that there are important – and insufficiently recognized – continuities, at both the strategic and the tactical levels, between the work of postcolonial critics such as Chinua Achebe, Wole Soyinka and Wilson Harris on the one hand, and theorists like Said, Spivak and Bhabha on the other, even if at times important differences of emphasis must be recognized in their interpretation and deployment of some of the key analytic concepts and critical procedures which they share.

In my conclusion, I will suggest that many of the problems currently faced by postcolonial theory are common to postcolonial criticism more broadly, especially as regards the question of how to negotiate solidarity and alliance between different postcolonial social formations and interests, and the respective critical practices which these have generated, while at the same time respecting their historical and cultural particularities. For this reason, more than any other, I think that some of the current enthusiasm for and antagonism towards postcolonial theory are equally misguided. However, the scepticism which at times informs my own interest in postcolonial theory testifies to my acknowledgement that some at least of the objections of its detractors are serious ones, and must be taken seriously. I do not share Robert Young's optimism that dissemination of what he calls 'the new logics of historical writing', which he identifies above all with the work of Said, Bhabha and Spivak, can help inaugurate a brave new world of cultural liberation, while some of its exponents and supporters continue to ignore – or even deplore – what has been done before, and what continues to be done, in other arenas of struggle, political and critical, in the postcolonial field. On the other hand, precisely because of the many and profound continuities between postcolonial criticism and postcolonial theory, there can be no sensible reason for the exponents and supporters of the former to dismiss the latter out of hand.

1

Postcolonial criticism or

postcolonial theory?

Postcolonial criticism and theory alike comprise a variety of practices, performed within a range of disciplinary fields in a multitude of different institutional locations around the globe. Many of these long predate the period when the term 'postcolonial' began to gain currency[1] and have since been claimed retrospectively as continuous, or contiguous, with what are now commonly identified as postcolonial modes of cultural analysis. Anyone with the temerity to write a history of these practices would probably have to start at least as early as the beginning of this century with the work of figures as different as the African-American thinker W. E. B. Du Bois and the South African Sol Plaatje (and, arguably, much further back). S/he would need to discuss cultural formations as diverse as the Harlem Renaissance of World War One and the 1920s and the *négritude* movement of the 1940s and 1950s. Such a history would need to address figures as geographically, ideologically and culturally varied as the Trinidadian C. L. R. James, who lived much of his life in London, Frantz Fanon, originally from Martinique but a revolutionary activist in Algeria, African critics as different as Chinua Achebe and Anta Diop, and Ranajit Guha, the Indian historiographer long based in Australia. To do justice to what was never a smooth narrative of 'influence and development', such a history would also have to examine the claims of some Latin-American criticism, 'Commonwealth' literary studies of the 1960s and 1970s, and various kinds of aesthetic theory in non-European languages considered as precursors to, or variants of, what is now regarded as postcolonial criticism.

While postcolonial criticism has apparently had a long and complex history outside Europe and America, it arrived only belatedly in the Western academy and British university literature departments more particularly. (Much of the following account will be shaped by the fact that I am a literary critic working in Britain, though I shall try not to be too parochial in my range of reference.) One mark of this belatedness is that it was not acknowledged as a separate category of analysis in a number of relatively recent and influential works of cultural description and critical theory in Britain, from Raymond Williams's *Keywords* (1976, revised edition 1983), to Terry Eagleton's *Literary Theory* (1983) and Raman Selden's *The Theory of Criticism* (1988). Indeed, reconsideration of the 'crisis in English studies' engendered in British universities in the late 1970s and early 1980s indicates just how little part was played in rethinking the field of literary studies by what would now be described as postcolonial concerns and modes of criticism. Thus neither of the Methuen New Accents volumes which sought to redefine the discipline at this moment of turmoil – Peter Widdowson's *Re-Reading English* (1982) and Janet Batsleer's *Rewriting English* (1985) – found space to address in any detailed manner either the cluster of interests now identified with colonial discourse analysis or the already well-developed fields of 'new' or postcolonial literatures in English. It was not until 1989 that a preliminary survey of postcolonial criticism, Bill Ashcroft, Gareth Griffiths and Helen Tiffin's *The Empire Writes Back*, appeared; the first critical reader in the field, Patrick Williams and Laura Chrisman's *Colonial Discourse and Post-Colonial Theory*, was published as recently as 1993.

Given its short history as a practice in the Western academy, and literature departments in Britain more specifically, postcolonial criticism has nonetheless had – on the face of it, at least – a major impact upon current modes of cultural analysis, bringing to the forefront of concern the interconnection of issues of race, nation, empire, migration and ethnicity with cultural production. One measure of this impact is that while undergraduate courses on the new literatures in English or in areas such as 'empire and literature' were only exceptionally on offer in Britain in the late 1960s, for instance at Leeds and Kent universities, options in postcolonial literature, criticism and theory are now available as part of the curriculum of English departments in all but the most traditional (and these are often, not coincidentally, the most prestigious) institutions. By the middle of the 1970s, whole degree programmes combining English and the study of one or more of the 'new' literatures came onstream, and a recent development has been the appearance of a range of taught Master's degrees, providing various configurations of 'Postcolonial Studies', notably at the universities of Kent, Warwick and Essex.

These transformations have been accompanied by new kinds and patterns of scholarly production. For instance, there is now a variety of journals dedicated to the investigation of postcolonial culture and critical problems, including *The Journal of Commonwealth Literature*, *Ariel*, *Research in African Literatures*, *Kunapipi*, *The Journal of New Literatures in*

English, World Literature Written in English, Third Text and *Wasafiri*. The consolidation of the postcolonial field since the early 1980s is, moreover, reflected in the widespread attention being paid to it in special issues of non-'dedicated' journals: a by no means comprehensive list of examples would include *Critical Inquiry* (1985 and 1986), *New Literary History* and *Cultural Critique* (1987), *Oxford Literary Review* (1987 and 1991), *Inscriptions* and *South Atlantic Quarterly* (1988), *Genders* (1991), *Public Culture* and *Social Text* (1992), *Yale French Studies, The Cambridge Review, History Workshop* and *PMLA* (1993), *New Formations* and *Literature and History* (1994). Equally striking has been the proliferation of conferences which have engaged with various postcolonial concerns. In Britain alone, these range from the Roehampton Institute conference of 1983 on 'Literature and Imperialism' and the Essex University conference of 1985 on 'Europe and Its Others', to the University of Galway conference on 'Gender and Colonialism' (1992), the South Bank University conference on black writing in Britain entitled 'Out of the Margins' and the London University Institute of Commonwealth Studies conference on 'Empire, Nation, Language' (both in 1993), the Warwick University conference on Edward Said in 1994, the London Institute of Contemporary Arts conference on Fanon in 1995 and the University of North London conference on 'Border Crossings' in 1996. Professional associations and networks servicing those involved in the field of postcolonial criticism have also expanded in range and number; they include the Association for Commonwealth Literature and Language Studies, the African Literature Association, the Association of Teachers of Caribbean, African and Associated Literatures, the Open University Group for the Study of Post-Colonial Literatures and the London Inter-University Post-Colonial Seminar.

All this activity has been partly enabled by important institutional developments outside the university, notably in publishing, which have made available much of the 'primary' material to support many of these new activities. Heinemann started its African Writers series in 1962 and in the next decade launched a complementary Caribbean Writers series, which has been followed in turn by an Asian Writers series. Also, in the 1970s, Longman introduced its Drumbeat Series of 'Commonwealth' writing. More recently, the Women's Press launched a Black and Third World Women Writers Series. These initiatives have been complemented by the foundation by contemporary migrants of publishing houses specializing in postcolonial concerns like Karnak, New Beacon and Bogle L'Ouverture within the British context. In mainstream academic publishing, too, the interest in postcolonial studies is reflected in the lists of an increasing number of firms, including Routledge, Manchester University Press and Verso. As the notes in this volume indicate, there has been a rapid expansion in the number of monographs (and an explosion of articles) dedicated to the issues raised by post-colonial criticism and cultural production.

As much as by analysis and dissemination of the new literatures in English, postcolonial criticism has been increasingly preoccupied in investigating the complicity of a large part of Western culture, and the canon of English literature more specifically, in the attitudes and values underpinning the process of expansion overseas. From the more obvious figures like Defoe, Conrad and Kipling, attention has now spread to writers who were traditionally conceived of as having no immediately apparent connection to questions of empire.[2] Attention is now being devoted, moreover, to consideration of the interconnections between empire and literary production in whole periods and movements. Postcolonial perspectives have influenced many of the new interpretations of the Renaissance period[3] and have helped to produce important new interpretations of Romantic literature.[4] The traditional view of Victorian writing, represented by C. A. Bodelson's comment that 'the part played by the colonies in mid-Victorian fiction is surprisingly small',[5] is being radically reassessed[6] and there is increasing investigation of the links between Modernism and imperialism.[7]

Postcolonial criticism has not simply enlarged the traditional field of English studies, or refocused attention on neglected aspects or areas within it. It has also, in association with other relatively recent critical discourses as various as feminism and deconstruction, significantly altered the modes of analysis which were dominant within the discipline in the period from 1945 to 1980. Most notably, perhaps, it has helped to undermine the traditional conception of disciplinary boundaries. Configurations such as 'colonial discourse analysis' insist upon the importance of studying literature together with history, politics, sociology and other art forms rather than in isolation from the multiple material and intellectual contexts which determine its production and reception. In related fashion, postcolonial criticism has challenged hitherto dominant notions of the autonomy of the aesthetic sphere, helping to gain acceptance for the argument, advanced on a number of fronts since the 1960s especially, that 'culture' mediates relations of power as effectively, albeit in more indirect and subtle ways, as more public and visible forms of oppression. For example, postcolonial critics have characteristically worked to break down the formerly fixed boundaries between text and context in order to show the continuities between patterns of representation of subject peoples and the material practices of (neo-)colonial power. Moreover, postcolonial criticism has contributed to the interrogation of received distinctions between 'high' and 'popular' culture which has been such a feature of cultural criticism more generally in recent decades. For example, a recurrent concern for some postcolonial critics has been to challenge the assumptions governing traditional discriminations between literature and oral narratives, or *orature*. In colonial discourse analysis, meanwhile, there has been a proliferating interest in hitherto marginalized genres such as journalism and travel writing, a project initiated by Said's *Orientalism* (1978).[8]

Such developments suggest an extensive and continuing, if belated, response from within the West to the complaint of *Orientalism* that the systematic study of the relations between metropolitan culture and questions of race, empire and ethnicity was still considered to be off-limits by the Western literary-cultural establishment in the mid-1970s.[9] Indeed such has been the enthusiasm for postcolonial criticism in the two decades since then that it could be argued that it is now itself betraying a tendency to 'colonize' an evergrowing number of historical periods, geographical locations and disciplinary fields. As Aijaz Ahmad points out, the term was first used in the early 1970s in political theory to describe the predicament of nations which had thrown off the yoke of European empires after World War Two.[10] By the time of Ashcroft, Griffiths and Tiffin's *The Empire Writes Back* (1989), it was being used to describe 'all the culture affected by the [European] imperial process from the moment of colonization to the present day'.[11] 'Colonial discourse analysis' now operates across an ever broader range of fields, including the history of law, anthropology, political economy, philosophy, historiography, art history and psychoanalysis.[12]

The perspectives and approaches associated with postcolonial criticism are also being used increasingly to address the histories and current predicaments of 'internally colonized' cultures within the nation state in the 'developed' world. In the case of Britain, for instance, Michael Hechter's *Internal Colonialism* (1975) inaugurated a new phase of analysis which stresses a continuing, essentially (neo-)colonial, relationship of subordination of the 'peripheral' nations of Scotland, Wales and Ireland by the English 'centre'.[13] Similarly, while Fanon's *The Wretched of the Earth* (1961) disavowed the possibility of meaningful comparison between the historical and cultural predicaments of African America and the colonized peoples subject to European control, this same text, ironically, became an important reference point for the American Civil Rights and Black Nationalism movements of the 1960s. A new generation of African-American critics, represented by figures like Henry Louis Gates, has drawn on the work of older African contemporaries like Soyinka in attempting to elaborate both a 'black' poetics and literary theory. And the migration of African intellectuals as diverse as Anthony Appiah and Toks Adewale to the United States has further blurred the kind of barriers which Fanon assumed to exist, leading to a profound cross-fertilization between African-American and postcolonial cultural perspectives. Finally, as 'Commonwealth' literary studies has largely reconceptualized itself since around 1975, so many of its proponents have increasingly claimed a postcolonial identity for the old 'settler' colonies, formerly known as the British Dominions such as Australia, New Zealand or Canada.[14]

The example of Canada serves to suggest just how tangled and multi-faceted the term 'postcolonial' has now become in terms of its temporal, spatial, political and socio-cultural meanings. Here there are at least five distinct but often overlapping contexts to which the term might be applied. First of all, as Mary Louise Pratt suggests in *Imperial Eyes* (1992), until the 1960s at least, white Canada saw itself to a large degree as in a dependent relationship, culturally and politically, to Britain;[15] and the legacy of this relationship continues to have important repercussions for Canada's identity today. As a novel like Margaret Atwood's *Surfacing* (1970) intimates, many Canadians now see themselves as having fallen under the economic and political sway of the United States. A parallel process of subordination has been detected in the cultural domain, especially as a consequence of US domination of the continent's mass media; this was already being volubly protested against in the 1960s, for example in the criticism of R. D. Mathews.[16] Thirdly, there is the issue of Quebec, which has often been seen in recent times as an oppressed culture or, indeed, a nation within Canada – in a manner analogous to Atwood's conception of the relationship of Canada to the United States. As Pierre Vallière's *Nègres Blancs d'Amérique* (1968) suggests, for three decades at least Quebecois critics have been using what would now be considered as postcolonial frameworks and perspectives, in this case drawn from Fanon's work, to describe the predicament in which Quebec finds itself *vis-à-vis* Anglophone Canada. However, as the bitter three-way conflict over land rights in the early 1990s between federal and state governments and the Mohawk people suggests, a state like Quebec (or, indeed, Canada as a whole) which seems to be postcolonial from one perspective can be simultaneously (neo-)colonial in its relationship to other groups within its jurisdiction. The example of the Mohawk, then, points to a fourth such context in modern Canada, the predicament of the indigenous inhabitants who predated white colonization, sometimes described as the 'First Nations' of Canada. As Julia Emberley's *Thresholds of Difference* (1993) suggests, the increasingly voluminous and self-assertive nature of the cultural production of these groups is fully amenable to analysis within postcolonial frameworks. A final context is provided by the arrival of significant numbers of 'New Commonwealth' migrants to Canada, whose relocation has taken place since the formal decolonization of Britain's former empire and the relaxation of the 'white Canada' policy which governed immigration strategies until the 1960s. To these is now being added a new wave of a quite different kind of economic migrant from Hong Kong, whose arrival is having a significant impact on cities like Toronto and Vancouver in particular.

As writers from Austin Clarke in the 1960s to Bharati Mukherjee in the 1980s suggest, Canada's treatment of such minorities raises many questions about its claims to be a genuinely pluralistic or 'multi-cultural' society.

QUESTIONING THE POSTCOLONIAL

Such has been the elasticity of the concept 'postcolonial' that in recent years some commentators have begun to express anxiety that there may be a danger of it imploding as an analytic construct with any real cutting edge. As one might infer from the last section, the problem derives from the fact that the term has been so variously applied to such different kinds of historical moment, geographical region, cultural identities, political predicaments and affiliations, and reading practices. As a consequence, there has been increasingly heated, even bitter, contestation of the legitimacy of seeing certain regions, periods, socio-political formations and cultural practices as 'genuinely' postcolonial. As will be seen, the term has even been taken by some recent observers to indicate an essentially complicit mode of political (dis)engagement from the coercive realities of colonial history and the current neo-colonial era.[17] Equally, there has been at times violent disagreement over whether the proper object of postcolonial analysis as a reading practice should be postcolonial culture alone, however this is defined, or whether – or to what degree – it is legitimate to focus on the culture of the colonizer. While such disagreements have accompanied postcolonial criticism from its inception, the intensity of such disputes has now reached a pitch which suggests that, despite the institutional gains noted in the last section, it would be wrong to infer that postcolonial criticism is now necessarily as securely established or as readily identifiable as some of the older and more prestigious contemporary modes of cultural analysis like feminism, psychoanalytic criticism or post-structuralism, contested as these themselves often continue to be. (And the relations of these discourses to the postcolonial field also, of course, are being vigorously debated.) Indeed, despite abundant evidence of the successes of postcolonial criticism, it is arguable that these conflicts have attained sufficient weight and charge to raise the question of whether it is not now splintering into a series of competing, mutually incompatible or even antagonistic practices.

Such challenges to postcolonial criticism as a coherent field of practice perhaps derive in the first instance from what, following Henry Louis Gates, one might describe as the 'multiplication of margins' which perhaps inevitably accompanies the 'coming to voice' of increasing numbers and kinds of national, linguistic, religious or ethnic groups, communities or sub-cultures in the contemporary era.[18] It is not a principal aim of my text to define which of these are, or are not, 'properly' postcolonial. As the example of Canada suggests, there are many different degrees, forms and (characteristically intertwined) histories of colonization and there are going to be many different degrees, forms and histories of postcoloniality as a consequence. While these differences must always be respected, it seems invidious and distasteful to insist on a kind of beauty parade in which the competitors are made to press their claims to have been the most oppressed colonial subjects or to be the most 'truly' postcolonial subjects. Unlike some commentators, therefore, I am not troubled by this 'multiplication of the margins' (though I agree with Gates that it involves some unfortunate, although probably only temporary, consequences), primarily because it attests to the increasing success of the manifold struggles against neo-colonialism (which itself, of course, takes many forms).

Moreover, just as feminist criticism need not be confined to analysis of women's or feminist texts, or to geographical regions or socio-cultural formations in which feminism is an influence, or to the period since the technical political emancipation of women (if this has, indeed, happened) in the area under discussion, so it seems to me that postcolonial criticism can in principle be legitimately applied to any number of different contexts. In my view, postcolonial criticism can still be seen as a more or less distinct set of reading practices, if it is understood as preoccupied principally with analysis of cultural forms which mediate, challenge or reflect upon the relations of domination and subordination – economic, cultural and political – between (and often within) nations, races or cultures, which characteristically have their roots in the history of modern European colonialism and imperialism and which, equally characteristically, continue to be apparent in the present era of neo-colonialism. Even such a broad definition may be unnecessarily restrictive. One of the best papers at the 'Empire, Nation, Language' conference in London in 1993 addressed the cultural histories of classical Greek colonies within broadly postcolonial perspectives, and Deepika Bahri has recently called for more work on '"native" breeds of colonization and oppression'[19] before, during and after the era of European conquests overseas. Such projects seem genuinely worth while in their own right and not simply in order to understand the distinctive nature and legacies of European colonialism better. Just as the wide variety of modes of feminist cultural analysis, which often have very different objects, preoccupations and methods, does not make the concept of feminist criticism meaningless, so it seems to me quite unnecessary to be exclusivist and narrow (in the way that colonialism constructed and reproduced minute discriminations and hierarchies amongst its subjects) in defining the remit of postcolonial criticism. (I realize that there are many possible objections to this argument and I will return to some of them in due course.)

Before describing some of the disputes within the field in more detail, it is necessary to note the fact that postcolonial criticism has by no means been fully recognized as an important or even distinct mode of cultural analysis within the Euro-American academy. For critical texts like those by Williams and Eagleton, to which I alluded earlier, postcolonial criticism as it is currently understood had not as yet, perhaps, attained sufficient shape or mass – in the West, at least – for separate consideration. However, given its increasing visibility over the last fifteen years, it is significant that it still does not always feature in more recent accounts of modern literary criticism, like Jeremy Haw-thorn's *A Concise Glossary of Contemporary Literary Theory* (1992), volume eight of *The Cambridge History of Literary Criticism*, subtitled *From Formalism to Post-Structuralism* (1995), which covers the twentieth century, simply ignores postcolonial criticism altogether (though Spivak is discussed in passing as a deconstructionist). By contrast, Chris Baldick's *Criticism and Literary Theory: 1890 to the Present* (1996) refers twice to postcolonial criticism, which is chiefly represented by a half-page discussion of Said's *Orientalism* (something less than half the space devoted to what is described as Walter Raleigh's 'disappointing' Shake-speare criticism). More troubling, perhaps, than the indifference (or what Spivak would call the 'sanctioned ignorance') of such ostensibly authoritative institutional histories is the outright hostility of some traditionalists within English studies. A representative figure in this respect is Peter Conrad, of Oxford University. His *Observer* review of Said's *Culture and Imperialism* in 1993 dismissed the project of colonial discourse analysis with which Said has become so closely identified as symptomatic of the contemporary 'culture of gripes and grievances'[20] unleashed in the wake of the liberation movements of the 1960s. As the tone of Conrad's remarks might suggest, postcolonial critics have suffered from the wider backlash against what the New Right has caricatured as 'political correctness'. In a recent interview, Spivak recounts being shown a piece by the art historian Hilton Kramer in *The New Criterion*

> which suggests that my appointment, in what he describes as a once-distinguished department [Columbia English department, where Said, too, is a professor], is a violation of every principle of the university, the assumption being that I was appointed because I was merely politically correct rather than an expert in the field of literary criticism.[21]

Critics working within other disciplines, like Kramer, have often judged postcolonial criticism harshly. Another example is Ernest Gell-ner, until recently Professor of Social Anthropology at Cambridge, whose review of *Culture and Imperialism* in *The Times Literary Supplement* at around the same time as Conrad's was also scathing. It was ostensibly motivated by the argument that – not for the first time – Said was straying into academic fields not proper to the literary critic and claiming competence on issues which were, in fact, beyond his jurisdiction. In the course of a subsequent bitter exchange of letters with Said (which embroiled a number of other scholars), and perhaps stung by Said's insistence on anthropology's historical complicity in techniques of colonial management, and the discourses of Orientalism more specifically, Gellner went on to dismiss not just *Culture and Imperialism*, but *Orientalism*, too, as 'quite entertaining but intellectually insignificant'.[22] Similar doubts have been expressed more recently by the historians Russell Jacoby and John MacKenzie. Jacoby, for example, also questions the interdisciplinary ambitions of postcolonial critics:

> As they move out from traditional literature into political economy, sociology, history, and anthropology, do the postcolonial theorists master these fields or just poke about? Are they serious students of colonial history and culture or do they just pepper their writings with references to Gramsci and hegemony?[23]

MacKenzie's *Orientalism: History, Theory and the Arts* (1995), the most substantial (by volume, at least) of the critiques from those working in other disciplines, gives a resoundingly affirmative answer to the latter question. Asserting on the one hand that *Orientalism* deals in truisms that had long been common currency among historians, MacKenzie also argues that Said and his followers fail at a fundamental level to understand both imperial history and historiography. Indeed, the reader is informed, 'nothing better represents the naïveté and lack of sophistication of the left-wing literary critics'[24] than their shortcomings in these two areas.

POSTCOLONIAL CRITICISM OR POSTCOLONIAL THEORY?

What makes it impossible to dismiss the hostility of critics like MacKenzie and Jacoby as simply the product of traditional disciplinary jealousies, however, is that elements of their critique are repeated by others working *within* approximately the same discursive terrain as Said, Bhabha and Spivak. In fact, the interventions of MacKenzie and Jacoby have simply exacerbated an already heated 'internal' debate over appropriate methods of analysis of the cultural production generated by the histories of (neo-)colonialism. In focusing their attacks on postcolonial studies on the work of Said, Bhabha and Spivak, MacKenzie and Jacoby thus reinforce a divide between postcolonial criticism and postcolonial theory which was already becoming marked as a consequence of the publication of earlier texts as different in method, political affiliation and subject matter as Stephen Slemon and Helen Tiffin's *After Europe: Critical Theory and Post-Colonial Writing* (1989) and Aijaz Ahmad's *In Theory: Classes, Nations, Literatures* (1992).[25]

To some degree, this apparent rift is the responsibility of Said, Bhabha and Spivak themselves. Aijaz Ahmad comments justifiably in *In Theory* that

> one is struck by the fact that neither the architecture of *Orientalism* nor the kind of knowledge the book generally represents has any room in it for criticisms of colonial cultural domination of the kind that have been available . . . on an expanding scale, since the late nineteenth century.[26]

Said's next major work of criticism, *The World, the Text, and the Critic* (1983), contains a single reference to Fanon, but it is not until 'Orientalism Reconsidered' (1985) that he makes any extensive acknowledgement of the work of such predecessors:

> At bottom, what I said in *Orientalism* had been said before me by A. L. Tibawi, by Abdullah Laroui, by Anwar Abdel Malik, by Talal Asad, by S. H. Alatas, by Fanon and Césaire, by Pannikar, and Romila Thapar . . . who in challenging the authority, provenance, and institutions of the science that represented them to Europe, were also understanding themselves as something more than what this science said they were.[27]

While this is generous, if belated, recognition of the earlier critical tradition, it is only in the essays collected in *Culture and Imperialism* (1993) that Said engages in detail with any of these precursors. Similarly, while Bhabha addresses a limited range of Fanon's work with some consistency from the early 1980s, there is scarcely any citation of other predecessors in the field apart from Said himself in the initial phase of his career. 'Representation and the Colonial Text' (1980) alludes to Achebe's 'Colonialist Criticism', though this piece is omitted from the recent selection of essays comprising Bhabha's *The Location of Culture* (1994). 'Commonwealth' literary studies is the object of somewhat lazy jibes in both this essay and in 'Signs Taken for Wonders',[28] reinforcing the impression that Bhabha's methodology is shaped almost entirely by European 'high' theory. The same pattern is discernible in Spivak's career. *The Post-Colonial Critic* (1990) refers in passing to Ngugi's *Writers in Politics*, and there is a single reference to Achebe in *In Other Worlds* (1987). Moreover, while many of the interviews which make up *The*

Post-Colonial Critic were given in Australia, it is clear that for Spivak, the 'white settler' histories of such countries make their presumption of a 'postcolonial' identity, and consequently of a role in postcolonial criticism, deeply problematic.[29]

Some of what has been written about these figures by their admirers also encourages the idea that a radical break exists between their work and the rest of postcolonial criticism. At times, indeed, such accounts suggest that postcolonial criticism is something which begins with Said. Thus in *Colonial Discourse and Postcolonial Theory* (1993), Williams and Chrisman make the following claim: 'It is perhaps no exaggeration to say that Edward Said's *Orientalism*, published in 1978, single-handedly inaugurates a new area of academic inquiry: colonial discourse, also referred to as colonial discourse theory or colonial discourse analysis.'[30] The looseness of this formulation apart (colonial discourse is not the same as colonial discourse analysis), it is apparent from the voluminous extracts which they themselves have so usefully collated that the analysis of colonial systems of representation and cultural description long predates Said's intervention in the field. What Said inaugurates, rather, is an approach to such analysis from within methodological paradigms derived, as already suggested, from contemporary continental European cultural theories. Similar problems also beset what is still the best account of Said, Spivak and Bhabha, Robert Young's *White Mythologies: Writing History and the West* (1990), a text to which all subsequent evaluations of postcolonial theory must express a debt. Young argues that the novelty of this trio's work is its engagement with 'the discursive forms, representations and practices of contemporary racism, together with their relation to the colonial past'.[31] Young does recognize the importance of Fanon as a precursor to the work of these three critics, naming *The Wretched of the Earth* (1961) as the text which initiates the attempt to decolonize European philosophy and historiography. However, while this work is privileged in a somewhat arbitrary way (many of its concerns were anticipated in *Black Skin, White Masks* almost a decade earlier), Young's discussion of Fanon is extremely brief, barely longer than that devoted to Barthes, whose appearance in such company seems particularly contentious.[32] Fanon is certainly not given space on the scale deemed appropriate to Said, Spivak and Bhabha, the last of whom, at the time Young's book appeared, had written a bare handful of essays, as compared with several substantial and influential books by Fanon. In this sense, ironically, Young's account of the emergence of postcolonial criticism parallels the Marxist model of global history, deconstruction of which is a primary aim of *White Mythologies*. While Marxism, according to Young, only sees the periphery's history in a dependent and imitative relation to that of the metropolis, he seems unwittingly to imply that postcolonial analysis only 'comes of age' once it becomes a practice of the Western academy and learns to theorize itself in ways which derive from a European context.

Moreover, it is arguable that Young does not question the claims of postcolonial theory with sufficient scepticism. For instance, in somewhat cursorily discounting the criticisms made of Bhabha's politics by Abdul JanMohamed, on the grounds that they result from a simple misunderstanding of his work, Young closes off important areas of debate, which this book seeks to reopen as a central concern. JanMohamed's 'The Economy of Manichean Allegory' (1986) inaugurates the critique of postcolonial theory from a counter-hegemonic political perspective. He has been followed in this respect by a large number of critics, as diverse as Ketu Katrak, Stephen Slemon, Anne McClintock and Arif Dirlik. While other points of disagreement, for example over periodization of the 'postcolonial', or the cultures to which it might be taken to refer, are by no means to be discounted, perhaps the most heated current debate concerns the political implications of the incorporation of French-derived 'high' theory into postcolonial analysis. Indeed the unity of what I have more narrowly defined as postcolonial criticism, rests to a surprisingly large measure on a shared hostility towards the supposedly reactionary politics of postcolonial theory, as a comparison of Aijaz Ahmad with some latter-day exponents of 'Commonwealth' literary studies suggests.

The attack on postcolonial theory from within approximately the same discursive field has perhaps become most notoriously associated with Ahmad's In Theory. While Said's work has long been subject to modification and elaboration, both by himself and by 'disciples' like Bhabha and Spivak, the effect of these revisions has generally been to reinforce rather than undermine his status as the pre-eminent figure in the field. By contrast, Ahmad's critique of Said is so hostile that Said's sympathizers have at times condemned In Theory in terms as violent as those in which Ahmad excoriates the work of Said. Thus in The Times Higher, Bryan Cheyette expressed outrage at the appearance of what he described as 'this extraordinarily offensive volume' and concluded: 'It is to Verso's discredit that they have published a volume that will be grist to the mill of those who wish to dismiss out of hand any kind of theoretical thinking about "race" and "nation" in literary studies.'[33] The alarm evident in such pronouncements testifies to the scale of Ahmad's challenge, which is expressed in his desire to 'break with the existing theoretical formation both methodologically and empirically',[34] a formation for which he holds Said, despite generous personal praise, primarily responsible. In some ways, In Theory is as comprehensive an attack on postcolonial theory as MacKenzie's. In contrast to MacKenzie, however, Ahmad sees postcolonial theory not as politically radical or even 'correct' but as deeply conservative in its ideas and effects. In fact,

Ahmad goes as far as to suggest that postcolonial theory is simply one more medium through which the authority of the West over the formerly imperialized parts of the globe is currently being reinscribed within a neo-colonial 'new world order' and is, indeed, best understood as a new expression of the West's historical will to power over the rest of the world.[35]

There are five main elements to Ahmad's critique, all of which are anticipated or repeated, albeit generally in more temperate terms, by others working in the field. First of all, *In Theory* explores the implications of the institutional location and affiliations of figures like Said. From this perspective, Ahmad interprets postcolonial theory as the activity of a privileged and deracinated class fraction, which is cut off from the material realities of 'Third World'[36] struggles, the dynamic energies of which are appropriated and domesticated into a chic but finally unchallenging intellectual commodity which circulates largely within the Western academy. In Ahmad's eyes, postcolonial theorists reproduce within the academic sphere the contemporary international division of labour authorized by global capitalism. According to this argument, Third World cultural producers send 'primary' material to the metropolis, which is then turned into a 'refined' product by the likes of Said, principally for the metropolitan cultural elite, which they in fact regard as their primary audience; a certain amount of such work is in turn re-exported as 'theory' to the Third World. Ahmad's conclusion is scornful: 'The East, reborn and greatly expanded now as a "Third World", seems to have become, yet again, a *career* – even for the "Oriental" this time, and within the "Occident" too.'[37]

Given his deep scepticism about 'Commonwealth' literary studies,[38] it is somewhat ironic that comparable criticisms of postcolonial theory were being articulated from within that critical sub-formation prior to Ahmad's intervention in the debate. For example, Slemon and Tiffin's *After Europe* (1989) argues that postcolonial theory relegates other forms of postcolonial criticism, which do not rely on French-derived 'high theory', to an inferior category of analysis which is assumed to be both an anterior, or more 'primitive', stage in its own emergence and to be incapable of self-consciousness about its epistemological assumptions or methodological procedures. Postcolonial theorists are, moreover, represented as having the tendency to appropriate to themselves the subversive energies which they have discovered in the postcolonial cultures that they mediate:

> When reading for textual resistance becomes entirely dependent on 'theoretical' disentanglement of contradiction or ambivalence within the colonialist text – as it does in deconstructive or new historical readings of colonialist discourse, – then the actual locus of subversive agency is necessarily wrenched

away from colonised or post-colonial subjects and resituated within the textual work of the institutionalised western literary critic.[39]

As primary evidence of postcolonial theory's reinscription of the West's traditional cultural authority, Ahmad points to the hierarchy which organizes its choice of objects for study. The favoured field for analysis in the work of Said and his followers is identified as colonial discourse. In Ahmad's eyes, this privileges the Western canon over Third World culture and, moreover, represents a politically disabling shift of attention from the facts of current neo-colonialism to the less contentious area of fictions produced in an era of formal imperialism now safely past. According to Ahmad, postcolonial theory subsequently favours the work of the migrant intelligentsia of Third World origin based in the West. Said and his followers are taken to task for assuming that writers like Salman Rushdie (to whom Ahmad is consistently hostile) represent the authentic voice of their countries of origin. Instead, Ahmad locates them within the politically dominant class fraction of their host society, to which texts like Shame, like postcolonial theory itself, are in the first instance deemed to be addressed. Ultimately, Ahmad implies, a lot of such work needs to be placed within metropolitan discursive traditions such as Orientalism and Ahmad takes Said severely to task for failing to see how a text like Satanic Verses belongs to a long tradition of anti-Islamic sentiment in the West. When Third World culture 'proper' is addressed in postcolonial theory, Ahmad argues, most attention is given to those texts which 'answer back' to imperial and neo-colonial culture – for instance, the fictional ripostes to Heart of Darkness by figures as diverse as Chinua Achebe, Wilson Harris and Tayib Salih. According to In Theory, this attention to work that has been, in a crucial sense, interpellated by Western culture simply reinforces the traditional relationship between centre and periphery which underlay all discourse, political and cultural, of the colonial period. There is thus a damaging tendency 'to view the products of the English-writing intelligentsia of the cosmopolitan cities as the central documents' of the national literature of the country in question.[40] In the process those aspects of Third World culture which are most genuinely independent of metropolitan influences and of allegiance to the national bourgeoisie, such as literatures written in regional Indian languages, are either neglected or ignored.

Such objections are echoed in recent versions of 'Commonwealth' literary studies. In 'New Approaches to the New Literatures in English' (1989), for instance, Diana Brydon also argues that so much energy is expended by postcolonial theory on engaging with colonial discourse that the new cultural production of the postcolonial world is in danger of being overlooked or even silenced in a process which unwittingly replicates the operations of colonial discourse itself. Objecting to 'the narrowing of focus to the imperial/colonial relation as if it were all that there were', Brydon concludes that: 'Deconstructing imperialism keeps us within imperialism's orbit.'[41] Brydon also anticipates Ahmad in pointing to two other important lacunae in postcolonial theory which qualify its claim to be performing radical kinds of cultural analysis. She argues that postcolonial criticism addresses the areas of class and gender in a way that postcolonial theory characteristically fails to do.[42] Ahmad, by comparison, suggests that insofar as postcolonial theory does address non-Western cultures, its habitual focus on the problematics of the Third World nation overlooks these other important sites of mobilization against (neo-)colonialism – which may often be in conflict with nationalist discourse and programmes of liberation. Ahmad detects similar shortcomings in postcolonial theory's approach to the work of metropolitan-based migrants. In his view, it persistently fails to recognize the customarily hostile representation by writers like Rushdie of 'women, minorities, servants, and others who are not of the ruling class'.[43]

Above all else, however, Ahmad organizes his attack on postcolonial theory around the argument that its methodological procedures derive from contemporary Euro-American critical theories which are politically regressive in a number of ways. To Ahmad, Western cultural criticism in general has become increasingly detached from any concrete connection with popular political struggle, whether at home or abroad, since the 1960s. Post-structuralism is then represented as the most striking and debilitating instance of this divorce, especially in its American versions in which, according to Ahmad, material forms of activism are replaced by a textual engagement which sees '*reading* as the appropriate form of politics'.[44] Ahmad attaches Said's criticism to post-structuralism and consequently reads his model of postcolonial analysis as similarly cut off from any real engagement with popular liberation movements in the Third World. The prestige of postcolonial theory is then attributed to its emergence in the wake of post-structuralist theory which itself reached the peak of its influence at a particularly conservative historical and cultural conjuncture, the period 'supervised by Reagan and Thatcher'.[45]

In this respect, too, there are parallels between *In Theory* and texts like Slemon and Tiffin's *After Europe* (1989), which is chiefly concerned with exploring how a 'genuinely' postcolonial literary criticism may be developed, a preoccupation which runs through many of the contributions to the volume. Integral to this inquiry is a critique of postcolonial theory as represented by Spivak and Bhabha in particular, who are arraigned for evading the real politics of the postcolonial predicament as a consequence of their obsession with 'a set of philosophical questions whose cultural and historical specificity within postmodern Anglo-American culture is rarely admitted'.[46] In an essay published in the same year as In Theory, Helen Tiffin takes this argument further:

> For all its potentially useful insights, post-structuralist philosophy remains the handmaiden of repression, and if I may mix metaphors, serves as District Commissioner of the 1980s, his book title now changed from The Pacification of the Primitive Tribes of the Lower Niger to Enjoying the Other: or Difference Domesticated.[47]

Adapting some of the perspectives and terms of Said's critique of Derrida in The World, the Text, and the Critic to his followers (to which I will return in chapter 3), Slemon and Tiffin's volume attempts to recuperate a number of analytic concepts, strategies and figures which Spivak and Bhabha deconstruct, on what many of the essays see as the mistaken assumption that they articulate the epistemological or political values of the dominant order. For many of the contributors to After Europe, the centred subject, the aesthetic sphere, foundational identities, the nation and nationalism, 'master'-narratives of liberation and emancipation, and authorial intention are all variously and at different times considered to be legitimate means of organizing resistance to (neo-)colonialism, whether in the spheres of politics or cultural criticism. More than anything else, After Europe seeks to recuperate the referential properties of language, which the volume presents as consistently side-lined by post-structuralism's characteristic fracturing of the traditional conception of the relationship between signifier and signified. In the view of many of the contributors, this theoretical priority leads to an occlusion of 'the real' which constantly defers the attempted engagement of postcolonial culture with pressing social and political problems. The strategic logic of such arguments is comparable, once more, with that which informs Ahmad's resistance to post-structuralism's 'debunking of all myths of origin, totalizing narratives, determinate and collective historical agents – even the state and political economy as key sites for historical narrativization'.[48]

Finally, the surface discourse of postcolonial theory is often no more palatable to such critics than it is to the historians considered earlier in this introduction. Like MacKenzie's Orientalism, and in contradiction of Jacoby's claim that stylistic clarity and coherence are of concern only to 'conservative' critics, Ahmad's In Theory laments the 'very arcane' nature of Homi Bhabha's style and the 'inflationary rhetoric'[49] of postcolonial theory more generally. Likewise, from within the ambit of contemporary versions of 'Commonwealth' literary studies, Graham Huggan complains of 'the often mystificatory vocabulary'[50] of European post-structuralism which subsequently seeps into postcolonial theory. For many within the field of postcolonial criticism, the complexity of the language of postcolonial theory is one more symptom of its will to power over other kinds of postcolonial analysis. Consequently such figures insist on the importance of writing in what Ketu Katrak describes as 'a language lucid enough to inspire people to struggle and to achieve social change'.[51]

METROPOLITAN APPROACHES TO THE 'LITERATURE OF EMPIRE', 1945–80

In order to assess the justice of some of the charges brought against postcolonial theory, it is necessary to begin with a comparison between its critical focuses, practices and assumptions and those which were traditionally involved in the study of the relations between culture and imperialism in the Western academy. As will be demonstrated later, a number of earlier non-Western critics anticipated the argument of Said's *Orientalism* (1978), in asserting a direct and material relation between the political processes and structures of (neo-)colonialism on the one hand and, on the other, Western regimes of knowledge and modes of cultural representation. Within Europe and America, however, these interconnections were almost completely ignored throughout the period from 1945 to the early 1980s. This provides the first context, then, in which postcolonial theory must be placed in order to determine whether it is indeed complicit with dominant ideologies in the more recent history of the post-war era.

This occlusion of the political meanings and effects of colonial discourse in the metropolitan English department is – with hindsight – clearly apparent in 'traditional' critical writing on the literature of empire such as Molly Mahood's *The Colonial Encounter: A Reading of Six Novels* (published the year before the appearance of *Orientalism*). Abdul JanMohamed proposes that 'Mahood skirts the political issue quite explicitly by arguing that she chose those authors [who include Conrad, Forster and Graham Greene] precisely because they are "innocent of emotional exploitation of the colonial scene" and are "distanced" from the politics of domination'; he concludes that such an approach 'restricts itself by severely bracketing the political context of culture and history'.[52] Benita Parry makes similar criticisms of Alan Sandison's *The Wheel of Empire*, which was considered a ground-breaking study when it first appeared ten years earlier in 1967. In Parry's opinion, Sandison recuperates the literature of empire as a body of existential allegories in which 'man' faces and overcomes the threatening 'otherness' of a hostile universe. To Parry, Sandison's mythic approach is 'calculated to drain the writings of historical specificity' and 'naturalizes the principles of the master culture as universal forms of thought and projects its authorized representations as truth'.[53]

There is certainly some justice in such comments, as is suggested by the post-war history of Kipling criticism, to take a single representative case study.[54] Sandison, for example, sees Kipling's protagonists as engaged in a 'conflict between their personal lives and the empire they serve [which] is only a reflection of that more fundamental dialectic between self and destructive non-self'.[55] But he is far from alone in this kind of approach in the period in question. Thus Bonamy Dobree interpreted the imperial narratives as an engagement with 'the enduring problems of humanity' and concluded that the Indian government represented for Kipling 'the most superb instrument to cause man to out-face the universe. . . . Since it unifies the impulses needed to do this, it is Mr Kipling's Catholic Church.'[56] Elliot Gilbert's *Kipling and the Critics* (1965), meanwhile, complained that 'politics notoriously has a way of making it difficult to arrive at sober judgements'[57] of any artist's work, especially of Kipling's, and urged a more 'objective' approach, which would focus on his craftsmanship. Gilbert's next work was *The Good Kipling* (1970), which, while continuing to concentrate primarily on formal issues, nonetheless also followed Dobree and Sandison in seeing empire in Kipling's Indian stories as a metaphoric device which allowed the author to develop a quasi-mystical philosophy of work and action in the face of an absurd universe.

Such approaches have crucial implications for one of the key problems of Kipling's work, its recurrent representation of violence. Ever since Robert Buchanan complained in 1899 that Kipling had created 'a carnival of drunken, bragging, boasting Hooligans in red coats and seamen's jackets, shrieking to the sound of the banjo and applauding the English flag',[58] critics have consistently deplored what they see as the sadism and cruelty of Kipling's Indian writings. In the existentialist-inspired critical readings of the 1950s and 1960s described in the paragraph above, however, the violence in Kipling's work is often treated as some unavoidable concomitant of the 'human' (which we can now understand as the Western white middle-class male's) struggle for meaning, rather than being recognized at face value as evidence of Kipling's awareness (often much more troubled than Buchanan or some Kipling critics of the 1980s have suggested) of the force required to uphold imperial rule in India.

The occlusion of the political contexts of imperialism in traditional literary criticism prior to *Orientalism* is equally apparent in the way that the problem of Kipling's violence is recurrently explained, or even excused, as the expression of a damaged individual's psychopathology. Edmund Wilson's *The Wound and the Bow* (1941) inaugurated this pattern of interpretation, seeing the 'sadism' of Kipling's work as a reaction to his traumatic childhood experience of abandonment in England by his parents. J. M. S. Tompkins, Philip Mason and Lord Birkenhead, together with more recent figures like Martin Seymour-Smith, have all reiterated Wilson's argument in more or less the same terms. Tompkins's *The Art of Rudyard Kipling*, for instance, concludes that, as a result of his childhood traumas, Kipling was left scarred for life, 'not, as has been loosely said, a cruel man, but certainly with an emotional comprehension of cruelty and an intellectual interest in it'.[59]

While Kipling's psychobiography no doubt played some part in his interest in the violence of the colonial context, to over-emphasize it is to overlook the consistency of his awareness of the political realities within which he was situated. Tompkins astutely picks up on Kipling's interest in revenge tragedy, but does not see the implications for Kipling's writing that the genre's interest in violence and cruelty reflects upon the unstable political and social contexts within which it was produced. A story like 'On the City Wall' (1888), for instance, is quite explicit about the way that peace, and British control, are ultimately maintained in India. Overlooking the northern city is the British-garrisoned fortress, on the walls of which are mounted 'the line of guns which could blow the City to powder in a half an hour'.[60] Indeed, the tale is at some pains to set up an ironic comparison between the 'fundamentalism' of the local religious rioters and the 'enthusiasm' of the white soldiers: 'The Garrison Artillery ... to the last cherished a wild hope that they might be allowed to bombard the city at a hundred yards' range.'[61] Haunting many of Kipling's narratives is the memory of the 1857 uprisings, and the fear of a recurrence of these events, as is suggested by the nationalist conspiracies which are dramatized both in this story and in *Kim*. Equally important was the fear of a Russian invasion of India throughout much of the 1880s; in *Something of Myself*, his autobiography, Kipling recalled being summoned in his capacity as a journalist to report on 'reviews of Armies expecting to move against Russia next week'.[62] All these factors at least partially explain Kipling's recurrent representation of violence in the colonial context. The failure in much 'traditional' criticism of his work to take account of them typifies its characteristic denial of the legitimacy of 'political' readings of aesthetic work, even when such narratives deal so explicitly with political matters.[63]

Far from being an activity 'innocent' of overt political affiliation, however, traditional 'literature of empire' criticism has at times been underpinned by a distinctly chauvinistic cultural politics, as is the case with Martin Green's influential text, *Dreams of Adventure, Deeds of Empire* (1980). Much of Green's analysis is taken up with the interesting and important argument that the literature of empire constitutes a distinct genre, even tradition, within the history of the English novel.

Green attempts to challenge, even reverse, the habitual pre-eminence given in criticism to what he calls the 'courtship' or 'domestic' novel over the 'novel of adventure', which he sees as habitually involved in questions of territorial expansion and exploration. According to Green, the former type of novel has achieved its prestige by being defined against the apparent triviality and excesses of the adventure novel. Green argues that this involves a systematic simplification of the latter tradition: 'The adventure novel has one large advantage in seriousness, in that it deals with that body of historical fact which Simone Weil called "force".'[64] However, it is soon apparent that what animates Green's attempt to revalue the adventure novel, as much as anything else, is regret for the loss of Britain's status as a great power which the genre, as 'a history of the WASP hero',[65] is deemed to celebrate. Green's text can thus be interpreted in part as an attempt to preserve or even reconstruct what he sees as an important part of the national self-image and ideological heritage, a heritage which is now threatened by foreigners and immigrants alike. Green suggests that whereas empire formerly existed as 'a free space outside England, waiting for use, it has [now] moved inside, in the form of immigrants, who are instead an impediment on our freedom of movement'.[66] In Green's view, indeed, Britain is now itself being colonized; thus London has become 'a city organized to service foreigners richer than ourselves, a tourists' city, culturally a colonial city'.[67] Green's text, then, resonates with the kind of cultural politics which underpinned the nationalism of the early Thatcher years, one symptom of which, according to Salman Rushdie's 'Outside the Whale' (1984), was nostalgia for the vanished empire, a phenomenon which he labelled the 'Raj revival'.[68] (It is in this nostalgic line of cultural criticism that John MacKenzie's Orientalism also needs to be placed and in which his attack on postcolonial theory must be contextualized.)

As the trajectory of the career of a critic like Benita Parry suggests, however, metropolitan critics of the literature of empire have been increasingly responsive, in the last fifteen years, to the political positions and methodological procedures associated with Said's Orientalism. The radical development between her early, fairly traditional (but nonetheless important) critical work on British writers in India in Delusions and Discoveries (1972) and the article on Kipling in 1988, moreover, should give one further reason to be wary of some of the more extreme criticisms of the Western academy for its supposed inability to challenge the dominant regimes of knowledge and associated modes of cultural analysis. Thus a lot of Kipling criticism which has been undertaken in the Western academy since around 1980 is markedly different in emphasis and approach from the work done in the period from 1945 to 1980. John McClure's Kipling and Conrad (1981), my own Kipling and 'Orientalism'

(1986), Patrick Williams's '*Kim* and Orientalism' (1989) and Zohreh Sullivan's *Narratives of Empire* (1993) typify the new kinds of Kipling criticism which have emerged in the Western academy in the wake of *Orientalism* – though it must be noted that such developments have in turn engendered problems of their own.[69]

METROPOLITAN APPROACHES TO POSTCOLONIAL LITERATURE, 1965–80

The second context in which the emergence of postcolonial theory needs to be placed involves metropolitan approaches to the study of the culture of the decolonizing nations in the post-war period. It is once again no surprise that such approaches should now appear, from a postcolonial perspective, to be as unsatisfactory as established modes of analysis of the literature of empire in this era. One kind of early response to the newly emerging literatures of the former empire is neatly illustrated in the reminiscences of the 1988 Nobel laureate Wole Soyinka. In *Myth, Literature and the African World* (1976) he records how, as a visiting fellow of Churchill College, Cambridge, in 1973, he offered to give some lectures on contemporary African writing. The English Faculty declined his proposal, directing him instead to the Faculty of Anthropology as a more suitable venue. However, while the most prestigious centres of English studies simply ignored the new literatures in English in this way (and largely continue to do so), the field did begin to be studied systematically elsewhere, notably at the universities of Leeds and Kent, from the mid-1960s onwards. These early kinds of analysis, under the aegis of 'Commonwealth' literary studies, as the new sub-disciplinary field became known, have themselves come to seem increasingly problematical – indeed, for many currently working in the field, quite untenable.

The reasons for this are varied. The term 'Commonwealth literature' was initially coined to describe the writing of those regions which were formerly part of the British empire; this implicitly constructed a critical paradigm in which the status of British literature was to be considered as culturally equivalent to its dominant position within the new political grouping of the Commonwealth. John Press's *Commonwealth Literature* (1965), the proceedings of the first conference on Commonwealth literature to be held in Britain, at Leeds University in 1964, is indicative of the ethos within which the new sub-discipline was formed. Welcoming the conference delegates, the Vice-Chancellor expressed the hope that new writers from the decolonized empire would 'contribute enrichment and new traditions to the great body of English literature'.[70] Moreover, the legitimacy of the field was largely theorized, initially, through the argument that Commonwealth literature was distinguished by a shared language and a common history vis-à-vis the experience of British rule, which distinguished it from non-British literatures in English as well as postcolonial literatures in other European or 'local' languages. While Press acknowledged 'that the vernacular literatures of the Commonwealth are, for millions of men and women, the most effective means of embodying ... the values of their societies',[71] and expressed the hope that such work might one day come to be studied under the aegis of the new sub-discipline, his call was never more than very fitfully taken up in 'Commonwealth' literary studies prior to the reformulation of the field as a branch of a recognizably postcolonial criticism from the mid-1970s onwards.

Press's volume very much stressed the first term in its subtitle, Unity and Diversity in a Common Culture. It tended to assume that a shared political and cultural history generated both a common repertoire of styles and a common metaphysic or world-view which overrode particular national variations or individual idiosyncrasies among writers in the field. This key premise of 'Commonwealth' literary studies – which remained largely unchallenged until the 1970s, as later critical texts such as K. L. Goodwin's National Identity (1970), William Walsh's A Manifold Voice (1970) and Commonwealth Literature (1973), and William New's Among Worlds (1975) suggest – was initially formulated by the organizer of the 1964 Leeds conference, Norman Jeffares. In his introductory speech, Jeffares argued that 'all of us are members of a common culture';[72] the cultural/political sub-text of that commonality, however, was revealed by the way in which Jeffares constructed British literature as the norm against which 'local' Commonwealth literatures were to be measured. Thus he deplored any significant deviation from 'the great tradition' of the metropolis, rejecting anything 'too local in interest, too diminished in continuity, too immediately appealing, and therefore, in the long run, too unacceptable throughout the world'.[73] This argument largely determined the direction initially taken by the emerging subdiscipline. Rather than looking to define a Nigerian national literature, for example, critical emphasis was to be placed on establishing the connections between individual writers like Soyinka or Achebe and, firstly, the British tradition, secondly, other Commonwealth novelists and only last, if at all, between such figures and other Nigerian authors. British critics, as one might expect, adopted Jeffares's position with particular enthusiasm. B. Argyle's essay on Australian fiction is representative in this respect, arguing that: 'It is ... a pity in these universal times to find so many modern Australian critics bogged down in being Australians ... much native criticism constitutes the greatest problem to a study of Australian fiction.'[74]

The Anglocentrism underlying Jeffares's ostensibly ecumenical approach to Commonwealth literature was equally manifest in other prescriptions for the new sub-discipline. Implicit in his demand that writers like Soyinka should be read 'for the supranational qualities of their work'[75] was a rejection of the role of the politically engaged artist which writers like Achebe had aspired to from the beginning of their careers. For Jeffares, material struggles such as the various African liberation and independence movements were by definition only of 'local' or temporary interest and were not to be understood as crucial contexts within which the new literatures should be read. He required instead that critical effort be directed primarily to elucidation of the 'human truths' mediated by Commonwealth writers and called for the Commonwealth critic to operate by 'universal' standards, by which Jeffares in fact meant those which continued to dominate the metropolitan English department at the time. Indeed Jeffares tried to insist that the criticism of the new literatures be entrusted to the old centres of cultural authority: 'The younger literatures are a little short of good critics, who can recognize talent and guide taste towards it.'[76]

A number of other aspects of the proceedings gathered in volumes such as Press's *Commonwealth Literature* or Goodwin's *National Identity* (1970), which collected the proceedings of the next Commonwealth literature conference in Brisbane in 1968, suggest a subtle reinforcement of the authority of the 'centre' over the margin. For instance, the privileged place of 'white Dominion' literature in the new sub-discipline was implied by the fact that in the former text it was the subject of the first five chapters consecutively. While R. D. Mathews argued passionately in Press's volume that Canada was increasingly coming under the cultural and economic tutelage of the United States, there was no real discussion in either volume of the role of Dominion cultures as colonizing formations *vis-à-vis* their own aboriginal populations. Also notable is the fact that of the twenty-two critics whose papers were published by Press, eight were from Britain, six from the 'white' Dominions and only eight from the rest of the non-white Commonwealth. Moreover, when comparisons were made between the literature of the white and non-white Commonwealth, in the manner encouraged by Jeffares, these were done overwhelmingly by white rather than non-white critics, who preferred to focus on 'national' issues. Perhaps the most significant, and sinister, development between the two volumes, however, was Jeffares's call in *National Identity* for 'standard British English' to be adopted as the medium of Commonwealth writing. Arguing that 'the literary man [sic] must demand good language teaching', Jeffares concluded: 'Our ultimate job may well be to keep the language homogeneous, so that when somebody writes in one part of the Commonwealth he or she will retain an audience in another part.'[77] This perspective was reinforced by metropolitan 'Commonwealth' literary critics, like William Walsh, who condemned the leading African novelist Gabriel Okara in the following terms: 'This kind of prose gives the impression of bending unnaturally against the bias of English and strikes the reader [Walsh automatically assumes this to be a British reader] not with its primitive simplicity but perversely by its mannered artificiality.'[78]

While such attitudes are representative of the dominant vision of early 'Commonwealth' literary studies, it would be misleading to pretend that they remained uncontested until the advent of postcolonial theory in the form, initially, of *Orientalism*. (Moreover, it should be pointed out that postcolonial writers from Achebe to Wilson Harris were happy to speak at such conferences as 'Commonwealth' writers and have their contributions lend authority to the emerging sub-discipline.) Right from the beginning, at the Leeds conference, elements of an alternative rationale and method to Jeffares's were being articulated. Thus S. Nagarajan complained of Commonwealth literature that: 'The diversity is striking enough. . . . But the unity, I am afraid, is not equally obvious.'[79] The last essay of Press's volume, Chinua Achebe's 'The Novelist as Teacher', rebutted many of the critical assumptions about the relationship between literature and politics evident in Jeffares's opening address, emphasizing the divergence between African critics like himself, for example, and the normative critical values operating in the metropolitan English department. D. E. S. Maxwell, moreover, foreshadowed later arguments in postcolonial criticism by questioning the legitimacy of comparing even such seemingly closely aligned literatures as those of Australia and New Zealand. Insisting that each country had quite different histories of settlement and cultural development, he went on: 'Place the settlement of Canada against the settlement of West Africa – never "settled" in at all the same sense – and the divergence appears at its widest.'[80] Questions of periodization were raised at the Queensland conference, too, in debates over whether the new field was to be limited to cultural work produced after the achievement of political independence from Britain or whether much earlier figures such as Olive Schreiner could legitimately be included. Indeed, there was increasing disagreement as to whether South Africa, which had left the Commonwealth in 1960, could be included at all within the emerging subject area. (When it was, as in William New's *An Introduction to Modern Commonwealth and South African Fiction* of 1975, the emphasis tended, symptomatically, to be almost entirely on white South African writing.)

By the mid-1970s, Jeffares's paradigm of 'Commonwealth' literary studies was beginning to implode under the weight of disagreement over such issues, which were taking on an increasingly political character. In the non-white former colonies, especially, there was growing exasperation that emphasis on a common political and cultural history foreclosed exploration of other productive areas of critical inquiry, particularly into the development of individual national traditions. There was also an increasing realization, developing out of the implications of essays like Maxwell's, that African writing in English, for example, might have closer links to Francophone African literature than to the British tradition or even to the culture of the former 'white' Dominions, with their very different colonial histories and roles within both the Commonwealth and the larger global economy and polity. As early as Goodwin's *National Identity* (1970), Lloyd Fernando had pointed out that the political paradigm underpinning the label 'Commonwealth literature' also unnecessarily and damagingly precluded comparisons between Commonwealth and other Anglophone postcolonial literatures, for instance between Singaporean literature in English and the regionally adjacent English writing of the Philippines.

In Anna Rutherford's *Common Wealth*, which appeared three years later, critics like Peter Quartermaine and Hallvard Dahlie extended this kind of inquiry to consideration of possible points of comparison between American and Commonwealth literatures. In Dieter Riemenschneider's *History and Historiography of Commonwealth Literature* (1983) this was taken a stage further. Firstly, Bruce King included discussion of the dialect poems of the Harlem Renaissance poet Paul Dunbar in his theorization of the fraught and complex relationship between 'Nationalism, Internationalism, Periodisation and Commonwealth Literature'; then Helen Tiffin argued that 'we can only gain by including the literature of the United States in our comparisons'.[81] Such interventions marked a significant move towards an expanded field of study, variously designated as 'New Literatures in English' or 'Literatures of the World in English', depending on how strongly the links with the United States were stressed, as a more appropriate framework within which the literature of the former British empire might be studied. This debate over the spatial model implied in the sub-discipline's name entered a distinctive, even decisive, new phase in the mid-1970s with urgent reconsideration of the relations of British literature to the new Anglophone writing. Initially the issue centred on whether the continuities between British and non-British literatures should be stressed or, instead, the ways in which Commonwealth literature supplied new kinds of narrative technique and language uses which constituted a 'counterdiscourse' *vis-à-vis* metropolitan traditions and practice. Increasingly, however, the argument was about whether British literature should be included at all within the field. In Rutherford's *Common Wealth* (1973), the Welsh critic Ned Thomas had insisted that it should, but for quite different reasons to those adduced in the past. In 'An Introduction to Saunders Lewis' he raised – for the first time in the history of the subdiscipline – the question of 'internal colonialism' within Britain and the possible proto-national status of Welsh or Irish literatures along the lines of the emerging non-white Commonwealth literatures. Despite the force of Thomas's intervention, the general trend was, increasingly, to exclude the study of British literature altogether. The more this happened, the more British-based critics like Jeffares also began to lose their institutional sway over the field and the closer 'Commonwealth' literary studies came to reconstituting itself as a branch of 'postcolonial' criticism.

Other developments helped this transformation to take place fairly quickly from the mid 1970s onwards. Firstly, there was a broad revaluation of the history of colonialism, so that critics questioned ever more fiercely the official account of the benefits which imperialism had supposedly brought to the former colonies, which had more or less implicitly informed early versions of 'Commonwealth' literary studies. Notable examples include Walter Rodney's *How Europe Underdeveloped Africa* (1972) and Chinweizu's *The West and the Rest of Us: White Predators, Black Slaves and the African Elite* (1975). Secondly, there was a re-examination of the ideological underpinnings of early formulations of 'Commonwealth' literary studies, which began to be interpreted more or less explicitly as a neo-colonial attempt to reconstitute the West's cultural authority after formal decolonization. Both developments began to influence the work of an increasing number of white Commonwealth critics by 1975, as the proceedings of a further conference, collected in Hena Maes-Jelinek's *Commonwealth Literature and the Modern World*, testify. The editor's preface, for example, develops questions raised in Wilson Harris's contribution to the volume about the 'unconscious prejudices in the complacently "humanistic" approach'[82] to issues of cultural difference and exchange. While Jeffares once more provided the keynote address, reaffirming yet again the principal elements of the vision he had first articulated in Press's *Commonwealth Literature* a decade earlier, there is a real sense in the volume as a whole of a paradigm shift in the methodology and political affiliations of the sub-discipline, especially insofar as the editorial is guided much more by Harris's anxieties than Jeffares's urbane confidence in the future.

The changes of direction and emphasis in the writing of a representative 'Commonwealth' critic like the Australian Helen Tiffin (which have parallels with those in Benita Parry's work in the domain of 'literature of empire' over approximately the same period) are indicative of the impact of such developments. In Riemenschneider's *History and Historiography of Commonwealth Literature* (1983), she defended 'Commonwealth' literary studies thus: 'The demonstrable value of this implicit comparative "umbrella" is I think sufficient rebuttal to those who decry Commonwealth Literary Studies as a factitious discipline based upon a political anachronism.'[83] In the same article, however, there is a symptomatic sliding between the terms 'Commonwealth' and 'postcolonial', the former of which largely disappears in her subsequent work. As with the new modes of colonial discourse analysis circulating in the metropolitan academy in the wake of Said, this reorientation is not, however, without its own problems. Thus *The Post-Colonial Studies Reader* (1995), edited by Ashcroft, Griffiths and Tiffin herself, is remarkable for the fact that well over a third of the articles it collates are by critics from the former 'white' Dominions, or about cultural concerns which derive, in the first instance at least, from those specific contexts. Not only does this raise many questions about the legitimacy of seeing Australian and Canadian culture, for example, as equivalent in genuinely meaningful ways to the cultures of non-white regions of the former European empires,[84] but it may even represent a process of subtle marginalization of the concerns of the latter regions.

The title of Anna Rutherford's *From Commonwealth to Post-Colonial* (1992) clearly suggests the degree to which the category 'Commonwealth' has now been subsumed into the postcolonial field as a consequence of such interventions – and, no doubt, by the waning importance of the Commonwealth as a political grouping in recent years. The declining prestige of the category 'Commonwealth literature' and, as a consequence, of the academic field of 'Commonwealth' literary studies – at least in its early formulations – has been accelerated by the hostile attitude of a number of writers who might once have been deemed suitable for inclusion within its remit. Even in the 1960s, figures as diverse as Lloyd Fernando, Clark Blaise and V. S. Naipaul had rejected the label of 'Commonwealth' writer, a rebuttal which is vigorously repeated by more recent authors, most notably by Salman Rushdie in 'Commonwealth Literature Does Not Exist' (1983). The category has also come under attack from critics like Aijaz Ahmad, who sees a neo-colonial cultural agenda, mediated primarily by the British Council, behind attempts to persist with its deployment, and concludes that 'all that is wrong with the category "Commonwealth Literature" begins with the *notion* that it should exist at all'.[85]

Nonetheless, the former conceptualization of the field, and its traditional nomenclature (the *Journal of Commonwealth Literature* continues to be published under the same name with which it began life in 1965, for example), retain the allegiance of many. Riemenschneider's defence, in *The History and Historiography of Commonwealth Literature*, of the comparative method of 'Commonwealth' literary studies as preferable to an exclusive focus on theorizing the nature of individual national literatures, on the basis that the latter exercise leads to substitution of aesthetic by ideological categories and a futile reliance on essentialist myths of identity, also remains persuasive for many in the field. In more recent times, Diana Brydon has confidently taken issue with Homi Bhabha's attack on the sub-discipline in 'Signs Taken for Wonders'

(1985), objecting with some justice that: 'Bhabha lumps all practitioners of Commonwealth history and literature together as stereotypically nationalist, expansionist and moralising, denying them the very specificity he accuses them of suppressing, and without providing any evidence for his claims.'[86] Indeed, as pointed out in the Preface to this volume, Edward Said, no less, has given new legitimacy to the sub-discipline, albeit with the caveat that the old model of a harmonious symphony of complementary literatures must give way to a paradigm represented by the concept of the 'atonal ensemble'.[87] And Cambridge University now seeks funds for a centre for Commonwealth Studies in which literary criticism is to play a significant part, an initiative which is, ironically, most closely associated with Churchill College, Soyinka's host college when he suffered his embarrassing snub in 1973. Whether this development signals the beginning of a counter-revolution against the success enjoyed by postcolonial modes of analysis in reorienting the study of the 'new literatures' inaugurated in the West by 'Commonwealth' literary studies remains to be seen.

2

Edward Said:

Orientalism and beyond

It is in the context of this institutional network of literary-critical practices – and the values which underwrote them – that the emergence of postcolonial theory, in the shape of Edward Said's *Orientalism* (1978) needs to be situated. Said's importance was initially considered to derive primarily from his mediation of the critical methods associated with certain kinds of French 'high theory' into the Anglo-American academic world of the 1970s. *Orientalism*, moreover, provided one of the first examples of a sustained application of such modes of analysis to Anglophone cultural history and textual tradition. More specifically, *Orientalism* was to adapt elements of this new theory (which in certain respects reinforced, as well as challenged, an older Marxist tradition) to the study of the connections between Western culture and imperialism, to argue that all Western systems of cultural description are deeply contaminated with what Said describes as 'the politics, the consider-ations, the positions, and the strategies of power'.[1] It is this insistent emphasis on the relationship between Western representation and knowledge on the one hand, and Western material and political power on the other, which underwrites the decisive push *Orientalism* gave to the transformation of earlier metropolitan approaches to the study of the literature of empire and the new literatures which began to emerge from the decolonized regions, into what is now known as the postcolonial field of study. At the same time, however, Said is also seminal for bringing to bear – again for the first time – issues associated with race, empire and ethnicity on that same 'high theory' in a manner which pointed to its complicities in culture-specific, even ethnocentric, ways of thinking. As Robert Young puts it in *White Mythologies*:

The appropriation of French theory by Anglo-American intellectuals is marked, and marred, by its consistent excision of the issue of Eurocentrism and its relation to colonialism. Not until Edward Said's *Orientalism* (1978) did it become a significant issue for Anglo-American literary theory.[2]

It is, then, difficult to overestimate the impact of Said's text in helping to reorient the disciplinary sub-fields described in the last two sections of chapter 1. As Joseph Bristow's *Empire Boys* (1991) suggests, for 'the majority of white academics',[3] the debate about postcoloniality began with Said. A large debt is also acknowledged by Homi Bhabha and Gayatri Spivak. Bhabha's 'Postcolonial Criticism' (1992), for instance, asserts that '*Orientalism* inaugurated the postcolonial field' and Gayatri Spivak describes it in similarly glowing terms as 'the source book in our discipline'.[4] As such praise might imply, Said's work has provided a spring-board for many of those coming after him. For instance, Robert Young's critique of Western historiography (particularly of its Marxist incarnations) in *White Mythologies* is rooted in what Said describes as his desire to redress the West's 'homogenizing and incorporating world historical scheme that assimilated non-synchronous developments, histories, cultures, and peoples to it'.[5] And as chapter 4 will demonstrate, Bhabha's essays in the period up to around 1988 can be understood at least in part as an effort to develop Said's treatment of questions of psychic affect and identification in colonial relations, issues which *Orientalism* raises without engaging with in any great detail. Such work is often revisionary, of course; for instance (as will be argued in more detail in the next chapter), what is arguably Gayatri Spivak's most important single essay, 'Can the Subaltern Speak?' (1988), can be seen in large measure as an attempt to effect a reversal of the terms of Said's critique of Foucault and Derrida in *The World, the Text, and the Critic* (1983). The point is, however, that it is Said who so often sets up the terms of reference of subsequent debate in the postcolonial field.

Even among those who are essentially hostile to Said, like John MacKenzie or Aijaz Ahmad, *Orientalism* is recognized as a seminal text, the influence of which must be undone before what are considered to be more adequate modes of analysis of the relation between culture and (neo-)colonialism can be elaborated. Thus in the course of Ahmad's attempt in *In Theory* to advance Marxism as the most fruitful framework within which to study such questions, much the longest chapter is devoted to analysis of *Orientalism*. Nor, despite his polemic against Said, is Ahmad easily able to escape the influence of Said's own thinking. The force of *In Theory*'s critique derives in large measure from attention to Said's privileged position within an institutional framework which, Ahmad argues, is compromised by the Western academy's complicity in the reproduction of the current international division of labour. This, however, repeats the thrust of some of Said's own arguments even as it redirects them against Said himself.[6] For one of the most notable and novel aspects of *Orientalism*, at least as regards the Anglo-American context at the particular moment that it appeared, is Said's continuous insistence on the importance of attention to the political and material effects of Western scholarship and academic institutions, and their affiliations to the world outside them. Said rejects the traditional liberal understanding of the humanities as organized round the pursuit of 'pure' or 'disinterested' knowledge. Instead he sees such practices as deeply implicated in the operations and technologies of power, by virtue of the fact that all scholars (and artists) are subject to particular historical, cultural and institutional affiliations which are governed in the last instance by the dominant ideology and political imperatives of the society in question. Consequently, Said argues, 'ideas, cultures and histories cannot seriously be studied without their force, or more precisely their configurations of power, also being studied.'[7]

In advancing these arguments Said draws on two principal methodological sources, Foucault and Gramsci. For Said's early work at least, the more important influence is probably Foucault. Orientalism follows Foucault in two principal ways; first of all, in its conception of what power is and how it operates. As is now well known, Foucault rejects the conception of power as a force which is based upon simple repression or even juridical sanction in (post-)Enlightenment (Western) societies, or as something which percolates downwards pyramid fashion from institutions at the apex like royalty or the state. In place of what *The History of Sexuality* (1976) describes as the 'repressive hypothesis',[8] Foucault sees power as an 'impersonal' force operating through a multiplicity of sites and channels, constructing what he calls a 'pastoral' regime, through which it seeks to control its subjects by 're(-)forming' them, and in so doing, making them conform to their place in the social system as objects of power. In a series of studies, he has demonstrated this proposition in relation to the psycho-sexual domain, the regime of punishment and the discourses surrounding madness and reason. The key instrument of power in all these domains is 'knowledge' insofar as the subjects of power are first identified as such, whether 'deviant' or not, and consequently made available for 're(-)forming'. From these case studies, Foucault develops a powerful argument linking all forms of 'the will to knowledge'[9] and all modes of cultural representation of 'the Other', or marginal constituencies, more or less explicitly, to the exercise of power. Secondly, Said adapts from Foucault the argument that 'discourse' – the medium which constitutes power and through which it is exercised – 'constructs' the objects of its knowledge. As Foucault puts it in *Discipline and Punish* (1975), discourse 'produces reality; it produces domains of objects and rituals of truth.'[10] In Said's work, then, the regime of disciplinary power inscribed in Orientalism transforms the 'real' East into a discursive 'Orient', or rather substitutes the one for the other.

Nonetheless, there are some important differences between Foucault and Said, notably concerning the issues of intention and, to a different degree, the possibilities and forms of resistance to the dominant. In these respects, Said inaugurates the 'catachrestic' reading of Western methodological sources which is a distinguishing feature of much subsequent postcolonial theory. For Foucault, power is in a sense an anonymous network of relations which is strategic only insofar as it seeks to maximize itself by all means possible. Governments, for example, are simply its agents and not its authors (and for Foucault, of course, individuals – authors included – are only ever 'functions' of the systems within which they operate, not the sovereign agents conceived of in traditional humanism). For Said, by contrast, Western domination of the non-Western world is not some arbitrary phenomenon but a conscious and purposive process governed by the will and intention of individuals as well as by institutional imperatives. Moreover, in theory at least, Said retains a conception of the individual's capacity to evade the constraints of both the dominant power and its normative 'archive' of cultural representations: 'Yet unlike Michel Foucault, to whose work I am greatly indebted, I do believe in the determining imprint of individual writers upon the otherwise anonymous collective body of texts constituting a discursive formation like Orientalism.'[11] Said thus clearly reinscribes a model of agency and intentionality drawn not just from Marxism, but from a humanist tradition to which, judging by the generous praise accorded to scholars like Erich Auerbach, he remains deeply attached.

Said attempts to synthesize these aspects of Foucault's thinking with the work of the Italian Marxist Gramsci, seeing cultural (re)production – of which practices like 'humanistic' research or fiction writing are only one, albeit important, part – operating alongside more obvious and 'public' mediations of power such as government and the law to position classes in hierarchical relations to each other. As with Foucault, Gramsci is ostensibly less concerned with the repressive apparatuses of state power and more with the way that the consent of the subordinate (or 'subaltern') sectors of society is 'solicited' in the domain of 'civil society' through such channels as education and cultural practices. Thus he argues that 'one should not count only on the material force which power gives in order to exercise an effective leadership.'[12] (Having said this, Gramsci also warns against 'a neglect of the moment of political society, of force, of domination'.[13]) *Orientalism* owes much to Gramsci's conceptualizations of the dynamics of domination. For instance, Said argues that: 'It is hegemony, or rather the result of cultural hegemony at work, that gives Orientalism the durability and the strength I have been speaking about so far.'[14]

It is this focus on the 'civil domain' of cultural relations as the medium through which power operates most effectively which largely underwrites Said's attempted synthesis of Foucault and Gramsci. More particularly, the urgent aim of *Orientalism* is to expose the degree to which Western systems of knowledge and representation have been involved in the long history of the West's material and political subordination of the non-Western world. Said is preoccupied especially by the relationship between the West and the East and the particular discourse which mediated that relationship, which he calls Orientalism. In using this term, Said appropriates a label which had hitherto been used in two contexts in particular. Firstly, it described those East India Company officials who opposed the programmes of the Westernizing radicals represented by figures like T. B. Macaulay and Lord Bentinck, whose influence was dominant from the 1820s to the 1850s.[15] These opponents of the modernizing 'Anglicists' were closely associated with the group of scholars, also known as Orientalists, who were at work in India in the period 1780–1830. These scholars were generally understood, at least until Said's text appeared, as enthusiasts for Indian culture and learning, and as cultural relativists who recognized the West's debts to the civilizations of the East.[16]

For Said, what is at issue is not so much the question of whether identification with Eastern culture in such scholarship was sympathetic or not, but the fact that (as he sees it) all Western discourse about the East is determined in the last instance by the will to domination over Oriental territories and peoples. For Said, the pursuit of knowledge in the colonial domain cannot be 'disinterested', firstly because the relationship between cultures on which it depends is an unequal one, and secondly because such knowledge, whether of the language, customs or religions of the colonized, is consistently put at the service of the colonial administration. From this perspective, even the kind of scholarship associated with Sir William Jones ultimately expresses a '*will* or *intention* to understand, in some cases to control, manipulate, even to incorporate, what is a manifestly different (or alternative and novel) world'.[17] Said supports his argument by analysis of the work of a wide range of scholars and writers, principally in the period from the eighteenth century to the present, who were employed as either imperial administrators or advisers. Building on the research of predecessors like Jacques Waardenburg, Said demonstrates the often intimate relations between Western texts of cultural description, representation and scholarship on the one hand and specific institutions and techniques of colonial management and surveillance on the other. Thus Said concludes that figures as diverse as Gertrude Bell, T. E. Lawrence and St John Philby were 'posted to the Orient as agents of empire ... formulators of policy alternatives because of their intimate and expert knowledge of the Orient and of Orientals'.[18]

In Said's view, Orientalism (in the sense in which he uses the term) operates in the service of the West's hegemony over the East primarily by producing the East discursively as the West's inferior 'Other', a manoeuvre which strengthens – indeed, even partially constructs – the West's self-image as a superior civilization. It does this principally by distinguishing and then essentializing the identities of East and West through a dichotomizing system of representations embodied in the regime of stereotype, with the aim of making rigid the sense of difference between the European and Asiatic parts of the world. As a consequence, the East is characteristically produced in Orientalist discourse as – variously – voiceless, sensual, female, despotic, irrational and backward. By contrast, the West is represented as masculine, democratic, rational, moral, dynamic and progressive. The regime of stereotype does not always, or necessarily, mediate the East in such ostensibly negative terms. As Said points out, the East is also at times vaunted in the West for its spirituality, longevity and stability. In describing these qualities as 'overvalued', however, Said suggests that the vision inscribed in such motifs is as distorted as its negative counterpart and similarly produced, above all else, by Western projections onto the Other.

Such patterns of description – and the power relations they inscribe – are illustrated with reference to an enormous diversity of Western representations. The geographical scope of Said's inquiry is extensive. While centred primarily on the West's relations with the Islamic world of the Middle East, *Orientalism* ranges over much of the rest of the Eastern world and at times suggests that its arguments bear on the imperialized world as a whole. Said's analysis is also ambitious in terms of the range of fields of knowledge and representation which he covers. The scope of the text in this respect is described as follows: 'I set out to examine not only scholarly works but also works of literature, political tracts, journalistic texts, travel books, religious and philological studies.'[19] *Orientalism* initially addresses these diverse fields in relation to the imperial histories of Britain and France, before moving on to explore their influence on the contemporary neo-colonial global order supervised by the United States. The historical range of Said's inquiry is even more comprehensive than this might suggest, however, stretching as it does from US interventions in Islamic regions in the 1970s right back to the era of classical Greece and the conflict between Athens and Persia. In this respect, it is important to remember that *Orientalism* is 'simply' the first part of a trilogy made up of *The Question of Palestine* (1979) and *Covering Islam* (1981). These two works convincingly demonstrate the continuing influence of the historical discourses analysed in *Orientalism* on the West's current dealings with the Middle East.

The formidable weight of Said's argument is reinforced by the intimate and homologous relationship he uncovers between three ostensibly discrete aspects of the Western cultural formation. Firstly, Orientalism refers to the 'primary' representations of the East and Eastern peoples which have circulated in Western discourse since classical times, the basic patterns and tropes of which have embodied the West's 'knowledge' of the Orient. Secondly, the term refers to the 'style' in which such tropes are conceived and presented, by which Said appears to mean something deeper than surface rhetoric or convention – invoking more, perhaps, questions of political positionality and moral attitude. Thirdly, it describes the systems of scholarship and the set of cultural institutions refining, commenting upon and circulating those primary representa-tions. Moreover, by virtue of Said's stress on the indivisible relationship between knowledge and power, Orientalism at times seems to include the material structures and processes – military, political and economic – which have since the eighteenth century at least kept the East subordinate to the West. Each aspect of the Orientalist formation reinforces the others. Thus military conquest makes available new peoples and cultures for study. Such study in turn enables hegemony to be confirmed or extended, for instance by providing knowledge of the customs of subject peoples, which then forms the basis for administrative policy and action. Meanwhile 'primary' representations of the colonized (the fictions of Rider Haggard or Kipling, for example) circulate in the metropolis, encouraging support for intervention in, or further Western-ization of, the conquered territories.

CONTRADICTIONS IN ORIENTALISM

For five years or so after its first appearance, the argument of Orientalism remained largely uncontested – a tribute to its power and the originality, or unfamiliarity, of the terms in which it was constructed. Inevitably, however, critiques of it began to appear from the early 1980s onwards. These analyses became progressively more searching, to the extent that by the end of the decade not only were Said's interpretations of individual writers or disciplines within Orientalism being questioned, but the text's very premises – political and methodological – had been thrown into doubt. Said was to lend authority to such challenges himself by fundamentally reconsidering the approach to colonial discourse analysis which Orientalism had elaborated. As has been seen, Said is by no means an uncritical disciple of Foucault, even in Orientalism. 'The Problem of Textuality: Two Exemplary Positions', published the same year as Orientalism, also signals dissatisfaction with aspects of the Foucauldian methodology which is such a distinctive feature of the latter text. His turn away from discourse theory is even more decisive in the revised version of this essay, 'Criticism Between Culture and System'

(1983). In 'Orientalism Reconsidered' (1985), 'Foucault and the Imagination of Power' (1986) and *Culture and Imperialism* (1993), Said moves ever further away – in theory at least – from the Foucauldian perspectives elaborated in *Orientalism*. Equally, while *Culture and Imperialism* continues to pay tribute to Gramsci as a seminal modern thinker, the arguments about hegemony developed in *Orientalism* play a less central role in the latter text.

The commentaries on *Orientalism* which appeared in the period up to 1990 cumulatively exposed various and deep-rooted contradictions in its arguments. These were explained principally in terms of Said's attempt to combine aspects of the Marxist tradition of cultural theory, with its realist epistemology and conventional vision of power as repressive and working on behalf of certain material interests, together with Foucauldian theory, which privileges discourse and language as the prime determinants of social reality and which sees power as 'decentred', 'impersonal' and arbitrary in terms of its 'social interests'. A subsidiary pattern of contradiction was identified in Said's asymmetrically related attempt to marry together the anti-humanism of Foucault, on the one hand, with the traditional humanist scholarship represented by figures like Auerbach, whom *Orientalism* holds up as the exemplary twentieth-century Western scholar, on the other – and both of these with Gramsci, who occupies an intermediate position in respect of the questions of intention, agency and the possibility of resistance to the dominant. In the eyes of Dennis Porter, James Clifford and Robert Young, who provided the most influential critiques of *Orientalism* prior to Ahmad's *In Theory*, Said fails convincingly to synthesize or harmonize these various methods of cultural analysis, each with its own distinct epistemology, social values and political assumptions, leading to what Clifford describes in *The Predicament of Culture* (1988) as a persistent hermeneutical short-circuit at the very centre of his thesis.[20]

These short-circuits may be briefly summarized as follows. First of all, there is an at times radical contradiction in *Orientalism*'s discussion of the relationship between discursive Orientalism and the material practices and politics of imperialism, which derives in part from Said's attempt to abolish the distinction between the two terms. On the one hand he suggests that the traditions of Western scholarship and representation of the Orient preceded and even determined expansion into the East, laying the foundations, for example, of Napoleon's invasion of Egypt. He also argues at other moments, however, that the latter determined the former, so that 'modern' French Orientalism derives from the new knowledge which Napoleon's expedition made available. This issue is never resolved, any more than the deeper contradiction in the epistemology of *Orientalism* to which it is related. At certain moments Said follows the logic of discourse theory in his insistence that the Orient constructed by Orientalism is not so much an objective or reliable representation of the 'real' East as an essentially imagined or constructed space. On the other hand, Said also claims that the West has, in fact, consistently misrepresented the Orient, thus implicitly conceiving of it in materialist terms as a real place which is independent of and prior to its representation by the West. From this perspective, Orientalist discourse is to be understood as a form of ideological knowledge in the traditional Marxist sense, which could in theory be corrected by a changed form of consciousness of the Orient.

The second major methodological difficulty in *Orientalism* centres on Said's own position as a critic of the system he analyses. He often strongly rejects the premise of traditional humanist criticism that the critic can remain outside the 'text' or discursive field that is being analysed and consequently provide a 'disinterested' account of it. At the same time, Said is in practice persistently able to escape the constraints of the all-enveloping system which he criticizes – and of which he is part, insofar as the Western academy is complicit in (neo-)colonial forms of knowledge production; and he is also in practice able to provide an 'objective' and 'truthful' critique of the history of Western representations of the East. Said negotiates his way to this privileged space outside the system partly by recourse to traditional humanist arguments about his own 'lived experience' as an exile and to a conception of the critic as occupying 'a sensitive nodal point'[21] in his culture, a formulation which would not be out of place in the work of a critic like F. R. Leavis. Even more problematically, Said sees Orientalism as a 'department' of humanism,[22] yet at the same time proposes a reconstituted version of humanism, adumbrated in the work of certain Orientalists themselves in the first instance, as the way forward beyond the disablingly dichotomizing and essentializing vision which is characteristic of Orientalism.

The contradictions between Said's humanism and his recourse to Gramsci, on the one hand, and his anti-humanism on the other, are most sharply revealed in what is probably the knottiest methodological problem in *Orientalism*. This derives from Said's discrimination between what he calls 'latent' and 'manifest' Orientalism. This analytic distinction recalls the binary arrangements which underpin a number of essentially structuralist modes of critique. Thus Marxist cultural analysis was traditionally organized round the relationship of base to superstructure, Freudian psychoanalysis around the relationship of conscious to unconscious (as well as around the distinction between 'latent' and 'manifest' content in dream interpretation) and Saussure's system of linguistics around the relationship of *langue* to *parole*. In Said's scheme, 'latent' signifies the 'deep structure' of Orientalism, the political positionings and will to power which supposedly remain constant in the discourse, whereas 'manifest' signifies the 'surface detail' – the individual discipline, cultural work, scholar or even national tradition. While the force of Said's strategic argument depends largely on demonstrating the determining force of the former aspect of Orientalism over the latter, there are enough moments in the text when this is not the case to suggest a deep-rooted tension in Said's thinking over the degree to which the underlying will to power of Orientalism organizes the particulars of which it is constituted.

The conflicts involved in Said's attempt to theorize the relationship between 'latent' and 'manifest' Orientalism are signalled at the most basic level in his divided view of how Orientalist texts are to be read. Insofar as he focuses on 'manifest' Orientalism, he elaborates a reading strategy characterized by close readings of the individual text, to highlight the ways in which particular writers diverge from the patterns established by 'latent' Orientalism:

> What interests me most as a scholar is not the gross political verity but the detail, as indeed what interests us in someone like Lane or Flaubert or Renan is not the (to him) indisputable truth that Occidentals are superior to Orientals, but the profoundly worked over and modulated evidence of his detailed work within the very wide space opened up by that truth.[23]

By contrast, when Said emphasizes 'latent' Orientalism as the privileged term in the opposition he draws, he argues that the appropriate reading practice is one which 'does not entail analysis of what lies hidden in the Orientalist text, but analysis rather of the text's surface ... I do not think that this idea can be overemphasized.'[24] In practical terms, the difficulties these arguments pose are immense, since they are presented as alternative, and not as dialectically linked, ways of reading. One is left with a stark choice. Is one to approach Kipling, for instance, simply in terms of how he reflects the dominant ethnographic, anthropological and political thought of his period and in terms of the way in which he reinforces the vision of India in earlier fictional representations of the sub-continent? Or is one to approach him as a writer whose 'unique' personal style and vision question and even challenge the dominant ideologies of imperialism and received traditions of writing about empire? Said never quite solves the problem of how to conceptualize the relationship between the 'latent' and 'manifest' aspects of Orientalism, a failure which certainly partially explains his often radically contradictory accounts of a number of key thematic issues in the discourse which he analyses.

In contrast to earlier critics like Porter, Clifford and Young, however, I would argue that the often profound paradoxes, even confusions, within the argument of *Orientalism* do not derive in the first instance from Said's incompatible epistemological positions and methodological procedures, important though these undoubtedly are. Instead, I would suggest that they arise primarily from Said's recognition, conflictual and uneven as this often is, that colonial discourse is in fact fractured in its operations, aims and affective economy. Said's recognition of the divided nature of Orientalism is already apparent from the very beginning of his text, which suggests that 'European culture gained in strength and identity by setting itself off against the Orient as a sort of surrogate and even underground self.'[25] This is a somewhat confusing formulation; on the one hand, it seems to imply that the West consciously defines the East as outside itself and radically different or Other; at the same time, the East is also apparently located intimately within the West as an integral, if generally unacknowledged, part of its own constitution and identity. While the relationship between West and East remains conflictual, whichever interpretation one wishes to favour, it certainly confirms that Said does conceive of the West as divided – on the analogy of the tension between the conscious and unconscious elements of the psyche.

Said's acknowledgement of a dichotomy within Western representations of the non-West in fact recurs throughout his text. For instance, aside from the basic division between 'latent' and 'manifest' Orientalism, he differentiates between two forms of the discourse that are generated respectively by the 'textual attitude' and by 'lived experience' of the East. Towards the end of *Orientalism*, Said notes a tension between what he calls 'vision' and 'narrative' in Orientalist discourse (a particularly important discrimination to which I shall return in due course). At another point, he distinguishes between what he calls the 'scientific' attitude which informs certain kinds of Orientalist discourse and the 'aesthetic' approach characteristic of other parts of the archive. At other moments, as already implied, Said points to a conflict between the conscious aims, will or intentions of Orientalism and what he describes as the 'battery of desires, repressions, investments and projections'[26] operating in the affective realm of the colonizing formation. The first term of each of these sets of binary oppositions is in conflict with the second, producing distinctly different patterns of representations of the Orient. This points to a persistent inner dissonance throughout the history of the discourse and across its varied fields of knowledge, a perception which prepares the ground for later work like Bhabha's.

These varied instances of Said's recognition of the conflictual nature of colonial discourse in part reflect the prevarication of *Orientalism* over the larger question of the degree to which 'manifest', or 'surface', Orientalism is determined by its 'latent', or 'deep', counterpart. Such evidence also, however, suggests the need for a second modification of the early critiques of *Orientalism*. While these see the text as conflictual in terms of its method, they tend to argue that at a thematic level, Said's vision of Orientalism is itself homogenizing and totalizing, and that in this respect he replicates the operations of the discourse which he criticizes. For instance, Young claims in *White Mythologies* that, for Said, conflict can only 'arise [within the dominant discourse] from the intervention of the outsider critic, a romantic alienated being battling like Byron's Manfred against the totality of the universe'.[27] Instead, I would argue that Said commutes uncertainly between a recognition of the heterogeneity of colonial discourse on the one hand and a conviction of its essential consistency on the other.

Said's first major prevarication over the consistency or otherwise of Orientalism derives from the fact that the discourse is produced by different national cultures, in particular those of Britain, France and the United States. His insistence on the overriding importance of 'latent' Orientalism leads him at moments to underplay the differences between the various national traditions. For instance, at times there seems to be little distinction between nineteenth-century French and British Orientalism and their American equivalent a century later; all these Said proposes to consider 'as a unit'. Thus, despite the vastly changed material and political circumstances which underpin the rise of the USA to superpower status, Said detects a fundamental continuity in the system of knowledges which continues to enable Western dominance of the East. Thus far in his argument, Said is justifiably accused of homogenizing the sites of enunciation of Orientalist discourse, and in the process of suppressing important cultural and geographical, as well as historical, differences in the varied cultures of Western imperialism. Indeed, in this respect it can certainly be argued that Said repeats in reverse the alleged tendency of colonial discourse to homogenize its subject peoples, by implying that colonizing cultures 'are all the same'.

By contrast, Dennis Porter suggests in 'Orientalism and Its Problems' that the distinctions between 'national' discourses of empire and the divergent patterns of representation to which they give rise are much greater than Said recognizes. While he does not explore this argument in any detail, it is subsequently advanced substantively by Lisa Lowe's *Critical Terrains: French and British Orientalisms* (1991), which demonstrates much more marked variations between French and British Orientalism than Said apparently allows, especially if one looks outside the relatively narrow historical field of the nineteenth century to which much of *Orientalism* is devoted. By comparison of figures as diverse as Lady Mary Wortley Montagu, E. M. Forster, Gustave Flaubert and Roland Barthes, Lowe demonstrates the degree to which not just different styles, but different thematic preoccupations, characterize the respective national traditions. Equally, she demonstrates that each national tradition is internally more varied than Said suggests. For instance, she points to a profound modification of Flaubert's initial conceptions of the Orient as the writer's career advanced and suggests that his later 'Orients' are in some ways diametrically opposed in terms of their political meanings to his earlier representations of the East.[28]

As early critics of *Orientalism* from C. F. Beckingham to James Clifford pointed out, moreover, German Orientalist scholarship poses a particular problem for Said's scheme, which, as has been seen, depends in a fundamental way on the argument that there is no 'pure' or disinterested knowledge of the Orient which is politically innocent or not complicit in the process of overseas expansion.[29] In 'Orientalism Reconsidered' (1985), Said somewhat irritably dismisses such objections as superficial or trivial, a position which may initially seem fair enough given the clear delimitation of his field in *Orientalism* as British, French and American colonial discourse. Nonetheless, the absence of a German empire (or even of a German nation), throughout much of the historical period that Said considers, weakens his claim about the intimate relationship between Orientalist knowledge and the will to power overseas. Indeed, in *Orientalism* Said explains that he decided to exclude German scholarship precisely because Germany was not an imperial power and therefore had 'no *national* interest in the Orient', as well as on the more contentious grounds of the allegedly superior 'quality, consistency, and [greater] mass'[30] of Anglo-American-French Orientalism.

Such critics nonetheless tend to overlook the fact that Said does in fact concede a certain amount of difference between the various national versions of colonial discourse on which he concentrates, though at times the terms in which such distinctions are framed are somewhat vague and schematic. For instance, he suggests that 'English writers on the whole had a more pronounced and harder sense of what Oriental pilgrimages might entail than the French.'[31] Later on, Said distinguishes between these two inflections of Orientalism in stylistic terms. The British tradition, represented by Edward Lane, is generally impersonal and scientific in emphasis, representing the subject peoples in a detached mode which corresponds to a desire to classify in order to control; consequently, there is little attention in such work to the positionality or dramatic role of the observer himself (it is almost invariably a he), and not much self-reflection in a stylistic or methodological sense about how to mediate the Orient. The French tradition, represented by Chateaubriand, is distinguished by its 'aesthetic' quality and sympathetic identification with subordinate cultures. The observer is characteristically an important part of the subject matter in question and there is greater self-consciousness about the text as artefact. For Said, such contrasts are more or less historically consistent, producing a similar set of differences between the work of figures like Sir Hamilton Gibb and Louis Massignon in the following century. More than anything else, the distinctions between these two branches of Orientalism are explained in terms of the different political histories of each nation's involvement in the Orient. Thus while the nineteenth-century British traveller in the Middle East was imbued with a sense of power which derived from the continuing expansion of British influence in the East, the French pilgrim was afflicted with a sense of acute loss as a result of the collapse of French influence in the region after the fall of Napoleon. As a consequence, Said suggests, the emphasis of French Orientalism in terms of its political vision was essentially on developing strategies of cultural influence, whereas the British version, by contrast, was more intimately and directly concerned with the material exigencies of actual rule.

While Said's evident desire to acknowledge the distinctions between British and French Orientalism partly answers the objection that he homogenizes colonial discourse in this respect, his explanation for the differences is not wholly convincing. There seems no good reason to exclude North Africa from his account of the West's relationship with the Islamic world in the modern period. If the *Maghreb*, much of which was within the French sphere of influence by the mid nineteenth century, is inserted into Said's scheme, many of the assumptions on which he bases his comparison between French and British Orientalisms are called into question. For example, given that his main focus is on the Arabs and Islam, Said cannot correctly claim that at the time of Lord Cromer's administration in Egypt, as far as 'the actual space of the Orient was concerned ... England was really there, France was not, except as a flighty temptress of the Oriental yokels'.[32] By the time of Massignon, moreover, much of the Middle East itself had fallen under French control as a consequence of the defeat of the Ottoman empire in World War One. Thus the predominance of the 'aesthetic' attitude in French Orientalism cannot convincingly be attributed to its lack of direct involvement in the Arab world. Moreover, Said's evidently greater sympathy for French Orientalism seems paradoxical in the context of his general desire to valorize narratives based on 'lived experience' over those which embody the 'textual' attitude. For the attitude of French Orientalism must necessarily be more 'aesthetic' or 'textual' in nature than its British counterpart if one accepts for the moment the argument that French Orientalists had less direct involvement in the Middle East than the British writers examined by Said. Finally, one must ask whether Said does not himself reproduce the kind of stereotyping which he condemns in Orientalism in making such distinctions. British Orientalists, as epitomized by Lane, come across as characteristically repressed, correct, unemotional and solitary; Gerard de Nerval and Chateaubriand by comparison seem spontaneous, emotional *bon viveurs*, happy to participate in their 'host' cultures.

A second major prevarication over the consistency or otherwise of Orientalism can be noted in Said's analysis of the historical development of the discourse. Early on, he asks the question: 'What changes, modulations, refinements, even revolutions take place within Orientalism?'[33] At times he appears to answer himself by arguing that there are distinct phases in the discourse, even radical transitions, which one might expect, given the methodological debts to Foucault, to correspond to the latter's notion of changing epistemes. One such shift is located with surprising precision in 1312, a date one must suppose is shorthand for the onset of the Renaissance, and another, as for Foucault, in the last third of the eighteenth century. While this seems to mark the most important moment of transition within Orientalism, corresponding as it does to a period in which the West's influence in the East is materially and rapidly enlarging, another shift in the discourse is identified as early as the 1840s, another in the late nineteenth century, yet others in both the 1920s and 1940s, at which point there had allegedly been 'such changes in [Orientalism] that it became scarcely recognizable'.[34]

On the other hand, it often seems that the continuities within colonial discourse are much stronger than these discontinuities so that in Said's account Orientalism at times has the unchanging consistency which the discourse itself allegedly projects onto the Orient. In this sense Said diverges markedly from Foucault's argument that changes in the Western regime of knowledge were violent and discontinuous. For Said the main difference in the discourse between the mid eighteenth century and the beginning of the nineteenth century is not a qualitative one at all, it transpires, but rather a question of its increased scope or range. In fact 'as a set of beliefs, as a method of analysis, Orientalism cannot develop. Indeed, it is the doctrinal antithesis of development.'[35] As already suggested, such claims enable Said to tie together Aeschylus' *The Persians*, as an early example of the discourse, with Jimmy Carter's Middle Eastern policy making two millennia later, positing an essentially constant rearticulation of the same intrinsic vision in Orientalism throughout the written records of Western culture. And to the extent that Said can then claim that 'Orientalism, in its post-eighteenth-century form, could never revise itself',[36] of course, he completely contradicts the arguments outlined in the previous paragraph about the radical changes in twentieth-century versions of the discourse.

The question of the historical consistency of Orientalism is bound up with the crucial issue of the possibilities of resistance to the dominant order and its regimes of representation. However, Said's conflicting account of such issues arises primarily from his recognition of certain kinds of resistance to Orientalism, rather than from contradictions between his methodological sources (which certainly exacerbate this crucial instance of Said's general equivocation over the relationship of 'latent' to 'manifest' Orientalism). Perhaps the sharpest difference of all between Gramsci and Foucault is in their conception of resistance. To some degree, it is justifiable to see Foucault as a profoundly pessimistic thinker in this respect. While he argues in *The History of Sexuality* that '[w]here there is power, there is resistance', *Discipline and Punish* presents disciplinary power as 'the non-reversible subordination of one group of people by another'.[37] Moreover, his next book, *Language, Counter-Memory, Practice* (1977), explicitly sees human history not as progress to emancipation but as a cyclical process which leads from 'domination to domination'.[38] By contrast, Gramsci – as a Marxist – envisions the possibility of (self-)liberation for subaltern and 'emergent' groups and the overthrow of the traditionally hegemonic orders. Indeed, Gramsci could be seen as being as optimistic as Foucault is the reverse. For Gramsci, no form of despotism is invulnerable: 'Even the history of the oriental satrapies was liberty, because it was movement and a process of unfolding, so much so that those satrapies did fall.'[39]

To a large degree, it is arguable that a pessimistically Foucauldian perspective on the question of resistance predominates in *Orientalism*. To this extent, as Porter suggests in '*Orientalism* and its Problems', a particular weakness of Said's account is its failure to take account of how Orientalist discourse reproduced itself as a hegemonic form of knowledge. In this respect, Said overlooks Gramsci's argument that one hegemonic principle only 'triumphs after having defeated another hegemonic principle. . . . Not to enquire into the reasons for this victory means writing an externally descriptive history, without bringing to the fore the necessary and causal links.'[40] At times, Said seems to abandon the materialist method in his assumption that Orientalist discourse was always, somehow, simply there; in other words, he fails to explain how or why Orientalism arose, or the struggles in which the dominant forms and vision of Orientalist discourse were necessarily involved in order to become, and remain, dominant. For example, Said's scheme would be unable to explain how the relatively positive vision of Eastern culture associated with the Orientalists (as defined prior to Said) in India came to be superseded by the much more hostile one inscribed in the programme of Macaulay and the Anglicists, which led to the fundamental policy changes in colonial governance described by Gauri Viswanathan's *Masks of Conquest* (1989). As Porter concludes: 'Such a sense of hegemony as process in concrete historical conjunctures, as an evolving sphere of superstructural conflict in which power relations are continually reasserted, challenged, modified, is absent from Said's book.'[41] Said makes some attempt to explain how Orientalism in the late eighteenth century displaced earlier paradigms,[42] but there is no real recognition, even in this instance, of any *struggle* accompanying the emergence of the new version or how it suppressed competing visions of the East. The most unfortunate consequence of this omission is that Orientalism is itself perpetuated as a permanent, inevitable, even 'natural', mode of apprehending the non-Western world.

Said's characteristically deterministic vision of the operations of power in colonial relations leads him, in the first instance, to take insufficient account of resistance or contradiction *within* imperial culture itself. At moments he suggests that even those who were most critical of colonialism, like Marx, cannot escape the determinations of 'latent' Orientalism so that 'in the end it is the Romantic Orientalist vision that wins out, as Marx's theoretical socio-economic views become submerged in [a] classically standard image'[43] of the East. At such points, moreover, *Orientalism* seems to reinscribe the very forms of cultural essentialism for which Said condemns Orientalist discourse. Indeed, the Western observer is on one occasion presented as ontologically unable to know or represent the Orient in a truthful or sympathetic manner: 'It is therefore correct that every European, in what he could say about the Orient, was consequently a racist, an imperialist, and almost totally ethnocentric.'[44] Even figures like Chateaubriand and Nerval are compromised; their personal identification with Islamic peoples fails in the end to offset their 'perverse' reinscription of Orientalist 'vision'. Among modern Orientalists a similar complicity emerges, so that Gibb's 'extraordinarily sympathetic powers of identification' are overwhelmed by his 'reversion to the old Orientalist habit of speaking for the natives'.[45]

A further problem entailed by Said's failure to heed Gramsci's warning is that he does not take account of the abundant evidence that Western discourse itself registered the history which resisted its encroachments (as the Subaltern Studies group of historiographers have subsequently demonstrated in considerable volume and detail). Even in more recent times, when the West certainly has generally dominated the East, one can discern a distinct flexibility in patterns of Orientalist representation which corresponds to a recognition of the varying degrees and kinds of contestations of Western power by the colonized. Thus in nineteenth-century India, as I have argued in *Kipling and 'Orientalism'* (1986), British constructions of Islam and Hinduism shifted markedly according to changes in the perceived threat which each category of Indian subject posed to imperial control at different periods. For example, the 1857 uprisings in India radically modified the century-old stereotypes of the 'ravening Muslim' and of the 'mild Hindu' who was supposedly unmanly, meek and pliable.[46] Equally, as the largely Hindu-organized nationalist movement gathered strength in the last quarter of the century, Islam came to be considered a potential counterweight to nationalist agitation, and it began to be represented in significantly different and more positive ways to those current in the first half of the century. Meanwhile the educated urban Hindu was increasingly constructed in the *new* stereotype of the seditious and cunning 'babu'. In a more recent period still, Lisa

Lowe demonstrates that for French theorists such as Julia Kristeva and Barthes, Maoist China was for a while conceived of as utopian precisely because it was the only part of the world which genuinely seemed to escape the determinations of Western power. Similarly, the rise of anti-Japanese sentiment in the United States since the 1980s attests to the emergence of a new regime of representation which is clearly related to a growing sense of the relative economic enfeeblement of the West *vis-à-vis* its Eastern competitors.[47] Such evidence suggests that the West has always engaged in (re)negotiations of power with the East, which it never conceived of as absolute.

By contrast, the pessimistic Foucauldian in Said leads him at times to propose a model of colonial political relations in which all power lies with the colonizer. Thus according to one passage in *Orientalism*, imperial discourse operated 'with very little resistance on the Orient's part'.[48] This contentious claim leads to the almost total effacement of traces of opposition to Orientalist discourse from *outside* the dominant order. Indeed, when it is mentioned in *Orientalism*, subaltern counter-discourse is often treated somewhat dismissively, as in Said's description of the testimony of Oriental travellers to Europe: 'Eastern travellers were there to learn from and to gape at an advanced culture.'[49] Criticism of Said in this respect has been sharp, especially from critics based outside the West. Thus both Zakia Pathak et al.'s 'The Prisonhouse of Oriental-ism' (1991) and Ahmad's In Theory, for example, discern in Said's almost exclusive attention to the discourse of the colonizers a particularly worrying instance of his replication of the will of Orientalism itself to efface oppositional voices. As Said himself points out, Orientalism generally promotes an idea of the colonized subject as passive, silent and incapable of resistance. Said seems to accept at face value the power relations inscribed in the colonialist trope of 'surveying as if from a peculiarly suited vantage point the passive, sensual, feminine, even silent and supine East'.[50] As Zakia Pathak and her co-authors argue: 'The history that *Orientalism* helps recover from the white text is thus monologic; it does not help us to recuperate the other narratives which interrupt the hegemony of the narrative of Imperialism.'[51] In 'Oriental-ism Reconsidered', Said answers such criticism by arguing that it is largely irrelevant. Recognizing that 'what for the most part got left out of Orientalism was precisely the very history that resisted its ideological as well as political encroachments', Said nonetheless justifies his approach in *Orientalism* by reminding his audience that his focus was on Western discourses of subject peoples; consequently, he repeats his earlier argument that in imperial discourse the Orient was 'not Europe's interlocutor, but its silent Other'.[52]

It would be misleading, however, to claim that Said fails to register *any* signs of resistance to the authority of Orientalist discourse. First of all, he does recognize external resistance in the form of increasingly organized opposition to imperialism and neo-colonialism among the subject peoples. Indeed, the first page of *Orientalism* expresses a sense of the impending end of the era of Orientalism as the culmination of a long historical process of struggle. Later on Said argues that in the sixteenth century, 'the center [sic] of power shifted Westwards and now in the late twentieth century it seems to be directing itself back towards the East again'.[53] The fragmentation of Orientalist authority accelerates in the aftermath of World War One (despite the defeat of Turkey and the West's appropriation of its former imperial possessions – an apparent complication which Said does not address) when the Orient increasingly 'appeared to constitute a challenge . . . to the West's spirit, knowledge, and imperium'.[54] Indeed so successful had been resistance to Orientalism by the middle of this century that Said is prepared to risk generalizations of the kind that lay him open to the complaints of imperial historians like John MacKenzie about the accuracy of his scholarship. Thus Said claims that by 1955 'the entire Orient had gained its political independence from the Western empires' (an argument which is not only inaccurate in itself but which also, of course, contradicts the equally global statement at the end of Said's text about the 'triumph of Orientalism' in the post-war era).[55] Again, what is missing from this account of resistance is any sense of process, or analysis of how the colonized negotiated and challenged the authority of Orientalism, such as might have been available through favouring Gramsci rather than Foucault (or attending to colonial archives themselves). The challenge to Orientalism is never contextualized sufficiently, so that it, too, emerges abruptly, without any apparent rationale and with no sense of the variety of forms it took.

Secondly, Said at times concedes that the challenge to Orientalism has been embodied not just by the colonized in mass liberation movements, or by oppositional non-Western scholars such as himself, but by certain Orientalist scholars, from Chateaubriand in the nineteenth century to the American Middle East Studies Association today. To this extent, the inconsistency of Said's own position is dictated once more by a tension that he discerns in the hegemonic discourse itself.

For insofar as Said admits the possibility of 'good' Orientalists like Massignon, he does in fact recognize resistance from *within* the colonizing culture to the dominant regimes of Orientalism. What is so strikingly paradoxical about *Orientalism* from this perspective is the number of Orientalist scholars who seem to operate in an oppositional way within the archive. As well as Nerval and Flaubert, Said also praises the work of scholars like George Sale, Simon Ockley and William Whiston in the eighteenth century, of Antoine-Isaac de Sacy and Lane in the nineteenth century and of Gibb, Jacques Waardenburg, Jacques Berque and

Maxime Rodinson in the twentieth, all of whose careers suggest that 'scholars and critics who are trained in the traditional Orientalist disciplines are perfectly capable of freeing themselves from the old ideological straitjacket'.[56] Moreover, throughout the period of modern Orientalism first established in the eighteenth century, a significant and consistent counter-discourse defined by a 'sympathetic identification' with subject peoples is apparent. Indeed, one characteristic of 'modern' Orientalism, according to Said, was 'a selective identification with regions and cultures not one's own [which] wore down the obduracy of self and identity, which had been polarized into a community of embattled believers facing barbarian hordes'.[57] Insofar as Said privileges 'manifest' over 'latent' Orientalism at these points, he also suggests – in complete contradiction to the argument outlined earlier – that one culture can represent another in non-coercive or even non-judgemental ways, even when an unequal relation of power is involved. Thus he declares: 'I certainly do not believe the limited proposition that only a black can write about blacks, a Muslim about Muslims, and so forth.'[58] In fact the more negative kinds of Orientalist discourse are not the prerogative of white Westerners, judging by Said's acid comments on the work of Majid Khadduri ('a well-known Orientalist'), Sania Hamady and E. Shouby.[59]

REREADING *ORIENTALISM*

If such evidence implies that Said is rather more divided and conflictual on a number of important issues relating to Orientalism than earlier critics have suggested, it is nonetheless true that in certain respects he does homogenize, essentialize and totalize the operations of colonial discourse. This is particularly true of two main issues. The first concerns the place of gender in Orientalism. Since this has been addressed in detail by a number of other critics,[60] I will instead focus on the second, which has received less attention. This concerns Said's conflation of the various modes of cultural representation through which the non-Western world has been constructed. Ostensibly, Said does allow for some variations between the fields of knowledge which constitute Orientalism. In particular, he makes the following crucial discrimination between what he describes as 'vision' and 'narrative' in an insufficiently discussed passage towards the end of his text:

> Against this static system of 'synchronic essentialism' I have called vision because it presumes that the whole Orient can be seen panoptically, there is constant pressure. The source of pressure is narrative, in that if any Oriental detail can be shown to move, or to develop, diachrony is introduced into the

system. What seemed stable – and the Orient is synonymous with stability and unchanging eternality – now appears unstable.... Narrative, in short, introduces an opposing point of view, perspective, consciousness to the unitary web of vision; it violates the serene Apollonian fictions asserted by vision.[61]

A few preliminary points need to be made about this passage, which can be understood from one perspective as a further rearticulation of the problematic relationship of 'latent' to 'manifest' Orientalism. First of all, Said seems to imply that 'vision' exists prior to, and independently of, its mediations, so that it constitutes some kind of essence prior to its representation in individual texts (the same might be said of his conception of the relationship between power and discourse more generally). Secondly, by 'narrative', Said does not mean literary narrative but, more than anything else, the writing of history, against which is set the allegedly synchronic vision of discourses such as law, political economy, and anthropology. The argument is not really developed in any detail, partly, one must conclude, because the distinction is unsustainable. History cannot be privileged in the manner Said suggests, as is evident if one examines some of the great historiographical works of the Anglicist movement, like James Mill's *History of British India* (1817). The index of this seminal text contains an entry for 'Hindus' which is sub-divided into a whole series of transhistorical and essentialized categories, such as 'their falsehood ... cruelty ... timidity ... avarice', stereotypes which led one of Mill's own later editors to complain in 1840 that he had portrayed Indians in such a fashion as to 'outrage humanity'.[62]

While Said appears to exempt history writing from the determining influence of 'vision' (or the Western will to power), he assumes that all other kinds of colonial textuality operate uniformly and equivalently as mediations of Orientalist 'vision'. *Orientalism* is largely concerned to prove this thesis in respect of travel writing. Said in fact discriminates between different kinds of travel writing, which range, as already suggested, from the 'scientific' to 'aesthetic' in emphasis, with Lane and Nerval representing the extremes of each tendency and Richard Burton an intermediate position. Thus Lane's account of modern Egypt is characterized by 'sheer, over-powering, monumental description' which 'foils narrative movement', a problem which also overtakes T. E. Lawrence's *Seven Pillars of Wisdom*.[63] At the same time, Said implies that the more a text foregrounds itself as an 'aesthetic' artefact, as in Nerval's work, the more scope there is 'for the play of a personal – or at least non-Orientalist – consciousness'[64] which allows it to challenge or transgress the 'vision' inscribed in the 'scientific' paradigm of travel writing which Said sees as predominant in the colonial context.

But while Said seems to be gesturing at this point towards the recognition of an 'aesthetic sphere' which might be resistant to Orientalist 'vision', the crucial point is that these categories are not so distinct as one might imagine. Primarily, this is because 'aesthetic' modes of travel writing are often heavily dependent on prior work in the 'scientific' mode – for instance, the citation by Nerval and Flaubert of the work of Lane: 'What Orientalists like Lane . . . made available, the literary crowd exploited', so that Nerval's *Voyages*, for example, are characterized by 'the lazy use of large swatches of Lane'.[65] Moreover, the preoccupation with 'the observing self' which is a primary focus of 'aesthetic' modes of travel writing is still generally shaped by an overriding concern to provide an authoritative mediation of Oriental reality. For example, in Chateaubriand, 'the imperial ego makes no secret of its powers' and in Burton, too, the imperative of domination 'effectively overrules'[66] the eccentricities of his personal style.

However, as Dennis Porter has suggested in '*Orientalism* and its Problems', ascribing even the quasi-documentary form of travel writing as categorically as Said does to the realm of 'vision' is highly contentious. Focusing on the work of Marco Polo and T. E. Lawrence, Porter seeks to demonstrate that the radical stylistic heterogeneity of their discourse is accompanied by conflictual visions of non-Western peoples. The former is largely the consequence of each author's mixing of different genres with the latter essentially a result of the often complex positioning of the writer or his narrative persona. Lawrence, for instance, is situated within a double and contradictory location by virtue of being engaged in both a war between imperial nations and an anti-colonial war of independence on behalf of the Arabs against the Turks. Most interestingly, perhaps, for those engaged in literary studies, Porter sees such contradiction as deriving primarily from the deployment of particular kinds of 'literary' language use and style. He analyses passages from *The Seven Pillars of Wisdom* to argue that the excess of the signifier over signified at such moments produces a complex of meanings which cannot be stabilized in the service of a presumed Orientalist will to power in any easy or straightforward way. These expressions of Lawrence's 'literary sensibility' point, in Porter's eyes, to a 'potential ideological irresponsibility'[67] which Said's analytic model is unable to register. Following Althusser, Porter ascribes the possibility of counter-hegemonic qualities in this kind of writing to the 'relative autonomy' of the aesthetic work *vis-à-vis* the dominant ideology of the society within which it is produced. This relative autonomy is manifested in its internal distantiation of hegemonic values at the moment that it stages them.

The particular passages that Porter cites may not always in themselves convince the reader either of his general thesis, or even that *The Seven Pillars of Wisdom* is, indeed, 'a product of the literary instance'. Nonetheless, the virtue of Porter's essay is to suggest how the kind of 'ideological' critique developed in *Orientalism* is primarily thematically oriented and therefore generally oblivious to the complications and instabilities apparent in different kinds of textuality, notably in 'literary' instances of colonial discourse. Said does ask the following quesion: 'How did . . . novel-writing, and lyric poetry come to the service of Orientalism's broadly imperialist view of the world?'[68] However, the very terms within which this question is framed, of course, exclude the possibility that Western literature might at times have had a critical function *vis-à-vis* the juridical or political elements of Orientalist discourse or the material practices of imperialism. To all intents and purposes, then, Said treats literature as simply one more example of Orientalist discourse working harmoniously and homologously with the rest. While the principle behind this is the laudable one of reminding his reader that literary texts act in and on the world, it is on the face of it highly problematic to collapse a novel like Kipling's *Kim*, written in 1901, with legal edicts proscribing the immolation of Hindu widows in the 1820s, for example, or Dr Thievenot's travel writing about India from the eighteenth century, as equivalent instances of colonialist 'vision'. In general, *Orientalism* is remarkable for how little it engages with imaginative literature, despite Said's claim early on that he would be giving due consideration to its place in Orientalist discourse more broadly. Thus the Anglo-Indian poet Alfred Lyall is considered in passing, but only in terms of a corroboration of Cromer's executive policy in Egypt, and Kipling, too, is seen always as an ideologue and never as an artist. In this respect, once again, Said repeats a fault of which he complains in Orientalism itself – a failure to engage with literary evidence: 'What seems to matter far more to the regional expert are "facts", of which a literary text is perhaps a disturber.'[69]

To the extent that *Orientalism* stresses the determining role of 'latent' Orientalism over its 'manifest' counterpart, Said's theory of colonial discourse, like Orientalism itself allegedly, certainly has 'the self-containing, self-reinforcing character of a closed system, in which objects are what they are *because* they are what they are, for once, for all time, for ontological reasons that no empirical facts can either dislodge or alter'.[70] At such moments, *Orientalism* can all too easily resemble a vast synchronic structure whose own unvarying vision detects, in any given Western text on the Orient, an invariant will to power – no matter what its historical context or setting, its specific discursive mode (whether ethnology, law or literature), the cultures from which it originates or the cultures it represents. Said's repetition of the supposed tendency of colonial discourse to homogenize its subjects is particularly apparent in his own increasingly totalizing gaze, so that India and Indonesia – and even Japan – are brought in one by one to confirm his argument. Indeed, when Said ends his text with a reference to the 'world-wide hegemony of Orientalism',[71] it indicates the enormous distance he has travelled from his initial conception of Orientalism as a discourse generated to deal with the Arabs and Islam in the Middle East specifically. Such evidence indicates that Said is perhaps best described not in Ferial Ghazoul's words as 'a paradigmatic postmodernist', nor in Ahmad's terms as an exemplary post-structuralist,[72] but as a more or less unreconstructed structuralist.

As is well known, deconstruction challenges structuralism in a number of ways, particularly by its technique of reading for what is repressed or left out in order to make the structure, or the structuralist's narrative, centred, comprehensive and coherent. As Derrida put it in the course of his controversy with John Searle:

I do not 'concentrate' in my reading ... either exclusively or primarily on those points that appear to be the most 'important', 'central', 'crucial'. Rather, I deconcentrate, and it is the secondary, eccentric, lateral, marginal, parasitic, borderline cases which are 'important' to me and are the source of many things, such as pleasure, but also insight into the general functioning of a textual system. ... I note with astonishment that Searle chooses to ignore 'marginal fringe' cases. For these always constitute the most certain and decisive indices wherever essential conditions are to be grasped.[73]

As will be seen in the next chapter, Said has little sympathy for Derrida's work. Nonetheless, this aspect of Derrida's method is a fruitful means to understand how *Orientalism*'s impressively systematic theory of colonial discourse is put together and on what 'repressions' its symmetries and authority depend.

The medieval and early Renaissance literature that I will now discuss (I am by no means an expert – indeed, it could hardly be further from my own field of interest – but the risks seem worth taking) is certainly marginal to Said's main arguments. It makes an appearance in *Orientalism* principally in the shape of a very compressed discussion of Dante, whom Said presents as a figure expressing not just the hostility to Islam supposedly typical of his day but the core vision of the much longer tradition of discursive Orientalism. The texts I address (*The Song of Roland* is also mentioned by Said in passing) are marginal in at least three other important ways. First of all, they are literary works, a genre to which – as has been seen – Said pays little attention. Secondly, three of them come from Germany and Italy, nations (if one can use that term in this historical context) to which Said also pays little regard. Thirdly, they are written in a period which Said skates over unnecessarily hastily, in order to focus on the era of post-eighteenth-century imperialism when Europe was certainly ascendant over the Orient. As Said himself suggests, however, 'from the eighth century to the sixteenth, Islam dominated both East and West'[74] (in comparison, the West has dominated the East only for the last 250 years). Anxieties about Islam are evident in all these texts, particularly in *The Song of Roland*, which makes much of the fact that the Christians are faced by a Muslim army of 400,000 soldiers which threatens to pursue Charlemagne right into the heart of France.

  While Said is undoubtedly right in general terms in respect of Dante's predominantly negative vision of Islam in *The Inferno* (begun *circa* 1308), his interpretation needs to be refined for several reasons. In particular, Said fails to register the fact that Mohammed is situated where he is on account of the fact that he is a heretic, responsible for introducing a schism within the true and 'original' faith. As David Higgins suggests, this reflects Dante's belief, common in his time, that Mohammed had once been a Christian.[75] Thus Islam is implicitly seen as interlinked with Christianity, at least historically speaking, and not simply as some utterly Other or alien faith. Moreover, while Said acknowledges that Mohammed is not confined to the lowest valley of the Malebolge, or even to the lowest circle of Hell, it is worth pointing out that Mohammed's crime is considered no more (or less) disgraceful than Bertran de Born's instigation of rebellion against Henry II of England. Indeed, further down in Hell are one of Dante's own relatives (Geri de Bello), a counterfeiter (Capocchio) and a spendthrift (Caccia of Asciano). Only two circles higher than Mohammed is Frederick II of Swabia, who led a crusade to win back Jerusalem in 1227. Certain Muslims, such as Saladin, Averroes and Avicenna, as Said himself acknowledges, are considered to be on the same level as other 'virtuous pagans' like Socrates, Plato and Aristotle. All this suggests a more complex and nuanced vision of Islam in Dante's work than Said allows.

  More significantly, Dante's allegedly demonic portrayal of Islam cannot be said to exemplify the vision of 'all who have thought about the Orient in the West' even in the limited context of his own period. For example, Boccaccio's *The Decameron* (*circa* 1350) represents Saladin in very different ways from the later stereotypic vision of 'the wily Oriental' or 'Oriental despot'. The Third Story of the First Day insists on his 'extraordinary munificence' in the course of an account of his entirely honourable dealings with Melchizedek ('despite' the fact that the latter is a Jew). The theme is taken up again in the Ninth Story of the Tenth Day, where Saladin – again identified as 'an outstandingly able ruler'[76] – repays in abundant fashion the earlier hospitality of Messer Torello, who has been taken captive in the course of a crusade. (The politics of representation are more complex here. The fact that Saladin first meets Torello in disguise, in the course of a spying mission, might confirm the idea of 'the wily Oriental'. This is offset, however, by the ruses which Torello himself employs to get Saladin into his house, and Saladin's magnanimity once his captive's identity becomes known.)

A similarly conflicting pattern of representation is evident in the medieval period. *The Song of Roland* (*circa* 1100, roughly contemporary with the First Crusade, which led to the Christians' capture of Jerusalem) is Orientalist insofar as it blames the defeat of Charlemagne's rearguard primarily on the treachery of the Muslim armies occupying northern Spain. The historical truth was that Roland was ambushed by (fellow-Christian) Basque opportunists. Equally, the focus on the disaster at Roncesvalles might be understood as a means of deflecting attention from Charlemagne's much more serious defeat at Saragossa in 778 in consequence of his intervention in an internal struggle for control of Muslim Spain, which in turn precipitated the retreat through the Pyrenees. The poem certainly at times insists monotonously upon the wiliness and bad faith of Charlemagne's Muslim foes. But there is also persistent recognition of the positive qualities of certain Muslims. Marsile himself is 'like a true baron', and of Baligant the poet exclaims: 'O God, what a noble baron, if only he were a Christian!'[77] And, despite Charlemagne's final victory over the Muslims (a narrative turn informed, once more, by wish-fulfilment rather than accurate historical record), the poem has a strongly critical vision of the conduct of the Christian side, from which Charlemagne himself is not fully absolved. Thus the treachery at Roncesvalles derives in the first instance from Roland's stepfather Ganelon, who intrigues with the Muslim side as a way to repay his relative for various slights. Moreover, the representation of Roland strongly suggests that his heroic qualities are more than offset by a reckless pride which means that catastrophe is inevitable. From the outset, Oliver counsels Charlemagne against sending Roland, who is stubborn and lacks diplomatic skills, to treat with Marsile (again, this implies criticism of the king). Once battle is joined, Roland delays repeatedly before blowing the oliphant to alert Charlemagne, despite Oliver's entreaties to do so. Boasting emptily of the glorious victory which awaits the rearguard, Roland in fact consigns them to death at the hands of vastly superior forces, a disaster for which Oliver blames Roland unequivocally.

While the Muslims in *The Song of Roland* are generally depicted as belonging to a lesser order of civilization (despite their greater military skills) than the followers of Charlemagne (it is, however, important to note that Marsile's armies contain Slavs and Armenians, as well as a champion called Jurfaleu the Blond), no such hierarchical distinction is drawn in von Eschenbach's *Parzifal* (begun *circa* 1200, shortly before the Fourth Crusade of 1204). In this text, the 'magpie' Muslim Feirefiz, precisely because he is (at least) Parzifal's equal, is a worthy opponent for him. Both Gawan and Arthur himself acknowledge Feirefiz's worth and welcome him to their court. Nor is Parzifal unique among the non-Christians in this respect. Isenhart, Belacane's first suitor, is the epitome of courtly virtues and particular stress is laid on the fact that he is 'untutored in the ways of perfidy'.[78] The King of Zazamac is similarly noble and the King of Baghdad is known as 'the Blessed' for his magnanimity and generosity to his followers, among whom is included Gahmuret. In this text 'wiliness' is at least evenly divided. While Gahmuret is killed treacherously, he himself abandons the Moorish queen Belacane to a broken heart, and spirits himself back to Europe.

The cultural politics of von Eschenbach's representation are complex. On the one hand one might argue that Feirefiz's nobility can be attributed to his white ancestry, for it finally transpires that he is Parzifal's half-brother (this has parallels with Dante's conception of Islam as a schism within what was once the one true faith), the son of Gahmuret and Belacane, whom his father met in the course of a crusade and later defends against Vridebrant's *Christian* army. (What the later Said might call the 'inter-twined histories' of Islam and Christianity is further suggested by the fact that Isenhart is himself at once a 'blackamoor' and cousin to the King of Scotland. Similarly, Gahmuret meets his death fighting for the ruler of Baghdad.) Most interestingly, perhaps, von Eschenbach explores the possibility of reconciliation between Islam and Christianity in the highly symbolic duel between Parzifal and Feirefiz. The narrative prepares for the revelation about the combatants' true relationship by stressing the deep unity of which they are as yet unaware: 'Whoever wishes to name them "two" is entitled to say "Thus did *they* fight." Yet they were no more than one. Any brother of mine and I make one person, as do a good man and his good wife.'[79] The fight is unresolved and the pair agree to a truce with a kiss. The reconciliation is sealed by Feirefiz's marriage to Repanse de Schoye (he has been an extreme object of desire among the ladies of the Round Table ever since his arrival), after what seems to be a purely nominal conversion to Christianity. Feirefiz makes his true motive for 'conversion' abundantly clear: 'If I were baptized for your sakes, would Baptism help me to win love?'[80]

Ironically enough this resolution anticipates Said's later work in advancing respect for cultural difference and peaceful coexistence as the way forward for the Western and non-Western worlds (except of course for the fact that Feirefiz and Repanse then go off to rule India!). The emphasis on reconciliation is reinforced in another way. *Parzifal*, like much postcolonial fiction, indeed, conceives of itself as a hybrid mixture of Western traditions such as *chanson de geste* on the one hand and non-Western narratives on the other. According to von Eschenbach's narrative persona, the story of Parzifal is of Arabic provenance and comes to him through a French translation. In elaborating this prov-

enance, great pains are taken to stress the high refinement of Moorish/
Islamic culture. The same mixed provenance is true of the *Decameron*.
According to G. H. McWilliam, 'the most obvious of the *Decameron*'s
antecedents were the collections of stories that had originated in the
East during the early Middle Ages and were circulating, in translation,
throughout Western Europe in Boccaccio's own lifetime'.[81] In particular,
McWilliam argues, Boccaccio is indebted to the Sanskrit *Panchatantra*
for the device of the frame-story containing other tales within it. He
suggests that Boccaccio knew of this in a Latin translation based 'by way
of a Hebrew translation, upon the eighth-century Arabic version of the
text, *Kalilah wa Dimna*, which in turn was based upon a sixth-century
Pahlave, or old Persian, translation from the original Sanskrit'.[82] An
even more important source was the widely translated series of Eastern
stories commonly known as *The Seven Wise Masters*. McWilliam is at
pains to suggest not just formal similarities between the *Decameron* and
these earlier works, but also thematic affinities. In each case, for example,
story telling is the means whereby the spectre of death is held at bay.
Such 'borrowings' do not attest to their authors' blind conviction of the
superiority of Western culture. Rather, they seem to be appropriations
from non-Western cultures which are recognized by some of these writers
to be at least in certain respects the equal of their own.

This analysis – compressed as it is – suggests that Western representations of Islam may be much more complex than *Orientalism* characteristically assumes. As regards the imaginative literature of this period and of
these varied regions at least, Orientalism cannot be considered uniformly
either as a discourse of mastery or even as the consistent and unvarying
expression of the Western will to power through knowledge and
representation – *despite* the extent and immediacy of the conflict between
West and non-West which is certainly registered in them (as one would
expect of texts produced in the times of the Crusades). The projection
of desire as well as disavowal in such works suggests that it is ambivalence
rather than a simply dichotomizing and essentializing attitude which
more accurately characterizes the Western vision of the East. And what
is true of this early European literature often applies in later periods,
through different national traditions and across other fields of cultural
description, even when the West is at its most politically dominant and
oppressive.

BEYOND *ORIENTALISM*:
CULTURE, IMPERIALISM, HUMANISM

The essays collected in Said's *Culture and Imperialism* (1993) represent
both an extension and a modification of many of the arguments

elaborated in *Orientalism*. On the one hand, the later volume seeks to broaden discussion of the relations between culture and the histories of imperialism considerably. Thus it gives space to a wider range of geographical areas, social formations and cultural forms (including opera) and pays much more detailed attention than *Orientalism* to developments in the contemporary period. (There is also a notable, but still perhaps insufficient, increase in the space devoted to gender issues.) In terms of Said's continuing engagement with colonial discourse more specifically, there is a distinct shift of emphasis from non-literary to literary forms and an engagement with the canonical figures of metropolitan culture rather than comparatively marginal work such as travel writing in the imperial period. Most strikingly, perhaps, the later Said pays much more attention to non-Western forms of cultural production,[83] an area almost wholly ignored in *Orientalism*, which, as suggested earlier, tends to conceive of the colonized as 'the silent interlocutor' of the dominant discourse. In the later volume, there is discussion of – for example – the African novel, Caribbean criticism, and Subaltern Studies historiography. (However, it is noteworthy that the writer to which the chapter entitled 'Resistance and Opposition' devotes most space is W. B. Yeats.)

Compared with *Orientalism*, the architecture of *Culture and Imperialism* is much less deliberately systematic, despite the fact that Said's gaze is more synoptic. In *The World, the Text, and the Critic* (1983), Said in fact renounces any further ambition to provide totalizing frameworks and explanations of the kind offered in *Orientalism* and advances the essay – 'a comparatively short, investigative, radically skeptical form'[84] – as the best medium for investigation of the kind of questions he is interested in. *Culture and Imperialism* is, then, best approached as a series of interlinked pieces rather than a consistently developed thesis. *The World, the Text, and the Critic* also advances two important reasons for Said's growing unease with Foucault which have a particular bearing on *Culture and Imperialism*. Firstly, Said suggests that, in stressing a text's worldly affiliations, Foucault illegitimately homogenizes quite different kinds of discourse by stripping 'the [individual] text of its esoteric or hermetic elements'.[85] This implies that Foucault is unlikely to be of continuing help in Said's increasing engagement with the metropolitan literary canon's relations to imperialism and the specific 'esoteric' conventions and modes of signification which distinguish literature from other discourses.

The World, the Text, and the Critic also suggests that Foucault's often deterministic and pessimistic vision of how power operates raises insurmountable problems *vis-à-vis* Said's growing conviction of the need to move beyond the unequal and oppositional relations between Western and non-Western cultures which characterized the colonial era. Thus, well before *Culture and Imperialism*, Said is persuaded that Foucault offers no account of historical change which might advance the current world into the new, less conflictual relationship he increasingly desires to encourage. Moreover, it is clearly impossible for criticism (or art itself) to perform its part in developing this new cultural world order if, as some parts of Foucault's writing would seem to suggest, the categories of will and intention are to be discarded and the critic or artist is simply unable to challenge the operations of the hegemonic system within which s/he functions. It is no surprise, therefore, that in *Culture and Imperialism* Said's position on the question of the relationship between the discursive 'archive' and the individual work, writer or national tradition – or, indeed, between material base and cultural superstructure – promises, at least on first reading, to have tilted decisively away from the account provided in *Orientalism*, to the advantage of the latter terms.

As this might suggest, the changes of style, tone, method and thematic focus in the later text can be ascribed in the first instance to an apparently fundamental shift in Said's political perspectives. *Orientalism*'s predominant vision of future world history is essentially one in which relations between the West and the non-West would continue to be characterized by pervasive divisiveness and conflict as the inevitable and continuing consequence of, and reaction to, the violence engendered by the history of colonialism. In the later volume, he conceives of the histories, cultures and economies of the formerly dominant and subordinate nations as increasingly and systematically interdependent and overlapping. Said recognizes that this is in part the effect of an ever more integrated global economy which testifies to the West's continuing ascendancy over the non-Western world. This perception is, however, at least to some degree offset by the array of evidence he adduces which testifies to the success of both material and cultural forms of decolonization in the post-war era. In Said's eyes, the unprecedented global predicament now apparent requires a new discourse of liberation, largely developed out of leads offered in Fanon's work, which will free both sides from former antagonisms. Said's later work is broadly, though not naively, optimistic about effecting a reconciliation between the West and the non-West, based on both mutual recognition and respect. For this to happen, however, the West must accept an equitable redistribution of the world's resources and face up to the facts of its past histories of involvement overseas. Equally, however, the non-West must eschew the 'politics of blame', which Said sees as characterizing the discourses which accompanied formal decolonization.

Perhaps Said's most radical suggestion in *Culture and Imperialism* is that the contemporary world now has something approaching a 'common culture', which is rooted in this shared experience of colonialism and imperialism. In order to demonstrate this, Said argues that an innovative paradigm for 'humanistic' research is needed. What he proposes is 'counterpoint'. This is a mobile, eclectic method at a number of levels, and is specifically designed to combat the dichotomizing vision which Said identified in Western scholarship of the kind represented by Orientalism. It eschews any one 'specialized and separatist knowledge' as its guiding logic, drawing instead on a range of work including comparative philology, feminism, post-structuralism and Marxism as well as the more traditional kinds of humanist scholarship represented by Matthew Arnold and T. S. Eliot in Britain and Leo Spitzer and Erich Auerbach on the continent. For Said the value of counterpoint is that it crosses disciplinary boundaries and received divisions of discursive fields, reading culture together with politics and history as intimately related spheres in the same manner as *Orientalism* in fact does in practice, but with quite different aims and results. Said now lays greater stress on the links rather than the divisions between cultures, for instance by opening 'dialogues' between the Western canon and non-metropolitan production. Thus Yeats's (and Eliot's) poetry is read against the work of Césaire, and Albert Camus's fiction in the context of that of native Algerians. (Equally, *Culture and Imperialism* brings together quite discrete parts of the Western canon, making connections between ostensibly quite unrelated writers like Jane Austen and Kipling, for example, to suggest that each belongs to a culture continuously shaped by Britain's interventions overseas.[86])

One decisive shift in Said's vision between *Orientalism* and *Culture and Imperialism* is apparent in relation to the question of resistance to the dominant. The later text acknowledges, to a far greater degree than before, the tradition of metropolitan resistance to imperialism, though Said is right to stress that until the colonized themselves began the struggle for liberation, it was generally quite ineffective in the period between the abolition of slavery and World War Two. Nonetheless there is recurrent praise for figures like Jean Genet, 'who have, in effect, crossed to the other side'.[87] As further recent evidence of metropolitan opposition to Western domination, Said cites the self-reformation of scholarly bodies such as the American Middle East Studies Association, which, he argues, was formerly aligned in direct and sinister ways to US State Department programmes for regional 'influence'. While such activism is largely confined to the cultural domain in the West, Said nonetheless sees a complementary relationship between the kind of scholarship exemplified by Basil Davidson's historical researches on Africa since the 1950s and the material struggle of liberation leaders such as Amilcar Cabral.

Culture and Imperialism also recognizes resistance to the dominant from outside to a much greater extent than *Orientalism*. It addresses the histories of decolonization in the contemporary era, giving accounts of a number of struggles in the course of a broad-ranging analysis of nationalist discourse. While Said acknowledges the crucial role that cultural nationalism has had in ending the era of formal empires, he nonetheless persistently expresses unease that it may prevent the kind of reconciliation between West and non-West on which the future depends. The suspicion that nationalism can all too easily replicate the essentializing and dichotomizing vision of the culture of the former imperial powers organizes some of the most interesting parts of *Culture and Imperialism*, those which seek to discriminate between different kinds of anti-colonial and postcolonial critic. Said praises the work of 'cultural nationalists' like Ngugi and Chinweizu, and acknowledges that 'rejectionism' was an important stage in the struggle against colonization and one which cannot simply be either written off as misguided or, indeed, skipped. Nonetheless, it is clear to Said that the best way forward now is a mode of cultural criticism which reflects, indeed espouses, the hybridity engendered by the ever more intertwined histories of the modern world, and which eschews conceptions of identity which are based in fixed ontological categories, whether of race, ethnicity or national identity. To anchor cultural projects in such models is, for Said, to risk remaining for ever stuck in the posture of confrontation.

In practice, Said most values those 'Third World' intellectuals who have migrated to, or been exiled in, the metropolis, a trajectory which he describes as 'the voyage in'. The value attached to these critics rests on two propositions. Firstly, that there is an oppositional quality to the consciousness of such figures, characteristically expressed in the way that they appropriate the dominant metropolitan discourses and turn them back against the West to deconstruct its attempts at mastery over the regions from which such critics came. At the same time, by virtue of this 'border crossing', the 'unhoused' postcolonial critic escapes the impasses in which many nationalist 'Third World' critics are assumed to be trapped. Said explains these advantages in terms of his own 'lived experience' in a way which is at times reminiscent of *Orientalism*: 'This has enabled me in a sense to live on both sides, and to try to mediate between them.'[88] This emphasis on interconnection and cross-fertilization is reinforced through comparison between two pairs of critics – C. L. R. James and George Antonius, on the one hand, and Ranajit Guha and S. H. Alatas on the other. While all are praised for their vigorous challenge to Eurocentrism, Said clearly prefers the first pair to the second. In the first instance, this is because James and Antonius are more directly connected to broader political struggles, whereas the second pair are seen as primarily preoccupied with methodological problems in academic fields of study. Secondly, while the first pair are – as Said somewhat paradoxically expresses it – 'honourably dependent upon the West', the second are deemed to be rejectionist in its work, so that an 'act of [intellectual] separation repeats the basic gesture of decolonization'.[89] Finally, while the tone of Antonius and James is optimistic, revealing their faith in the persuasive powers of the liberation narrative, Alatas and Guha allegedly work in a darkly ironic mode, their pessimism expressed in 'a hermeneutics of suspicion'.[90]

Said's own suspicion of cultural nationalism leads him into some unexpected arguments. One involves the (partial) rehabilitation of V. S. Naipaul, often regarded in postcolonial criticism as the quintessential 'brown-skinned Englishman' who has internalized the West's tradit-ionally negative or derogatory vision of the Third World. Moreover, Said's general suspicion of literature which acts as a direct expression of political interests perhaps sheds light on *Culture and Imperialism*'s comparative neglect of the creative work of the 'Third World', certainly when measured against his attention to the metropolitan or 'migrant' canon. Ahmad is possibly right to suggest that Said's apparent preference for Western 'high' culture derives precisely from a relative ideological independence and aesthetic distance in the former, compared with the more immediate affiliation of the latter to the politics of the liberation struggle. Certainly, in a 1989 interview Said denies any interest in dispensing with, or even reformulating, the canon in the light of its supposed complicity in (neo-)colonial history – or, indeed, in the face of the growing volume of non-metropolitan cultural production. Said rests his disclaimer on a traditional humanist rationale: 'I have this strange attachment . . . to what I consider in a kind of dumb way "great art".' Pressed by Michael Sprinker to define what he means by this, Said replies, somewhat limply: 'There is an intrinsic interest in [canonical works], a kind of richness in them.'[91]

In seeking to defend a Western canonical figure like Joseph Conrad from the charge of racism brought against him by some African critics, notably Achebe, the later Said advances arguments which seem almost inconceivable from the author of *Orientalism*. While he recognizes that Conrad is not altogether innocent of complicity in Orientalist-style representations of the Other, failing to recognize signs of subaltern resistance, for instance, *Culture and Imperialism* argues that it is because of the 'complex affiliations' of works like *Heart of Darkness*, with their real setting, that they are interesting and valuable as works of art. Said clearly wants to keep straightforward propaganda out of the canon by virtue of his stress on *complexity*. This is what redeems Kipling, too. Thus, while there are 'few more imperialist and reactionary than he',[92] according to Said, Kipling nonetheless bears comparison *as an artist* with such major figures as Marcel Proust, Henry James and George Eliot. At such moments, *Culture and Imperialism* appears to see the canonical Western work as a 'space of resistance' inside the dominant order; its characteristic 'complexity' suggests that it escapes being mechanically determined by the 'latent' power of the base, whether this is considered as residing in the discursive archive, or in the material relations of (neo)-colonialism.

This seems difficult to square, however, with other arguments in *Culture and Imperialism* which are strongly reminiscent of those of *Orientalism*. (The later volume describes itself, in fact, as a 'sequel' to the first.[93]) Thus while Said now focuses on more 'literary' kinds of text, the later volume is thematically and ideologically consistent with the former in its paradoxical insistence, at certain moments, that no distinction can be made between the spheres of politics and culture, arguing that the two are not only connected but ultimately the same'.[94] Said's exploration of Western 'high' culture is organized largely by what – following the precedent of Raymond Williams – he calls an analysis of 'the structures of attitude and reference' in the field of 'high' culture which prepare for and endorse, wittingly or not, the imperial project. Restoring this frame of reference, Said asserts, will prevent us from spending 'a great deal of time elaborating Carlyle's and Ruskin's aesthetic theories, for example, without giving attention to the authority their ideas simultaneously bestowed on the subjugation of inferior peoples'.[95] These relations of power, he attempts to show, are embodied in the unlikeliest parts of the metropolitan canon. To this end, there is a particularly suggestive reading of Austen's *Mansfield Park*, which demonstrates how the hierarchies and moral values epitomized by the social economy of the 'great house' (which here, as in so much of English literature, symbolizes England itself) are intimately bound up with the repressive political economy of Sir Bertram's plantations in Antigua: 'What assures the domestic tranquillity and attractive harmony of one is the productivity and regulated discipline of the other.'[96] By concentrating on what would conventionally be considered as material which is marginal to the novel's main themes and bringing this to the centre of discussion (a technique which is associated with Derrida and Marxist critics such as Pierre Macherey alike), Said constructs a largely persuasive argument about the 'worldliness' of one of the apparently most politically unconcerned masterpieces within 'the great tradition'.

The continuities between *Orientalism* and *Culture and Imperialism* are nowhere so apparent, perhaps, as in the recurrence in the latter volume of problems which had plagued the former. For example, from 'Orientalism Reconsidered' (1985), through certain passages in *Culture and Imperialism*, to 'East Isn't East: the Impending End of the Age of Orientalism' (1995), Said is at pains to retract the assertion in *Orientalism* that Westerners are ontologically incapable of 'true' or sympathetic knowledge of the non-West. On the other hand, *Culture and Imperialism* at moments repeats the same kind of 'Occidentalism' apparent in the earlier text. Citing a particularly unpleasant example of Ruskin's views on race from his Slade lectures, Said asserts that such attitudes are 'readily at hand in almost any text one looks at in the nineteenth century'.[97] To this extent, *Culture and Imperialism* remains strongly attached to the idea that the individual Western writer or work of art cannot escape the determinations of the dominant ideology and is always marked by its production within the context of a system of (neo-) colonial relations. This is the rationale behind the approach which Said takes towards individual works within the Western canon, such as *Mansfield Park*. Yet the representative weight which Said gives such texts raises serious questions. It is contentious to suggest, as Said does, that *Mansfield Park* epitomizes Austen's work when it is more accurately regarded as distinctive, even exceptional, in her *oeuvre*. The usually becomes even more problematic when Said then uses this one work by a single author to generalize about the existence of a whole developed system of ideas about empire across the entire range of nineteenth-century literature. In this respect at least, Said seems to reaffirm his earlier Foucauldian position in *Orientalism* that it is 'discourse, whose material presence or weight is really responsible for the texts produced out of it'.[98]

The same problem is more acutely apparent in Said's interpretation of Verdi. The structure of argument is similar to that which informs the analysis of *Mansfield Park*. *Aida* is taken to represent the whole of Verdi's canon; that canon is in turn taken to stand for all of nineteenth-century opera. Finally, opera is read as an example of the imbrication of the whole of European 'high' culture in support for empire: '*Aida*, like the opera form itself ... belongs equally to the history of culture and the historical experience of overseas domination.'[99] (All this in fact radically contradicts the argument with which Said begins the essay, which is that *Aida* is exceptional, even within Verdi's canon.) The exorbitant nature of the larger (and unsupported) argument about opera as a genre is obvious; but even at a more local level, Said's reading of *Aida* is often unconvincing. For instance, he sees the opera somewhat over-literally as allegorizing Western fears of Egypt's expansionist ambitions in Ethiopia, an argument somewhat contradicted by the fact that Radames, the Egyptian military commander, is an unambiguously sympathetic, even heroic figure. Said's argument about the imperialist cultural politics of *Aida* seems questionable on other grounds. Firstly, Italy had itself only very recently become an independent unified nation state and the celebrated aria 'O patria mia' serves as a reminder that Verdi had long been an important figurehead in the struggle against foreign domination. Secondly, Verdi's antagonism to European imperialism underlay his increasing disaffection with Italian politics after Cavour. Hostile as he had always been towards British rule in India, Verdi was appalled by later Italian ambitions in Eritrea, to the extent that he welcomed the shattering defeat at Adua in 1896. As Julian Budden comments of the ageing Verdi, 'however much he had modified the political views of his early days, he retained the Mazzinian belief that no nation had a right to rule another.'[100] To read *Aida* as Said does, as merely the operatic arm of 'Orientalism', simplifies the full complexity of its historical and biographical contexts.

Perhaps most contentious of all is Said's ambitious attempt to extend his analysis of the complicity of Western culture in imperialism to questions of form and genre, particularly in respect of the debate over the 'rise of the novel'. That the relationship of its emergence to the development of Western imperialism is an intimate one, Said is adamant:

> Without empire, I would go so far as saying, there is no European novel as we know it, and indeed if we study the impulses giving rise to it, we shall see the far from accidental convergence between the patterns of narrative authority constitutive of the novel on the one hand, and, on the other, a complex ideological configuration underlying the tendency to imperialism.[101]

Yet it is never entirely clear in the end which of the two terms in this somewhat opaque formulation is the determining force, in part because of a recurrent ambiguity of phrasing (compare the comment that *Mansfield Park* is 'a novel based in England relying for the maintenance of its style on a Caribbean island'[102]). At times, Said seems to claim that the genre was a by-product of empire; at others, as when he cites Blake's dictum that 'Empire follows Art and not vice versa as Englishmen suppose',[103] the reverse. Consequently, the prevarication familiar from *Orientalism* between the relative influences of discourse and material imperatives in the acquisition and maintenance of empire is repeated in the later text.

Insofar as Said links the discourse of the novel to the colonial imperative, the argument rests on what he sees as a primary concern in both with spatialization and the control of space. This is an interesting idea but Said overstates it, as in his discussion of *Clarissa* (1748) and *Tom Jones* (1749). He sees each text as 'a domestic accompaniment to the imperial project for presence and control abroad, and a practical narrative about expanding and moving about in space that must be actively inhabited and enjoyed before its discipline or limits can be accepted'.[104] This loosely expressed and conceptualized argument is reiterated in discussion of George Eliot and Emily Brontë, where it is even less convincing; and pretty much unravels completely in Said's analysis of *Kim*. For to read Kipling's text not as a novel but as romance, which one is undoubtedly invited to do, reminds one that the latter genre, which has no obvious historical basis in or connection with empire, is perhaps even more characterized by concern with questions of travel and space than the novel. (And when Said conversely later claims that imperialism was already an influence in English culture from the time of the twelfth-century invasions of Ireland, the connection between the emergence of the novel and empire seems even more accidental.) While reading *Robinson Crusoe* (which he assumes is the inaugural Western novel in a rather unquestioning way) within the matrix of empire and spatialization may be convincing, a large number of other possible determinants of both this novel and the genre as a whole are simply ignored.[105] Thus while *Culture and Imperialism* at first promises a more flexible model of the relationship between base and superstructure, or between archive and individual text or writer, it all too often accords the former terms the privileged status generally assigned to them in *Orientalism*. Consequently, there is some justice in the criticism made by Abdul JanMohamed that, despite his apparently profound rethinking of the question of agency after *Orientalism*, 'Said's equivocation about the relations between a subject and the determining socio-political situation has reached an infinitely periphrastic refusal to come to terms with the issue.'[106]

Culture and Imperialism, while an apparently more immediately accessible work than *Orientalism*, remains in many respects a more enigmatic text than its predecessor. Its inconsistencies no doubt owe something to its piecemeal production in lecture and article form over a number of years. This also makes placing it in terms of the larger debate over the current divide between postcolonial theory and criticism a difficult task. On the one hand, the text at times strongly confirms the disillusion with Foucault evident in *The World, the Text, and the Critic*. Indeed at one point, Foucault is accused of abandoning political engagement altogether.[107] *Culture and Imperialism* is also harsh about other aspects of the 'high' theory on which *Orientalism* and some of Said's own successors draw, accusing it both of persistent neglect of the issue of (neo-) colonialism and – anticipating Ahmad – of a disengagement from the world which entirely suited the epoch of Reagan and Thatcher. At the same time, Foucault is praised highly for his attention to questions of genealogy. (Indeed, in praising him in the same breath as Raymond Williams, Said once again seeks to reconcile aspects of Marxist criticism with discourse theory.) On several occasions, moreover (in the discussions of Conrad and Camus, for instance), Said explicitly reaffirms the conventionalist epistemology of discourse theory. Thus the failure of both writers is ascribed to their inability to challenge the 'textual attitude' inscribed in the archive of 'Africanist' discourse; consequently, they are unable to imagine an alternative to Western domination, however much they may criticize the ways in which this power is actually mediated.

At the same time, however, the relation of this later text to Marxist and cultural materialist thinking is also equivocal. On the one hand, the debt to Gramsci is reaffirmed (though there is little reference to hegemony in *Culture and Imperialism*) and this is complemented by recourse to the Marxist historiography produced by figures like Eric Hobsbawm and V. G. Kiernan. Said is also strongly materialist in his vision of the economic and political realities underpinning the intertwined cultural histories which he analyses and in his perception that culture plays its role in what was historically in the end a struggle for land and territory and is now one for surplus profits. At such moments, Said sits squarely within a realist epistemology which is characterized by an attention to structural and institutional forms of, and struggles for, power. However, *Culture and Imperialism* again repeats the objections of *Orientalism* to Marx and chides Raymond Williams, to whose work more than anybody else's the later text nevertheless pays tribute, for a failure to attend to issues of imperialism in his criticism. Moreover, while Said emphasizes the necessity for a global view of present cultural relations, he clearly rejects the systematic, indeed, totalizing explanatory models of 'globalization' to which Marxists like Ahmad lay claim.

This eclecticism, which is perhaps both the strength and the weakness of *Culture and Imperialism*, is further evident in Said's continuing recourse to the humanist tradition which plays such an ambiguous part in *Orientalism*. The text begins with the seemingly extraordinary collocation of T. S. Eliot and Fanon, and Eliot remains an important point of reference throughout the text. (Indeed, while Said seems by instinct predisposed to left-leaning paradigms of cultural analysis, he is quite happy to draw (without demur) on work by conservative critics, such as D. K. Fieldhouse's imperial historiography or Martin Green's studies of the 'literature of empire'. While Said in this way continually enacts his own prescriptions about the importance of interconnection and reconciliation, and in the process makes many genuinely illuminating cross-references, he also at times comes close to reinscribing some of the problems involved in the older humanist model of a 'common culture' – but this time on a global, not national, scale. At times one is inescapably reminded of Arnold's project in *Culture and Anarchy* (Arnold is, in fact, invoked several times, albeit in passing and not always in completely positive terms). Confronted by the urgent problem of increasing global conflict, Said proposes to mitigate it by stressing the value of a common 'heritage'. In place of the contending Philistines and Barbarians of Arnold's vision, one has cultural nationalists of various kinds in many parts of the globe (including the West). Instead of reading English together with French and classical literature, however, Said reads the Western canon together with non-Western culture. The stewards of this 'common culture' are, by analogy with Arnold's classless 'aliens' (a term with nicely ironic connotations in the present context), essentially without strong national affiliations. They are figures who – wherever they are physically located – have made 'the voyage over' to a new transnational cultural identity.

While it is clear that the vision underlying the 'new humanism' which Said advances as the premise and goal of a new discourse of liberation is not to be confused with its historical Western counterpart, it is not so clear whether Said's prescriptions are any less vulnerable than Arnold's were in a different epoch and a much more limited cultural frame of reference. The key question, in this respect, concerns the problem of constructing a common culture which also recognizes and respects legitimate differences and which does not preserve the political status quo by attempting to negotiate away real and material conflicts of interest by appeals to a 'higher' reality embodied in a quasi-spiritual sphere of shared texts. Arnold's scheme in practice largely reaffirmed the cultural and ideological authority of the centre through its choice of texts and definitions of what culture was. In doing so, it discounted the place of women, the working class and regional minorities within a reconceptualized national culture. On the basis of Said's reluctance to reformulate or extend the Western cultural canon (which he has been at such strains to stress has, to a very considerable degree, been complicit in domination over the rest of the world), his conception of a new common culture on an international scale may equally well confirm, or even engender, a whole series of margins and outsiders.

I have tried to subject Said's criticism to a rigorous but, I hope, sympathetic critique. (I, like most others now working in this academic field, am greatly in his debt.) I wish, then, to conclude by strongly endorsing the importance which many other critics have attributed to his work. Said's influence has been evident in a number of disciplinary fields, to an extent matched by only a handful (at most) of other contemporary cultural critics. In comparative literature, anthropology, sociology, area studies and political science, as well as English literature, Said's ideas have aroused widespread interest and excitement and enabled a very considerable amount of subsequent work. As Michael Sprinker comments: 'Specialists in these fields have often been critical of his interventions, but they have on the whole not been able to ignore or dismiss him out of hand.'[108] This attests to the importance of many of the questions which Said has asked in his long and distinguished career. Perhaps the most challenging of these, certainly in terms of the directions in which postcolonial theory – and postcolonial criticism more generally – has moved since *Orientalism* first appeared, is whether it is possible to represent cultural difference without, on the one hand, resorting to essentialist models of identity or, on the other, reducing different cultures to the status of exchangeable terms in a system of more or less arbitrary equivalences. More pressingly still, Said's work asks whether 'true' knowledge – or even non-coercive and non-reductive representation of the Other – is indeed possible. Behind these inquiries lies another, deeper preoccupation, which Said expresses as follows: 'Can one divide human reality, as indeed human reality seems to be genuinely divided, into clearly different cultures, histories, traditions, societies, even races, and survive the consequences humanly?'[109] It is for raising questions like these, about some of the most urgent issues of our time, in the terms he does, and for ensuring that they have remained in the forefront of contemporary cultural debate in the West, that Said's reputation remains secure – whatever criticism he has subsequently received for the particular answers he himself has given to some of them.

3

Gayatri Spivak:

the deconstructive twist

The work of the US-based critic of Indian origin Gayatri Spivak constitutes one of the most substantial and innovative contributions to postcolonial forms of cultural analysis, though her essays are also some of the most elusive, complex and challenging in the field. Indeed, even the editors of *The Spivak Reader* confess that 'the experience of the Spivakian page often seems one of insurmountable difficulty, and its effect [may be] to exaggerate one's sense of one's own ignorance or dimness, and one's sense of the ineffectuality of theory'.[1] In order to bring out the distinctive nature of Spivak's work, it may be worth beginning by identifying some of the ways in which her criticism contrasts with Said's. These differences are apparent in how Spivak writes, what she writes about and the critical methods and values she espouses.

To begin with, Spivak's style at times challenges in a quite fundamental way the accepted conventions of academic discourse to which Said generally adheres. At one point in *In Other Worlds*, Spivak describes her attempt at writing in the traditional academic mode before frustration drives her to one more suited to her temperament and purposes. What Rey Chow describes as the 'rough and unfinished' quality of Spivak's writing derives in part from her frequently provisional and informal mode of composition, and Spivak herself draws attention to the 'musing style'[2] adopted at moments in *Outside in the Teaching Machine*. *The Post-Colonial Critic*, meanwhile, takes the *ad hoc* form of a series of interviews. (Paradoxically, however, such informality often does little to make Spivak more accessible; many of these interviews bear witness to her interlocutors' struggle to keep abreast of her arguments.)

Even Spivak's more formal pieces often have the somewhat fractured feel of an 'event', as she acknowledges in describing 'French Feminism in an International Frame' (1981) as these 'fragmentary and anecdotal pages'.[3] In part, this is because her stance as a critic, whether in person or on the page, is characteristically interventionist – even combative; and Robert Con Davis and David Gross usefully describe her practice as 'performative'.[4] It is also in part a function of the eclectic collocations of subject matter that Spivak sometimes conjures up. 'Imperialism and Sexual Difference' (1986), for instance, brings (or throws) together Baudelaire, Kipling and eighteenth-century East India Company archives, and Spivak herself comments that there is an element of chance in her choice of these texts. The apparently fragmentary quality of Spivak's work derives equally from her theoretical strategies, in particular her deployment of the deconstructive practice of 'persistent critique'. In marked contrast to the totalizing, system-building 'architecture' of *Orientalism*, this method 'follow[s] the logic of the rhetoric – the tropology – [of the text under analysis] wherever it might lead',[5] which may well at times be into, and involve back-tracking out of, dead-ends. Spivak is particularly suspicious of the conventional kind of academic narrative which purports to build coherently to a closure which has by then established the whole and definitive 'truth' about the particular text or theoretical problem in question.

At a thematic level, there are equally clear differences between Said and Spivak. Broadly speaking, Spivak reverses the emphasis in early Said (and early Bhabha as well) on colonial discourse as the principal object of attention. Despite some quite brilliant examples of colonial discourse analysis like 'The Rani of Sirmur' (1985), 'Three Women's Texts and a Critique of Imperialism' (1985) and 'Imperialism and Sexual Difference' (1986), Spivak instead more characteristically focuses on various manifestations of counter-discourse. This has involved her in projects as diverse as the historiography of the Indian Subaltern Studies group, collaboration with the Algerian feminist Marie-Aimée Hélie-Lucas, criticism of a broad range of postcolonial creative work, especially in visual and verbal media (Aissa Djebar, Rushdie and Hanif Kureishi, for example), and analysis and translation of the Bengali-language fiction of Mahasweta Devi.

This broad range of interests is consistent with Spivak's demand that postcolonial analysis should embody above all else a 'persistent recognition of heterogeneity'[6] in respect of the cultures of (post)colonialism. Thus 'The Rani of Sirmur' warns that India cannot be taken to typify the rest of the Orient (contrary to what *Orientalism* assumes about the Middle East), and that differences within the colonizing formation(s) must be respected (contrary to Said's tendency to a uniform vision of Western Orientalism, at least at certain moments in his text). Spivak also argues that variations in the historical experience of oppression must be honoured (contrary to *Orientalism*'s tendency to homogenize the subject peoples – insofar as they are addressed at all). For Spivak there

are positive dangers in ignoring the differences or even at times conflictual relations between, for example, migrants to the metropolis and
postcolonial subjects who remain in the Third World; between the modes
and phases of diaspora (the export of slaves before 1850 as against
patterns of voluntary migration in the period since 1945, for instance);
between the cultural affiliations, locations, economic functions and social
status of diasporic groups; between the class or caste identities of
social constituencies in the Third World; or between writing of the
postcolonial diaspora in metropolitan languages and 'local' vernacular
traditions. In attempting to register the heterogeneity of the (post)-
colonial subject, Spivak insists most particularly on the importance of
attention to the 'female (sexed) subject' as a distinct category of analysis
and her work is always scrupulous in differentiating between (post)
colonial subjects according to gender. While *Orientalism* pays only
limited attention to the position of women on both sides of the colonial
divide, and while *Culture and Imperialism* remains within an essentially
masculine/ist conceptual horizon, issues of gender are central to Spivak's
writing throughout her career and across her range of interests.

There are also important differences in the political vision of early
Said and Spivak which can be illustrated in two principal ways. Whereas
Orientalism sees colonial history as an uninterrupted narrative of oppression and exploitation, Spivak tends to offer a more complex vision of
the effects of Western domination (as *Culture and Imperialism*, by
comparison, also does). While never underestimating the destructive
impact of imperialism, she nonetheless insists on a recognition of its
positive effects too, so that it is recurrently described in her work, in a
characteristic paradox, as an 'enabling violence' or 'enabling violation'.[7]
Equally, while remaining one of the sternest critics of the inequities of
the current international division of labour, Spivak claims that it is
impossible to deny the civilizing power of 'socialized capital' in the
contemporary era. This is illustrated in the first instance in the mapping
of her own emergence as one of the leading figures in the field of the
humanities today, in the course of which she recognizes that 'it is the
structures of cultural imperialism that has [sic] enabled me'.[8] By contrast,
whereas *Culture and Imperialism* offers a much more generous conception
than *Orientalism* of the potential of alliances between Western radicals
and the (formerly) colonized, Spivak is much less sanguine about the
material effects and political significance of such alliances. More than
any other postcolonial critic, perhaps, Spivak subjects the 'benevolence'
of Western engagements on behalf of the (post)colonial subject to
rigorous critical scrutiny. Whether organized by a liberal-humanist
vision, or by the anti-humanism of Foucault and Gilles Deleuze, Spivak
concludes that such interventions characteristically embody the same
kind of vision as that which informs the imperialist narratives promising

redemption to the colonized subject. Perhaps the most striking aspect of this element of Spivak's work is her scepticism about any easy or intrinsic fit between the aims and assumptions of First and Third World, or postcolonial, feminism. Indeed, Spivak suggests that First World academic feminism in particular often, albeit unconsciously, runs the risk of exacerbating the problems of the Third World gendered subject.

A final broad thematic difference is that Spivak's work is notable for its consistent concern with the practices (as well as politics) of pedagogy, an area which is rarely addressed in any detail in the work of Said (or, indeed, of Bhabha). Many of Spivak's most celebrated essays are framed in the context of the teaching environment and the problems which it involves. 'Imperialism and Sexual Difference' (1986) and 'How to Teach a Culturally Different Book' (1991), for example, explore the difficulties of teaching literary forms of colonial discourse without unconsciously perpetuating values which are the object of critique in the texts under discussion. In particular, her work seeks new ways to admit non-Western cultural production into the Western academy without side-stepping its challenges to metropolitan canons and modes of study and consequently perpetuating the '"subalternization" of so-called "third-world" literatures'.[9] In more recent writing, Spivak elaborates a number of ways in which what she calls a genuinely 'transnational study of culture' can be facilitated, particularly at the postgraduate level, suggesting measures as diverse as the phasing out of single-author studies, broadening the range of language requirements to include non-Western languages, greater attention to non-literary media and 'popular' cultural forms and integrating critical theory more effectively into postcolonial studies. Such proposals often involve a fundamental challenge to the traditional assumptions of disciplinary formations such as literary studies, as is suggested in such arguments as: 'Reading literature "well" is in itself a questionable good and can indeed be sometimes productive of harm and "aesthetic" apathy within its ideological framing.'[10] (What is implied by this is that an exclusive attention to developing the close reading skills of the kind promoted in New Criticism – which 'The Rani of Sirmur' claims was still the dominant approach in the discipline as late as 1985 – may discourage the reader from engaging with the wider material contexts out of which the text in question emerges and to which, in Spivak's view, it characteristically responds – in some measure at least.)

In terms of critical method, the comparison between Said and Spivak is equally revealing. In the first place, in contrast to early Said (and Bhabha), Spivak consistently and scrupulously acknowledges the ambiguities of her own position as privileged Western-based critic of (neo-) colonialism, and draws attention quite explicitly to her 'complicitous' position in a 'workplace engaged in the ideological production of neo-colonialism'.[11] In contrast to what is sometimes implied in *Orientalism*,

Spivak rejects the idea that there is an uncontaminated space outside the modes and objects of analysis, to which the postcolonial critic has access by virtue of 'lived experience' or cultural origin. A recurrent motif of Spivak's work, consequently, is 'negotiation' with, rather than simple rejection of, Western cultural institutions, texts, values and theoretical practices. This is by no means to suggest that Spivak's attitude to such institutions and practices is uncritical. But as she explains in 'Neocolonialism and the Secret Agent of Knowledge' (1991), opponents often have to be fought on their own ground with their own methods being used against them, at least in the first instance. And because of her recognition of the at least potentially beneficial aspects of 'socialized capital', another recurrent motif in Spivak's criticism is her recognition that postcolonial counter-discourse – whether critical or creative – is characteristically a 'persistent critique of what you cannot not want'.[12]

What may initially seem the elusive and fragmentary nature of Spivak's work derives in considerable measure from the multiplicity of the 'negotiations' she conducts at a methodological level and her refusal to espouse any one critical school or cultural/political master-narrative at the expense of others. Spivak's theoretical affiliations are an extremely complex matter. For instance, she played an important role in the emergence of the French cultural theory of the 1960s and 1970s in the Anglo-American academic world by virtue of her translation of Derrida's *Of Grammatology* (1967, translated 1976). However, while *In Other Worlds* acknowledges the seminal influence of Derrida's work on her own (and on more than one occasion she has described him as her teacher), she has also insisted that 'I'm not a deconstructivist'.[13] Her relationship to Marxism is equally difficult to fix. On the one hand she confesses to Sara Danius and Stefan Jonsson, 'I'm not really a Marxist cultural critic', while to Robert Young she asserts, 'I'm an old-fashioned Marxist'.[14] In part this evasiveness can be understood as a way of drawing attention to the unorthodox ways in which she uses such theories. For example, she refers to herself as someone working in 'the nooks and crannies of Marx', to her desire 'to translate Freud ... otherwise', and she argues that deconstruction 'is among the things that have to be catachretized'.[15]

Spivak's expertise in a variety of methodologies is reflected in the fact that in Greenblatt and Gunn's *Redrawing the Boundaries* (1992), a text designed to demonstrate the impact of the new critical and cultural theories of the previous twenty-five years on the discipline of English studies, her work is discussed under five different headings – more than for any other critic I could trace. Such fluency has led Colin McCabe to describe her as 'a feminist Marxist deconstructivist'.[16] Apt though this label is, it should not be taken to imply a desire on Spivak's part to synthesize these various discourses into a new, internally consistent, form of cultural critique which one might describe simplistically as 'post-colonial theory'. Indeed, she insists that the critic must proceed in 'the absence of a totalizable analytic foothold'.[17] Moreover, an important characteristic of Spivak's criticism is her desire to 'to stake out the [various] theories' limits'.[18] A case in point is 'The Rani of Sirmur' in which analyses of the Rani's subject-position informed by the perspectives of class and gender are performed separately, in part to demonstrate their points of incommensurability, in part to emphasize the irreducible heterogeneity of the Rani's identities. More particularly, Spivak's characteristic attention to what the essay describes as 'the thematics of imperialism' brings Western theory to crisis by revealing its characteristic blindness to questions of empire, race and ethnicity. This is what underlies her desire to 'open up the texts of Marx beyond his European provenance',[19] for example.

Certain of Spivak's theoretical affiliations indicate some degree of continuity with Said's work. Thus 'The Rani of Sirmur' draws heavily on Foucauldian discourse theory in describing a paradigmatic case of what she calls the 'worlding' of subject peoples and territories under colonial rule. By this, Spivak means not only the process through which the 'reality' of Sirmur came to be constructed for the British, through the techniques of geographical and ethnographic 'mappings', for instance, but the way that the local population was in turn 'persuaded' to substitute that version of reality for its own modes of understanding and structuring its social world. Spivak analyses what she calls 'three random examples of Othering' from official colonial archives in a way which largely corroborates Said's argument that Orientalism was a means by which the West constructed the colonial arena in terms which had little to do with the 'reality' (as understood by the local inhabitants) of the territories in question. As a later section of this chapter will show, Spivak is particularly interested in the implications that such processes have for the subject-constitution of the colonized subject and, in turn, for the question of (post)colonial identity.

There is further methodological continuity between Spivak and Said in terms of a shared interest in Marxism, more specifically the work of Gramsci. The debt in Spivak's work is most evident in her key analytic figure of 'the subaltern', a term derived via the Subaltern Studies group of historiographers from *The Prison Notebooks*, where Gramsci characteristically employs it to describe rural labour and the proletariat. As Ranajit Guha's 'Preface' to *Selected Subaltern Studies* (1988) explains, he and his colleagues adapted the concept 'subaltern' to designate non-elite sectors of Indian society, primarily the rural constituencies which range from impoverished gentry to the 'upper-middle' ranks of the peasantry. Spivak extends the reach of the term in essays like 'Can the Subaltern Speak?' by using it to figure social groups 'further down' the social scale and consequently even less visible to colonial and Third World national-

bourgeois historiography alike; she is especially preoccupied by 'subsistence farmers, unorganized peasant labour, the tribals and communities
of zero workers on the street or in the countryside'.[20] More particularly,
her analysis is directed at the subject-position of the female subaltern,
whom she describes as doubly marginalized by virtue of relative economic
disadvantage and gender subordination. At moments, indeed, Spivak
seems to wish to exclude the male urban proletariat from the category of
subaltern and to confine it to women of the Third World 'urban sub-
proletariat' alone; and in more recent work, the scope of the term is
further extended to include the female urban 'homeworker', whether in
the Third World or the metropolis, a change of focus which has sig
nificant implications for the argument of earlier essays like 'Can the
Subaltern Speak?' – as will be seen.

These shared theoretical affiliations should not, however, disguise the
fact that in many respects Said and Spivak interpret their sources in very
different ways. For instance, they often take a quite different line on the
heritage of Marxist social and cultural criticism. As was suggested in the
last chapter, *Orientalism* is highly critical of Marx's interpretations of
colonialism. Indeed, Marx's writings on India are presented as not only
determined by the discourses of Orientalism but as contributing, in the
end, to their further consolidation. In strong contrast to Said (and also
Bhabha), Spivak consistently seeks to assert the usefulness of classical
Marxist analysis for contemporary postcolonial work (a strategy which
probably saves her from the kind of assaults which Ahmad mounts on
Said and Bhabha in *In Theory*). Indeed, the apparent contradiction
noted earlier in Spivak's statements about her affiliations to Marxism is
resolved if one bears in mind that she finds the orthodox tradition of
Marxist political economy more useful than the 'culturalist' strands of
Marxism associated with figures like Raymond Williams and Fredric
Jameson. Far more than Said (and Bhabha), Spivak gives detailed
attention to the economic structures of the international division of
labour in the age of 'micro-electronic capitalism' – as well as their 'superstructural' cultural/political consequences. However, Spivak is certainly
also indebted to certain kinds of revisionist Marxism – as her recourse to
Gramsci suggests. Thus her interest in the 'itineraries of silencing' – the
ways in which political, cultural and literary narratives alike attain their
coherence and authority through the exclusion or marginalization of
certain kinds of experience or knowledge – owes much to the work
of Pierre Macherey, notably *A Theory of Literary Production* (1978) and
later essays like 'The Text Says What It Does Not Say'.

One of Spivak's principal attempts to recuperate Marxism from the
kind of critique mounted in *Orientalism* comes in 'Can the Subaltern
Speak?' in the course of the essay's broader inquiry into whether the
subaltern can speak for him- or herself, or whether the subaltern is

condemned only to be known, represented and spoken for in a neccessarily distorted or 'interested' fashion. Indeed this essay undoes the general convergence which Said seeks to promote between the methodology of Gramsci and Foucault in *Orientalism* precisely by bringing to bear on Foucault (and Deleuze) various modes of Marxist critique. From this perspective, Spivak makes three main criticisms of their work. Firstly, she insists that the reference by Deleuze to 'the workers' struggle' as the organizing principle in his political theory and practice is flawed by his unconscious Eurocentrism so that, characteristically, Deleuze 'ignores the international division of labour, a gesture that often marks poststructuralist political theory'.[21] Spivak goes on to argue that Foucault and Deleuze typically privilege micrological structures of resistance, determined by local conflicts and operating through voluntaristic associations, at the expense of macrological and 'objective' determinations like class interest, global capitalism and nation-state alliances. While she does not wholly discount the effectiveness of micrological patterns of resistance, Spivak argues that they must not be allowed to efface these larger configurations of power and other potential sites and modes of resistance.

Thirdly, Spivak reintroduces the concept of ideology in order to challenge Foucault and Deleuze's construction of the subject according to what she sees as a simplistic economy of 'desire'. In her view, this renders subjectivity, agency and identity coherent and legible in a manner which is, ironically, in some ways comparable with what is proposed in liberal humanism: 'In the name of desire, they reintroduce the undivided subject into the discourse of power.'[22] By contrast, Spivak's theory of the subject draws equally on the classical Marxist model of the 'divided and dislocated subject' (at the level of both individual and class identity) and on Althusser (in whose work the decentred subject is only held together, and given the illusion of free subjectivity, by the interpellation of ideology). In Spivak's view, it is both the disavowal of a theory of ideology and a simplistic resolution of necessarily asymmetrical relations between desire and interest which lead Deleuze and Foucault to the assumption that the 'marginal' can act resistantly, have full self-knowledge and speak for him/herself in unmediated fashion. Their 'unquestioned valorization of the oppressed as subject' thus inevitably leads them to 'an essentialist, utopian politics'.[23]

Even more striking is the difference between the attitudes of Said and Spivak to Derrida. Broadly speaking, Spivak reverses Said's preference for Foucault over Derrida, at least in her work up to 1990. As she argues in 'Can the Subaltern Speak?':

> I find [Derrida's] morphology much more painstaking and useful than Foucault's and Deleuze's immediate, substantive involvement with more

'political' issues . . . which can make their influence dangerous for the United States academic as enthusiastic radical.[24]

This is not to suggest, however, an uncritical endorsement on Spivak's part of every aspect of Derrida's work, which explains why she argues that deconstruction must be 'catachretized'. She attempts to both 'use and go beyond' Derrida, primarily by testing his ideas against non-Western cultural problematics and predicaments. Nonetheless, Spivak's work can be understood from one perspective as an attempt to rehabilitate deconstruction for use in postcolonial analysis after the attacks mounted on Derrida by others working in the postcolonial field.[25] More particularly, her work offers a studied riposte to Said's interpretation of Derrida in The World, the Text, and the Critic.

As suggested in chapter 2, The World, the Text, and the Critic marks Said's first sustained expression of unease about the directions in which 'radical' cultural and critical theory appeared to be developing by the early 1980s. Said salutes the deconstructive analysis of Derrida as a remarkable project and absolves him from the 'new orthodoxy' emerging in the work of some of his disciples. Nonetheless, he criticizes Derrida on several counts. First of all, Derrida is accused of promoting a kind of 'negative theology' rather than providing 'positive knowledge' of the world. By this Said means that Derrida is more concerned with rhetoricity and the conditions of possibility of textuality and meaning than with what texts speak to – and of – the world outside them. In particular, the positive knowledge which Said sees as being ignored is the way that texts mediate, refract or suppress the contexts of power which produce them. Said describes this as 'an extremely pronounced self-limitation, an ascesis of a very inhibiting and crippling sort'.[26] A further criticism which Said makes is that Derrida places himself beyond the play of textuality which he describes, so that his own writing is assumed to provide authoritative and 'objective' analyses of earlier writers and philosophers. Said suggests that 'we must ask how . . . he can systematically place himself outside the logocentric world when every other writer somehow could not'.[27]

In mounting this critique, Said closely follows Foucault's earlier analysis of Derrida in an appendix to a new edition of Madness and Civilisation (1972), entitled 'My Body, this Paper, this Fire'. This was itself a reply to Derrida's own critique of Foucault in Writing and Difference (1967), on which in turn Spivak relies substantially in her account of Foucault. As this might imply, despite the misgivings noted in the last chapter, Said's essay marks a clear preference for Foucault over Derrida. While both figures are deemed to challenge the orthodoxies of the dominant culture and each inaugurates ambitious new intellectual projects, the key difference for Said is that 'Derrida's criticism moves us *into* the text, Foucault's *in* and *out*.'[28] Said illustrates his argument by discussion of their respective treatments of *aporia*. For Derrida, he claims, it is a purely formal problem, while in Foucault's work the overriding interest of the *aporia* is that it reveals what cannot be thought 'because certain other things have been imposed upon thought instead'.[29] Above all, Said sides with Foucault because of his concern with 'the process of exclusion, by which cultures designate and isolate their opposites, and its obverse, the process by which cultures designate and valorize their own incorporative authority'.[30] Insofar, then, as cultural descriptions produce or confirm particular and concrete kinds of political discrimination, Said sees Foucault's work as providing a far better means than Derrida's to understand culture – especially (neo-) colonial culture – as a material network of connections between knowledge and power.

Said's critique raises a number of problems. As suggested in chapter 2, *Orientalism* itself employs a base/superstructure model in which it is implied that power exists prior to and independently of its mediations (in textuality, especially) in some pure, unmediated and accessible form. Secondly, Said himself posits a privileged independence of system for the right kind of critic, who is somehow able to exist between 'the power of the dominant culture, on the one hand, and the impersonal system of disciplines and methods (savoir), on the other'.[31] (That criticism is an institutional practice first and foremost is precisely the rationale of much of *Orientalism*.) More importantly, it is arguable that Said has misunderstood Derrida in a number of important ways, not least in misconstruing the notorious phrase 'there is no outside-the-text', which in fact demands a suspension of the traditional distinction between text and context and not, as Said appears to presume, to reinforce it.[32]

PRACTISING DECONSTRUCTION IN
POSTCOLONIAL THEORY

It is in the context of such attacks on Derrida, which owe so much to the terms of debate established by Foucault, that 'Can the Subaltern Speak?' announces an intention to correct what Spivak sees as the common misapprehension that 'Foucault deals with real history, real politics and real social problems; Derrida is inaccessible, esoteric and textualistic.'[33] By contrast, Spivak attempts to identify 'aspects of Derrida's work that retain a long-term usefulness for people outside the First World'. For the purposes of discussion, Spivak's application of deconstruction to post-colonial issues can be divided into two strands (though the distinctions between them would in the end, of course, be unsustainable to a decon-structionist). On the one hand, she sees it as a kind of 'negative science', the purpose of which is not to produce 'positive knowledge' in the sense of establishing the 'authoritative truth' of the text or problem in question; nor is it to be understood (in contrast to the approach at times taken in *Orientalism*, for example) as a form of ideology-critique or the 'exposure of error'. Rather, Spivak's emphasis is on revealing the assumptions, strategies and rhetoric through which a given narrative, whether political, literary, historical or theoretical, is grounded and mediated. Moreover, following the lead of her teacher Paul de Man in *Allegories of Reading* (1979), Spivak is equally interested in the ways that the rhetoric or style of texts, whether in colonial discourse or contemporary modes of cultural analysis, interrupt and contradict their logical or thematic propositions. Many of her essays analyse what she calls the 'cognitive failures' which ensue from such ruptures, while disclaiming any intention 'to suggest a formula for correct cognitive moves'.[35]

Central to this kind of 'negative critique' is Spivak's habit of 'reading against the grain' of the ostensible logic or surface meaning of the text in question. This is often effected by attention to what she calls the 'tangents' of a text; thus in 'Three Women's Texts and a Critique of Imperialism', Spivak concentrates on minor characters, sub-plots or seemingly marginal motifs in order to bring out the unconsciously racialized nature of the conceptual frameworks which operate in a variety of canonical nineteenth-century women's texts. Equally characteristic are the techniques of 'reconstellation' or 'catachresis'. By the first term, Spivak means the manoeuvre by which a whole text is taken 'out of its proper context and put . . . within alien arguments'.[36] For instance, the 'subaltern material' of Mahasweta Devi's story 'Stanayadini' is used in 'A Literary Representation of the Subaltern' (1988) to test a variety of 'elite' Western theoretical discourses, thereby revealing their limitations and 'absences'. 'Catachresis' is a more local, tactical manoeuvre, which involves wrenching particular images, ideas or rhetorical strategies out of their place within a particular narrative and using them to open up new arenas of meaning (often in direct contrast to their conventionally understood meanings and functions). As has been seen, she redefines Gramsci's concept of the 'subaltern' in quite radical ways. Meanwhile in 'Can the Subaltern Speak?', she takes a very particular definition of 'Otherness' in Derrida's writing, elaborated in the context of an eschatological sense of the 'Other', and reconceptualizes it to criticize metropolitan notions of the (post)colonial Other.

From another perspective, however, Spivak sees deconstruction as having a more directly 'affirmative' mode. While arguing that it can never in itself provide the basis of a political programme – as 'The Rani of Sirmur' puts it, deconstruction 'does not wish to officiate at the grounding of [new] societies, but rather to be the gadfly' – and while warning that 'claims to the built-in radicalism of deconstruction'[37] are ill advised, Spivak sees it nonetheless as having the potential to act in a number of politically enabling ways. In the first place, she ascribes to deconstruction precisely the qualities which Said at moments values in Foucault, the potential to generate greater awareness of – and, possibly help in the liberation (or 'coming to voice') of – excluded or marginalized social constituencies. There is thus a parallel between her attention to what is suppressed or ignored in order to allow a particular theory or text to function as a coherent or authoritative narrative, and her focus on the way that dominant social fractions operate hegemonically. What is crucial in both these respects is to follow 'the itinerary of the silencing'[38] of the subject(s) which are written out (or off). More obviously, Spivak also uses deconstruction to subvert the systems of binaries on which dominant discourses characteristically rely to legitimize their power. Spivak is equally convinced of the 'affirmative' potential of deconstruction insofar as it can act as a 'political safeguard' by preventing radical political programmes and forms of cultural analysis alike from reproducing values and assumptions which they ostensibly set out to undermine. The danger of what Spivak describes as this kind of 'repetition-in-rupture' arises from her belief that reversal of the dominant discourse alone (for example, valorizing East over West as a means of counter-manding the hierarchies of Orientalism) involves remaining within a logic defined by the opponent (as is the case, at times, with *Orientalism*). Spivak suggests – like the later Said – that while reversal must be effected (one cannot skip this stage), it must be succeeded by displacement of the terms in opposition: 'Without this supplementary distancing, a position and its counter-position ... will keep legitimizing each other.'[39] For Spivak, like Derrida, directly counter-hegemonic discourse is more liable to cancellation or even reappropriation by the dominant than a 'tangential', or 'wild', guerrilla mode of engagement. For this reason, too, she advocates the modes of 'negotiation' and 'critique', which unsettle the dominant from within.

For Spivak there are two areas in particular in which such reinscriptions of the dominant ideology take place in counter-hegemonic discourse. These involve definitions of identity and the role of the investigating subject. To take the former problem first: for Spivak, Derrida's conception of the decentred subject is extremely useful in preventing postcolonial struggle from lapsing into a fundamentalist politics through its critique of traditional ways of understanding 'identity', 'belonging' and 'origins'. In Spivak's view, the self or subject must be understood not as innate or given, but as constructed discursively and therefore as inevitably 'decentred':

A subject-effect can be briefly plotted as follows: that which seems to operate as a subject may be part of an immense discontinuous network ('text' in the general sense) of strands that may be termed politics, ideology, economics, history, sexuality, language and so on. . . . Different knottings and configurations of these strands, determined by heterogeneous determinations which are themselves dependent upon myriad circumstances, produce the effect of an operating subject.[40]

While principally indebted to Derrida for this definition of the 'dispersed' subject, Spivak also draws on Lacanian theory to describe the necessary decentredness of the subject in consequence of its emergence through the symbolic order inscribed in language. She also cites Foucault in order to suggest the inevitable multiplicity of subject-positions with which textuality inscribes both author and reader and, by extension, the subject in general. Textuality, then, is 'where the self loses its boundaries' and this 'trace of the other in the self'[41] prevents identity and consciousness from ever becoming fully self-present.

It comes as no surprise, therefore, that Spivak rejects all definitions of identity which are fixed in essentialist conceptions of origins or belonging. However, the bitter denunciation of 'roots' seekers in The Post-Colonial Critic, for example, also rests on the argument that any notion of a 'pure' or 'original' form of postcolonial (or subaltern) consciousness and identity implies that (neo-)colonialism has had no role in constructing the identity of its subjects. To ignore the 'epistemic violence' involved in constituting the (post)colonial subject is simply to efface, in a naively utopian way, the long and violent history of the effectiveness of (neo-)colonial power. As Spivak points out, the very term 'Indian' is the product of colonial discourse and as a category of identity involves a particular material history of subject-constitution by alien forces which cannot be wished away: names 'like "Asian" . . . are not anchored in identities. They are incessant fields of recoding that secure identities.'[42] In this respect, Spivak strongly corroborates Gyan Prakash's argument that the postcolonial subject has been thoroughly 'worked over' by colonialism and its legacies.[43] The tendency towards a 'fundamentalist' conception of non-Western identity is not, however, exclusively a trait of the Third World. Spivak sees the nostalgia for the 'authentic' Third World subject as deriving in part from the West, where many 'radicals' (like consumers who prize the genuine 'ethnic' product) prefer the subjects of their benevolent attention to be as 'pure' as possible. This, of course, has parallels with the paradoxical nostalgia of colonial discourse for the 'noble savage' who is being 'redeemed' (or even extirpated) precisely by the imposition of Western models of civilization on the colonial arena.

A crucial corollary of Spivak's theorization of identity according to 'dispersed' and 'textual' models is that she dismisses the argument that only the postcolonial subject can address the subject of postcoloniality, a perspective which she dismisses as 'nativism' or 'reverse ethnocentrism'. While Spivak accepts that all too often the postcolonial subject continues to be spoken for largely by the metropolis, there is no question of assuming that s/he necessarily has privileged insight into her/his own predicament. For Spivak, Indians who work in English departments in India, for example, have no more privileged access to 'Indian reality' than their counterparts in the West. Consequently, she strongly defends the use of 'elite' (i.e. Western) critical theory to analyse postcolonial and subaltern material and resists the 'nativist' argument that only 'local' theory or forms of knowledge validly apply in this context. In 'Neocolonialism and the Secret Agent of Knowledge', Spivak satirizes Third World women who refuse the designation 'feminist' because they see feminism as a discourse which originates in the West. By contrast, Spivak dismisses as an alibi the argument of some 'progressive' Westerners that they should not address the subject of (post)coloniality on the basis of a lack of expertise:

> What we are asking for is that ... the holders of hegemonic discourse should de-hegemonize their position and themselves learn how to occupy the subject position of the other rather than simply say, 'O.K., sorry, we are just very good white people, therefore we do not speak for the blacks.' That's the kind of breast-beating that is left behind at the threshold and then business goes on as usual.[44]

In 'Subaltern Studies: Deconstructing Historiography' (1985), Spivak illustrates in detail the practical implications of such arguments about identity – and the potentially homeopathic remedies of 'affirmative' deconstruction – through examination of the attempt of the Indian Subaltern Studies group of historians to recover expressions of subaltern consciousness in the colonial period. Spivak begins by paying generous tribute to the revisionist historiography of the group, which emphasizes not transition but conflict and discontinuity in its analytic model of the development of India from imperial possession to independent nation state. Spivak also recognizes the importance of the way that it brings 'hegemonic' (i.e. colonial and national-bourgeois) historiography to crisis by virtue of its stress on the role of the subaltern as historical agent. However, despite her collaboration in, and evident sympathy with, the group's work, Spivak criticizes the attempt to restore the subaltern's voice in isolation from both the colonizing formation and other sectors of local society, such as the native elite, to which it is necessarily, if differentially, linked. As Gyan Prakash argues, the subaltern, insofar as it is constructed by the hegemony of the dominant,[45] by definition cannot be autonomous. For Spivak, the problem is compounded by the group's assumption that there is a 'pure' or 'essential' form of subaltern consciousness, the 'truth' of which can be reached independently of the colonial discourses and practices which have in fact constructed the subject-position of the subaltern as a social category. Such factors have in fact precipitated an 'epistemic fracture' which means that the subaltern only enters colonial textuality as an 'intending subject of resistance', for example, at the behest of colonial officials or historiographers who have their own interests foremost in ascribing motivation (and therefore 'subjectivity') to the subaltern. In Spivak's view, the Subaltern Studies group's failure to take sufficient acount of this 'epistemic fracture', as well as its reinscription of a bourgeois/ humanist model of subaltern agency, reveal the degree to which the group replicates aspects of the regime of knowledge which underpinned colonialism itself. Consequently, 'one must see in their practice a repetition of as well as a rupture from the colonial predicament'.[46]

In a seemingly paradoxical way, Spivak nonetheless excuses the work of the Subaltern Studies group for its 'cognitive failures'. In the first instance her criticism is mitigated on the grounds that the group attempts to explore the experience of the most marginal social groups, in contrast to nationalist historiography's focus on local elites or the West's customary attention to the Third World groups that are directly accessible to the First World. Secondly, Spivak suggests that the idea of a 'pure' (and accessible) subaltern consciousness is a necessary 'theoretical fiction' which enables a critique of the dominant models of colonial and national-bourgeois historiography to be begun. She points out that a variety of similarly productive 'fictional' constructs operate in the work of Marx, Gramsci and Derrida himself. The idea of the sovereign subject, then, is 'among the conditions of the production of doing, knowing, being'.[47] In one of her most often quoted lines she argues that its deployment in the work of the Subaltern Studies group may therefore be legitimate: 'I would read it, then, as a *strategic* use of positivist essentialism in a scrupulously visible political interest.'[48] But while it is permissible to 'strategically take shelter in essentialism' and Spivak herself often does so, particularly when writing as a feminist, the concept must always he kept 'under erasure' and not mistaken for a 'universal truth'.

As suggested earlier, 'affirmative' deconstruction is also embodied in Spivak's attention to the role and politics of the 'investigating subject'. In 'Subaltern Studies: Deconstructing Historiography', Spivak argues that the group mistakenly assumes that it can side-step the implications of its creation of a space from which the oppressed can speak. In this respect, it repeats the problem identified in 'Three Women's Texts and a Critique of Imperialism': 'If, however, we are driven by a nostalgia for lost origins, we too run the risk of effacing the "native" and stepping forth as "the real Caliban", of forgetting that he is a name in a play, an inaccessible blankness circumscribed by an interpretable text [i.e. the discourse of imperialism which has constituted Caliban].'[49] 'Can the Sub-altern Speak?' develops this argument much more forcefully in the context of Western 'radical' theory. Spivak contradicts the assumption of Deleuze and Foucault that they are 'transparent', in other words that they are able to escape the determinations of the general system of Western exploitation of the Third World – in which Western modes and institutions of knowledge (such as universities and cultural theory) are deeply implicated – in order to intervene 'benevolently' to further the struggle of the subaltern for greater recognition and rights. To Spivak, this is a classic instance of the West representing, in the sense of speaking for or standing in for, subaltern experience – a gesture which is continuous with (even though it also ostensibly challenges) the historical process of constructing subject-positions for the subaltern in the era of formal imperialism.

Spivak argues this by juxtaposing the work of Foucault and Deleuze with an account of how the British assumed the prerogative to speak for the oppressed native woman in the discourse surrounding the prohibition of *sati* in early nineteenth-century India. The key manoeuvre – as in the case of the Rani of Sirmur – was to construct a figure of the Indian female which 'justified' the imposition of the 'modernizing', 'liberating' and 'progressive' regime of empire, a process which also consolidated imperial Britain's self-image as civilizationally superior in comparison with both the 'degraded' native woman and her local oppressors. As Spivak points out in 'Three Women's Texts and a Critique of Imperial-ism', the missionary St John Rivers in *Jane Eyre* justifies his missionary project as one which involves bettering his own race as much as the 'liberation' of India. Such attitudes continued to operate well into the present century, even among opponents of colonial rule. Spivak instances Edward Thompson, writer and missionary campaigner (and father of E. P. Thompson), who, despite his at times strong criticism of imperialism, in her view still often 'appropriates the Hindu woman as his to save against the [Indian patriarchal] "system"'.[50]

Central to this process of appropriation in the discourse surrounding *sati* was the ascription of a 'voice' – representing free will and agency – to the subaltern woman. In the case of the British, this voice supposedly called out to the imperialists for liberation; according to the native male, the voice assented voluntarily to the practice. Neither version, according to 'Can the Subaltern Speak?', can possibly be trusted as authentically representing the 'true' voice of the female subaltern. Spivak points out that, on the one hand, the British were unable even to spell the names of those they had 'saved' and often translated proper names into common nouns. On the other hand, she notes that the rigour with which *sati* was enforced in Indian society was in direct proportion to the amount of property the widow held – thus poor women were often spared the ordeal of their richer sisters. In both discourses of *sati*, the voice of the subaltern is ventriloquized; 'spoken for' as she is, Spivak suggests, one 'never encounters the testimony of the women's voice-consciousness'.[51] Thus between colonialism and indigenous patriarchy (and in the contemporary period, the conflict may instead be between nationalism and local patriarchies), 'the figure of the woman disappears, not into a pristine nothingness, but into a violent shuttling which is the displaced figuration of the "third-world woman" caught between tradition and modernization.'[52]

In Spivak's view, neither Foucault nor Deleuze is sufficiently aware of how their intervention as 'benevolent' modern Western intellectuals soliciting the agency and testimony of the 'marginal' ties them into this history of appropriation, or of how their definition of the marginal *as* marginal reinforces their own prestige as interpreters of subaltern experience: 'The banality of leftist intellectuals' lists of self-knowing, politically canny subalterns stand revealed; representing them, the intellectuals represent themselves as transparent.'[53] Whether the object of 'ethnocentric scorn' in the imperial period, or of 'hyperbolic admiration' today, the subaltern's function (and subject-position) remains primarily constituted by the West. Spivak's critique of Foucault and Deleuze is summarised by the brilliant analogy she draws between their construction of the subaltern and the production of 'woman' in mainstream male Western psychoanalytic discourse:

> As Sarah Korfman [*sic*] has shown, the deep ambiguity of Freud's use of women as a scapegoat is a reaction-formation to an initial and continuing desire to give the hysteric a voice, to transform her into the *subject* of hysteria. The masculine-imperialist ideological formation that shaped that desire into the 'daughter's seduction' is part of the same formation that constructs the monolithic 'third-world woman'. ... Thus when confronted with the questions, Can the subaltern speak? and Can the subaltern (as woman) speak?, our efforts to give the subaltern a voice in history will be doubly open to the dangers run by Freud's discourse.[54]

While Spivak recognizes that the application in unmodified form of work like Derrida's *Of Grammatology* to analysis of the subaltern may involve some of the same problems as Foucauldian or even traditional empirical analysis of marginal constituencies, she argues nonetheless that Derrida demonstrates a critical self-awareness as investigating subject which promises to prevent the kind of impasse reached by Foucault and Deleuze. Spivak argues this principally through analysis of a passage in *Of Grammatology* where Derrida dissects the use made of Chinese in the course of attempts by Western scholars such as Warburton and Leibniz to describe the principles of a 'universal language'. The practical 'writing out' of the specific properties of Chinese (even while it is the object of admiration) in the service of a 'higher goal', from which all mankind will supposedly benefit, is used to warn the contemporary Western intellectual of the continuing dangers of claiming objectivity or disinterestedness in relation to the culture of the Other. According to Spivak (in strong contrast, once more, to Said's interpretation of him in *The World, the Text, and the Critic*), Derrida demonstrates – by scrupulous attention to the paradoxes of his own position – a solution to the problem of 'how to keep the ethnocentric Subject [in particular, the Western observer] from establishing itself by selectively defining an Other':[55]

> To render thought or the thinking subject transparent or invisible seems, by contrast, to hide the relentless recognition of the Other by assimilation. It is in the interest of such cautions that Derrida does not invoke 'letting the other(s) speak for himself' but rather invokes an 'appeal' to or 'call' to the 'quite-other' (*tout-autre* as opposed to a self-consolidating other), of 'rendering *delirious* that interior voice that is the voice of the other in us'.[56]

Rather than assimilating the Other by 'recognizing' it in the terms that Derrida criticizes, or 'benevolently' assigning it identity in the manner of Foucault and Deleuze, in Spivak's eyes it is in fact better to preserve subaltern experience as the 'inaccessible blankness' which serves instead to reveal the horizon and limits of Western knowledge.

'TRANSPARENT' FEMINISM IN THE POSTCOLONIAL FRAME

A further criticism which Spivak makes of counter-hegemonic modes of cultural analysis relates to their failure to attend sufficiently to questions of gender. Of Subaltern Studies historiography, for example, she comments that 'the crucial instrumentality of woman as symbolic object of exchange'[57] is at times overlooked, and she complains of a similar lack of attention to the 'sexed subject' in the work of Foucault and Deleuze. In seeking to correct this kind of gender-blindness, however, Spivak finds little comfort in some of the interventions of Western feminism. Indeed, much of the substance her critique of figures like Deleuze and Foucault is prefigured in essays such as 'French Feminism in an International Frame' and 'Three Women's Texts and a Critique of Imperialism', which address the 'transparency' of Western feminism and its equally (self-)interested intervention on behalf of the subaltern woman. The occasion of the former essay is the publication of the anthology edited by Elaine Marks and Isabelle de Courtivron entitled *The New*

French Feminisms (1981), which Spivak uses to announce an investigation of the way in which 'the discourse of the world's privileged societies dictates the configuration of the rest'[58] and the place of 'radical' feminism within that discourse.

Spivak's argument is broached somewhat tangentially through discussion of the positionality of the female postcolonial intellectual *vis-à-vis* (Western) cultural theory. The career of the young Sudanese woman academic whom Spivak identifies (with?) at the outset of her essay is offered as emblematic of the way that dominant Western discourses of knowledge and academic method – in this case the 'objective' methodology of 'structural functionalism' – can seduce the non-Western academic into what may be blatantly Eurocentric values and assumptions. In this respect, the Sudanese lecturer acts to reveal Spivak's own intellectual trajectory: 'In my Sudanese colleague's research I found an allegory of my own ideological victimage.'[59] Spivak describes how, once landed as a postgraduate student in the USA, she found 'a commitment to feminism was the best of a collection of accessible [political] scenarios'.[60] Nonetheless, Spivak records, her initial enthusiasm for 'International Feminism' soon gave way to scepticism about a number of its (largely unexamined) assumptions, particularly its implicit claims to speak of and to Woman as a universal category. Spivak suggests that 'International Feminism' is in fact first and foremost a discourse of, and about, the developed West, and its engagement with Third World women disguises an often patronizing mission of intervention on behalf of its 'disadvantaged' sisters.

In this respect, the work of Julia Kristeva comes in for the most detailed criticism, with *About Chinese Women* (1977) arousing Spivak's particular antagonism. Kristeva's interest in the Oriental subaltern woman is, for Spivak, an example *par excellence* of the manner in which the involvement of First World intellectuals in the Third World actually functions *self*-interestedly as a process of *self*-constitution. Thus Kristeva's curiosity in the face of her objects of study 'is about *her* identity rather than theirs':

> This too might be a characteristic of the group of thinkers to whom I have, most generally, attached her. In spite of their occasional interest in touching the other of the West, of metaphysics, of capitalism, their repeated question is obsessively self-centred: if we are not what official history and philosophy say we are, who then are we (not), how are we (not)?[61]

Spivak sees such problems as arising in part from Kristeva's methodological shortcomings, for example her reliance on systems of binary opposition between the Orient and the 'Indo-European world'. In Spivak's view, this leads Kristeva to reinforce (since even when she reverses their traditional coding, she does not displace) stereotypes familiar from Orientalist discourse about the immemorial and unchanging nature of Chinese life, especially in terms of its patterns of gender and religious power and experience. Kristeva is also deemed to ignore a variety of non-Western cultures (like India's) in order to make the whole of the East approximate to one of the binary terms being employed. Spivak further objects that Kristeva's work proceeds without regard for archival evidence, so that speculation is paraded as historical fact, and that it relies on translated anthologies and Western theses (indeed Kristeva's treatment of the role of Chinese family structure is presented as derived principally from a single literary-critical academic article, as well as dependent on questionable aspects of Freudian theory). This, more than anything else, leads Kristeva to what Spivak sees as an extremely naive belief that Chinese women, having supposedly preserved pre-patriarchal forms of power through the millennia, were not in fact (further) marginalized under Maoism.

Spivak ends by placing Kristeva's 'research' in the long history, broached by Derrida's *Of Grammatology*, of the West's attempts to appropriate Chinese culture for its own various ends. At best, she concludes, this misguided intervention can be understood as another case of 'colonialist benevolence'. However, a more accurate interpretation, in Spivak's view, is to see it as a determinate stage in the evolution of a post-Marxist intellectual formation in post-1968 Paris. This more than anything else indicates the essential irrelevance of Kristeva's work to a genuinely 'International Feminism'. In this interpretation, Kristeva's work represents the disillusioned turn, after the failure of the May 1968 *événements*, to 'the individualistic avant-garde rather than anything that might call itself a revolutionary collectivity. . . . The question of how to speak *to* the "faceless" women of China cannot be asked within such a partisan conflict.'[62] As a corrective to Kristeva's deficiencies, Spivak suggests a quite different kind of approach to the women of the Third World: 'The academic [Western] feminist must learn to learn from them, to speak to them, to suspect that their access to the political and sexual scene is not merely to be *corrected* by our superior theory and enlightened compassion.'[63] In short, the Western feminist must learn to stop feeling privileged *as a woman* once contexts of racial difference, in particular, come into play.

In keeping with her demand for greater recognition of 'the immense heterogeneity' of women's experiences and discourses about women, however, Spivak does distinguish between different elements of French feminism. Thus while some of its theory is 'part of the problem' of the West's current attempt to know the East, other elements may provide 'something like a solution'; this reinforces her consistent argument against 'the tired nationalist claim that only a native can know the scene'.[64] Thus Spivak looks to the feminist models of 'symptomatic reading' developed by Hélène Cixous and others out of, and sometimes in reaction to, the deconstructive thematics elaborated by Derrida as one means to initiate the kind of inquiries she prescribes, especially insofar as these involve a critique of essentialist or biologistic models of women's identity. Above all, Spivak seeks to 'translate' those Western feminist narratives which, in her baroque phrase, engage with 'the suppression of the clitoris in general as the suppression of woman-in-excess',[65] out of their 'original' context and see them applied to, and modified by, the very different material conditions of subaltern women in the Third World – such as those researched by her young Sudanese colleague. Unless such 'translations' are made, Spivak concludes, even the best of such theory cannot 'escape the inbuilt colonialism of First World feminism toward the Third'; to make such 'translations', by contrast, would be to 'promote a sense of our common yet history-specific lot'.[66]

While Spivak concentrates on continental theory in 'French Feminism in an International Frame', she stresses at the outset that in respect of their treatment of subaltern women, there is little substantive difference between the politics of Anglo-American and French versions of feminist critique. In 'Three Women's Texts and a Critique of Imperialism', Spivak develops this position in considerable detail. The essay begins in Saidian fashion by observing a continuing and systematic failure to explore the interrelationships between metropolitan culture and power overseas. Indeed, Spivak anticipates *Culture and Imperialism* by broadening the field of colonial discourse analysis from texts generally recognized to be directly connected with the representation and mediation of imperialism to areas of the canon which seem only tangentially related to such questions. Thus 'Three Women's Texts' centres on 'mainstream' nineteenth-century British women's fiction in order to reveal its complicity in rearticulating 'the axioms of imperialism'.

Spivak's argument focuses initially on a rereading of *Jane Eyre* (1847), a work which constitutes a 'cult text' of contemporary Anglo-American feminism. She suggests that the current high valuation of *Jane Eyre* in such criticism depends in part on a failure to situate Brontë's feminist project in its historical context. In short, stress on Jane's emergence as both triumphant proto-feminist and autonomous individual(ist) ignores the role forced on the 'native female' in the constitution of these enabling new identities for the metropolitan woman. For example, the construction of the 'degraded' native woman as a subject to be 'redeemed' creates a role for the benevolent Western woman (as missionary, for instance), which provides a new public space or role in citizenship into which she can emerge. Spivak elaborates her argument principally through analysis of the function of Bertha Mason within *Jane Eyre* (to which Said had already alluded suggestively, albeit in a very compressed fashion, in *The World, the Text, and the Critic*[67]). While recognizing that Bertha is in fact a white Creole and a member of the plantocracy which built its wealth on slavery, Spivak reads her 'catachrestically' as occupying the position of the colonized subject ('the woman from the colonies') within the text, a reading partly invited by the insistence in Brontë's novel not only on Bertha's origins in the West Indies, but on her dark features and 'animal' qualities. For Spivak, it is only through the effacement of this resistant colonial female subject 'that Jane Eyre can become the feminist individualist heroine of British fiction [and subsequent Anglo-American criticism]'.[68]

This critique of the unconscious politics of Western proto-feminism in *Jane Eyre* is partly mobilized through comparison of Brontë's text with its 'rewriting' at the hands of Jean Rhys in *Wide Sargasso Sea* (1966). In certain respects, Spivak sees contemporary feminism as an advance on its nineteenth-century equivalent in terms of its treatment of the racial Other. Thus Rhys's text demonstrates much more explicitly, in the relationship between Antoinette and black women colonial subjects like Tia and Christophine, the way in which 'so intimate a thing as personal and human identity might be determined by the politics of imperialism'.[69] Spivak grounds this aspect of her argument in analysis of the motifs of mirrors and dreams which run through *Wide Sargasso Sea*, focusing particularly on the ways in which they bring the subject-positions of Antoinette and the black servant girl Tia into alignment with each other. For Spivak, the great strength of Rhys's novel is that it demonstrates that this Other cannot be 'selfed' (attain coherent subjectivity or identity) 'because the fracture of imperialism . . . intervened'.[70] Insofar as Antoinette, who is read 'allegorically' as the colonized subject (she is from the outset ambiguously positioned between the English imperialists and the black ex-slaves), occupies the position of the Other to the 'Rochester' figure (who represents the metropolis), she is forced to adapt her world-view and sense of identity to the perspective of the colonizer. This process of self-alienation radically disorients Antoinette and is exacerbated by her 'translation' (reversing the trajectory of the 'middle passage') to England. There, forced by the 'Rochester' figure to assume the new persona of Bertha Mason, Antoinette is unable to deal with the variety of conflictual subject-positions assigned to her and catastrophe follows. Antoinette's arson is an act of rebellion against the dominant, which recalls the attack by the ex-slaves on her own family plantation house in the West Indies. In these respects, in Spivak's view, *Wide Sargasso Sea* provides a quite different aetiology of 'Bertha's' crisis from the biologically determined (because of factors related to heredity/racial mixing in her family) 'madness' into which Brontë's Bertha descends: 'At least Rhys sees to it that the woman from the colonies is not sacrificed as an insane animal for her sister's consolidation.'[71]

Although Rhys recognizes at the level of this individual instance the problem of identity formation in respect of the gendered colonized subject, Spivak suggests that *Wide Sargasso Sea* also reveals the finally limited degree to which even the most sensitive contemporary Western woman writer is able to deal with the difficulties of 'representing' the racial Other. Spivak praises Rhys on the one hand for creating in Christophine a colonized female subject who can, within the determinate limits imposed by imperial law, provide a critique of, and resistance to, the patriarchal process by which 'Rochester' appropriates Antoinette. (This may seem paradoxical; however, Christophine is not strictly a speaking subaltern – she belongs rather to the category of 'good servant', as Spivak points out.) At this point, nonetheless, the argument becomes ambiguous. On the one hand, the manner in which Christophine is made to leave the text abruptly, 'with neither narrative nor characterological explanation or justice',[72] suggests to Spivak a kind of violence on Rhys's part. On the other, she seems nevertheless to regard Rhys as redeeming herself precisely through *not* giving Christophine a larger or more directly oppositional role, since this would fall into the trap of 'selfing' her as 'the intending subject of resistance' with a coherent and unproblematically accessible subjectivity.

In the third and concluding section of the essay, Spivak offers a further perspective on such issues by reconsideration of Mary Shelley's *Frankenstein* (1818). This text at first sight seems a surprising choice for comparison with the first two. For while 'there is plenty of incidental imperialist sentiment in *Frankenstein*' (for instance, Clerval's ambition to fashion a career in India), 'the discursive field of imperialism does not produce unquestioned ideological correlatives for the narrative structuring of the book'.[73] Nonetheless, Spivak insists, it is possible to 'reconstellate' the text within the history of imperialism in ways that may be politically useful. Spivak engenders a postcolonial perspective by reading 'the monster' allegorically, like Bertha Mason, as a symbol of the colonized subject. Thus Frankenstein's experiment in 'constructing' the 'monster' is seen as an instance of the project of subject-constitution of the colonial Other in which 'the dark side of imperialism understood as social mission'[74] is bodied forth. In denying the monster the right to reproduce itself, *Frankenstein* embodies the ambivalence of colonialism (and the whole Enlightenment project which it represents) in particularly sharp form. Having refused the 'monster' independence in the form of a new life in South America, and having failed to turn 'the monster'/ colonized subject into a domesticated version of himself (in accordance with the model offered by the 'Westernization' of the Oriental subject Safie), Frankenstein seeks to efface it in a manner which recalls the repressive manoeuvres of imperial power in the face of the recalcitrant 'nationalist' or 'fundamentalist' native.

Just as she discriminates between the work of the French feminists by largely absolving the work of Cixous from the general thrust of her critique, so Spivak claims that Shelley's text is significantly different from the others she analyses in the essay. Unlike Brontë and even Rhys, Shelley discriminates between different orders of racial Otherness and subordination (as just implied, Safie is the Ariel figure who represents the incorporated colonized elite, while the 'monster' is the rejectionist Caliban figure). More importantly, in Spivak's view, Shelley attempts to keep the subject-position of the latter kind of Other open or 'blank' (the 'monster' has no name), 'uncircumscribed' and therefore uncontrolled by both the literal text which represents it and the 'social text' of an emergent imperial formation. (Spivak perhaps discounts too readily the process of subject-constitution involved in the 'education' which the 'monster' vicariously acquires.) This is implied in Spivak's second catachrestic reading of the 'monster', which aligns 'him' with the position of the female subject represented by Walton's sister, who, as addressee of his letters, remains crucial to, but also 'outside' Franken-stein's narrative. In contrast to Rhys's Christophine, then, 'the monster' is not simply expelled from a ('social' as well as literary) text that cannot contain 'it', but remains hovering beyond its discursive reach as a continuously disturbing counter-knowledge. Shelley remains a more productive model than her successors insofar as she 'reminds us that the absolutely Other cannot be selfed, that the monster has "properties" which will not be contained by the "proper" measures'.[75]

CONCLUSION: SPIVAK'S 'REPETITIONS-IN-RUPTURE'

One of the problems in assessing Spivak's achievement as a critic is that there are very considerable changes of position and direction in the course of a career as long as hers. She herself demands that the heterogeneity of critics as prolific as Barthes and Foucault must be honoured and this seems a useful reminder in attempting to organize a critical evaluation of her own work. In recent years, moreover, Spivak has signalled major changes of direction in respect of each of the areas which the first section of this chapter began by identifying. Firstly, she has expressed a desire to find a more simple and accessible style and (unlike Bhabha) now recognizes the difficulties caused by the opacity of some of her essays, particularly for those constituencies which she would most like to engage, students and non-academic Third World audiences. Secondly, significant new interests have been announced. For instance, without surrendering the principle of 'negotiation', Spivak has begun to explore a number of alternatives to the dominant cultural/critical narratives in the Western academy. Thus she is currently assessing the potential of the Hindu concept of *dharma* as an alternative to Western conceptions of ideology and is offering psychoanalytic perspectives developed out of the discourse of *sati* as an alternative to what she describes as the 'regulative psychobiographies' of Western psychoanalysis (a topic to which I will return in the next chapter). Equally, Spivak is now interested in reconceptualizing the idea of the ethical subject outside its histories in the Judaeo-Christian tradition.[76] Spivak explains some of her more recent interests in terms of the changing geo-political order and new patterns of economic 'super-exploitation' in what has been over-optimistically described as the era of 'late' capitalism. This, in particular, underlies her new interest in the possibilities of 'an ecologically just world'.[77]

These changes of thematic focus are also reflected in Spivak's growing tendency to revise some of the arguments which have been analysed in preceding sections of this chapter. Such revisions to some extent exemplify what Spivak has described as the necessity of the 'unlearning of privilege', in other words the imperative to reconsider positions that once seemed self-evident or natural. These revisions are fully consistent with her aim of employing an analytic framework which is open – even contradictory – rather than totalizing. However, some of them are radical, pointing to a distinct break in her career around 1990. For instance, Spivak now expresses impatience with the way that subsequent critical discussion has taken up, or even fetishized, her celebrated concept of 'strategic essentialism'. She claims that an excessive preoccupation with the decentring of the subject can 'turn into precious posturing'[78] which may deflect postcolonial analysis from more pressing problems. In the case of 'Can the Subaltern Speak?', which I have treated as Spivak's single most important essay in that it seems to draw together the arguments of many of her other pieces in the 1980s, this rethinking has been so profound that she has forbidden its inclusion in *The Spivak Reader* (1996). One reason is that Spivak has tired of the way that the concept of the 'subaltern' has been so far (mis)appropriated that 'the word has now lost some of its definitive power'.[79] (Until the promised revision appears, however, one has to make to do with the current version of the essay, which remains of seminal importance for the number and variety of debates which it has generated within the postcolonial field. In any case, Spivak also claims – somewhat paradoxically – that the conclusions to the new version will be substantially the same.)

Spivak's current work also signals some important methodological reorientations. One striking instance (which perhaps is a prime reason for the refusal to grant permission for 'Can the Subaltern Speak?' to be reproduced) is her profound reconsideration of Foucault, which begins almost immediately after the appearance of the fairly scathing critique of his politics which is offered in that essay. *The Post-Colonial Critic* (1990), in strong contrast, begins by acknowledging Foucault's seminal importance in contemporary cultural theory and, indeed, praises him precisely because of his attention to the politics of his own positionality as a critic. Moreover, this text even claims that Foucault 'brilliantly tried to represent the oppressed'.[80] And in contrast to Said's increasing, even terminal, disaffection with Foucault by the time of *Culture and Imperialism*, Spivak's more recent work attempts to displace her own earlier reversal of Said's preference for Foucault over Derrida. Thus the essay 'More on Power/Knowledge' in *Outside in the Teaching Machine* not only again retracts major elements of her earlier critique of Foucault, but goes on to explore ways in which his work and Derrida's might be brought to a mutual accommodation. Similarly, in 'French Feminism Revisited' (in the same volume), Spivak reconsiders some of the objections raised in 'French Feminism in an International Frame', seeing French feminism now as in large measure useful for the kind of work being produced by the Algerian critic Marie-Aimée Hélie-Lucas, for example.

Spivak herself usefully discriminates between contradiction and evolution in intellectual work and one needs to avoid collapsing such developments too hastily under the former rubric. The most productive approach in an evaluation of Spivak's work is not necessarily, in any case, to search out in a punitive spirit the paradoxes in the arguments of a critic who, true to the spirit of deconstructionism, declares: 'As for contradictions . . . I'm not afraid of them.'[81] As has been seen, Spivak is suspicious of coherence for its own sake and suggests that contradictions, tensions or *aporia* in a text can also be the places where they become most productive for subsequent intellectual or creative work. Nor is there anything sacrosanct for Spivak about conventional notions of a neat fit between theory and practice. Indeed, she repeatedly insists that theory and practice should bring each other to productive crisis. Much of what is apparently contradictory in Spivak's work exemplifies Derrida's argument in *Of Grammatology* that 'the enterprise of deconstruction always in a certain way falls prey to its own work'.[82] What she describes as the inevitability of such 'cognitive failure' arises in the first instance from the necessarily 'fictional' nature of founding concepts such as 'origins', 'totalities' and 'the subject', which, while the object of the deconstructionist's 'persistent critique', are nonetheless also the indispensable tools which enable theoretical work to begin. It also derives, as was suggested earlier, from Spivak's refusal to presume the possibility of an Olympian objectivity outside the terms of the 'text' being analysed, or the institutional location in which that analysis is performed. As Spivak admits: 'My explanation cannot remain outside the structures of production of what I criticise.'[83]

It may be more appropriate, instead, to follow Spivak's own analytic procedures and identify the 'itinerary' which leads to her 'cognitive failures' and to consider the ways in which these may nonetheless be enabling for subsequent postcolonial criticism. At the same time, one needs to distinguish between these potentially productive problems and those instances of 'repetition-in-rupture' of ideas and positions that Spivak is ostensibly undermining which seem, by contrast, to be quite paralysing. At the root of the latter kind of difficulties, perhaps, lies the very eclecticism of method which Spivak prizes so highly. For instance (as in Said's early work), Spivak's Marxism seems at times to conflict severely with her recourse to discourse theory and some of the assumptions governing her deconstructive work. She does, of course, often attempt to bring the two methodologies into alignment. 'Can the Subaltern Speak?', for instance, sees the processes of subject-constitution and material exploitation as complementary components of the 'vast two-headed engine'[84] of European imperialism, which respectively require discourse theory and the materialist forms of Marxist analysis to unpick. Equally, she engineers a convergence between these two forms of analysis and deconstruction by stressing the parallels between their respective critiques of positivism, realism and the categories of the concrete and experiential, all of which Spivak sees as central to the epistemological and philosophical framework underpinning (neo-)colonialism itself.

Conflict nonetheless arises because of Spivak's inconsistent, even equivocal, treatment of such categories. On the one hand, she follows the logic of discourse theory by insisting that the 'real' is constructed, and not 'just' mediated, by sign-systems. Thus facts or events 'are never not discursively constituted'.[85] Historical reality (like the life of the Rani of Sirmur) is only available through textual sources and cannot be recovered independently of the processes of construction and manipulation which those involve. However, Spivak argues in other parts of her work that 'the real' has an existence independent of its mediations. The most obvious case in point is the world economy built on the international division of labour, for an understanding of which only a fairly traditional kind of Marxist economic theory is adequate. Western antihumanists such as Foucault are consequently reproved for their ignorance of the 'real history' of colonialism and the 'objective' determinations of the current global order. It is this material 'base' which is responsible 'in the last instance' for shaping subject-constitution through 'superstructural' sign-systems and, consequently, how people see themselves and the world. This emphasis on the 'independent' or 'prior' status of 'the real' also underpins Spivak's criticism of Kristeva's failure to do 'primary research'; the fact that About Chinese Women is flawed by her insufficient existential experience of China clearly implies that the 'true' and 'prior' reality of the 'real' position of Chinese women has escaped Kristeva. A similar epistemology underpins her praise for Mahasweta Devi's fiction; for Spivak it is 'representationally accurate to the last degree' and her protagonists 'could have existed as subalterns in a specific historical moment imagined and tested by orthodox assumptions'.[86] From this perspective, Spivak attempts a negotiation between Marxism and deconstruction in terms quite contradictory to those proposed earlier. The convergence is possible because Marxism is premised upon a clear acceptance of the materiality of the world; by comparison, deconstruction, too, is never fully above 'mere empiricism'.[87] In more recent work, moreover, 'lived experience' is recuperated in the manner of much 'culturalist' Marxism (and, indeed, liberal humanism); for instance, Spivak now claims that the postcolonial critic must 'learn to honour empirical work' and lays great stress on the importance of 'face to face' work with the subaltern.[88]

Perhaps the most important immediate problems to which this methodological eclecticism leads occur in the context of Spivak's conceptions of subaltern identity, positionality and agency. The paradoxical treatment of such issues derives in the first instance from the fundamentally contradictory epistemological status of the subaltern in Spivak's work. As has been seen, in her attempt to resist the appropriation of the subaltern, Spivak at times conceives of him/her as 'wholly Other', as the radically different term which reveals the horizon or limits of Western systems of knowledge. For instance, in 'Supplementing Marxism' (1993) she writes:

> Subalternity is the name I borrow for the space out of any serious touch with the logic of capitalism or socialism. . . . Please do not confuse it with unorganized labour, women as such, the proletarian, the colonized, the object of ethnography, migrant labour, political refugees, etc. Nothing useful comes out of this confusion.[89]

In such formulations, the subaltern seems at times not to be part of the global economy at all and, to a considerable degree, escapes its determinations. There is a consistent pattern of this kind of vision of the subaltern in Spivak's career. Thus – as has been seen – she treats the 'monster', the allegorical figure of the subaltern in *Frankenstein*, as the 'wholly Other' which finally evades the determinations of the 'social' as well as literary text. Equally, her discussion of Mahasweta Devi in 'A Literary Representation of the Subaltern' assumes, to begin with at least, that characters like Jashoda are 'outside' the global economic system. From this angle, then, the subaltern seems to be primarily a conceptual category, rather in the manner that Spivak describes the proletarian as being a 'theoretical fiction . . . a necessary methodological presupposition'[90] which enables particular kinds of analysis to begin. This all suggests that the subaltern is to be seen above all else as an (empty) 'space', or rather 'inaccessible blankness', from which an interrogation of the dominant conceptions of subject-constitution and practices of subject-positioning, whether in the international division of labour or Western 'radical' cultural theory, can potentially be mounted.

In order to construct the subaltern in these terms, however, Spivak is forced into a paralysing series of the 'repetitions-in-rupture' which she complains of in other kinds of cultural analysis. Thus the more the subaltern is seen as *wholly* other, the more Spivak seems to construct the subaltern's identity neither relationally nor differentially, but in essentialist terms, thus repeating precisely the failure of the Subaltern Studies group to consider the subaltern in context of adjacent constituencies like the native elite. Even more bizarrely, the idea of the subaltern being essentially 'untouched' by the global economy would seem to imply that the subaltern is not actually in a subordinate position, insofar as s/he cannot be exploited by a system of which s/he is not part. And the more the subaltern is seen as a 'theoretical' fiction, of course, the more the suffering and exploitation of the subaltern becomes a theoretical fiction, too. Finally, in insisting on occasion on seeing the subaltern in this way, Spivak leaves the would-be non-subaltern ally of the subaltern in a seemingly impossible predicament, simultaneously unable to represent the subaltern in an 'uninterested' fashion insofar as this necessarily, at least to begin with, entails assigning the subaltern subjectivity and a (subordinate) subject-position and yet – as ethical and political agent – unable *not* to represent the subaltern.[91] In other words, the non-subaltern must either maximally respect the Other's radical alterity, thus leaving the status quo intact, or attempt the impossible feat of 'opening up' to the Other without in any way 'assimilating' that Other to his/her own subject-position, perspectives or identity.

Spivak has long been aware of this problem. Nonetheless, whereas *In Other Worlds* disclaimed any intention to 'paralyse' the non-subaltern investigator, 'Neocolonialism and the Secret Agent of Knowledge' deliberately refuses to offer a 'solution' to the dilemma.[92] However, it seems that Spivak now recognizes that her catachrestic redefinition of Derrida's notion of the 'tout-autre' is in itself untenable. In the first place, this is because the appeal to the 'wholly Other' logically requires the Other to have already been identified as such in differential relation to that which is not 'wholly Other'. In Derrida, or more accurately Derrida's account of Kant's 'On a Newly Arisen Superior Tone in Philosophy' (1796), the voice of the 'Other' (in Kant, the Oracle) is expressed through an *inner* voice.[93] Consequently as Todorov comments in his critique of Spivak in *'Race', Writing and Difference*, 'Otherness is never radical' in the way that Spivak (and others) sometimes seem to suggest.[94]

In more recent work, Spivak retreats further from the concept of 'the wholly Other', accpeting that the 'wholly Other' is literally unnameable and unimaginable; Outside in the Teaching Machine cites Derrida again, this time much more in conformity with the spirit of his commentary on Kant, to the effect that 'the completely other is announced as such . . . within what it is not'.[95] This confirms the existence of a second conception of the subaltern which was, contradictorily, already apparent in 'Three Women's Texts and a Critique of Imperialism' and 'A Literary Representation of the Subaltern'. The former essay suggests that insofar as Frankenstein's anonymous 'monster' is structurally related to (and at first literally dependent on) his creator, he cannot be read as the 'absolutely Other' (thus the common misapprehension that the 'monster' shares Frankenstein's name). In the latter piece, Spivak points out that Jashoda's employers' granddaughters-in-law are part of the post-indepen-dence diaspora and international brain-drain. This places Jashoda, retrospectively at least, within a system which is, after all, not inaccess-ible to an analysis which addresses capitalist dynamics.

Such evidence signposts a second and quite distinct pattern of description of the subaltern which recurs throughout Spivak's career. In this reading, Spivak treats the subaltern as a 'real' and concrete historical category, more particularly as a material effect of the export overseas of Western capitalism. Moreover, Spivak sees the current international division of labour as consolidating the process of subalternization inaugurated by colonialism: 'Woman's body is thus the last instance in a system whose general regulator is still the loan: usurer's capital, imbri-cated, level by level, in national industrial and transnational global capital.'[96] This account of the subaltern – perhaps paradoxically – implies a much more optimistic and enabling potential role for the would-be ally of the subaltern. As Steven Cole argues,

> while Spivak's general account of the relation of knowledge to that which is known is itself rendered indeterminate by the ultimate inscrutability of its objects, here instead it is precisely because we know the truth of the female [or subaltern] body that we are able to judge the adequacy . . . of how that body is represented in legal definitions of 'woman as object of exchange.'[97]

From this second perspective, Spivak concedes that 'it is not possible for us as ethical agents to imagine otherness or alterity maximally. We have to turn the other into something like the self in order to be ethical.'[98] To be able to give 'the name "woman" to the other woman',[99] which Spivak sees as the ethical task of the Western feminist vis-à-vis the Third World woman, for example, to some extent necessarily involves assimi-lating that other woman to a 'higher' term (Woman) or to the 'giver's' more specific cultural identity.

Spivak's contradictory conception of the subaltern generates two quite incompatible accounts of subaltern 'voice' (which for Spivak figures will and agency), each of which generates its own further pattern of 'repetition-in-rupture'. Thus insofar as Spivak stresses the 'wholly Other' nature of the subaltern, she generally insists that there is no position from which the subaltern can speak. The first problem with this is that Spivak is, of course, repeating the gesture of constituting and speaking for, or in place of, the subaltern – the very manoeuvre for which she criticizes Foucault and Deleuze. As Bruce Robbins observes in defending Said against such charges: 'The critic who accuses another of speaking for the subaltern by denying that subalterns can speak for themselves, for example, is of course also claiming to speak for them.'[100] Moreover, where Deleuze and Foucault conceive of a marginal who can speak, Spivak reverses but does not displace their vision, thereby reconstituting what is historically one of the most fundamental and enduring binary oppositions between the West and the Third World constructed by metropolitan forms of knowledge (such as Orientalism). Like Said's *Orientalism*, which is also ostensibly so concerned to undermine the equation of the West with 'voice' and the East with 'silence', an essay like 'Can the Subaltern Speak?' actually ends up by constructing the subaltern as the West's 'silent interlocutor'. Perhaps the greatest irony of 'Can the Subaltern Speak?' in this respect is that if Spivak's account of subaltern silence were true, then there would be nothing but the non-subaltern (particularly the West and the native elite) left to speak to or write about. This may explain the apparently extraordinary change of focus in the conclusion of the essay, where Spivak abruptly switches attention from her general theory of subalternity to discuss a concrete historical case of an 'ad hoc *subaltern* rewriting of the social text of *sati*-suicide'.[101] As Bhuvaneswari Bhaduri is a member of the urban property-owning classes (Spivak described her recently her as 'middle class'[102]) with family connections to Spivak's own landowning family, it seems on the face of it incredible that she can be assigned to the same class fraction as the groups defined as subaltern earlier in the essay. If, however, she is not strictly representative of the subaltern, then Spivak is herself obscuring subaltern experience by focusing on the experience of a member of what might (at least from the perspective of Subaltern Studies historiography) be understood to be the bourgeois-nationalist elite.

Nevertheless, it may be Spivak's intention in part to suggest the inaccessibility of 'truly' subaltern experience by focusing on the 'silencing' of a figure who, as an unmarried woman, was still relatively marginalized *vis-à-vis* the male nationalist elite, certainly in nationalist historiography. In other words, one needs to see Bhaduri being used allegorically or catachrestically, in the way that – despite her 'objective' status as member of the white plantocracy – Bertha Mason is used in 'Three Women's Texts and a Critique of Imperialism' to figure the fate of the colonized female subject within the context of the emergence of Western feminism. However, to read the essay in this way itself involves further reinscriptions of ideas which Spivak ostensibly sets out to undermine. Assuming that Bhaduri does indeed allegorically figure the subaltern, one can argue that Spivak restores to her all the qualities of self-consciousness and free will which she has dismissed in Western humanist (and anti-humanist) models of the oppressed subject. Thus Spivak not only disregards her own warning against nostalgic representations of the subaltern as 'intending subject of resistance' and her praise for Rhys's refusal, in Wide Sargasso Sea to 'romanticize individual heroics on the part of the oppressed',[103] but she claims to reveal the 'true' motivation behind Bhaduri's suicide: 'She had finally been entrusted with a political assassination. Unable to confront the task and yet aware of the practical need for trust, she killed herself.'[104] Spivak claims Bhaduri's death as an act of insurgency against British rule on the basis of what seems, on the face of it, fairly flimsy evidence. The authority of phrases like 'Bhuvaneswari had known' is offset by the fact that the 'text' which Spivak relies on is hearsay, and is interpreted several decades later; thus the inevitable qualifiers like 'no doubt', 'perhaps', 'tentative explanation' and 'possible melancholia'. Moreover, this politically comforting reconstruction of motive (close family members in fact ascribe the suicide to emotional problems) makes Bhaduri 'signify' (if not literally speak), in apparently blatant contradiction of the assertion that the subaltern 'as female cannot be heard or read' and of the praise in the final paragraph of the essay for Derrida's alertness to 'the danger of appropriating the other [assuming Bhaduri can, indeed, be read as the subaltern] by assimilation'.[105] Finally, while Spivak accuses Kristeva of a 'wishful use of history', her treatment of the Bhaduri case seems itself to be precisely an instance of the way 'positivist knowledge' which claims to be able to (re)produce the 'truth' of experience, engenders the kind of 'utopian politics' for which Kristeva is criticized.[106]

A further instance of 'repetition-in-rupture' evident in this aspect of Spivak's account of the subaltern is the way that in 'Can the Subaltern Speak?' (as so often elsewhere) Spivak not only addresses the West primarily but in fact focuses on the metropolitan intellectual as privileged object of investigation. Though one appreciates the irony of her reversal of the West's anthropological gaze, this focus nonetheless reinscribes the West as subject, laying Spivak open to the kind of accusation she makes against Foucault and Deleuze. Equally, her polemics on the importance of 'unlearning privilege' are clearly directed at Western colleagues. Like Kristeva's About Chinese Women, then, many of Spivak's essays function as 'a set of directives for class- and race-privileged literary women'.[107] Similarly, while 'French Feminism in an International Frame' begins by disavowing any desire to patronize her young Sudanese colleague (not altogether convincingly, given the tone of her comment that 'I was ready to forgive [her] sexist term "female circumcision"'[108]), Spivak is nonetheless speaking over the head of this 'misguided' Third World academic to her feminist peers in the West and, indeed, using her as an object-lesson in the perils of 'ideological victimage'. The patronage this implies is most marked in the conclusion, where, quite astonishingly, Spivak offers the essay as 'a theme that can liberate my colleague from Sudan'.[109]

A final major problem in 'Can the Subaltern Speak?' is the fact that Bhaduri cannot be entirely representative of the subaltern in another crucial sense. She is, of course, dead and therefore literally unable to speak or – in the absence of any archival evidence (such as diaries) she might have left – to have her views recovered or reconstructed. Clearly, as 'Subaltern Studies: Deconstructing Historiography' concludes, there are pretty much insuperable problems in attempting to recuperate the 'true' experience of those who have historically been denied a place in history, especially the 'illiterate'. It is for this reason more than any other that the Subaltern Studies historians do not (or are unable to) extend their researches to social fractions below the level of the 'upper-middle' peasantry whose fate is recorded in colonial archives. But whether the same constraints apply to the subaltern living today is another matter, particularly when she is defined as including the (metropolitan) 'urban home-worker'. (Moreover, the focus on a historical case like Bhaduri's seems somewhat incompatible with Spivak's complaint in 'The Rani of Sirmur' that the lives of the contemporary subaltern are going unrecorded.)

While one must acknowledge the force of Spivak's argument about the dangers of constructing 'a monolithic collectivity of "women" in the list of the oppressed whose unfractured subjectivity allows them to speak for themselves',[110] there seem to be equivalent dangers in seeing the contemporary female subaltern, equally monolithically, as *incapable* of coming to the point of voice or self-representation. While Spivak is excellent on 'the itinerary of silencing' endured by the subaltern, particularly historically, there is little attention to the process by which the subaltern's 'coming to voice' might be achieved. Spivak often appears to deny the subaltern any possibility of access to the (self-)liberating personal and political trajectories enabled by the growth of the modern women's movement in the West, for instance. Thus she rejects successively a number of different accounts which offer a potential teleology of subaltern emancipation. Most obviously and persistently, she refutes the claim of (neo-)colonial discourse that the West will effect the liberation of the rest of the world. While accepting that both Gramsci and Marx envision the subaltern's rise to hegemony, Spivak herself rejects the Marxist modes-of-production narrative of the emergence of the oppressed to voice as a consequence of the transition from feudalism to capitalism and beyond.[111] Finally, she dismisses the nationalist narratives of the native elite, which promise liberation for all sectors of the indigenous population once colonialism is ended.

In so hastily discounting the possibility of class-based modes of solidarity and alliance politics as an option for the subaltern, Spivak at times seems to present him/her as a forever passive and helpless victim of forces beyond his/her control. This makes it rather difficult to understand, let alone accept, her complaint about the West's historic 'refusal to acknowledge the colonial peoples, post-colonial peoples, as agents'.[112] Ironically, dominant discourse records the subaltern's resistance to a far greater degree than Spivak's own work, albeit that such resistance may be coded in all manner of negative terms (most often as criminality), as the Subaltern Studies historians have demonstrated in detail. From Nanny, the guerrilla leader of the Maroon uprisings of 1773, through the bazaar prostitutes' role in the 1857 'Mutiny' and the Nigerian market women protesters of 1929 to the 'bandit queen' Poolan Devi today, the resistance of the subaltern woman has always been acknowledged in dominant historiography. Equally, there are many less 'spectacular' but nonetheless effective instances of subaltern women's mobilization, particularly around issues of health (or the body), in both the colonial period and today.[113] Such evidence suggests that the subaltern woman has not always accepted as inevitable the hapless immiseration represented by Mahasweta Devi's character Jashoda. (Symptomatically, Spivak praises Devi precisely because she, too, does not construct the subaltern woman as an 'intending subject of resistance'.)

On the other hand, a quite different and far less deterministic vision of the subaltern's voice (and agency) is also elaborated in Spivak's work. This account takes two forms, the first of which, however, ostensibly reinforces the proposition that the subaltern cannot speak. Thus while In Other Worlds recognizes the possibility of the subaltern's emergence from subalternity, it also insists that this trajectory is impossible to record or analyse.[114] By contrast, when the text also acknowledges that subordinate groups can 'start participating in the production of knowledge about themselves',[115] it is surely too simple to imply, as Spivak does, that by the very process of having found a voice, such figures have automatically become part of the hegemonic order or are now members of the constituency of stooge-like 'privileged native informants'. Spivak's contention that 'If the subaltern can speak then, thank God, the subaltern is not a subaltern any more'[116] does not sufficiently recognize that there may be a number of intermediate positions between 'full' subalternity and hegemony. In this respect, Spivak's characteristic hostility to 'culturalist' Marxism means that she is deaf to the powerful argument made by Raymond Williams about 'emergent' and 'residual' social forms and communities, a theory itself in part derived from Gramsci's conception of the possibility of transition between subalternity and hegemony.[117]

In any case, as early as 'French Feminism in an International Frame' (1981), the subaltern woman (as represented by the washerwomen on her grandfather's estate) can be clearly identified as speaking subject, albeit through Spivak's mediation, by the Western intellectual who cares to read the piece (though interestingly, Spivak does not herself speak *to* them). In more recent work, particularly, Spivak argues in no uncertain terms that the subaltern can indeed speak – and act resistantly. Thus she dismisses Richard Rorty's account of the later Foucault's alleged pessimism on this score as a misinterpretation:

> It is the disenfranchised who teaches us most often by saying: I do not recognize myself in the object of your benevolence. I do not recognize my share in your naming ... she tells us if we *care* to hear ... that she is not the literal referent for our frenzied naming of woman in the scramble for legitimacy in the house of theory.[118]

This does not, however, detract from the force of Spivak's argument that the subaltern is still, characteristically, only heard through the mediation of the non-subaltern, or that while the subaltern can speak, the West may choose not to hear, or that the terms in which the subaltern speaks may be overdetermined, so that no 'pure' form of subaltern consciousness can be retrieved. For example, insofar as the washerwomen on her grandfather's estate continue, as late as 1949, to assert the claim of the East India Company to the river, Spivak reveals them as already 'coded' by imperialism, and consequently as conceiving of their social being (or subject-position) within terms set out so many decades earlier.

Spivak's conception of the speaking subaltern, however, in turn generates its own pattern of conceptual 'repetition-in-rupture'. For instance, insofar as the process of 'coming to voice' is recognized, Spivak at times seems to imply that it derives in the first instance from the interventions of 'benevolent' outsiders, a process which is perhaps inevitable given the implications of statements like 'the subject of exploitation cannot know and speak the text of female exploitation'.[119] For instance, Spivak describes Mahasweta Devi as a writer who is working 'actively to move the subaltern into hegemony' through her fiction, and she praises Cixous, who gives 'the name woman to *the other*

woman',[120] as an example of how the First World feminist can empower
the Third World woman. To her great credit (and in contrast to the
relative silence about such matters in Said and, especially, Bhabha),
Spivak's account of her own advantages is consistent and disarmingly
frank. As an 'academic feminist' based in the United States, Spivak
recognizes that she is, by comparison with most of the world's women,
already infinitely privileged. She refers to herself as 'an upper-class young
woman' and describes her 'caste-fix' as Brahmin; as a consequence, she
admits, 'in India, whatever I do, I'm recognisable, marked socially as,
you know, "up there"'.[121] Thus her affiliation to the subaltern is inevitably both 'class-determined and determining'. For these reasons it is
difficult to escape a sense of Spivak's own 'benevolence' when she
describes herself as acting from this position of privilege as 'sort of
Mahasweta Devi's henchwoman with the tribals'.[122] And to the extent
that Spivak's treatment of Bhaduri could also be understood as a
restoration of agency and intention to a figure who, allegorically at least,
represents the subaltern – Spivak is herself moving her, if not into
hegemony, at least into history. In this sense, too, Spivak repeats the
gestures she criticizes in the 'benevolent' West, whether in its humanist,
anti-humanist or feminist incarnations.

Nor is it easy to see how Spivak always escapes what Robert Young
describes as 'the inevitable risk of presenting herself as the representative
of that very "Third World Woman"'.[123] She clearly wishes to preserve
her distance from what 'Can the Subaltern Speak?' scornfully describes
as certain varieties of the Indian elite who are native informants for First
World intellectuals interested in the voice of the Other. Yet in mediating
what the subaltern can(not) say, her own work would seem to belong
with precisely the kind of text which she criticizes in 'French Feminism
in an International Frame': 'The pioneering books that bring First World
feminists news from the Third World are written by privileged informants and can only be deciphered by a trained readership.'[124] A more
recent instance of Spivak's continuing role as native informant comes in
Outside in the Teaching Machine, in the context, once more, of the
problem of the 'invisibility' of subaltern experience to the West: 'I know
the kind of woman I am thinking about. And I also know that this
person is not imaginable by most [Western] friends reading these
words.'[125]

There must also be a suspicion that some of the paradoxes of Spivak's
position are at times only resolved by her apparent reinscription of
varieties of 'nativism'. Spivak is at pains to suggest the fallacy of the
proposition that only the subaltern can know the subaltern, because it
predicates the possibility of knowledge on knower and known being
'identical'. But at other moments Spivak comes close to rearticulating a
version of cultural essentialism. Thus while postcolonial writers (and

critics) as members of a bourgeois class fraction 'can claim . . . little of subaltern status',[126] and 'A Literary Representation of the Subaltern' mounts a powerful critique of Devi's authority as a guide to her own work, Spivak nonetheless also appears to suggest that Devi's cultural and geographical proximity to the 'sexed subaltern' enables her to produce representations of that constituency which avoid the problems which beset benevolent Westerners. Spivak, too, seems consistently able to avoid such difficulties by virtue of her origins and existential experience of the Indian context, despite a vast intervening caste, class and linguistic/ cultural chasm between herself and subaltern communities. And one must note that Spivak is not above reproving Benita Parry's criticism of her supposed deafness to the 'native' voice by reference to her own status as a 'native',[127] as if this in itself, irrespective of her many 'elite' identities and affiliations, was sufficient answer. Moreover, the only Westerner in Spivak's work who seems to escape the traps of 'benevolence' is Gail Omvedt and even she does not fully transcend the customary ethno-centrism of the Western investigator.[128] This raises the same problem as *Orientalism*, the question of whether Westerners are *ontologically* incapable of 'disinterested' or 'true' knowledge of the non-West.

Finally, perhaps, questions must be asked of the general conception of the 'political' (and its effectiveness) in Spivak's critique. In 'Subaltern Studies: Deconstructing Historiography', Spivak charges the group (as she does Kristeva in 'French Feminism in an International Frame') with insufficient attention to the collective and 'objective' material forces underlying social change. However, despite her consistent attention to the material realities and structures of the international division of labour, Spivak's own work also often seems to discount material forces in the aetiology of social development or crisis. These are consistently presented in her work as being instigated at a discursive level, and depend upon provoking changes in 'the function of the sign-system'.[129] If, as often seems the case in Spivak's work, it is interventions such as deconstructive criticism which primarily produce violent disruption of the sign-system, then this inevitably privileges critical work over more 'direct' forms of intervention such as insurgency or peaceful political organization against the dominant. For example, in 'Can the Subaltern Speak?' Spivak criticises Deleuze for a naive belief that such forms of political intervention can precede, or take precedence over, disruptions of the 'sign-system'; and 'French Feminism in an International Frame' praises Catherine Clément's axiom that one must first 'change the imaginary in order to be able to act on the real'.[130] Moreover, and extremely contentiously for someone who describes herself as an 'old-fashioned' Marxist, Spivak attributes to Marx himself scepticism about the possibility and effectiveness of conscious collective agency.[131] Indeed, a fundamental incompatibility between Marxism and deconstruction is apparent in her argument that 'a political programme cannot base itself upon affirmative deconstruction'.[132]

On the other hand, Spivak disclaims the argument that she is 'trying to reduce hard reality to nothing but signs', and argues that deconstruction of 'the symbolic order' can in fact support the politics of a 'great-narrative' such as Third World liberation.[133] It is in this context that she claims: 'I call "politics as such" the prohibition of marginality that is implicit in the production of any explanation.'[134] Nonetheless the ambiguities in her conception of 'the political' have elicited some sharp criticism from postcolonial colleagues. In the course of a somewhat acrimonious interview with several Indian women critics, Spivak steadfastly refused to answer what 'pragmatic political usefulness'[135] her work has to Third World struggle. Meanwhile, Benita Parry has complained of the 'exorbitation of the role allotted to the post-colonial woman intellectual'[136] in Spivak's work. On the other hand, in assessing the political relevance of Spivak's work, one must acknowledge the modesty in her advice to 'be aware of the limits of your power rather than dramatize yourself' and the honesty of her own refusal of the temptation of some 'radical' academics' 'tendency to offer grandiose solutions with little political specificity, couched in the strategic form of rhetorical solutions'.[137] However, in the absence of any concrete account in Spivak of how the subaltern can transcend subalternity – a process which is, albeit unevenly, observable in much of the contemporary Third World, side by side with increasing immiseration for many other subaltern groups – accepting such 'cognitive failure' as inevitable can all too easily seem to legitimate political apathy. Thus one might be tempted once again to adapt Spivak's explanation of the ineffectiveness of Kristeva's feminist project to her own work, while substituting the term 'racism' for 'sexism': '[Even] if one knows how to undo identities, one does not necessarily escape the historical determinations of sexism.'[138]

Such criticisms might suggest that Spivak's work issues in a series of major short-circuits in the way that *Orientalism* sometimes seems to. Perhaps the strongest criticism in this respect has come from Richard Freadman and Seamus Miller, who argue that

> her deconstructive discussion, whilst trying to displace the binary oppositions it finds, to effect some fruitful renegotiation of categories, is in fact beset by contradictions which ultimately defuse its political force. Thus, Spivak wants to discern politically expedient ideological falsehoods where there can allegedly be no truth; she wants to help reconstruct the history of female literary marginalization whilst denying the possibility of authentic histories; she wants to assert the claims of emancipation whilst at the same time repudiating ethics and postulating only the most minimal conception of individual agency imaginable; she wants to employ psychoanalytic concepts

without conceding, at least in principle, a real history of her analysee; and so on.[139]

This is forceful, but perhaps exaggerated. Spivak might legitimately counter such an argument in the following terms:

> Deconstruction does not say there is no subject, there is no truth, there is no history. It simply questions the privileging of identity so that someone is believed to have the truth. It is not the exposure of error. It is constantly looking into how truths are produced. ... Deconstruction, if one wants a formula, is, among other things, a persistent critique of what one cannot not want.'[140]

Arguably, Spivak's work characteristically exemplifies the concept of the 'success-in-failure' that she sees as an inevitable consequence of deconstructive work in the postcolonial field, which at its best nonetheless produces 'constructive questions, corrective doubts'.[141] Certainly her criticisms of western radical critical theory for its failure to attend to questions of (neo-)colonialism are forceful and productive, as is her analysis of the problems of counter-hegemonic intellectual projects such as the Subaltern Studies group. While one might not agree with every aspect of her interpretation of the canonical metropolitan texts she analyses, the feminist framework which Spivak elaborates in essays such as 'Three Women's Texts and a Critique of Imperialism' has been proved extremely fruitful for many subsequent women critics in the field, as the work of Firdous Azim, Laura Donaldson, Lisa Lowe, Rey Chow and Jenny Sharpe attests.

Certainly Spivak forces all those working in the field of postcolonial criticism to consider scrupulously their political positionality and affiliations as well as the 'interests' of their critical assumptions and approaches. Perhaps the most enabling element in all of Spivak's work is the emphasis on the importance of trying to recognize and hear the Other woman in *her* terms (even if this involves, quite literally, learning *her* language) and not simply assimilating her unproblematically to Western values, histories and regimes of knowledge: '[There] has to be another focus: not merely who am I? But who is the other woman? How am I naming her? How does she name me? Is this part of the problematic I discuss?'[142] After Spivak, there can be no question of 'innocent' or intrinsically politically correct denunciations of (neo-)colonialism derived from an unexamined identification with, or 'benevolence' towards, the oppressed:

> Those questions – political (what is it to vote?), economic (what is it to hope to save?), social (what is the good life?) – and their answers cannot

teach her [the critic/researcher] enough to make up an account of the ethical subject distinguishable from the celebration of a transcoded, anthropological subject/object. How can the questioner not acknowledge that the arrival of the moment between her and the other woman is not just good chemistry between the two, but also vast aggregative violating systemic work which is precisely from that hotel lobby that she is trying to leave?[143]

In these respects, Spivak's work exemplifies what she eventually comes to value most in Foucault's work, 'the new making-visible of a "success" that does not conceal or bracket problems'.[144]

4

Homi Bhabha:

'The Babelian Performance'[1]

The republication of most of Homi Bhabha's essays (sometimes in heavily revised form) in *The Location of Culture* (1994) has greatly facilitated reconsideration of his contribution to contemporary analysis of the cultural and political issues raised by (neo-)colonialism, race, ethnicity and migration. When they are considered as a developing body of work, rather than as a series of discrete articles published in journals which are widely dispersed in different disciplinary and geographical locations, it becomes much easier to appreciate the degree to which Bhabha challenges the vision of his predecessors in the postcolonial field and those of Fanon and Said in particular. Seeing Bhabha's work collected in this way suggests that, thus far at least, his career falls into two principal phases. From around 1980 to 1988, his principal interest is in colonial discourse analysis. Whereas Said's *Orientalism* focuses on the Middle East, however, Bhabha's particular interest – like Spivak's – is in the cultural exchanges involved in the history of British rule in India. Since then, Bhabha has become more preoccupied with the issues raised by the cultural consequences of neo-colonialism in the contemporary era and the complex and often conflictual relationship of postcolonial discourse to postmodernism.

While I have divided Bhabha's work into two phases for the purposes of analysis, the break between them should not be over-emphasized – if only because much of the discussion of contemporary cultural problematics in later essays, such as 'By Bread Alone' (1994), is illustrated in terms of colonial history. As this might suggest, Bhabha's discussion of postcoloniality assumes a relationship of continuity rather than rupture between the era of colonialism and the contemporary period, which he refers to as 'the on-going colonial present'.[2] The continuity between the two phases of Bhabha's career is also evident at a conceptual and methodological level, so that his distinctive theoretical insights are constantly revised and elaborated upon as his work develops. Thus he describes one of his key analytic figures, the 'time-lag' – which first appears in 1990 – as 'a structure of the "splitting" of colonial discourse that I have been elaborating and illustrating – without giving it a name – from my very earliest essays'.[3]

Reading Bhabha's work involves a number of difficulties familiar from Spivak's criticism. One of these is the often extremely dense (or clotted) texture of his style. At times, indeed, his characteristically teasing, evasive, even quasi-mystical (or mystificatory) mode of expression seems designed to appeal primarily to the reader's intuition. 'The Postcolonial and the Postmodern' (1994), for example, argues thus: 'If you seek simply the sententious or the exegetical, you will not grasp the hybrid moment outside the sentence – not quite experience, not yet concept; part dream, part analysis; neither signifier nor signified'.[4] Equally challenging is Bhabha's methodological eclecticism, typified by the comments at the end of 'DissemiNation' (1990): 'I have attempted no general theory . . . I have taken the measure of Fanon's occult instability and Kristeva's parallel times into the "incommensurable narrative" of Benjamin's modern storyteller to suggest no salvation, but a strange cultural survival of the people.'[5] These difficulties are compounded because Bhabha often bends his sources – at times radically – to his own particular needs and perspectives. Of his engagement with Bakhtin, for instance, he comments: 'As with Guha [the Subaltern Studies historian], my reading will be catachrestic: reading between the lines, taking neither him at his word nor me fully at mine.'[6] Moreover, Bhabha is not above rewriting his sources for the purposes of advancing his own arguments. In 'The Postcolonial and the Postmodern', for instance, he cites Roland Barthes's description, in *The Pleasure of the Text* (1973), of languages overheard in a bar. However, Bhabha not only alters the original, but supplements Barthes's account with details of his own, to produce the impression that Barthes is actually in Tangiers and not evoking it through the mediation of another writer. *Caveat lector!* This is not to dismiss these procedures as altogether or intrinsically illegitimate. In the first place, as is now generally recognised, all interpretations of texts necessarily involve an element of 'misreading'. More germanely, perhaps, it has always been a common postcolonial strategy to inflect Western narratives in new ways, as is evident in the many 'rewritings' of metropolitan literary texts by non-Western artists. One could argue that Bhabha (and Spivak) are simply extending this subversive process of 're-citing' and 're-siting' to the critical and theoretical arena.

The first phase of Bhabha's work might be approached initially in terms of its attempt to move beyond the analysis of colonial relations in terms of systems of binary oppositions of the kind which underwrite both Said's *Orientalism* and the later, better known work of Fanon, such as *The Wretched of the Earth* (1961). While 'The Other Question' (1983) recognizes that Said 'hints continually at a polarity or division at the very centre of Orientalism', Bhabha's description of Said's analysis as 'undeveloped' in this respect[7] expresses his belief that such tensions as *Orientalism* does note in colonial relations are finally (and illegitimately) resolved and unified by Said's assertion of the unidirectionality and intentionality of colonial knowledge as will to power. As chapter 2 suggested, this – ironically – re-establishes the very division between colonizer and colonized which Said deplores in colonial discourse itself. Bhabha meanwhile suggests that, under the increasing pressure of political exigencies (particularly the Algerian war of independence), Fanon reinstates models of colonial identity which are psychically and phenomenologically fixed in a similar way to *Orientalism*.

Whereas early Said concentrates almost entirely on the colonizer, and later Fanon almost entirely on the colonized, Bhabha seeks to emphasize the mutualities and negotiations across the colonial divide. For Bhabha the relationship between colonizer and colonized is more complex and nuanced – and politically fraught – than Fanon and Said imply, principally because the circulation of contradictory patterns of psychic affect in colonial relations (desire for, as well as fear of the Other, for example) undermines their assumption that the identities and positionings of colonizer and colonized exist in stable and unitary terms which are also absolutely distinct from, and necessarily in conflict with, each other. One could argue that, *pace* Bhabha's disclaimer in 'Dissemi-Nation', there is in fact a 'general theory' organizing his varied analyses of colonial discourse. This is that the colonial relationship is structured (on both sides) by 'forms of multiple and contradictory belief'[8] (a phrase which recurs in many of the essays up to 1988).

In seeking to shift the focus of colonial discourse analysis to questions of identity-formation, psychic affect and the operations of the unconscious, Bhabha's main methodological debts are to Freud and – more particularly – Lacan, whose radical revisions of Freud underlie Bhabha's principal theoretical premise in his treatment of such issues. This is that, as 'Remembering Fanon' (1986) puts it, 'identity is only ever possible in the *negation* of any sense of originality or plenitude, through the principle of displacement and differentiation . . . that always renders it a liminal reality'.[9] As this essay acknowledges, Bhabha's adaptation of Lacanian theory for analysis of colonial relations was anticipated in Fanon's *Black Skin, White Masks* (1952), which for Bhabha offers a strikingly different, and much more enabling, approach than later work like *The Wretched of the Earth*. Fanon's first text is praised most particularly for its engagement with colonial relations at the inter-subjective level (rather than focusing on the 'public sphere' of law, economic structures and military campaigns, for instance) and for conceiving of them as dynamic and shifting rather than static in their modes of operation: 'That familiar alignment of colonial subjects – Black/White, Self/Other – is disturbed ... and the traditional grounds of racial identity are dispersed, whenever they are found to rest in narcissistic myths of Negritude or White cultural supremacy.'[10]

The unstable psychic sphere of colonial relations is illustrated initially in Bhabha's early work through analysis of the workings of colonial stereotype. In marked contrast to *Orientalism*, Bhabha is little concerned with noting, let alone correcting, mistaken definitions of the identity of 'the Other' on the part of a supposedly all-powerful metropolitan culture. Nor, as 'Representation and the Colonial Text' (1984) suggests, is Bhabha much concerned with offering more positive images (or 'reverse stereotypes') of the colonized, as he suggests is the case with some post-independence 'cultural nationalist'[11] criticism. Instead, Bhabha is more anxious to challenge certain recent accounts of the psychic economy of stereotype. In 'The Other Question', for instance, he criticizes Stephen Heath's analysis of representations of racial difference in Orson Welles's film *A Touch of Evil*, suggesting that it is debilitated by a failure to register the *ambivalent* and conflictual nature of (neo-)colonial affective relations. For Bhabha, Heath's position demonstrates 'a limiting and traditional reliance on the stereotype as offering, *at any one time*, a secure point of identification'[12] on the part of the individual or group which circulates it.

By contrast, Bhabha interprets the regime of stereotype as evidence not of the stability of the 'disciplinary' gaze of the colonizer, or security in his own conception of himself, but of the degree to which the colonizer's identity (and authority) is in fact fractured and destabilized by contradictory psychic responses to the colonized Other. 'The Other Question' begins by observing the dependence of colonial discourse on concepts of 'fixity' in its representation of the unchanging identity of subject peoples (for example, in the stereotypes of the 'lustful Turk' or the 'noble savage'). However, for Bhabha there is a curiously contradictory effect in the economy of stereotype, insofar as what is supposedly already known must be endlessly reconfirmed through repetition. For Bhabha, this suggests that the 'already known' is not as securely established as the currency and rhetorical power of the stereotype might imply. This in turn points to a 'lack' in the colonizer's psyche, which is further exemplified, in Bhabha's view, by the way that stereotype requires the colonizer to identify himself in terms of what he is *not* while at the same potentially undermining him insofar as his identity then depends partly upon a relationship with this potentially confrontational Other for its constitution (notably the case in such stereotypes as the 'wily Oriental' or the 'untrustworthy servant'). Bhabha elaborates on the function of the colonial stereotype by analogy with Freud's conception of the role which the fetish plays for the fetishist. The stereotype not only shares the fetish's metonymic structure of substitution for the 'real' object but, like the fetish, is a means of expressing and containing severely conflictual feelings and attitudes. In Bhabha's gloss, 'fetishism is always a "play" or vacillation between the archaic affirmation of wholeness/similarity . . . and the anxiety associated with lack and difference'.[13]

For Bhabha, this structure of affective ambivalence on the part of the colonizer is partly manifested in a consistent pattern of conflict in colonial discourse. For example, the colonized subject can be simultaneously beyond comprehension (as in stereotypes about 'the inscrutable Oriental' or 'the mysterious East') and yet completely knowable as the object of the all-seeing colonial gaze. Similarly the colonized subject can be

> both savage (cannibal) and yet the most obedient and dignified of servants (the bearer of food); he is the embodiment of rampant sexuality and yet innocent as a child; he is mystical, primitive, simple-minded and yet the most worldly and accomplished liar, and manipulator of social forces.[14]

All this suggests a radical departure from *Orientalism*'s conception of colonial discourse; for Bhabha it is never as consistent, confident and monologic as Said (generally) implies but is, instead, riven by contradictions and anxieties which are evident, in the first instance, in these mixed modes of representation.

As well as psychoanalytic theory, Bhabha utilizes certain elements of post-structuralism to conceptualize the tension and disturbance within colonial discourse. Bhabha's enthusiasm for such theory is, however, by no means untempered. Like Spivak and Said, he is concerned by its characteristic blindness to questions of race and empire.[15] Thus Bhabha calls for the habitual attention of deconstruction to dissemination and *différance* to be reconfigured, so that it is focused not just on questions of semantic slippage *within* the text, but on how signification is affected by particular sites and contexts of enunciation and address, more specifically those pertaining to the peculiar conditions of (neo-)colonialism. This kind of 'departure from Derrida'[16] (which, like Spivak's, is more a matter of reorienting Derrida than really challenging him, as Said does) has its parallel in Bhabha's 'translation' of aspects of Foucault to the study of postcolonial problematics. Of particular significance in this respect is Bhabha's adaptation of Foucault's theory of 'repeatable materiality'. This is glossed as

> the process by which statements from one institution [or enunciative context] can be transcribed in the discourse of another . . . any change in the statement's conditions of use and reinvestment, any alteration in its field of

experience or verification, or indeed any difference in the problems to be solved, can lead to the emergence of a new statement: the difference of the same.[17]

Bhabha's recourse to Derrida and Foucault underwrites his second main conceptualizion of the various ways in which colonial authority becomes fractured. For Bhabha, colonial discourse is never quite as authoritative and unified as it claims to be because of the inherent tendency of meanings to slip, owing to the effects of both 'repetition' and *différance*. For example, the authority of what 'Signs Taken for Wonders' (1985) describes as the 'English Book' (by this Bhabha means in the first instance the Bible, which he then uses to figure the 'text' of English culture more generally) depends on the claim that it is originary, fully self-present, and unitary. According to Bhabha's synthesis of some of the arguments of Foucault and Derrida, however, such apparent 'essences' are revealed as already incomplete, by the very process of their 'repetition' in a new context. Since the 'repetition' of the 'original' can never be identical with the 'original' (otherwise it would be the 'original'), this process of 'translation' produces a destabilizing 'lack' in that 'original'.[18] Consequently, as 'Sly Civility' (1985) puts it, colonial discourse is always *'less than one and double'*.[19] The 'slippage' in colonial discourse is primarily, for Bhabha, a consequence of the process of 'translation' of particular ideas, narratives and theories from the metropolis and their 'hybridization' in the course of their rearticulation in a different context in the pursuit of imperial hegemony overseas.

'Sly Civility' also illustrates some more basic ways in which colonialism fragments the colonizer's identity and authority. The argument is advanced primarily through analysis of the contradictory career of the representative nineteenth-century figure, J. S. Mill. While employed in the despotic service of the East India Company, Mill also agitated on behalf of the principle of individual liberty and the extension of democratic rights in the metropolitan sphere. Bhabha points out that one of Mill's most famous essays, 'On Liberty', was actually written in response to Macaulay's proposals for the reform of Indian education. Mill (and many others like him) attempts to make domestic democracy compatible with overseas despotism, in a unified vision of Britain's identity and mission as a nation. In Bhabha's view, however, this generates only an 'an agonistic uncertainty' which 'puts on trial the very discourse of civility within which representative government claims its liberty and empire its ethics'.[20] The radical contradictions in nineteenth-century British discourses of the nation are typified, for Bhabha, in Macaulay's essay on Warren Hastings, which explains the principles of government espoused by the East India Company in the following manner: 'Be the father and the oppressor of the people; be just and unjust, moderate and rapacious'.[21] For Bhabha, the coherence of Macaulay's vision of Britain's cultural integrity is chronically destabilized by such processes as bringing peace and progress to India by violent forms of disruption, or effecting the emancipation of the Indian subject through absolute government:

> Why does the spectre of eighteenth-century despotism ... haunt these vigorous nineteenth-century colonial practices of muscular Christianity and the civilizing mission? Can despotism, however vigorous, inspire a colony of individuals when the dread letter of despotic law can only instil the spirit of servitude?[22]

Bhabha conceptualizes the fracturing of colonial discourse (and consequently of its will to power) through different kinds of 'repetition' in a number of other essays. In 'Of Mimicry and Man' (1984), he introduces one of the key concepts in his first phase of work, that of 'mimicry'. Bhabha sees this from one perspective as a form of colonial control generated by the metropolitan colonizer, which operates in conformity with the logic of the panoptical gaze of power elaborated in Foucault's *Discipline and Punish* (1975). The colonizer requires of the colonized subject that s/he adopt the outward forms and internalize the values and norms of the occupying power. In this sense, then, mimicry expresses the 'epic' project of the civilizing mission to transform the colonized culture by making it copy or 'repeat' the colonizer's culture. Precisely because it operates in the affective and ideological spheres, according to what Foucault might describe as the logic of a 'pastoral' regime, in contrast to policies of domination based on brute force, mimicry constitutes for Bhabha 'one of the most elusive and effective strategies of colonial power and knowledge'.[23] At the same time, however, the disciplinary gaze of the colonizer is destabilized anamorphically by a blind-spot, which is the consequence of the crucial differentiation which the strategy of mimicry requires between being English and being 'Anglicized'. The difference between the two terms sustains the distinction between the colonizing and colonized subjects on which colonial control depends. One element of colonial discourse, then, envisions the colonized subject's potential for reformation and gradual approximation to the elevated condition of the colonizer, through the redeeming experience of benevolent imperial guidance, while another contradicts this with a conception of the ontological difference (and inferiority) of the colonized subject. At the heart of mimicry, then, is a destabilizing 'ironic compromise ... the desire for a reformed, recognizable Other, *as a subject of a difference that is almost the same, but not quite*'.[24] The consequence of this, however, is quite contrary to the 'intention' of the colonizer, in that mimicry produces subjects whose 'not-quite sameness' acts like a distorting mirror which fractures the identity of the colonizing subject and – as in the regime of stereotype – 'rearticulates [its] presence in terms of its "otherness", that which it disavows'.[25] Perhaps most damaging of all for the will to power of colonial discourse is Bhabha's suggestion that 'Englishness' (what the colonizer's authority ultimately depends upon) is itself a belated 'effect' which emerges as a consequence of contact with alien cultures. In this early formulation of the problematic of the 'time-lag', Bhabha again points to a 'lack' at the heart of the colonizer's identity which, he argues, 'causes the dominant discourse to split along the axis of its power to be representative, authoritative'.[26]

MODERNITY, THE POSTCOLONIAL AND THE POSTMODERN

As suggested earlier, Bhabha's second phase of work is primarily devoted to the problems posed by colonial history and inherited discourses, of race, nation and ethnicity, for contemporary cultures. As Bhabha becomes increasingly (but not exclusively) engaged with the predicament of the postcolonial migrant in the Western metropolis, so some important changes of perspective are made. In the second phase, the questions of cultural exchange and identification are not overdetermined by problems of geographical distance between metropolis and periphery and overt forms of political inequality, but by the contiguity of cultures sharing the same (metropolitan) space and relations of ostensible, if often illusory, equality. Nonetheless, at a strategic level, the preoccupations of the second phase often run parallel with those of the first. These include the following questions: How is the relation of Western culture to its migrant (and non-Western) 'equivalents' to be understood? How is the identity of the contemporary migrant (or subaltern) to be conceptualized? In what terms should the agency of these constituencies be expressed? And what are the most appropriate forms of postcolonial or 'minoritarian' resistance to the dominant order?

Such issues involve Bhabha in a complex set of negotiations between the discourses of postcolonialism and postmodernism, which 'The Postcolonial and the Postmodern' describes as guided by a desire 'to rename' the postmodern from the perspective of the postcolonial. This emphasis on 'negotiation' (compare Spivak) between the two discourses sets Bhabha apart, in important respects, from many other postcolonial and 'minority' critics who see postmodernism as in fact writing out (or off) the predicament and problems of the non-Western world in a new universalizing discourse which parallels the implicit ethnocentrism of the 'humanism' which accompanied the colonial project.[27] However, if Bhabha attempts to modify aspects of these more hostile acounts of postmodernism, he is by no means uncritical of some formulations of the postmodern, which, he agrees, tend to take the cultural histories and predicaments of the contemporary West as normative. Bhabha gives several examples to support his argument. For instance, in '"Race", Time and the Revision of Modernity' (1991), he suggests that Mladen Dolar's argument that 'the persisting split [of the sovereign subject] is the condition of freedom'[28] overlooks the the way in which the authority of (neo-)colonialism depends precisely upon fracturing the subjectivity of its subordinates through encouraging the non-Western subject to identify with metropolitan cultural forms and values. Equally unsatisfactory, in Bhabha's view, is Fredric Jameson's exorbitation of the cultural predicament of America (or rather, in a successively diminishing series, California, or Los Angeles, or Bel Air, or, indeed, just the disorienting foyer of the Bonaventura Hotel) to describe a general global condition. Bhabha comments caustically that 'we are likely to find ourselves beached amidst Jameson's "cognitive mappings" of the Third World, which might work for the Bonaventura Hotel in Los Angeles, but will leave you somewhat eyeless in Gaza'.[29]

Bhabha's attempt to rearticulate postmodernism through postcolonial experience in fact begins by challenging two of the basic narratives through which the former has been mediated. The first argues that the project of modernity inaugurated by the Enlightenment has exhausted its promise in the face of the catastrophic events of twentieth-century history. The second suggests that it has completed itself more or less satisfactorily, with the alleged global triumph of Western models of social democracy and economic organization (as is implied by critics like Richard Rorty and – more notoriously – Francis Fukuyama). By contrast, like the Jürgen Habermas of 'Modernity – An Incomplete Project' (1983), an essay cited in '"Race", Time and the Revision of Modernity', Bhabha suggests that the contemporary world has not yet arrived in a new cultural dispensation. However, whereas for Habermas modernity is incomplete because it has not yet exhausted its potential to construct a juster and more rationally organized world (despite the Holocaust and Hiroshima), for Bhabha modernity cannot be considered complete for a number of quite different reasons.

In the first place, this is because in certain crucial respects, the putatively postmodern world simply replicates and perpetuates certain negative aspects of modernity. This is most obviously apparent in the contemporary West's continuation of the social, political and economic structures (and ideological forms of Othering) which characterized the colonial history accompanying modernity. Thus Bhabha argues that 'the language of rights and obligations, so central to the modern myth of a people, must be questioned on the basis of the anomalous and discriminatory legal and cultural status assigned to migrant, diasporic, and refugee populations'.[30] Secondly, modernity cannot be assumed to be 'complete' (and to have been, therefore, succeeded by postmodernity) because the role the non-Western world played in the constitution of modernity has never been properly acknowledged. In the material sphere, the contribution of slavery or colonial exploitation to the physical civilization of modernity has still not been fully recognised. This is equally true in the cultural and ideological spheres, inasmuch as insufficient attention has been paid to the way that many of the foundational ideas of modernity – such as 'Man', reason, progress and the nation – were developed by constructing the non-West in a differential fashion as 'premodern', not fully human, irrational, outside history or primitive/barbaric in terms of its social values and structures.

Bhabha is particularly concerned by the refusal in certain recent accounts of modernity to address these issues. This is exemplified by Foucault's failure to register how Social Darwinism not only prepared the way for Nazism but was itself first developed in the context of contacts with non-Western cultures made available through colonial history. Moreover, according to Bhabha, Foucault sees racism as a hangover from a 'premodern' episteme rather than recognizing it as 'part of the historical traditions of civic and liberal humanism that create ideological matrices of national aspiration, together with their concepts of "a people" and its imagined community'.[31] One such ideological matrix, critical to the emergence of modernity in Foucault's account, is the French Revolution, with its dreams of a universal brotherhood of Man guaranteed by the principles of liberty, equality and fraternity. Bhabha destabilizes this conception of the French Revolution, and the 'modern' aspirations and values it represents, by reconsidering it through the prism of the anti-colonial uprising led shortly afterwards by Toussaint L'Ouverture in Haiti. The necessity for this uprising suggests that, so far as the colonial context was concerned, the promises for 'Mankind' of emancipation, progress and brotherhood symbolized in the French Revolution were simply not held to apply. Indeed, Toussaint's revolt suggests 'the tragic lesson that the moral, *modern* disposition of mankind, enshrined in the sign of the Revolution, only fuels the archaic racial factor in the society of slavery'.[32]

This interrogation of current theorizations of modernity by the reinscription of the repressed histories and social experiences of the historically marginalized, which Bhabha describes as 'a postcolonial archaeology of modernity', has its precedent – as does so much of Bhabha's thinking – in Fanon's early work. For Bhabha, *Black Skin, White Masks* is concerned above all else with the ways in which 'the figure of the "human" comes to be *authorized*[33] at the time of the Enlightenment. Fanon's perception of the 'tardy' emergence of the black man as a human being (or the lag in time before he began to be recognized as such within Western discourse) problematizes the legitimacy of the universalized and transcendental category of Man 'as a unifying reference of ethical value' which underwrote the new episteme of modernity: 'What Fanon shows up is the liminality of those ideas – their ethnocentric margin – by revealing the historicity of its most universal symbol – Man.'[34] But for Bhabha, who, characteristically, appropriates established heuristic concepts to new ends, this 'belatedness' is not simply rejected, but reinscribed in positive terms, inasmuch as it opens up a new temporality or 'time-lag'[35] through which formerly colonized subjects can now rearticulate themselves in terms other than those to which they had historically been assigned (for instance 'primitive', 'savage', etc.). Through the 'time-lag', moreover, the formerly colonized can subvert and transform the centre's narratives of self-description, by revealing what has been left out or repressed in their constitution as 'monumental' symbols. (Bhabha's second phase of work, following Kristeva's 1979 essay 'Women's Time', consistently associates 'symbols' with the mediation and reproduction of the established forms of social authority.) Through the 'time-lag', the legacy of colonialism thus acts *projectively* from within the apparently 'historical' phenomenon of modernity, pointing to 'forms of social antagonism and contradiction that are not yet properly represented, political identities in the process of being formed, cultural enunciations in the act of hybridity, in the process of translating and transvaluing cultural differences'.[36]

As this might suggest, while keeping modernity open by means of a disjunctive temporality through which new sites, 'times' and kinds of enunciation are possible for the formerly colonized in the contemporary period, Bhabha scrupulously avoids a reinscription of this 'unfinished modernity' as progress towards synthesis and closure in the sense of a resolution of historical and cultural differences and conflicts. Bhabha strongly challenges the teleology which is implied in both the traditional liberal vision of the final emergence of 'the (united and equal) family of Man' and the Marxist vision of 'the end of history' which will be brought about by the (global) triumph of the proletariat. (Indeed, Bhabha is characteristically suspicious of the dialectic as a conceptual tool in itself insofar as the 'progression' its dynamic involves will tend to efface the cultural 'difference' of the formerly colonized within a 'higher' term.) Instead, Bhabha proposes a model of cultural difference which respects and preserves the peculiar and multiple histories and identities of the marginalized.

This underwrites other aspects of Bhabha's scepticism about some theories of the postmodern. Insofar as these address the relations of different cultures to each other, particularly when they inhabit the same geographical/cultural space, certain postmodern celebrations of 'pluralistic identities' are, in Bhabha's opinion, premature. In some respects the postmodern vision of cultural synthesis or bricolage is too close in its political implications, for Bhabha's liking, to dominant mainstream discourses of multi-culturalism and cultural relativism. Both of these, in their different ways, seek to minimize the challenges posed by cultural difference in order to preserve the 'organicist' mythology of the 'host' community or nation. Multi-culturalism does this by implicitly constructing cultures as essentially equivalent and therefore interchangeable in their various parts, leading inevitably to an emphasis on assimilation to the dominant. Cultural relativism, in Bhabha's eyes, necessarily manages cultural difference in relation to a normative centre, which also serves to reinforce the authority of the dominant culture. Both discourses also depend on 'consensual' agreement to what Bhabha, following Richard Rorty, describes as 'final vocabularies', in other words the concepts and values (inevitably shaped, Bhabha implies, in Western terms) which cultures must assent to share in order to engage dialogically with each other in the first place. For Bhabha, the difficulties in the idea of 'final vocabularies' are graphically illustrated by the incommensurable nature not just of different kinds of cultural production in its narrow sense (how does one conceptualize the 'equivalence' between 'orature' and literature for example?), but of the basic existential experiences of different social and cultural groups. In a way strongly reminiscent of Roland Barthes's *Mythologies* (1958), more specifically the essay entitled 'The Family of Man', Bhabha suggests that life and death themselves have different significations within different locations and social systems of value. 'The family', or 'mothering', or 'ageing', for instance, in practice may mean quite different things and embody quite different values in Cambridge and in Bridgetown, Bulawayo or Kota Kinabalu.

In asserting that the time for 'assimilating' minorities to the dominant values and social practices of the 'host' nation has passed, Bhabha illustrates his conception of 'cultural difference' in terms of what he describes as 'the language metaphor', which represents cultures in semiotic terms as functioning and assigning value in the same way that systems of language provide meaning. The problem of the 'integration' of migrants, then, is reconfigured, under the influence of Walter Benjamin especially, as the problem of 'translation'. The argument depends on the proposition that the narratives and symbols with which a given culture represents and understands itself are not amenable to attempts to translate them 'transparently' into the terms of another culture in the same way that it is impossible to make a perfect 'match' between, say, English and French: 'The work of the word impedes the question of the transparent assimilation of cross-cultural meanings in a unitary sign of "human" culture.'[37] What gets left behind in such transactions at the inter-cultural level embodies a productive resistance to the process of full appropriation or 'assimilation' to the dominant which older discourses of the plural-cultural society were in reality directed.

This argument, of course, suggests important modifications to the conception of identity which characterized the first phase of Bhabha's work. In opposing the colonialist claim to a foundational or essential identity, Bhabha suggests that identity is differential and, in theory at least, infinitely 'displaceable' – primarily through reference to Derrida's conception of *différance* and Lacan's conception of dependence on the Other as a necessary element of subject-constitution. This perspective is corroborated by Bhabha's reading of Fanon: 'In destroying the "ontology of man", Fanon suggests that "there is not merely one Negro, there are *Negroes*".'[38] In Bhabha's first phase, moreover, 'black nationalism', whether in the form of *négritude* or black separatist movements in the United States, reverses but does not displace the models of subject-constitution and social identification in the discourses of Western racism itself. By contrast, Bhabha's second phase of work rereads Lacan through Slavoj Žižek to suggest that there is, in fact, an irreducible element to identity. 'How Newness Enters the World' (1994) puts it thus: 'Unlike Derrida and de Man, I am less interested in the metonymic fragmentation of the "original". I am more engaged with the "foreign" element that . . . becomes the "unstable element of linkage" between cultures and groups'.[39]

Nonetheless, cultural difference is not to be understood simply as that which remains beyond the attempt of one culture to 'integrate' or 'translate' another. While Bhabha is at pains to deny both the cultural relativist concept of 'the family of man' and what he sees as postmodernism's sometimes simplistic valorization of 'multiple selves',[40] he stresses that the relationship of postcolonial or migrant experience to the dominant culture is not simply antagonistic. For this reason he opposes what he calls the doctrine of 'cultural diversity' which, like the regime of *apartheid*, seeks to inscribe absolute and ontological relations of difference between cultures. Bhabha cites Derrida's figure of the hymen to elucidate the ambivalent working of the model of difference he has in mind: 'It is an operation that *both* sows confusion *between* opposites *and* stands *between* the opposites "at once".'[41] This kind of exchange is not, then, intrinsically antagonistic, but instead supplies (in both senses) a 'lack' *without* sublating either of the cultures concerned into a new synthesis. Many of Bhabha's characteristic terms in the second phase of his writing, like 'indeterminism', 'difference', 'the third space' and 'the in-between' (all of which develop from, and bear comparison with, the term 'hybridity' and the functions of 'hybridization' from the first phase), are means to conceptualize the relationship between cultures in the terms described above.

Such conceptions of the 'ambivalent' relations between migrant or postcolonial culture and its traditional metropolitan counterpart are elucidated at greatest length in 'The Postcolonial and the Postmodern' through a complex elaboration on Roland Barthes's conception in *The Pleasure of the Text* of the relation between the 'sentence' and the 'non-sentence'. Whereas for Barthes the distinction between the two terms is absolute (the non-sentence is 'what is eternally, splendidly, outside the sentence,'[42] Bhabha tries to establish a relationship of contiguity between them. In order to mount this argument, Bhabha cuts the word 'eternally' out of the phrase from Barthes cited above and disarticulates the 'non-sentence' from 'outside the sentence', which thus becomes a third term or space 'in-between' the sentence and non-sentence. Bhabha's inflection of Barthes suggests, then, that what is outside the sentence supplies alternative possibilities to a polarity between non-sentence and sentence because these two terms are necessarily linked in the general system of the conditions of intelligibility, which, while in one sense necessarily 'outside the sentence', is also necessarily inside the sentence, thus allowing it to function as a sentence. (This perhaps owes something to the way that *langue* is irreducibly different to, but also inextricably bound up with, *parole* in Saussure's work.)

For Bhabha, the practical advantage of his reorientation of contemporary theories of the postmodern through the two 'general theories' of his second phase, the ambivalent temporality represented by the 'time-lag' and cultural difference, lies in a potential reconceptualization of both *inter*-national and *intra*-national cultural relations in terms of what 'The Commitment to Theory' describes as 'a different engagement in the politics of and around cultural domination'.[43] Bhabha's goal is to provide a new space and time for the politics of culture in the contemporary era which transcends any conception of relations between cultures – whether or not situated in the same nation space – either in terms which approximate to the US model of *e pluribus unum* (this simply disguises the continued domination of the old centres of authority) or in terms of an aggregate of confrontational, fundamentalist particularisms. Bhabha's political vision will be subjected to closer scrutiny in the next section of this chapter. Before turning to that, however, it is necessary to consider some of the problems in Bhabha's reconceptualization of the relations between modernity, postcoloniality and postmodernism.

Enabling and productive as Bhabha's treatment of these issues undoubtedly is, certain deep-rooted problems present themselves. First of all, despite his genuflection to the argument that postcolonial criticism emerges from 'those who have suffered the sentence of history –

subjugation, domination, diaspora, displacement',[44] the most distinctive essays of the second phase, such as 'The Postcolonial and the Postmodern', are referenced almost exclusively in terms of contemporary Western thinkers, in this particular instance Hannah Arendt, Bakhtin, Lacan and Barthes. Such is the extent of Bhabha's debts to metropolitan sources (despite some attempts to challenge and revise them) that one might be tempted to argue that the effect of the second phase of his career is – contrary to his professed intention – actually to rename the postcolonial from the perspective of the postmodern or, at times, to subsume the former within the latter. Bhabha's recourse to Barthes in 'The Postcolonial and the Postmodern' raises the problem in particularly sharp form. As Lisa Lowe has demonstrated in *Critical Terrains*, Barthes's treatment of the non-Western world moves from a critique of Western exoticism, as in several of the essays in *Mythologies*, to a rearticulation of it in his later career. More particularly, much of Barthes's work in the 1970s, including *The Pleasure of the Text* as well as the books on Japan and China published either side of it, can be understood as an unwitting reinscription of an older tradition of Orientalist ideas, in the way that Spivak suggests is true of Kristeva. In this tradition, as chapter 2 suggested, the non-West represents the female, the body, the pre- or a-social and the 'non-rational', albeit that in Barthes's account these qualities are recoded positively. Thus the non-West supplies Barthes with ways of undermining the values and epistemologies which underpin the West's symbolic orders. There seems to be a direct continuity between Barthes's conception of China or Japan in terms of what Lowe describes as 'a preverbal Imaginary space, before "castration", socialization, and the intervention of the Father'[45] and his construction of Tangiers, which provides a similar sort of space ('outside the sentence') in the passage from *The Pleasure of the Text* discussed earlier, out of which Bhabha generates so much of his argument about inter-cultural relations. While the East may function as a means by which to deconstruct the authority of the West (Barthes insists that the [western] sentence is 'hierarchical: it implies subjections, subordinations'[46]), it is still being appropriated (in the schematic and simplifying way which Spivak complains about in Kristeva's account of China) as a solution to 'internal' Western cultural problematics.

While it is surprising that Bhabha makes no comment on Barthes's exoticism, more problematic is the fact that he is in fact at times seduced by Barthes's rigid ontological distinction between the 'sentence', and what is 'outside the sentence'; consequently, despite himself, he reinscribes rather than displaces a whole series of binary oppositions between (neo-)colonial and postcolonial culture. The West, for Barthes and Bhabha alike, is associated with writing, the symbol, pedagogy (all of which denote monological, fixed and authoritarian qualities), abstract forms of thought and a conception of culture as an epistemological object of the kind associated with the museum, in other words divorced from everyday experience. Meanwhile, the postcolonial is associated with the 'text', the voice, the sign, performance (all of which denote dialogical, democratic and mobile properties), sensual modes of apprehension, and a conception of culture as active, present and enunciatory. The oppositions which Bhabha sets up between Casablanca (which he uses to figure the West, by virtue of the film of that name) and Tangiers are in fact schematic to the point of caricature, with the effect that the West itself then takes on all the qualities of fixity and repetition associated with the 'eternal East' of Orientalist discourse. This is nothing other than the 'reverse ethnocentrism' of which he (like Spivak) so often complains.

Moreover, while Bhabha claims that he is attempting to 'provide a form of the writing of cultural difference in the midst of modernity that is inimical to binary boundaries',[47] the great irony is that his conceptualizations of the means to move beyond the binary in fact depend for their effectiveness entirely upon the structures he is trying to undermine. Hybridity, perhaps the key concept throughout his career in this respect, obviously depends upon a presumption of the existence of its opposite for its force. Not only does this involve a new set of binary oppositions, but it runs the danger that the hybrid (and the postcolonial space or identity it represents) will itself become essentialized. Kristeva warns in 'Women's Time' that an insistence that sexual difference is irreducible may eventually lead feminism to the practice of an inverted sexism. This is the same order of problem which Bhabha faces insofar as, more often than not, he presents the 'non-hybrid' alternatives to the postcolonial (Western neo-colonialism and Third World nationalism, most notably) in unitary terms which do not do justice to their manifest internal contradictions and differential histories. This immediately becomes apparent once issues of class and gender, as well as race, are brought to bear on the presumed 'unisonance' of the cultures or social fractions in question (an issue to which I will return in due course). Thus in tracking the ways that modernity constituted itself as such in terms of a non-Western Other, Bhabha makes only the most token reference to the parallel processes of Othering of women and subordinate classes in the domestic sphere within the discourses of the Enlightenment – as well as to modernity's initial impetus, its engagement with its own classical or premodern history.

At the same time, one must note that the issue is more complicated than this account might suggest. Precisely because of his attempt to avoid polarities, to stress contiguity and the productive dynamics of cultural 'translation', as well as on the grounds of plain common sense, Bhabha is forced to admit that *all* cultures are impure, mixed and hybrid.

As 'The Third Space' puts it, 'all forms of culture are continually in a process of hybridity'.[48] The question which this raises, however, is that if this is indeed the case, then what is the conceptual purchase of concepts like 'the third space', 'hybridity' and the 'in-between' (which operate in conformity to 'the *general* conditions of language')[49] and how can they be conceived of as specifically postcolonial modes or spaces of cultural intervention? If every culture is in fact 'in-between', and none is 'self-identical', the postcolonial loses the particular modes of agency and identity which Bhabha has earlier claimed for it. Such questions point to tensions and conflicts at the heart of Bhabha's project which are as damaging as the ones which chapter 2 identified in the early work of Edward Said.

'THE AGENT WITHOUT A CAUSE': AGENCY, RESISTANCE, POLITICS

The difficulties involved in Bhabha's daring attempt to think beyond the binary are perhaps most persistently evident in his account of the issues of political engagement, resistance and agency. In both phases of his career, Bhabha attempts a radical revision of the terms in which these three topics are customarily conceived of, whether in earlier post-colonial criticism or traditional 'liberal' and Marxist thinking as well. In the earlier essays, as has been seen, Bhabha sites the zone of the political not so much in the 'public sphere' of material relations between colonizer and colonized as in a shifting, and often unconscious, affective area 'in-between' the dominant and subordinate cultures, across which an unstable traffic of continuously (re)negotiated psychic identifications and political (re)positionings is in evidence. Nor is 'the political' neces-sarily a matter of confrontational modes of interaction: 'The place of difference and otherness, or the space of the adversarial ... is never entirely on the outside or implacably oppositional. ... The contour of difference is agonistic, shifting, splitting.'[50] Bhabha concludes, nonethe-less, that psychic ambivalence on the part of both 'partners' in the colonial relationship opens up unexpected and hitherto unrecognized ways in which the operations of colonial power can be circumvented by the native subject, through a process which might be described as psychological guerrilla warfare.

As this might suggest, concurrent with Bhabha's reconsideration of the 'spaces', 'times' and modes of the political is an attempt to re-formulate subaltern agency in terms other than those figured by either late Fanon or early Said. For Bhabha, the figure of the violent native insurgent in The Wretched of the Earth reinscribes the Western model of the individual as sovereign subject, by which Western modernity itself, together with the history of colonialism which accompanied it, is underwritten. In strong contrast to Fanon's account, *Orientalism* implicitly constructs the subaltern as an 'effect' of the dominant discourse with no agency which can operate oppositionally. For this reason, as chapter 2 suggested, the subaltern can only ever be the West's 'silent interlocutor' within *Orientalism*'s model of the operations of power.

In the first phase of his work, Bhabha explores a way forward through the opposed models of agency in Said and Fanon by positing various 'intransitive' models of resistance, which recuperate the resistance which is written out in *Orientalism*, without reinscribing the sovereign subject of Fanon's later work. As the first section of this chapter demonstrated, colonial power is immanently liable to destabilization, or what might be termed 'resistance from within', for three principal reasons. Firstly, following the Foucault of *The History of Sexuality* (1976), Bhabha suggests that, like other forms of power, colonial authority unconsciously and 'unintentionally' incites 'refusal, blockage, and invalidation'[51] in its attempts at surveillance. Secondly, synthesizing Foucault's theory of 'material repeatability' and Derrida's theories of 'iterability' and *différance* in *Writing and Difference* (1967), Bhabha argues that 'intransitive' resistance derives in part from the vicissitudes to which all language is intrinsically liable, especially through the processes of 'repetition', and 'translation'. Finally, following Lacan's *Four Fundamental Concepts of Psycho-Analysis* (1973), Bhabha argues that the gaze of colonial authority is always troubled by the fact that colonial identity is always partly dependent for its constitution on a colonized Other who is potentially hostile.

In contrast to these kinds of 'intransitive' resistance, however, the first phase of Bhabha's work also explores resistance in (ostensibly) more conventional terms as an expression of the agency of the colonized. There is a link to some extent between the two kinds of resistance insofar as Bhabha at times seems to suggest that it is the first kind which opens up a space for the second. In Bhabha's account, mimicry must be approached from the point of view not just of the subject who is mimicked (the colonizer), but also of the subject who mimics (the colonized); in this latter sense mimicry can be described as a defence 'exactly like the technique of camouflage practised in human warfare'.[52] Bhabha's perception of the 'transitive' and active nature of this kind of resistance is illustrated in two ways. Firstly, the colonized subject is empowered to return the colonizer's gaze: thus mimicry (and cognate processes like hybridization) is also 'the name for the strategic reversal of the process of domination . . . that turns the gaze of the discriminated back upon the eye of power'.[53] 'Signs Taken for Wonders' represents this in terms of the capacity of the native subject to question the foundational narratives and texts of Western culture and interpret them in ways other than were 'originally' intended or use them for purposes which were not foreseen by the colonizer. Bhabha illustrates this process of 'hybridization' through a native catechist's description of the ironic and subversive (mis)understandings which a group of his fellow-countrymen bring to the canonical Christian-imperialist text, the Bible. These ordinary Indians point in the first instance to contradictions in the scriptures at a textual level (the problem of the contradictory relationship between monotheism and the doctrine of the Trinity which historically proved such a stumbling block to missionaries in India), so that they pose 'questions of authority that the authorities – the Bible included – cannot answer'.[54] They also point to the conflict between the domestic metropolitan conception of the Bible as universal word of God and the Bible's deployment in the colonial arena as sign of the superiority of English culture specifically – a process which Bhabha states, in a characteristically baroque formulation, effectively 'disarticulates the structure of the God–Englishman equivalence'.[55]

Secondly, the subject who mimics can also refuse to return the colonizer's gaze, which, Bhabha suggests, destabilizes colonial authority just as effectively in a different way. As argued in the first section of this chapter, the colonizer's 'ambivalence' towards the colonized is expressed partly in the 'narcissistic colonialist demand that [he] should be addressed directly, that the Other should authorize the self, recognize its priority, fulfil its outlines, replete, indeed, repeat, its references and still its fractured gaze'.[56] In 'Sly Civility', for instance, the second type of 'transitive' subaltern resistance is figured in terms of the natives' refusal to satisfy the colonizer's 'demand' for such recognition. Thus resistance arises from the subaltern's apparently deliberate attempt to elude the subject positions to which the dominant order seeks to confine the Other in order to 'confirm' itself as dominant. Faced with this elusive Anglicized colonized subject, who inhabits a multiplicity of subject-positions, 'in-between' Englishness and an 'original' Indianness, the 'demand' of colonial authority can neither unify its message nor readily 'place' its subjects.

Bhabha's focus on the psychodynamic and discursive spheres of colonial relations thus constructs 'transitive' resistance in terms of psychological guerrilla warfare and subversion of the terms of the symbolic order which authorizes the colonizer's identity and consequently his control of overseas lands. However, Bhabha's attempt to find a way beyond the mutually incompatible accounts of resistance in his predecessors is fraught with problems. One principal objection is that, as Robert Young points out in White Mythologies, it is unclear 'whether these apparently seditionary undoings in fact remain unconscious for both colonizer and colonized'.[57] Moreover, Bhabha fails to clarify the degree to which the various kinds of resistance which he describes are in fact 'transitive' or 'intransitive', active or passive. The problem derives in part from Bhabha's equivocal definition of his terms. To describe ambivalence as a 'strategy of discriminatory power'[58] might be taken to imply that it is consciously deployed by the colonial power as an instrument of its authority. Bhabha's use of Foucauldian frameworks, however, would suggest that ambivalence is simply a more or less arbitrary conduit for the flow of power, enabling it to 'maximize' itself, regardless of the 'intention' of the colonizer.[59] Ambivalence is described equally ambiguously in context of the colonized. 'By Bread Alone' (1994) describes the circulation of rumour and panic on the Indian side prior to the 'Mutiny' of 1857 as a 'deliberate narrative strategy' and the 'strategic affect [sic] of political revolt'.[60] However, it is simultaneously made clear that, by its very nature, rumour is spontaneous, sporadic and – in accordance with the Foucauldian conception of the resistance which power incites – without any intending 'author(s)'.

Bhabha's recourse to Lacan tends to compound the problem. Lacan's own theory of psychic mimicry is illustrated in terms of analogies with the biological defences of insects (moths with the coloration of wasps, for instance), and thus the question of conscious intention or purposive planning simply does not arise, though the 'effectiveness' of such resistance is certainly assumed by both Lacan and Bhabha.[61] If the resistance inscribed in mimicry is unconscious for the colonized, however (and in Lacanian terms, the demand for – and presumably therefore refusal of – recognition is negotiated at an unconscious level), it cannot function for the colonized as the grounds on which to construct a considered counter-discourse, let alone as a means of mobilizing a strategic programme of material and 'public' forms of political action from within the oppressed culture. Bhabha, however, appears to vacillate on this issue. The passive construction used in 'Of Mimicry and Man' to describe the 'process by which the look of surveillance returns as the displacing gaze of the disciplined' suggests that such resistance may be 'intransitive'; by contrast, the description in 'Sly Civility' of the 'refusal to restore the image of authority to the eye of power' suggests a much more voluntaristic and pre-meditated form of subversion.[62] The confusion which Bhabha's account of resistance results in is particularly evident in 'Signs Taken for Wonders'. On the one hand, Bhabha seems to see the subaltern as actively and purposively 'hybridizing' the 'English Book'. But the peasants' questions to the catechist are based as much on category mistakes or misunderstandings as on a considered challenge to his teachings. Is this kind of response a mode of resistance and, if so, is it then conscious or unconscious, transitive or intransitive?[63]

More to the point, perhaps, is that it is far from certain that the various kinds of 'intransitive' resistance which Bhabha describes in his early essays debilitated colonial control in any serious way. The destabilization to which colonial discourse is immanently liable through 'rep-etition', *différance* or 'translation' is the condition of all language and discourses of power. However, history suggests that discourses like imperialism, fascism or homophobia are no less effective for the obvious contradictions and unconscious/affective conflicts that are inscribed in them. Thus while Sir Henry Maine describes colonial administrators as being 'men bound to keep true time in two longitudes at once',[64] this seems to be accepted by him as an existential fact rather than seen as an obstacle to effective colonial government. And Macaulay's comments on the radical paradoxes of Warren Hastings's programme of government did not in any way diminish his own belief in the validity of the imperial mission in itself. By contrast, the fact that these paradoxes seem to have remained unconscious for Hastings suggests that they cannot be said to have been destabilizing for his sense of authority either. Moreover, Kipling's reference to 'the tangled trinities' of Christian doctrine in the epigraph to 'Lispeth', the first story in *Plain Tales from the Hills* (1888), and one which bitterly satirizes missionary work, indicates that colonial discourse itself often and consciously performed the kind of 'insurgent interrogations' of Christian doctrine which Bhabha identifies with the Indian peasants in 'Signs Taken for Wonders'. This point is confirmed in Forster's depiction of the logical absurdities in the sermon of the missionaries Graysford and Sorley at the end of chapter 4 of A *Passage to India* (1924).

Equally, there is little material evidence that psychological guerrilla warfare of the kind which Bhabha describes as operating 'strategically' from within the subordinate formation was, in fact, particularly destabil-izing for the colonizer. His bald assertion in 'By Bread Alone' that 'historical agency is no less effective because it rides on the disjunctive or displaced circulation of rumour and panic'[65] suggests, quite illegiti-mately, that the British in India were as threatened by the pre-Mutiny rumours as by the armed uprising itself. In fact, Bhabha's account seems to vindicate Eric Stokes's 'traditional' analysis of the 'Mutiny', which he wants to rebut. Stokes argues persuasively that the failure of the rebellion lay in the absence of clear goals, common aims or purposive planning. Precisely because it remained sporadic, it was quite easily contained.

Moreover, Bhabha fails to give sufficient weight to the effectiveness of mimicry as a strategy of colonial control. Thus the most Anglicized of the Indians in 'Signs Taken for Wonders', the catechist Anund Messeh,[66] is the most amenable to colonial authority. It is the peasants, who are much less culturally assimilated to the dominant order, who provide the 'insurgent questionings' of the colonial text. In general, the Anglicized 'mimic man', represented most notoriously in the figure of the Western-educated 'babu', seems to have inspired much more scorn than fear amongst the British in India. While Ronny Heaslop in Forster's A

Passage to India expresses some anxiety that the 'educated Indians will be no good to us if there's a row',[67] the implication is that the 'row', if it does transpire, will be provoked by other, less assimilated, constituencies. In fact, there is a long tradition in colonial discourse which represents the surveying eye of colonial authority falling upon its mimic subjects which clearly suggests that the ostensible subversion of its authority which is made possible by the return, or refusal, of the gaze of power is cancelled out by the fact that such a challenge has already been registered and, in the process of being recognized, has been contained. In *India Inscribed* (1995), Kate Teltscher provides two instructive examples of the limitations of these kinds of challenge to colonial authority in travelogues of the late eighteenth century. In the first, an Englishman chances upon a satiric staging by some servants of his conduct as master. In the second, an Indian servant responds to his master's rage by lying face down on the floor and stopping his ears. Both the return, and the refusal, of the gaze of power in these examples lead to a change of attitude and behaviour on the part of the two masters. But, as Teltscher argues, the real relations of power remain unchanged or, indeed, are even enhanced in the colonizer's favour, by the more ostensibly 'humane' forms of servitude which result from the self-reflection which these incidents induce in the masters.[68]

Such evidence confirms the doubts which Bhabha himself expresses at the very beginning of the first phase of his work. While one version of 'The Other Question', subtitled 'Difference, Discrimination, and the Discourse of Colonialism' (1983), suggests that 'shifting positionalities will never seriously threaten the dominant power relations',[69] such doubts are never aired in later treatments of subaltern resistance, so that mimicry, for example, is consistently represented as a 'menace' to the dominant order. This is by no means, however, to suggest that Bhabha is wholly wrong in his general argument. One can certainly find examples of colonial discourse where the kinds of destabilization of authority which he describes in processes like mimicry do take place. From Kipling's 'On the City Wall' (1888) to Doris Lessing's *The Grass is Singing* (1950), the colonized subject's return of, or refusal of, the gaze of the dominant proves extremely unsettling. However, these are, of course, literary rather than official documents, often produced by figures with a deep ambivalence, or even hostility, towards official imperial ideology. Moreover, in these cases mimicry proves unsettling precisely because the principal protagonists of these stories are *not* fully representative of the colonizing societies but exist, like Antoinette in *Wide Sargasso Sea*, 'in-between' the dominant and subordinate social formations – at both the material and psychological/affective levels.

In making a renewed attempt more recently to work through the impasse between a humanist conception of agency and one which writes

out agency in the conventional sense altogether as simply an 'effect' of
the dominant ideology or discourse of power, Bhabha uses conceptual
frameworks and critical terminology which are in some ways noticeably
different to those deployed in his first phase of work. However, once
again it must be stressed that the discontinuities between the two phases
of Bhabha's work should not be exaggerated. Thus in one of his most
recent essays, 'By Bread Alone', Bhabha makes a startling (violent?)
connection between Toni Morrison and the nameless Indian peasants
on the eve of the Indian 'Mutiny'. This has the effect of suggesting that
the same model of agency is evident in both the historical subaltern and
the contemporary postcolonial artist. Moreover, as the discussion of the
impossibility of fully 'translating' cultural difference in the second section
of this chapter suggested, Bhabha retains a conception of immanent or
'intransitive' kinds of resistance in his theorizations of the relationship
between neo- and postcolonial cultures. Equally, his emphasis on the
'catachrestic gesture' of the postcolonial artist or critic, who interrogates,
turns round, (mis)appropriates the terms or symbols of Western discourse, has parallels with the 'insurgent' questionings performed by the
native Indian audience in 'Signs Taken for Wonders' (assuming that this
is, indeed, what their responses to the catechist represent).

In pieces like 'The Postcolonial and the Postmodern', Bhabha again
relies on aspects of the 'language metaphor' to explore the problem of
agency. Thus in order, as he puts it, both to 'transform our sense of the
"subject" of culture and the historical agent of change' and to conceptualize 'a new collaborative dimension' which enables forms of solidarity
in the 'public sphere',[70] Bhabha draws an analogy between the operation
of agency in social relations and intentionality in texts. In post-
structuralist theory, the author (and, indeed, the subject) is in fact an
effect of textuality insofar as s/he must enter a pre-existent language,
governed by rules and conventions which are not of the author's
choosing, in order to create meaning. For Bhabha, intentionality, and
by analogy agency, is therefore an effect of discourse (and/or the 'social
text') and not its cause or origin. In this sense, according to Bhabha, the
author, or agent, only re-emerges through 'a form of retroactivity', similar
to the way that in Lacanian psychoanalytic theory the subject becomes
'individuated' only *after* being positioned within the terms of the
symbolic order and called upon to speak (or act).[71] It is in this context
that one can perhaps more clearly understand Bhabha's conception of
'the [belated] return of the subject [or agent]' who is necessarily 'self-
alienated', because individuation, as the product of entry into the
symbolic order inscribed in language, is therefore necessarily 'an effect of
the intersubjective'.[72]

Bhabha's engagement with Bakhtin and Arendt in this essay also
enables him to propose a model of political solidarity which sharply

contrasts with that underpinning what he dismissively describes as 'the liberal vision of togetherness',[73] as well as with the more traditional models of agency and solidarity in Fanon or the work of the Subaltern Studies group. Bhabha seems to suggest that postcolonial agency, like authorial intention, necessarily implies forms of solidarity, since it is inter-subjective in two principal ways. Firstly, just as the meaning, or intention, of a text is constructed through a process of negotiation between author and reader, so agency involves a conception of the effects of that agency on others who then become 'authors' of that agency in the way that readers, too, might be understood to (help) construct the meaning of the author's text. (This again suggests that the agent is a 'time-lagged' or retroactive 'effect', this time of the effects which his agency can be understood, only in retrospect, as having had.) Secondly, just as the meaning of any text is linked through the play of allusions, genre and inter-texts to other texts, and thus contains 'traces' of them, and just as, in Bakhtin's terms, any speech text contains, in a variety of possible ways, traces of the prior speech of others, so Bhabha appears to suggest by analogy that all agency contains traces of the prior agency of others (insofar as all actions are the consequence of previous actions). The fact that in Bakhtinian theory, the speech act, or text, always assumes an addressee, and anticipates a response, also seems to suggest to Bhabha that agency works 'dialogically' in ways which also necessarily involve 'the social' dimension and, potentially at least, the possibility of solidarity.

This extremely problematic and unstable vision of agency (if I have understood it right) as simultaneously 'individuated', conscious, active or transitive on the one hand, and 'social', unconscious, passive or intransitive on the other, or rather 'in-between' the two sets of terms, does not really negotiate a clear way beyond the dichotomous visions of agency in Said and Fanon. Rather, it appears to offer an account of resistance and agency which is essentially circular. The model of agency for both historical subaltern and contemporary postcolonial subject is depicted in the following impersonal terms in 'The Postcolonial and the Postmodern': 'When the sign ceases the synchronous flow of the symbol [sic], it also seizes the power to elaborate ... new and hybrid agencies and articulations. This is the moment for revisions.'[74] Such revisions, however, are characteristically enacted in a much more conventional conception of the individual agent's intervention. For instance, Spivak is praised for advocating a '"seizing of the value-coding" ... that opens up an interruptive time-lag [which] enables the diasporic and postcolonial to be represented'.[75]

Bhabha's conception of the domain of the semiotic as the prime site of postcolonial resistance engenders two further important problems. Firstly, if the 'sign' conforms to the Derridean definition, it is necessarily potentially infinitely displaceable and differential; how, then, can post-colonial discourse ever attain sufficient stability to organize itself pro-grammatically? '"Race", Time and the Revision of Modernity' insists that the time-lag does not unleash 'a circulation of nullity, the endless slippage of the signifier',[76] because the postcolonial 'sign' is 'tied' to the monumental 'symbol' of the dominant social authority. One problem that this leads to is that if the agency of the 'sign' is so consistently directed to destabilization of the dominant, Bhabha is indeed – as Ahmad complains – privileging those forms of postcolonial discourse which 'answer back' to the centre. Those modes of critical and artistic activity which do not engage in this subversive dialogue with the symbols, texts and narratives of the centre are implicitly downgraded or ignored (usually on the grounds that they are 'cultural nationalist'). More importantly still, perhaps, this determining relation of sign to symbol suggests that Bhabha's conception of postcolonial agency and resistance in fact depends upon the continuing authority of the dominant for its operation and consequently risks reconstituting that dominant – which again corroborates one of Ahmad's objections to postcolonial theory.

Secondly, this emphasis on the semiotic domain has disturbing impli-cations for conventional ideas about political practice. Bhabha's concep-tion of critical or creative catachresis as the privileged form of political engagement is perhaps inevitable, given his reductive insistence that 'it is the realm of representation and the process of signification that constitutes the space of the political'.[77] In Bhabha's later work, politics is almost obsessively figured in (or reduced to) terms of discursive transactions, a pattern which is particularly notable in 'The Postcolonial and the Postmodern'. Thus the essay sees the question of solidarity, for example, as a problem of the 'the enunciation of discursive agency' and the textualization of political activity is quite explicit in phrases such as 'inciting cultural translations' and 'the agency of the social text'.[78] 'Remembering Fanon', symptomatically, turns Fanon the revolutionary into the kind of critic whose work 'opens up a margin of interrogation that causes a subversive slippage of identity and authority'.[79] In persist-ently privileging Black Skin, White Masks as Fanon's most important work, Bhabha almost completely discounts those later works of Fanon which call for violent action against the colonizer. Indeed, in reading his mentor's development as a thinker backwards, and so persistently ignoring his later work, Bhabha might even be accused not so much of 'remembering' as 'dismembering' Fanon.[80]

Some of the severest criticism directed against Bhabha relates to this apparent inflation of the critic's role at the expense of the obviously much more crucial role played by both armed resistance and conven-tional forms of political organization in ending the system of formal imperialism and challenging the current system of neo-colonialism. As early as 1987, Benita Parry was complaining of Bhabha's work in these terms. Aijaz Ahmad reiterated the charge in *In Theory*, a much more hostile pólemic against Bhabha's 'exorbitation of discourse' as a site of opposition.[81] Robert Young's defence of Bhabha against these charges in *Colonial Desire* is unconvincing. He argues that such objections are based on 'a form of category mistake', insofar as Bhabha's focus on 'the discursive construction of [neo-]colonialism does not seek to replace or exclude other forms of analysis, whether they be historical, geographical, economic, military or political'.[82] The point is, however, that while all of these other contexts are, albeit marginally and fitfully, present in Bhabha's account, the material contexts and negotiations of (neo-) colonial power are consistently presented in terms of, or overridden by, an economy of textual transactions.

At the same time, one has to recognize that Bhabha is seeking to undo the traditionally subordinate relation of discourse to 'material' forms of political action (without, in theory at least, simply reversing it), following Foucault's dictum that 'the relations of discourse are of the nature of warfare'.[83] Thus if he can be accused of textualizing politics, the obverse of this is that textuality, or cultural practice, is equally consistently politicized in Bhabha's work. Moreover, following certain strands of feminism, Bhabha strongly emphasizes the links between the psychic or personal domain and the political, rather than assuming, as is conventionally the case, that the political sphere is constituted in and confined to the public domain. Similarly, one must also consider seriously his argument, also derived from Foucault, that resistance is not necessarily always an '*oppositional* act of political *intention*'.[84] Parry is right to demand attention to the politics involved in undermining the binary oppositions by which the political is customarily understood to be structured,[85] but the assumptions on which her challenge rests would be vigorously contested by Bhabha. In the early essays there is a gathering weariness with political projects centred on the public domain, and with a conception of politics as necessarily confrontational, or enacted through apparently stable categories like class. By 1990, as 'The Third Space' suggests, Bhabha is arguing that on the left, 'there's too much of a timid traditionalism – always trying to read a new situation in terms of some pre-given model or paradigm, which is a reactionary reflex, a conservative "mind-set".'[86] In this respect, too, Kristeva seems the key influence. 'Women's Time' records 'an exacerbated distrust of the entire political dimension' (as traditionally conceived of) in post equal-rights feminism.[87] This distrust is apparent in her own essays, both here and in 'A New Type of Intellectual: The Dissident' (1977) – a piece cited in 'DissemiNation' – which argues, as does Spivak, that those who oppose the dominant power on its own terms or in its own language are necessarily caught up in its logic and thus perpetuate it. This may explain Bhabha's similar emphasis on contiguity rather than direct opposition as the most effective political position to inhabit, and his stress on infiltration of the dominant symbolic orders and systems, rather than more traditional forms of rejection or reversal of the dominant.

The charge often laid against figures like Kristeva (as the last chapter showed) and Barthes is that their turn to discursive forms of resistance and 'textual' revolution represents a collapse of political will after the failure of the May 1968 événements in France. The question to be asked of Bhabha is whether his textual engagements constitute an analogous swerve away from another moment which seemed to incarnate the 'end of socialism', in this case the triumph of Thatcherism and the institution of a new, more intense, phase of neo-colonialism (dressed up as 'the New World Order') under Thatcher and Reagan. The critique of confrontation or negation as an effective political tactic is, revealingly, first advanced in 'The Commitment to Theory' (1988), in context of a discussion of the failure of the miners' strike in the mid-1980s, the last great gesture of traditional mass oppositional resistance in recent British history. Both Kristeva and Bhabha are quite aware of the risks that their respective projects run. Kristeva's advocacy in 'Women's Time' of a 'third attitude', which will take feminism beyond programmes grounded in equal rights or biological difference, involves the possibility that 'this might quickly become another form of spiritualism turning its back on social problems, or else a form of repression ready to support all status quos'.[88] Bhabha's doubts about the effectiveness of his own prescriptions like 'the third space' and 'the in-between' surface in 'The Postcolonial and the Postmodern', which I have treated as the central essay of his second phase: 'Is the whole thing no more than a theoretical fantasy that reduces any form of political critique to a daydream?'[89] While one might be inclined to nod one's head, any simple affirmative must recognize that such an answer depends on traditional assumptions about the nature of the political, which as many cultural theorists including a good proportion of those affiliated to what used to be easily identifiable as the left (notably figures like Ernesto Laclau and Chantal Mouffe) suggest, have been overtaken by the events of recent global history.

'STUPENDOUS FRAUDS': POSTCOLONIAL THEORY AND THE POLITICS OF PSYCHOANALYSIS

I want to end by focusing on the implications of Bhabha's methodological reliance, throughout his career, on psychoanalytic theory as the principal means to figure and analyse (neo-)colonial relations. Robert Young's White Mythologies questions Bhabha's 'employment of the transcendental categories of psychoanalysis for the analysis of the historical phenomenon of colonialism',[90] without pursuing this objection in any detail. In contrast to other methodological sources which he employs, from Fanon to Derrida and Foucault, Bhabha tends to take psychoanalytic theory at face value, never questioning either its assumptions and premises or, more importantly, its applicability to non-Western psychic/ cultural problematics. As one of Spivak's interviewers puts it, a key question for those who use psychoanalysis in the context of postcolonial forms of analysis must be: 'Is the subject of the psychoanalytic model applicable world-wide, universally, or is it Eurocentric?'[91] Essentially, the problem with Bhabha's use of psychoanalytic theory is that such a question is never posed. There is no conception of psychoanalysis as a specifically *Western* narrative of knowledge which may have been complicit in the production of modernity and, more particularly, modernity's Others, in the same way as those various elements of the Western regime of knowledge (progress, reason and so forth) which Bhabha does subject to analysis from a postcolonial perspective. In this respect, there is a striking difference between his work and Spivak's. Spivak by no means dismisses out of hand the relevance of Western psychoanalysis for her own critical project. Indeed, she pays tribute to Freud as 'the most powerful contemporary male philosopher of female sexuality, and the inaugurator ... of the technique of "symptomatic reading"'.[92] Moreover, Spivak often has recourse to classical psychoanalysis, as both a technique of reading and in diagnosis of content, as in her application of 'the thematics of Narcissus' to uncover the repressed influence of 'the axioms of imperialism' in the work of Charlotte Brontë and other Western women writers in 'Three Women's Texts and a Critique of Imperialism'. Indeed, Spivak has recently explicitly reaffirmed the usefulness of adapting classical psychoanalysis to the study of colonial relations, citing Octave Mannoni and Fanon as important precursors in this respect.[93]

Nonetheless, Spivak points with equal consistency to the shortcomings of classical psychoanalysis, in the terms in which it was originally constituted, as a means of understanding the historically and culturally specific experience of the colonized. Thus she describes her essay 'Feminism and Critical Theory' (1985), for example, as in part designed to restore 'the dimension of race'[94] to the study of psychoanalytic discourse, and is persistently concerned with the ways that Western psychoanalysis reveals itself to be not a universal but a 'regional practice'.[95] Much of Spivak's attention in this respect is directed towards Freud's work, which she identifies as belonging to the 'masculine-imperialist ideological formation'.[96] In fact, even a cursory glance at a volume of Freud's like *On Sexuality* confirms the degree to which his work is imbued with the normative perspectives of racial and imperial theory contemporary to him. The 'non-rational', for instance, is characteristically represented in racialized terms. Bhabha himself quotes such a passage from 'The Unconscious' (1915) about the promptings of the id without, curiously enough, making any comment on Freud's choice of figurative language: 'We may compare them with individuals of mixed race who taken all round resemble white men but who betray their coloured descent by some striking feature or other and on that account are excluded from society and enjoy none of the privileges.'[97] Freud discusses sexual 'deviancy' in similar terms. A particularly important instance of this occurs in his treatment of fetishism, a narrative upon which Bhabha relies particularly heavily in 'The Other Question'. Freud's initial and brief discussion of fetishism occurs in the 'Three Essays on Sexuality' (1905), where the objects of affect are described in the following terms: 'Such substitutes are with some justice likened to the fetishes in which savages believe that their gods are embodied.'[98] While Bhabha 'translates' Freud's theory from the context of analysis of sexual affect to analysis of the psychic economy of colonial relations, it again seems strange that there is no comment on the ways that fetishism is implicitly racialized in Freud's discourse.

If it is such figurative language which reveals, in the first instance, what Spivak describes as 'the overtly imperialist politics of psychoanalysis',[99] it is also clear that Freud's general conceptions of normative and deviant psychic behaviour rests to a large degree on a binary opposition between Western and non-Western cultures, in which what is defined as deviant in the former is often the rule in the latter. For instance, neurosis in European society is equated with the psychic economy of non-Western societies, which supposedly conform to earlier stages of human evolution. Thus according to Freud, 'we find taboos among primitive peoples already elaborated into an intricate system of just the sort that neurotics among ourselves develop in their phobias'.[100] This clearly suggests how classical psychoanalysis constituted itself as a form of modern knowledge on morally loaded distinctions between metropolis and periphery which contributed significantly to the Othering of non-Western cultures, by defining them, explicitly or implicitly, as 'lacking' or 'anterior' in comparison with domestic metropolitan 'norms'.

Bhabha's more obvious indebtedness to Lacan than to Freud raises the question of whether Lacanian models of psychological development, identification and affect may not be opened up in a similar way from a postcolonial perspective (following the example set by feminist critics in respect of the gender bias in Lacanian theory). Spivak's work again provides an interesting point of comparison in this respect. Her career bears witness to a consistent and productive negotiation with Lacan as a framework for postcolonial analysis, for instance in 'A Literary Representation of the Subaltern'. Yet Spivak nonetheless suggests that Lacan's work must, like Freud's, be situated within the history of 'the institutionalization of psychoanalysis ... and its imposition upon the colonies'.[101] (In calling for a greater focus on the role of psychoanalysis in the subordination of the non-Western world, Spivak reiterates some of the arguments of Fanon, especially in texts such as A Dying Colonialism of 1959.) Spivak's doubts about Lacanian theory have been seconded by Anne McClintock, who argues that Lacan does not sufficiently recognize the crucial place of race (and class) as categories of identity. McClintock challenges Lacan's account of phallic fetishism by suggesting that certain kinds of fetish (such as national flags) cannot be fully understood within the narrow terms he proposes. Perhaps most radically of all, McClintock argues that by disavowing the often contradictory struggles for individuation and identity-formation in different gender, racial and class groups, in different historical and social contexts, Lacan's conception of the 'phallus' becomes another narrative of 'global order centred in a single, western authority'.[102] From this perspective, Lacan is seen as attempting to restore the power and prestige of 'the Law of the [white] Father' at precisely the moment that it is being challenged in the political realm in the era of post- or neo-colonialism. The culture-specific nature of Lacan's narrative is, for McClintock, particularly apparent in the monotheistic nature of his conception of 'the Law of the Father', which she sees as a secular reinscription of an older master-discourse and, indeed, as constituting 'a tragic, philosophical replica of the Judaeo-Christian narrative'.[103]

Bhabha's foreclosure of this kind of critique of psychoanalysis as both a method of cultural analysis and an institutional practice is especially surprising given the extent of his debts to Fanon's Black Skin, White Masks. Indeed, the debate about the politics of psychoanalysis opened up by Fanon himself suggests that this is a further area in which Bhabha consistently de-radicalizes his forerunner's treatment of colonial relations, by insufficient attention to the historical and material contexts in which Fanon's work always carefully situated itself. Contrary to Bhabha's extraordinary claim that 'It is one of the original and disturbing qualities of Black Skin, White Masks that it rarely historicizes the colonial experience',[104] Fanon is, in fact, scrupulously careful to historicize both the psychic and the cultural problematics which he addresses and, just as importantly, his own method. Thus from the outset of his argument, Fanon firmly rejects the possibility that psychic disturbances evident in the colonial context can be understood in existential or transhistorical terms:

> The analysis that I am undertaking is psychological. In spite of this it is apparent to me that the effective dis-alienation of the black man entails an immediate recognition of social and economic realities. If there is an inferiority complex, it is the outcome of [this] double process.[105]

Thus Mannoni's *Prospero and Caliban: The Psychology of Colonization* (1950) is described as 'dangerous' because it fails to take such circumstances into account. Instead of seeing the psychic disturbances which he analyses in post-war Madagascar as symptoms of the trauma induced by a specific phase of colonial oppression (the French were engaged in a particularly violent reimposition of colonial rule on the island in the late 1940s), Mannoni instead ascribes them to the innate 'dependency complex' of the natives of Madagascar, from which he then deduces their alleged unconscious 'desire' to be colonized. Despite Mannoni's evident sympathy for the suffering Madagascan, the logic of his argument inevitably serves to legitimize the restoration of French colonial rule.

For Fanon, Mannoni mistakes cause for effect. The psychic 'dependency' analysed by Mannoni – assuming it exists at all – is to be understood in the first instance as evidence of the change effected by colonialism in the outward structures of Madagascan social life, which then impact upon the psychic domain. In reviewing Mannoni's analysis of the dreams of a range of colonized subjects, research on which his predecessor largely based his theory of dependency, Fanon insists that

> the discoveries of Freud are of no use to us here. What must be done is to restore this dream *to its proper time*, and this time is the period during which eighty thousand natives were killed – that is to say, one of every fifty persons in the population; and *to its proper place*, and this place is an island . . . where the only masters are lies and demagogy. One must concede that in some circumstances the *socius* is more important than the individual.[106]

In this context the dream motifs of Mannoni's patients are not evidence of 'universal' fears and desires – or even those of a 'race' – in the way Mannoni assumes, but may have quite literal referents: 'The rifle of the Senegalese soldier is not a penis but a genuine rifle, model Lebel 1916.'[107] Mannoni's failure to attend sufficiently to what Fanon calls the colonial *socius* is, for Fanon, symptomatic of the culture-specific, if not downright ethnocentric, properties of Western psychoanalysis as a whole. This conviction underlies his patient and detailed critiques of the founding concepts and analytic frameworks of its major luminaries, from the 'Oedipus complex' and the 'inferiority complex' to the 'collective unconscious', on the grounds that 'Freud and Adler and even the cosmic Jung did not think of the Negro in all their investigations'.[108]

Perhaps the most curious aspect of Bhabha's appropriation of Fanon's arguments about the psychic economy of colonialism is the failure to record that Fanon's engagement with Lacan is more than simply an endorsement of the Lacanian reorientation of Freudian psychoanalytic critique. While Fanon's text contains considerable discussion of Lacan, he makes it clear that more often than not, 'I am departing from his conclusions'.[109] As is the case with Fanon's engagement with Freud, a major area of disagreement is over the question of whether the narrative of the Oedipus complex (and its revisions) can be applied universally. More significantly perhaps, in terms of an analysis of the place of Lacan in Bhabha's own work, Fanon reformulates Lacan's conception of the 'mirror stage' (which Fanon's translator labels the 'mirror period') to take account of the different psychic and material circumstances of the colonized. According to Fanon, while the black man is amongst his own kind, there is no occasion for him 'to experience his being through [racial] others', but in the context of colonized societies, the situation changes, so that he 'must be black in relation to the white man'.[110] What Fanon adds to the processes described in the 'mirror period', then, are elements of 'a historico-racial drama' which derives specifically from the context of colonial relations:

> When one has grasped the mechanism described by Lacan, one can have no further doubt that the real Other for the white man is and will continue to be the black man. And conversely. Only for the white man The Other [sic] is perceived on the level of the body image, absolutely as the not-self – that is, the unidentifiable, the unassimilable. For the black man, as we have shown, historical and economic realities come into the picture.[111]

Fanon further complicates the 'historico-racial drama' by insisting that factors such as gender and class, as well as geographical and cultural location, materially inflect the psychic economy of the colonized. While 'Remembering Fanon' contains a somewhat strained defence of Fanon against the charge of 'sexism' on the grounds that he uses the term 'man' in his writing to refer to both sexes, Bhabha in fact overlooks the quite different inflections, however problematically these are formulated, which gender does in fact give the affective economy of the colonized in Fanon's account. This is signalled in the chapter titles of Black Skin, White Masks, which discriminate pointedly between the experience of men and women of colour. Equally, it is an egregious mistake, in Fanon's eyes, to conflate the middle-class black doctor with the dock labourer in terms of their identification with the colonizer. Throughout his text Fanon also insists that the varying geographies and histories of colonialism inflect the psychic economy of colonial relationships differentially. Thus he argues that 'my observations and my conclusions are only valid for the Antilles' and insists on the importance of the 'the differences that separate the Negro of the Antilles from the Negro of Africa'.[112] While such divisions are seen as themselves partly constructed by the colonial process, Fanon argues that they must nonetheless be recognized as real and not falsely sublated into a greater unity. This, in his eyes, is the mistake of the negritudinists such as Senghor, who peddle an

essentialist myth of black identity, social or psychic, across the diverse
spectrum of black cultures and histories.

Problems with Fanon's application of a reformulated model of psychoanalytic theory to colonial relations undoubtedly remain. For instance,
the final and at times radical shortcomings of Fanon's analysis of gender
factors cannot be deflected in the way that Bhabha attempts to do in
'Remembering Fanon'.[113] Nor is Fanon's treatment of homosexuality as
a psychic 'deviation' either sympathetic or convincing. At a methodological level, it might be argued that Fanon makes the same category
mistake of which Spivak accuses the Subaltern Studies historiographers,
assuming that he can recover the psychic economy of the colonized as it
existed prior to 'the epistemic fracture' of colonization, as is clearly
implied in his argument that the Oedipus complex did not come into
being until the time of colonialism. Moreover, as Young (following
Deleuze and Felix Guattari) suggests in White Mythologies, if colonialism
did import its own psychic economy and impose it on the colonies, in
the same way that the West's cultural and material civilization was
imposed, then in fact Western psychoanalysis can, perhaps, relatively
legitimately be applied to questions of psychic disruption in the colonial
context. Nonetheless, there is little doubting the theoretical and
political force of Fanon's construction of psychoanalysis as a specifically
Western discourse. One might not necessarily agree that psychoanalytic
theory includes some of 'the most stupendous frauds of our period',[114] but
Fanon certainly raises disturbing questions about the ethnocentricity of
yet another apparently benevolent master-narrative. His comment on
Sartre's subordination of négritude to a Western model of class struggle
applies equally well to the claims of Western psychoanalysis: 'I have
barely opened eyes that had been blindfolded, and someone already
wants to drown me in the universal?'[115]

Thus while Bhabha attempts to follow Fanon in putting 'the psychoanalytic question of the desire of the subject to the historic condition of
colonial man',[116] the effect is arguably quite different from what emerges
from Fanon's account. In Bhabha, the colonial situation often seems to
provide new materials to illustrate and 'authorize' psychoanalytic theory
and rarely, if ever, evidence to trouble its habitual claims and procedures.
For example, while Bhabha devotes a section of 'The Other Question'
to analysis of the 'primal scenes' where the native subject becomes
racially marked in colonial discourse, this focus is soon subsumed into a
general theory of surveillance and the scopic drive which is not in any
way particular to the colonial situation. Indeed, Bhabha's recourse to
Lacan leads him to repeat the very existentialism which he (mistakenly)
complains of in later Fanon and to sublate the specificities of (neo-)
colonial relationships to the general conditions of relations between all
cultures. If 'to exist is to be called into being in relation to an Other-

ness',[117] then the psychic economy of fear and desire, recognition and disavowal, must operate in all situations where different cultural formations are brought into contact. 'The Other Question', significantly, describes ambivalence as 'one of the most significant discursive and psychical strategies of discriminatory power – whether racist or sexist [or, might one add, "classist"?], peripheral or metropolitan'.[118] This conception of ambivalence as a strategic production of both the metropolis and the periphery (and, by extension, of both neo-colonial and postcolonial formations, too) is confirmed in more recent essays such as 'Articulating the Archaic' (1990), where it is described as 'a form of persecutory paranoia that emerges from [all?] cultures' own structured demand for imitation and identification'.[119]

What sometimes seems to get lost in Bhabha's homogenizing and transhistorical model of the mutual (mis)recognitions of all cultures is Fanon's insistence that the psychic economy of colonialism mediates material, historically grounded, relations of unequal power. While one can appreciate the rationale behind Bhabha's reversal of Fanon's emphasis on attention to the psychic experience of the colonized, to the relative exclusion of that of the colonizer, and his interrogation of Said's conventional master–slave model of colonial relations, there are troubling political implications in the way Bhabha sees both colonizer and colonized as being equally caught up within – and similarly affected by – the psychic ambivalence which accompanies colonial exploitation and domination. Of the passage from *Black Skin, White Masks* where the white child fixes Fanon with its gaze, Bhabha comments: 'In each of them the subject turns around the pivot of the "stereotype" to return to a point of total identification'; moreover, what 'is denied the colonial subject, *both as colonizer and colonized*, is that form of negation which gives access to the [non-conflictual] recognition of difference'.[120] In more recent essays Bhabha has reiterated this model of the affective economy of colonialism, with similar political implications. Thus 'Articulating the Archaic' argues: 'In these instances of social and discursive alienation there is no recognition of master and slave, there is only the matter of the enslaved master, the unmastered slave.'[121] While from one perspective this line of argument is undoubtedly true, since for power to be exercised there must be two 'partners' in the relationship, it tends, as Abdul JanMohamed has argued, to produce an unwarranted unification of colonizer and colonized as a (single) 'colonial subject' which discounts the deep objective differences in the political power and material conditions of these 'secret sharers'. Consequently, there is considerable justice in JanMohamed's conclusion that Bhabha 'circumvent[s] entirely the dense history of the material conflict between Europeans and natives ... to focus on colonial discourse as if it existed in a vacuum'.[122] Terry Eagleton has drawn similar inferences from Bhabha's more recent work:

'One is allowed to talk about cultural difference, but not – or not much – about economic exploitation.'[123] Symptomatic of the crucial distinction in this respect between Fanon and Bhabha is their contrasting use of the Hegelian conception of the master–slave relationship. Whereas Bhabha sees the two terms collapsing into one, in a complex dialectic created by the mutual need of each protagonist in the relationship for recognition by the other, Fanon tartly observes: 'For Hegel there is reciprocity; here [in the colonial situation] the master laughs at the slave. What he wants from the slave is not recognition but work.'[124]

Perhaps the most unfortunate consequences of Bhabha's argument in this respect are evident in his comment in 'The Other Question' that: 'It is not possible to see how power functions productively as incitement and interdiction.'[125] Bhabha follows Foucault in this respect,[126] simply bypassing the fact that Foucault is addressing the disposition of power in the modern metropolitan West, not the 'archaic' scene of colonial despotism (a topic to which I shall return in the next chapter). Thus while the point is well made that colonial power could never rest entirely on force to be effective, there is a real danger in Bhabha's work of discounting the degree to which it *was* willing to resort to 'incitement and interdiction' to secure its rule. This is most obviously evident in the military campaigns which brought colonialism into being – and which were used to defend it in the era of decolonization – but is also apparent across the whole 'civilian' apparatus of colonial law, administration and education in the period of 'mature' or settled colonial rule. Conversely, Bhabha appears to discount those who refused the kind of identification with the imperial power which his concept of ambivalence involves. Such figures would include cultural and political 'fundamentalists' whose opposition to colonialism was based on a desire to revert to the cultural and political formations in place before the onset of colonial rule – and who often resorted to armed resistance in pursuit of their aims – as in the Indian uprisings of 1857 (and these 'fundamentalists' have always had their equivalents in the intransigent racial supremacists of the West). Throughout colonial history there appears to have been as much resistance to foreign domination as the subaltern's '"consent" in objectification'[127] which Bhabha believes necessary for the effective operation of colonial knowledge and power. In general, Bhabha gives far too little weight to material forms of resistance to (neo-)colonial domination, whether these take the form of insurgency, civil disobedience or peaceful democratic opposition.

Bhabha's unified model of 'the colonial subject', moreover, produces disturbing simplifications of the affective responses of both the colonizing and the colonized subject in themselves. Taking the former constituency first, an immediate objection is that while criticizing Said's alleged unification of colonial discourse within the colonizer's intentionality and will to power, Bhabha's recourse to psychoanalytic theory, and Lacan in particular, unifies them equally rigidly within the imperative of the colonizer's consistent and unvarying unconscious need/demand for psychic affirmation. (This seems to reverse, but not displace, Mannoni's conviction of the 'dependency' complex of colonized peoples.) Bhabha's arguments might be extended in a number of fruitful ways. For example, he does not sufficiently consider the complications which ensue from the ambiguous positioning of colonial society 'in-between' its metropolitan and local equivalents,[128] a fact which bears crucially on the process of the colonizer's subject-constitution and subject-formation. Anglo-Indian literature, for example, consistently demonstrates that the exiled community identified itself *against* the metropolis (often precisely through identifying *with* aspects of local Indian culture) even though it may have more characteristically identified itself as British against the Indians. In the former respect, it might be worth investigating how 'counter-mimicry' (whether expressed in the trope of 'going native' or that of adopting the disguise of local cultures for the purposes of surveillance or even pleasure) might also complicate Bhabha's scheme. Such investigations could be extended to to take greater account of how the colonizer's identity was negotiated – even within the colonial context – partly in terms of a displacement of intra-metropolitan forms of Othering into that sphere. Thus in *Heart of Darkness*, Marlow defines himself, and legitimizes the 'English' civilizing mission specifically, against European Others quite as much as in context of the 'cannibals', crucial as these are to the construction of his role as a representative of an advanced civilization. Equally, Bhabha's psychoanalytic model can neither recognize nor explain the long and varied tradition of opposition to empire from within metropolitan culture (which, as V. G. Kiernan suggests, goes back at least as far as Cicero's polemics against Verro's rule in Rome's North African colonies).[129] Such omissions tend to impose a uniformity on Western discourse which – as is the case with Said's *Orientalism* – too quickly discounts its internal differences, conflicts and historical variations.

The homogenization of the colonizer's affective sphere is also revealed in a lack of attention to gender in Bhabha's work. While recognizing the importance of his essay 'The Other Question' in the reformulation of established paradigms of colonial discourse analysis, Anne McClintock observes that Bhabha analyses 'symbolic knowledge and the fetishism of colonial discourse as if they were neutral with respect to gender'.[130] She points out that, in a footnote to the original *Screen* version of his article, Bhabha recognizes that the regime of stereotype is the product of 'male' affect specifically without, one might add, recognizing the complications which this ought to imply for his conception of the colonizer or, indeed, the (unified) 'colonial subject'. While Bhabha promises to defer more detailed attention to the issue of gender to a later occasion, McClintock nonetheless regrets that in this essay 'Bhabha does not concern himself with the possibility that returning the footnoted female to the body of the text might throw radically into question the Lacanian theory of phallic fetishism and the scene of castration itself'.[131] In her view, Bhabha's refusal to consider the place of gender in fetishism ties him into the reproduction of a discourse which, by historically denying the existence of the female fetishist, 'serves systematically to disavow female agency on terms other than those presented by men'.[132] This might help explain why the role and position of white women in imperialism is almost completely ignored in Bhabha's work (to an even greater extent than in *Orientalism*). And one must note that this deferral (or persistent evasion) of issues of gender (and, of course, class) characterizes Bhabha's more recent work. Indeed, the disclaiming footnote in the original version of 'The Other Question' to which McClintock refers has disappeared from the 'definitive' version of the essay republished in *The Location of Culture*.

Similar problems afflict Bhabha's model of the subaltern's affective responses and modes of engagement with the dominant formation. Thus resistance appears to operate quite uniformly within marginalized constituencies with extremely diverse cultural origins across very different historical conjunctures. As suggested earlier, 'By Bread Alone' elaborates a theory of the inter-subjective nature of subaltern agency through comparison of the best-selling contemporary African/American novelist Toni Morrison and the nameless peasants who circulated the chapati at the outset of the Indian Mutiny a century and a half ago. This particular instance of what Bhabha himself describes (without regret) as a propensity to 'reckless historical connection' is defended (unconvincingly) on the grounds that both cases illuminate, in genuinely comparable terms, 'the temporality of repetition that constitutes those signs by which marginalized or insurgent subjects create a collective agency'.[133] The psychic economy of ambivalence may be a particularly productive way to understand the effect of (neo-)colonial hegemony on certain sections of the (formerly) subaltern populations[134] – particularly, one suspects, on the native intellectual educated in (neo-)colonial systems of knowledge, whether locally or in the metropolis. But there is no recognition in Bhabha's scheme that the question of psychic identification in the native subject might be complicated by questions of gender, region, ethnic origin, religion, caste or class. Instead it is implied that the structures of psychic identification and affect which he theorizes apply equally in terms of their operations and results to the Western-educated rajah and the 'illiterate' female subaltern.

Bhabha's essays undoubtedly constitute a major contribution to the field of postcolonial analysis. However, despite his avowed wish not 'to reduce a complex and diverse historical moment [whether modernity or a putative postmodernity], with varied national genealogies and different institutional practices, into a singular shibboleth',[135] homogenization is precisely what sometimes results from the way that Bhabha interrogates complex and multiform realities such as (neo-)colonialism through the narrow and ahistorical analytic models of affective ambivalence and the discursive disturbance which accompanies it. Issues which Bhabha's approach would be unable, as a consequence, to elucidate (they are not, indeed, his stated brief) would include such crucial questions as: why did colonialism begin when it did? Why were some Western nations colonialist while others were not? What underlay the various transformations in the material history of empire – for instance the transition from mercantilism to colonialism, or from formal imperialism to neo-colonialism? How did the system of formal imperialism come to be overthrown? Even at the level at which Bhabha customarily works, his method would be unable to explain the varied patterns and expressions of affective structures like ambivalence in diachronic terms, thus registering the fact that certain stereotypes emerged in particular periods and locations, and often in response to specific socio-political developments. To take just one example: why did the Anglo-Indian vision of the educated Indian in the relatively positive terms of the 'pundit' or 'munshi' prior to 1857 give way by the 1880s to the stereotype of the 'babu', who, characteristically, malapropistically misappropriates the discourse of the colonizer? Why is there no real equivalent to the stereotype of the 'babu' in fiction about Africa? Such questions can indeed be answered, but only by a differential engagement with the complex histories and material processes of which imperialism is made up. This is *not* to suggest that using psychoanalytic theory in the field of colonial discourse analysis and postcolonial criticism more broadly is illegitmate in itself. But it emphasizes the necessity of the scrupulous attention demonstrated by Fanon (and Spivak) to the material and historical contexts of both (neo-)colonialism and psychoanalytic theory itself.

5

Postcolonial criticism *and* postcolonial theory

In the light of the detailed examination of the work of Said, Spivak and Bhabha provided in the last three chapters, it may now be possible to return to some of the issues raised in chapter 1 of this volume and, in particular, to reconsider certain of the objections levelled at postcolonial theory in recent years. I do not wish to dwell too long on the objections raised by those outside the discursive field, broadly understood, of postcolonial analysis. Many such attacks are transparently motivated by partisan political affiliations (with which I have no sympathy) and it is beyond the scope of this book to provide a detailed engagement with issues like 'political correctness' and affirmative action which have been brought into the debate by the spiritual heirs of the New Right and their sympathizers. Moreover, being more or less a strictly literary critic, I am not in a position to answer fully the accusations that postcolonial theory makes spurious claims to interdisciplinary competence. However, the arguments of historians like Jacoby and MacKenzie might have more weight if they provided examples of the supposed ignorance of imperial history and historiography which they purport to find in the trio's work, rather than relying on blanket condemnation of the shortcomings of their opponents in this respect. I have identified moments where the historical sense or accuracy of all three postcolonial theorists can be questioned, but my own feeling is that there is certainly not a problem of the order which Jacoby and MacKenzie assume to be the case. Significantly, neither makes any reference to the kind of revisionist historiography of imperialism being performed by the Subaltern Studies group (to which both Spivak and Said are, to different degrees, connected), which constitutes such a strong challenge to the assumptions on which their own work is based – partly because it often draws on the same 'high' theoretical sources which are decried in the work of the 'Holy Trinity'.[1]

The objections from within broadly the same discursive field are both more substantial and much more interesting. Chapter 1 identified five principal areas of contention, which I shall deal with in turn. Perhaps the most damaging charge laid against postcolonial theory is that, far from being a radical or liberatory form of cultural practice, it is in fact thoroughly complicit in the disposition and operations of the current, neo-colonial world order. This argument rests on a number of propositions. First of all, the institutional location of postcolonial theory is offered as *prima facie* evidence of its role in helping to consolidate contemporary forms of Western hegemony. Postcolonial theory is also sometimes seen by its critics as a practice which appropriates the cultural production of the Third World, and refines it as a commodity for the consumption of a metropolitan elite, while allowing some to trickle back for the edification of the national-bourgeois elites in the non-Western world. From this perspective, moreover, its practitioners are sometimes represented as intermediaries between the West and the non-West who participate in the acculturation of the latter to the values and cultural norms of the dominant order. Such attacks are most notoriously associated with Ahmad's *In Theory* but elements of his critique have been repeated by figures as diverse as Arif Dirlik and some of those working within contemporary versions of Commonwealth literary studies.

The characteristic institutional location of postcolonial theory certainly involves some ambiguities. As has been seen, Said can be quite equivocal as to whether the Western university may be considered conducive to genuinely oppositional kinds of scholarship. While Bhabha is largely (and strangely) silent about questions relating to his institutional affiliations, to her great credit Spivak consistently foregrounds the contradictions involved in working within a system which is complicit, at least to some degree, in the production of neo-colonial forms of knowledge. Leaving aside the 'moral' question which Ahmad raises concerning the personal career ambitions of the critics involved, it is certainly the case that postcolonial theorists are subject to institutional pressures, inducements and constraints. They are as circumscribed as any other Western academic by the need to attract research students, to publish, to perform at conferences and so forth. On the other hand, the not inconsiderable rewards for the 'international distinguished professor' are also available to them. These material factors must be recognized, and provide a necessary corrective to a naive or idealistic conception of the intrinsic ideological purity of postcolonial theory.

Such structural factors do not in themselves, however, automatically disqualify postcolonial theory from the radical roles which its exponents and supporters claim for it. Indeed, it is arguable that, in his attacks on the institutional politics of postcolonial theory, Ahmad – like others – repeats many positions and assumptions which he deplores in critics like Said. *In Theory* is centrally concerned to advance the argument that unlike Foucault, on whose work Said relies so heavily in *Orientalism*, Marxism recognizes human will and agency as the constitutive motor of human history: '"Determination" does not mean, in other words, the kind of entrapment of which structuralists and Foucauldians speak; it refers, rather, to the givenness of the circumstances in which individuals *make* their choices, their lives, their histories.'[2] Ahmad makes much of the fact that, at certain points in *Orientalism*, Said seems to argue that Western scholars and writers are incapable of anything other than a distorted, reductive or oppressive vision of the non-Western subject. He suggests that, in this respect, Said falls back on discredited kinds of essentialism and displays a determinism which reduces the entire Western cultural canon to an archive of bad faith and Orientalist deformation.

As chapter 2 suggested, Said is in fact more divided over the relationship of the individual to the archive, throughout his work, than Ahmad's account might suggest. Perhaps more to the point here is the fact that Ahmad's Althusserian model of the Western academy and culture industries as ideological state apparatuses *tout court* seems as totalizing as the Foucauldian theory he decries. In promising to reveal 'the objective determination of the [postcolonial] theory itself by these material co-ordinates of its production, regardless of the individual agent's personal stance',[3] Ahmad reduces a diverse range of postcolonial critics and theorists to the status of more or less willing stooges in the current phase of Western domination. This leads to the least fortunate parts of Ahmad's book, where the personal integrity of a number of leading migrant intellectuals, including Said, Bhabha and Rushdie, is impugned in a regrettably *ad hominem* manner. In seeing such work as irretrievably contaminated by its institutional affiliations, *In Theory* also implicitly delegitimizes the criticism of 'native' metropolitan intellectuals like Mary Louise Pratt or Peter Hulme who work in roughly the same field. Lamenting what he describes as the process of 'embourgeoisement' which has overtaken the black academic communities in the United States, Ahmad reads this as sufficient proof of the political co-option of the whole cadre of such figures, which would include critics like Henry Louis Gates and Cornel West. Such simplistic thinking not only homogenizes figures as diverse as Amiri Baraka, Kwame Anthony Appiah, Homi Bhabha and Toni Morrison in a way which is highly reductive, but also fails to account for how figures to whom Ahmad is himself intellectually indebted, like Raymond Williams or Perry Anderson, have managed to escape this process of incorporation. One should also note that, by implication at least, Ahmad's argument would mean that all those Third World writers and critics who take up temporary posts in the Western academy, from Chinua Achebe and Ngugi to Buchi Emecheta, automatically become part of the system of domination. In this sense, Ahmad reproduces the very essentialism and determinism of which he accuses Said.

In his deeply pessimistic reading of the effects of institutional location upon the political pretensions of postcolonial theory, Ahmad demonstrates a lamentable refusal to engage in one of the primary duties of the Marxist critic, which is to historicize the objects of his study. To reposition postcolonial theory in terms of the contexts out of which it first emerged, as chapter 1 of this book attempted to do, is to be reminded of the enormous changes it has helped to effect in terms of the way that a number of disciplinary fields are now studied. In the reformulation of traditional metropolitan approaches to the study of the connections between both Western and postcolonial culture and (neo-)colonialism, postcolonial theory – in the shape, initially, of Said's *Orientalism* – has played a decisive (if not exclusive) role. Seen in this historical perspective, the kind of accusations made by critics like Ahmad about postcolonial theory's complicity in sustaining the New World Order seem even more difficult to swallow.

Ironically enough, the assumptions governing Ahmad's attack raise doubts about whether his own criticism can claim to be the genuinely radical activity he assumes it to be. Ahmad condemns postcolonial theorists (and writers like Rushdie) for conceiving of the metropolis as their primary audience, and questions Said's praise for the migrant intellectual who addresses the West within the terms of its own discourse. He makes much of Said's ambivalent self-positioning, which is indeed evident in a characteristic pronominal shifting between 'us' and 'them' in some of the essays collected in *Culture and Imperialism*. But a similar ambiguity is evident in respect of Ahmad's own implied audience and point of enunciation. At times he appears to be addressing the formerly colonized cultures; elsewhere, however, he speaks as if from within the West to the Western academy – 'right here, within the belly of the First world's global postmodernism'.[4] Moreover, while Ahmad is now based in New Delhi (at what is probably India's most prestigious research centre), not only has he taught in the West himself (at Rutgers University) but many parts of his book were first presented as papers to Western audiences and *In Theory* is published by the same London firm as this text. Using Ahmad's own crude method of 'objective determination' of the material co-ordinates of his production, regardless of his own 'personal stance', such evidence would suggest that Ahmad belongs to an elite fraction of the same national bourgeoisie which he accuses of acting as the local agents of contemporary international capitalism.

Equally paradoxically, Ahmad is addressing the West not only in one of its principal languages but within the terms of its own critical narratives, especially when invoking Marxism as his guiding light. Ahmad's defence of Marxism, both as a practice of resistance to neo-colonialism and as an appropriate methodology for analysis of imperial and post-imperial cultural problematics, has undoubted merits. A long chapter on Marx largely succeeds in recuperating his mentor both from the charges of empiricism and historicism laid against him by certain exponents of post-structuralism and, equally importantly, from the charge of complicity in Orientalism levelled against him by Said. However, serious problems are involved in Ahmad's use of Marxism as a means with which to beat postcolonial theory. While expressing nostalgia for Brezhnevite socialism (and hostility or indifference to characteristically Third World inflections of Marxism such as Maoism or Nyererean *ujamaa*),[5] Ahmad's principal points of reference are, of course, *Western* Marxists such as Raymond Williams, Fredric Jameson (despite some important disagreements) and Perry Anderson. Unlike Said, Spivak and Bhabha, however, Ahmad makes no mention of this tradition's characteristic failure to address the deep-rooted historical relations between culture and imperialism. Nor does *In Theory* seem aware of work like Robert Young's *White Mythologies*, which graphically demonstrates the Eurocentric bias of Western Marxism's historiography. Indeed, Ahmad's own failure to take on board the long-established tradition of Third World engagement with Marxism, sometimes sympathetic, sometimes highly critical (a topic to which I will return in due course), ill accords with his violent attack on Said for not sufficiently acknowledging earlier forms of colonial discourse analysis performed by non-Western critics. Critics like Ahmad and Dirlik might, then, consider more carefully the implications of their own privileged institutional locations and the conceptual frameworks that they employ before pointing the finger at postcolonial theorists in an attempt to claim the high ground. They might remember, moreover, that attacks on postcolonial theory build careers just as surely as the production of postcolonial theory itself.

A second objection to postcolonial theory which was identified in chapter 1 relates to its alleged reinscription of the cultural authority of the West by virtue of a largely exclusive attention to colonial discourse as the privileged object of analysis. The premises of this objection are that such a focus not only displaces postcolonial culture 'proper' as the 'correct' object of analysis but also evades the more pressing and difficult issues involved in the West's current dealings with the formerly colonized regions, in favour of dissection of a discourse which is now safely historical. While it is true that Said and Bhabha tend to focus on colonial discourse in the earlier part of their careers, later on they engage increasingly with a wide variety of counter-discourses and other non-

Western forms of cultural production. By comparison, Spivak is concerned with the subaltern – and Western engagements with the subaltern
– throughout her career. The polemic against the attention paid to
colonial discourse in postcolonial theory has been effectively answered
by Benita Parry and Laura Chrisman.[6] Parry (who, as has been seen, is
far from completely sympathetic to the work of either Bhabha or Spivak)
argues that one continuing rationale for colonial discourse analysis is the
fact that historically it was never adequately performed in the West,
especially – as Said also suggests – by the left. By contrast, Chrisman
welcomes the focus of texts like *The Empire Writes Back* on the
postcolonial literatures, but suggests that to consider such work in
isolation from colonial discourse tends to essentialize both and (*pace*
Ahmad) itself encourages the impression that the era of colonialism is,
indeed, now simply historical, rather than having being reconstituted in
terms which have deep-rooted ideological origins. This argument can be
confirmed by looking at recent Western representations of Africa by
novelists as diverse as Paul Theroux, William Boyd and V. S. Naipaul,
journalists like Patrick Marnham or travel writers such as Shiva Naipaul.
In each case, the writer in question sits squarely within archival
traditions established in the colonial period – which are most readily
identifiable with Conrad and Evelyn Waugh respectively.

The argument against the preoccupation with colonial discourse seems
simplistic for other reasons. One would not, after all, suggest that the
attention paid by feminist criticism to the deconstruction of patriarchal
authority partially, or in the last instance, reinscribes the prestige of
patriarchy. Moreover, for cultural decolonization to succeed it cannot
skip, or prematurely foreclose, the stage which challenges the modes of
knowledge and representation underpinning imperialism. In any case,
the charge that the focus on colonial discourse is at the expense of
postcolonial culture 'proper' is difficult to sustain if one bears in mind
the exposure which the latter is now getting through the institutional
developments in educational courses, publishing, scholarly journals and
networks which were described in chapter 1, a process to which
postcolonial theory has made a significant contribution. In fact, insofar
as colonial discourse has been privileged by some postcolonial theory
(and criticism alike), the strategic aim has been to effect a revaluation
and expansion of the metropolitan canon, rather than to exclude the
study of postcolonial culture. This has involved, on the one hand,
rereading the canon to emphasize hitherto unseen connections between
it and the history of imperialism and, on the other, the promotion of
writers who have been directly concerned with the representation of
empire out of their habitual position in the second rank. Thus the
authors of *The Empire Writes Back* declare: 'Kipling and Haggard may
well take the place of George Eliot and Hardy, since their relationship

to historical and political realities may come to seem more important.'[7] This is one objective of Said's *Culture and Imperialism*, too, which declares an intention to restore 'valence' to writers like Conrad and Kipling, 'who have always been read as sports',[8] rather than as central to the canon.

To a significant degree, recent attacks on postcolonial theory's alleged complicity in the reproduction of neo-colonial forms of knowledge centre on a third argument, that the modes of cultural analysis on which it draws are deeply Eurocentric. As chapter 4 in particular has suggested (following Fanon's lead), there are certainly dangers in adapting to the postcolonial arena certain kinds of psychoanalytic theory without paying attention to the ideological freight which they carry. Similarly, it is questionable how far Foucault's theory of power can be taken to apply in context of the 'archaic' scene of colonialism, despite his claim that the colonized fall within the operations of the new dispensation which he describes.[9] It is undoubtedly true that the repressive aspects of the regime of colonial power were complemented by the kind of disciplinary processes of 'reform' which Foucault describes. Macaulay's theory of cultural filtration, which Gauri Viswanathan has anatomized so fully in *Masks of Conquest*, is one such example of the 'modern' technology of power; and, Said would argue, so is the whole system of colonial knowledge-gathering, whether ethnography, compilations of lexicons and grammars or physical surveys. What Bernard Cohn describes as the codification of Indian civilization by the imperial ruler was certainly in part designed to strengthen colonial rule by redefining the meaning of traditional culture *for Indians themselves*.[10]

However, the paradox of using Foucault as a means to analyse colonialism is that it was precisely as a modern 'disposition' of power was emerging in the West (in the shift from autocratic to democratic regimes) that the West began to impose new forms of despotism on the rest of the world. Indeed, when *Discipline and Punish* dates the emergence of the modern regime of power to 'about 1760',[11] this coincides almost too neatly with the emergence of Britain as the paramount power in India after Clive's victory at the battle of Plassey in 1757, an event which inaugurates the era of modern British imperialism. In this colonial context it is much harder to accept Foucault's argument that 'the function of power . . . was not that of interdiction' and that it is 'quite different from simple prohibition'.[12] Thus, while Foucault argues that the 'decline of the spectacle' associated with the exercise of older forms of power in Europe is one mark of the inauguration of a new episteme, in colonial space power as/in spectacle remained a crucial mechanism of domination. As Veena Das comments of British reprisals after the 'Mutiny' of 1857, 'the punishments meted out by the British were not intended to show the power of the "rule of law", but rather bore the marks of ritual death'.[13] Bernard Cohn argues powerfully that the staging of British power 'as a feudal order'[14] was never displaced by its programmes of modernization, as the succession of Imperial Durbars and Royal Visits suggests (George V crowned himself emperor in Delhi in 1911, as had Edward VII in 1903). Such evidence confirms David Scott's caution that one should not overlook, in the way that postcolonial theory at times too readily does, 'the differentials in the political rationalities through which colonial projects were constructed',[15] compared with the management of the domestic metropolitan sphere.

Problems of a similar order are involved in the recourse to Gramsci in postcolonial theory. While Said makes an issue of the Eurocentrism of classical Marxist analysis and its conception of world history, it seems curious that he makes no mention of this aspect of Gramsci's work. It is Gramsci and not Marx who makes the following proposition:

> Even if one admits that other cultures have had an importance and a significance ... they have had a universal value only in so far as they have become constituent elements of European culture, which is the only historically and concretely universal culture – in so far, that is, as they have contributed to the process of European thought and been assimilated by it.[16]

Moreover, while Gramsci himself implicitly 'authorizes' the application of his theory of hegemony and subalternity to the imperial context,[17] this has led to important difficulties for postcolonial theory. Said, for example, never suggests that Orientalism is a means for the ruling classes in European nations to secure the consent of the rest of their own societies in their rule, whether at home or abroad: this is an avenue which might have been interesting to explore in light of the common argument that many of the structural problems of modernization and democratization in British society between 1860 and 1960 were evaded precisely because imperialism worked to displace domestic social tensions and problems in the relations of production. Nor does he really explore how Orientalism worked to secure the consent of the Oriental subject in foreign rule (a topic which has, however, been addressed by Viswanathan and Cohn). Without consideration of the effects of the dominant discourse on the perceptions and allegiances of the dominated, whether the subordinate sections of the metropolitan populace or the colonized, it is difficult to see how Said can legitimately interpret Orientalism as an instance of hegemony in the Gramscian sense. For instance, if the Western travel writing with which *Orientalism* is so much concerned is to be understood as a mode of hegemonic reproduction *vis-à-vis* subject peoples, one would have to assume that such work was, if not produced primarily for an Oriental readership, at least circulated widely amongst it. This clearly was not the case with explorer/writers such as Richard Burton, who were, of course, addressing a domestic Western audience. Indeed, Said's emphasis is that much of the Orientalist archive was produced by Western experts for other Western experts. A comparable difficulty with the recourse to Gramsci is evident in Spivak's work. The more the subaltern is seen as being outside or beyond the international division of labour, the less the term has any real purchase in a Gramscian sense, in that subalternity is a relational term which only has meaning in context of the power of the dominant.

Perhaps the most serious objection to the use of Gramsci in postcolonial forms of analysis has been made by the Subaltern Studies historian Ranajit Guha, who questions whether hegemony is at all appropriate as a means of understanding the dynamics of colonial rule. For Guha the crucial element of consent which is associated with the process by which hegemony 'solicits' the subaltern's acquiescence in domination is precisely the alibi used in colonial historiography to excuse imperialism. The use of forced labour, the declarations of war on behalf of the subject peoples (and their conscription against imperial foes) and the abuse of *habeas corpus* are examples which Guha gives of the harsh realities of twentieth-century British rule in India. Consequently, he suggests that recourse to Gramsci leads to serious misrepresentation of the true nature of colonial power relations: '*The crux of that misrepresentation is that dominance under colonial conditions has quite erroneously been endowed with hegemony.*'[18]

Such objections must call into question the basic premise behind the invocation of both Foucault and Gramsci in postcolonial theory, namely a conviction of the determining role of knowledge in the constitution of power in the colonial arena and the privileged place of the cultural field as the channel through which that power is mediated. This points to a seemingly disabling conflict between two incommensurable models of colonial power, one of which sees it as based upon what Foucault would call the 'repressive hypothesis', the other of which sees it as mediated primarily through discourse and its various 'pastoral' strategies of 'reform'. Much of the hostility to postcolonial theory rests on the argument that it discounts material forms of colonial oppression and resistance to colonial power alike. While Bhabha warns that 'the rule of empire must not be allegorized in the misrule of writing',[19] this at times seems to be precisely the kind of category mistake which takes place in his work (as well as in Spivak's, though to a lesser extent). The consequence is that the deconstructive postcolonial critics, who, as Bhabha puts it somewhat portentously in *The Location of Culture*, 'live problematically, often dangerously, on the "left" margins of a Eurocentric, bourgeois liberal culture'[20] , too often and easily become the true heroes (in retrospect) of the liberation struggle. As Paget Henry and Paul Buhle argue, the lesson of the Marxist tradition represented by C. L. R. James's work, by contrast, is that it is essential for postcolonial analysis to remain alert to 'domains of social practice that are not governed by textual/communicative rules'.[21] This is one of the most recurrent and intractable problems in the whole field, not just in postcolonial theory. Postcolonial criticism is also at times prey to overvaluing the semiotic domain in the management of colonial relations, as in Stephen Slemon's somewhat extraordinary claim that 'in the settling of empire "out there" colonialism's chief technology ... has been the canonical texts of European literature'.[22]

Before addressing this issue in more detail, however, I want to identify other problems with the objections to the use of contemporary European methodological sources in postcolonial theory. For a start, Ahmad's description of Said as a post-structuralist is simplistic. While *Orientalism* has obvious debts to Foucault, and Said's more recent critiques of sectarian kinds of identity politics have aligned him with post-structuralist interrogations of the nation and 'myths of origin', Ahmad's description homogenizes Said's career in terms of its political meanings and discounts the eclecticism of his critical affiliations. Even when Said was most influenced by 'high' theory, his work was engaged in the obviously political project of a critique of Western forms of knowledge and the relation of those forms of knowledge to their executive power in imperialism. Since then, as chapter 2 suggested, Said has distanced himself increasingly from post-structuralism, for much the same reasons which animate Ahmad's hostility towards it: its wholesale failure to address the question of (neo-)colonial history and cultural relations, its inability to theorize resistance to dominant discourse and structures of power satisfactorily and its tendency to domesticate political activism in the course of translating it from its original base in popular movements to the academic arena. From *The World, the Text, and the Critic* (1983), through the interviews with Imre Salusinszky (1987) and Michael Sprinker (1989), to *Culture and Imperialism* (a specific instance here being the generally unfavourable comparison of Foucault with Fanon), this trajectory is patently clear. Equally, both Spivak and Bhabha provide a penetrating critique of European critical theory from the postcolonial perspective. Bhabha, for instance, acknowledges that for many observers, post-structuralism constitutes 'another power ploy of the culturally privileged Western elite to produce a discourse of the Other that reinforces its own power–knowledge equation'.[23] Even while decentring the claims of Western knowledge by the invocation of its Others, he argues, some contemporary Western theory then forecloses on those Others, usually by in some way essentializing them. Bhabha notes this tendency in figures as diverse as Foucault, Kristeva and Jean-François Lyotard – and sees it as aligning them, ironically, with earlier traditions of Orientalist discourse. Their failure to acknowledge the particular predicaments and cultural problematics of the Third World thus 'reproduces a relation of domination and is the most serious indictment of the institutional powers of critical theory'.[24]

This aspect of the work of these critics suggests that postcolonial theory is quite as much aware as other forms of postcolonial criticism and cultural analysis that, as Stephen Slemon puts it, 'although theory offers us an adept vocabulary for locating both the semiotic and the narrative slippages of colonialist settlement and post-colonial decolonisation, it also comes freighted with the cultural baggage of dominant Western culture'.[25] Some less sophisticated figures than Slemon, however, fall into the trap of what Spivak calls 'nativism' or 'reverse ethnocentrism' in assuming that because 'high' theory characteristically addresses other problematics than colonialism, it is inescapably complicit in the (neo-)colonial order and cannot be adapted to the analysis of postcolonial issues.[26] The objections to such theory are also often formulated in confused or contradictory terms. For instance, while Helen Tiffin complains that post-structuralism acts as the 'District Commissioner of the 1980s' in policing postcolonial culture, quite how it can play this role remains a puzzle, given her objection immediately afterwards that its practitioners also simply ignore that same postcolonial culture.[27] By comparison, Bill Ashcroft's 'Constitutive Graphonomy' provides what seem to me to be highly simplistic and distorted readings of both Derrida and Saussure.[28] Furthermore, while claiming that 'high' theory has now established a conception of language in which meaning is infinitely unstable and transmissible, Ashcroft also claims that Western epistemology continues to be characterized by a realism and positivism which are grounded in an empiricist philosophy of language. Finally, while Ashcroft questions the legitimacy of using Western post-structuralist models of language in postcolonial analysis, he does so by invoking the equally Western, and equally theoretical, linguistic models of Benjamin Whorf and Edward Sapir.

There are at least two further defences against such hostility to the application of Western 'high' theory to the postcolonial field. Firstly, one might argue that such theory has, of course, long been deployed in deconstructing the authority of the dominant ways of knowing and representation in the West and in this respect is quite compatible with what is being done by figures as varied as Said, Ahmad and some Commonwealth literary critics. Thus in claiming that postcolonial analysis 'adapts post-structuralist methodology to the critique of European cultural imperatives',[29] Graham Huggan – and many others – fail to acknowledge sufficiently post-structuralism's own decentring of such imperatives, for example the sovereign male, white, bourgeois subject around which imperial discourse ultimately mobilized. Its critique of the 'organicist' conception of the nation and essentialist 'myths of origin', moreover, is endorsed – if not acknowledged – in much of Ahmad's own text. Even though, as has been suggested, theorists like Kristeva and Barthes at times unwittingly reinscribe various Orientalist stereotypes in dealing with the modern Orient, they do so in the course of what is clearly an attempt to undermine the authority of Western epistemologies and regimes of representation. Since Derrida is usually the chief bogeyman in attacks on postcolonial theory's reliance on European methodological models, it may be worth pointing out that throughout his career he has made Western ethnocentrism a primary theme of his criticism. *Of Grammatology* (1967) argues quite explicitly that 'logocentrism is an ethnocentric metaphysics',[30] a theme taken up again in 'White Mythology' (1971). In 'Racism's Last Word' (1986), Derrida makes clear the relationship between apartheid and earlier European discourses of Othering, and in more recent work like *The Other Heading: Reflections on Today's Europe* (1992) his decentring of the authority of the West continues apace. It seems to me a grave misfortune that the attitude towards Derrida in a lot of postcolonial criticism, for example Slemon and Tiffin's introduction to *After Europe*, has been so influenced by Said's derivative and misleading account of him in *The World, the Text, and the Critic* rather than by engagement with his actual writings. Equally, it is all very well for Rosemary Jolly to attack Derrida in 'Rehearsals of Liberation' because 'Racism's Last Word' began life as a contribution to a museum catalogue and thus (by some curious logic) necessarily reinforces the hegemonic authority of Western cultural institutions. However, as Russell Jacoby gleefully points out in 'Marginal Returns', such claims demand attention to the contexts of Jolly's own denunciation which, of course, appeared in the august pages of another authoritative Western cultural institution, a special issue of the *PMLA*.

Secondly, as Spivak points out, deconstruction is not a political programme in itself but a reading practice and as such can, in theory, be put in the service of any manifesto. However, as her own work demonstrates, deconstruction's lack of an intrinsically 'correct' political agenda does not mean that its use in postcolonial analysis is innately illegitimate. Indeed her argument that deconstruction can be useful to postcolonial critique by acting as a safeguard against the dangers of 'repetition-in-rupture' seems amply confirmed if one looks at certain of the corollaries of the hostility to the 'intrusion' of 'theory' into the postcolonial field which have been expressed in recent years. For instance, it is as well to remember that an aversion to theory was a marked characteristic of the early models of Commonwealth literary studies analysed in chapter 1 (as well as the mainstream discourses of English studies on which they drew while also challenging them in other respects). In 1973, for example, William Walsh gloried in the absence of any coherent theoretical framework within which to understand the very object 'Commonwealth literature', bluffly asserting that 'I take it to mean what most people do'; and two years later, Jeffares called on the Commonwealth literary critic to eschew 'modern methods of attack' and 'tired professional thesis-style criticism' in evaluation of the new literatures from the former empire.[31]

Deconstruction can perhaps provide more important safeguards in respect of the discussion broached earlier about the relative importance of the semiotic and material domains in (neo-)colonial relations, particularly in relation to the more or less explicit assumption of some of those who decry postcolonial theory that theorizing is in itself a second-order activity which is less valuable than, or even parasitic upon, more direct forms of activism. (This charge tends to be levelled more at Spivak and Bhabha; given Said's prominent role in the Palestinian cause – he served for some years on the Palestine National Council[32] – few would challenge his credentials as an activist on the ground.) This argument assumes that a radical distinction – even opposition – exists between intellectual work and political engagement and in its more extreme forms implies that the domains of culture and the 'real' world (more specifically the relations of production) are divorced. This sort of argument risks a reinscription of traditional conceptions about the autonomy of the aesthetic sphere. Moreover, it involves the danger of constructing a division of labour in which the Third World acts, while the First thinks (or, even worse, in which the First World speaks, while the Third dumbly acts). As Jean Franco points out, there is already an all too prevalent sense that 'the Third World is not much of a place for theory'.[33]

Critics like Ahmad at times seem to imply that oppression is only, or overwhelmingly, mediated in concrete material forms. While I have earlier acknowledged the dangers of conflating the semiotic and the social, one must not go to the opposite extreme and dismiss any connection between the two. As Derrida reminds one in 'Racism's Last Word', racism cannot operate institutionally without a legitimizing discourse, and the various manifestations of racism need to be addressed together. And as Fanon argued so powerfully, decolonization cannot be considered fully effected until and unless the domain of culture is also included in the liberation struggle. From this perspective postcolonial theory can be seen as one activity, amongst others, which seeks to accomplish the goals set out in The Wretched of the Earth. There is thus considerable merit in Bhabha's argument that theory can, at least in principle, be seen as a form of political praxis. As he concludes, 'what is mistakenly labelled "pure theory"' need not, in fact, be 'insulated from the historical exigencies and tragedies of the wretched of the earth'.[34]

The paradox of the position of figures as diverse as Helen Tiffin and

Benita Parry is that their hostility towards some postcolonial theory for domesticating the material struggle against (neo-)colonialism is itself expressed at a discursive level and depends on similar institutional outlets to those on which their opponents rely. For instance, Parry's 'Problems in Current Theories of Colonial Discourse', which accuses Spivak and Bhabha of an exorbitation of discourse as the privileged mode of resistance, is a sophisticated textual intervention which first appeared in *The Oxford Literary Review*, an elite journal noted more than anything else – ironically enough – for its enthusiastic promotion of post-structuralism in the 1980s. Ranajit Guha's attack on the application of a Gramscian model of power to the colonial arena seems similarly paradoxical. In the first instance, Subaltern Studies historiography itself owes much to Gramsci's work in conceptualizing the field and objects of its study. Moreover, it is itself a counter-hegemonic activity in the Gramscian sense. The urgency of the group's challenge to colonial and national-bourgeois models of historiography is premised on the argument that these forms of cultural practice serve particular interests and social constituencies.

Colonial discourse itself acknowledges that imperial power was mediated in both the cultural and the material spheres. For example, a story like Kipling's 'On the City Wall' (1888) bears ample testimony to the fact that behind the literature, the schools and the cricket pitches imported to India as part of the 'pastoral' regime intended to 're-form' the Indian subject, lie the police – and behind them, the barracks. When the policy of acculturation fails, as it does in this story when the riots break out, the sanction of force is always available. Consequently, the kind of double optic evident in the work of the the Caribbean critic E. K. Brathwaite is necessary in the organization of counter-hegemonic forms of cultural analysis. He argues that on the one hand that 'it is not language but people, who make revolutions'; but he also recognizes that: 'It was in language that the slave was perhaps most successfully imprisoned by his master, and it was in his (mis-)use of it that he perhaps most successfully rebelled.'[35] To devalue the semiotic domain of colonial relations is on the one hand to simplify the complexities of the management of colonial relations. It is also implicitly to undervalue not just postcolonial theory, but other kind of postcolonial criticism (and 'primary' forms of cultural production as well) as forms of resistance, since it is precisely the semiotic sphere which they characteristically engage and within which they operate.

One way to prevent an excessive imbalance of critical focus on the semiotic as against the material domain – or vice versa – is offered in *The Nature and Context of Minority Discourse*, where JanMohamed and Lloyd quite rightly insist upon the necessity of 'a mutually complementary work of theoretical critique and practical struggle'.[36] To a considerable degree this is, in fact, the position which has been espoused by postcolonial theorists. Even Said, who becomes increasingly disaffected with theory *per se*, does not rule out a continuing place for it in postcolonial analysis as long as it is constantly interrogated by the practical exigencies and material realities of the struggle against the legacies of imperialism evident in the new international division of labour. In *The World, the Text, and the Critic*, he argues that

> it is the critic's job to provide resistances to theory, to open it up toward historical reality, toward society, toward human needs and interests, to point up those concrete instances drawn from everyday reality that lie outside or just beyond the interpretive area necessarily designated in advance and thereafter circumscribed by every theory.[37]

In similar vein, Spivak argues against vanguardist 'exorbitations' of the role of theory and, as has been seen, insists that theory and practice must continually attempt to 'bring each other to crisis'.[38]

The fourth pattern of objection to postcolonial theory identified in chapter 1 relates to the style and language in which it is mediated. Some observers see postcolonial theory as either wilfully obscure or simply poorly written. Others object that its at times intractable nature constitutes a will to power over other kinds of postcolonial criticism. Certain sceptics also suggest that the arcane language of postcolonial theory confines its consumption to a (largely metropolitan) elite and, whether deliberately or not, cuts out those who are at the sharp end of struggles against (neo-)colonialism. While Said is never especially difficult to read (even in *Orientalism*, which of all his texts draws most on continental theory), the case with Spivak and Bhabha is rather different. With Bhabha the question of clarity is a legitimate one to raise only insofar as, as has been seen, many of his key analytic concepts such as 'ambivalence' and the 'third space' are themselves so ambiguously (and at times contradictorily) defined. With Spivak, the issue arises in a particularly sharp form in the context of her demand that the Western intellectual must be able to speak to, and not simply about, the subaltern. (Attention to Spivak's style is also authorized by her own insistence on the importance of attention to the rhetoricity of criticism, for example in her discussions of Cixous and Luce Irigaray.) While *The Post-Colonial Critic* is disarmingly frank about her difficulties with writing in English, she has made a rod for her own back in attacking what she sees as other critics' pretensions to be speaking for 'the masses': 'On the other hand, how about attempting to learn to speak in such a way that the masses will not regard as bullshit?'[39] Far from always speaking (or writing) in such a way that the subaltern might understand her, Spivak, one is tempted to suggest, often exemplifies the 'unreadability in deconstruction' that she herself criticizes. On the evidence of many passages in Spivak's essays, or the struggles of a critic as acute and sympathetic as Robert Young to keep up with her in interview, her attack on what she calls 'clarity-fetishists'[40] seems seriously ill conceived.

Thus there is certainly merit in some objections to the style of some postcolonial theory. One can plausibly argue that Bhabha and Spivak are in fact more difficult to understand than their methodological mentors. Certainly Kristeva, for example, offers none of the difficulties I have experienced with Bhabha's work and I have found Derrida generally more lucid than Spivak, even if his actual ideas are no less complex. Moreover, the intrinsic difficulty of some continental cultural theory does not oblige those who draw upon it to re-enact its obscurities. For example, while Jacqueline Rose's superb *The Haunting of Sylvia Plath* (1991) deploys a good deal of the same kind of Lacanian theory as Bhabha, albeit applying it in the context of patriarchal rather than colonial forms of oppression, she produces a text which is a model of clarity – without in any way simplifying the material on which she draws. On the other hand, as suggested in chapter 3, there are signs in the recent *Spivak Reader* that Spivak now recognizes the problem that her style poses and is taking steps to address it. Some of Bhabha's more recent pieces, like 'Unpacking My Library ... Again' (1996), are also considerably more accessible than much of the work collected in *The Location of Culture*.

In any case, the issue of style and clarity is not as simple as is sometimes assumed by some of the critics of postcolonial theory's tendency to obfuscation (as they see it). For one thing, complaints about the 'macaronic' nature of 'foreign' cultural theory are all too often mediated in the indigestible domestic discursive equivalent of 'spotted dick'. Thus for all his bluster about the transparency of the historian's style, John MacKenzie himself persistently demonstrates that simplicity of style and fineness of thought are easier to promise than provide. What is one to make of statements such as: 'Historians can be lumpers and splitters, enthusiastic builders and sceptical doubters. ... By definition, discourse theorists must lump'?[41] Moreover, what some would see as rebarbative jargon is by no means the prerogative of postcolonial theory, as a cursory glance through a piece like Bill Ashcroft's 'Constitutive Graphonomy' soon demonstrates. And some postcolonial criticism which eschews such technical critical vocabularies altogether can be just as enigmatic or elusive as Spivak and Bhabha, as is the case with many of Wilson Harris's essays.[42] Finally, contemporary exponents of Commonwealth literary studies, who are amongst those who most loudly decry the obscurity of postcolonial theory, often seem to forget the ideological baggage which historically accompanied their forerunners' insistence on clarity of style. As was seen in chapter 1, A. N. Jeffares insisted on

Standard (i.e. British public-school) English as the norm for both critical and creative work in the decolonized Commonwealth and decried not just the jargon associated with theses and theory, but any departure from that norm amongst creative writers.

This is a problem that I myself have had to negotiate. While I have tried to write in a 'lucid' fashion (I don't claim to have always succeeded), I am reminded every time that I 'correct' the English of my students' essays that 'clarity' and 'coherence' are judged by conventions which are bound up with what are ultimately political values and imperatives. Against the objections of critics as diverse as Todorov, Ahmad or Huggan, one might suggest that Spivak and Bhabha are to some extent trying to construct a critical discourse which cannot easily be appropriated and recycled as the latest fashionable commodity by the Western academic industries (an aim which may nonetheless have been overtaken by subsequent events). The obvious parallel is with some French feminist theorists like Cixous and Irigaray, whose experimental form of critical writing is partly conditioned by the desire to escape forms and conventions which they see as contaminated by historic service on behalf of the dominant (in this case patriarchal) order. As Ian Saunders argues, there are advantages 'in adopting a writing practice that is itself – directly or implicitly – disruptive, that denies the protocols of order and legitimation that (conveniently enough for those it has empowered) constructs both gender and race as "properly" hierarchical'.[43] And one might also see some merit in Spivak's argument that a 'coherent narrative' of the complex relations between the West and the non-West may be less productive than a paratactic method of tangential or fragmentary, but persistent, critique in dealing with such questions.

Finally, critics as diverse as Aijaz Ahmad and Diana Brydon have detected an insufficient engagement with questions of class and gender in much postcolonial theory. This objection, too, has some force. As was noted earlier, many subsequent feminist critics have expressed dissatisfaction with the limited nature of Said's engagement with questions of gender. The lacuna identified by chapter 2 in Said's *Orientalism* in this respect is only partly rectified in both *The World, the Text, and the Critic* and *Culture and Imperialism*. Bhabha's work, too, fails to engage with the complicating effects of gender in any significant way. Both critics are, in general, similarly blind to the problems which issues of class might have for their work. Bhabha, for instance, assumes that the affective economies of mimicry and ambivalence operate equivalently for all colonial subjects irrespective of their positioning in the social hierarchy. While the next section of this chapter will show that there is a substantial tradition of suspicion about class-based forms of analysis in the field of postcolonial criticism as a whole – and with good reason, too – Ahmad is undoubtedly right that some postcolonial theory has prematurely foreclosed on the continuing potential of such approaches. For one thing, class plays a crucial and insufficiently considered role in Western representations of the Other. From von Eschenbach's *Parzifal*, through Aphra Behn and Lady Mary Wortley Montagu to Rider Haggard and Paul Scott, defining the class identity of the non-European subject is a primary concern; and where that subject is of sufficient social standing there are often significant modifications of the normative, racially based hierarchies which govern the moral and political vision of such writers. By contrast, postcolonial theory has also shown a marked reluctance to engage with the varied forms of 'popular culture', a reluctance graphically expressed in Said's interview with Michael Sprinker in 1989.

Spivak, however, applies a powerful corrective to the absence of attention to class and gender in her colleagues' work – as chapter 3 has tried to demonstrate. Indeed, she anticipates Ahmad's objection that a focus on nationalism as the privileged form of opposition to (neo-) colonialism occludes class and gender as alternative sites of resistance and alliance which may even be in conflict with the dominant discourses of nationalism.[44] Moreover, neither postcolonial criticism, *pace* Brydon, nor 'primary' forms of postcolonial culture more generally have been notably sensitive historically to questions of gender and class,[45] though the situation in both respects has improved markedly since 1990. And, while *In Theory* provides searching critiques of the representation of women in some contemporary postcolonial fiction (for instance Rushdie's *Shame*), the essentially patriarchal bias of Ahmad's own criticism is indicated by a complete absence of reference to women critics such as Gayatri Spivak, Chandra Mohanty or Lata Mani, to name just three figures originating in the same region, and working in broadly the same disciplinary area, as himself.

POSTCOLONIAL THEORY *AND* POSTCOLONIAL CRITICISM

As suggested in chapter 1, the hostility of some observers within postcolonial criticism, broadly understood, towards postcolonial theory (and, at moments, vice versa) has at times been sufficient to suggest that they should be considered as essentially separate fields of activity – having at best the same sort of relationship as quantum to Newtonian physics. While the example of certain sciences, or mathematics, suggests that forms of knowledge (production) with quite different assumptions, objects of study and methods can coexist within the same disciplinary rubric, I would prefer to argue that postcolonial theory and criticism are not so divorced from each other as certain commentators have suggested, more or less explicitly. In the first place, one might argue that there has been a growing methodological convergence between the work being done in the respective sub-fields. Sunday Anozie's *Structural Models and African Poetics: Towards a Pragmatic Theory of Literature* (1981) was perhaps the first of a number of attempts to apply elements of contemporary European cultural theory systematically to the analysis of 'primary' forms of postcolonial culture (leading the African-American critic Henry Louis Gates jr. to describe him as 'a veritable sub-Saharan Roland Barthes'![46]). From the early 1980s, by comparison, a distinct new interest in methodological concerns can be detected in Commonwealth literary studies. A consistent preoccupation of Riemenschneider's *History and Historiography of Commonwealth Literature* (1983) was the attempt to address the problem that, as Helen Tiffin put it, there were 'almost no theoretical and methodological studies of Commonwealth literature'.[47] In seeking to rectify these shortcomings, several contributors drew heavily on German and American versions of reader-response and reception theory to reconceptualize the field. By the time of Petersen and Rutherford's *A Double Colonization: Colonial and Post-Colonial Women's Writing*, three years later, a significant amount of French or French-derived cultural theory had also begun to be employed, notably the work of Hélène Cixous and Gayatri Spivak. Lacan made his first (brief) appearance in postcolonial criticism (that I have found, at any rate) in the shape of Paul Sharrad's contribution to Rutherford's *From Commonwealth to Post-Colonial* (1992), a title which symbolizes the important methodological and political shifts in the field. Since then, there has been a steady increase in the amount of such theory in both contemporary versions of Commonwealth literary studies and other branches of postcolonial criticism, for example in the work of Biodun Jeyifo and Kwame Anthony Appiah. The varied methodological affiliations of this younger generation of critics suggest that it is becoming increasingly difficult to sustain the distinction, which has for some time now been assumed to be self-evident, between postcolonial theory and the larger critical field. The situation is further complicated by the fact that – as a number of critics have pointed out – there is a strong case for seeing affinities between some 'primary' kinds of postcolonial cultural production and some of elements of postcolonial theory – particularly, perhaps, in respect of the use of catachresis and the hybridization of metropolitan narrative. As Helen Tiffin argues, 'Much post-colonial writing is not only creative but also critical and theoretical . . . distinctions between the two are rendered invalid by colonial and post-colonial conditions of literary production and consumption.'[48]

By contrast, whereas Said, Bhabha and Spivak characteristically seemed to find little connection between what they were doing and what had been – or was being done – in adjacent critical areas in the initial phase of their careers, all three have more recently demonstrated a far greater interest in the work of other, especially earlier, colleagues. As has been seen, Said addresses a diverse range of postcolonial, minoritarian and anti-colonial critics from W. E. Du Bois, through C. L. R. James and George Antonius, to Chinweizu and Ngugi in *Culture and Imperialism*. Meanwhile Spivak's *Outside in the Teaching Machine* engages with Fanon and *The Spivak Reader* pursues an interest in Ngugi first announced in *The Post-Colonial Critic*. Perhaps the most surprising change of emphasis takes place in Bhabha's work. 'The Commitment to Theory' (1988), which seems to me to announce the transition between the first and second phases of Bhabha's work, cites a long passage from *Tradition, the Writer and Society* (1973), where Harris elaborates a number of ideas which, as will shortly be seen, bear no little resemblance to some of Bhabha's apparently distinctive concept-metaphors. The importance of this text for Bhabha is suggested in the fact that it is cited once more in one of his latest essays, 'How Newness Enters the World' (1994). And other recent essays also allude variously to Derek Walcott, W. E. Du Bois and C. L. R. James, suggesting his increasing recognition of alternative methodological resources to those offered by the European theory which so dominates his early work.

Benita Parry rightly warns against a too hasty conflation of even seemingly complementary aspects of each sub-field of postcolonial analysis, but the difficulties of pushing her argument too far are indicated in the fact that she also criticizes 'the Holy Trinity' for insufficient attention to earlier work in the postcolonial field.[49] Similar inferences must be drawn from Ahmad's criticism of Said's failure in *Orientalism* to acknowledge prior forms of colonial discourse analysis. Such arguments only have force if, indeed, there are at least some elements of overlap. I have no wish to discount the important differences between (and within) the respective critical sub-fields and in the following acount will try to respect them. But my conviction is that these differences are less important than the convergences, which are evident in the way that a number of key strategic arguments, tactical manoeuvres and concept-metaphors often considered to be characteristic of postcolonial theory are in fact anticipated in earlier phases of postcolonial criticism. I must once more stress the corollaries of this argument. The first is that postcolonial theory is not entirely the radically new and original activity that it has sometimes been made out to be by its advocates. (This position must not, however, be confused with Arif Dirlik's, which is that there is nothing of substance which is new in postcolonial theory,[50] a charge which might be more palatable were his own argument not so thoroughly derivative from Ahmad.) Precisely because many of its perspectives and procedures have been anticipated in earlier critical history, however, postcolonial theory cannot simply be dismissed, in the way attempted by Ahmad and Dirlik, without the legitimacy of many other branches of postcolonial criticism and associated forms of cultural analysis also being called into question.

If one begins with the parallels between the two sub-fields at the strategic level, perhaps the most obvious and important is a shared concern to decentre the cultural authority historically enjoyed by the West through a critique of its dominant ideology, humanism. One notable earlier example is Aimé Césaire's broad-ranging *Discourse on Colonialism*, published in 1955 (which again makes one wonder why Young's *White Mythologies* locates the beginning of the movement to challenge Western historiography in Fanon's *The Wretched of the Earth*). This constitutes an attack as swingeing as anything in *Orientalism* on the West's pretensions to represent the benchmark of human progress and civilization. Césaire also anticipates Bhabha's arguments about the questions which empire posed to the West's 'discourses of civility' in a manner which in some ways is much more powerful, insofar as Césaire was writing at a time when formal imperialism was still in place. For Césaire, there is a contradiction which would be ludicrous, were it not so painful, in the fact that a decade after a war against the totalitarian system of Fascism, a doctrine premised of course on doctrines of racial superiority, Western European powers should still be clinging on to their colonies. More radically still, Césaire argues that Fascism, far from being an unexpected historical aberration, evolves quite predictably from the sort of assumptions which govern the work of revered 'liberal' scholars and social scientists of the nineteenth century like Renan. This inaugurates a theme which resurfaces in *Culture and Imperialism* and once more, in greater detail, in Young's *Colonial Desire* (1995).

Elements of Césaire's arguments were repeated by many other postcolonial critics prior to Said, in many different parts of the formerly colonized world, especially in the years immediately preceding the appearance of *Orientalism*. In 'Reflection and Vision' (1975), for instance, Wilson Harris pondered on the degree to which 'humanism is itself subconsciously aligned to the very colonial prejudices it claims to deride'.[51] In *Morning Yet on Creation Day*, published in the same year as Harris's essay, Chinua Achebe suggested that continued absorption by non-Western cultures of 'the *human condition* syndrome'[52] in reality meant reaffirming the very vision which underpinned imperial conquest. Similarly, in *The West and the Rest of Us* (also 1975), Chinweizu sees an essential continuity between the colonial and neo-colonial era in the ongoing attempt implicitly or explicitly to impose 'so called timeless, universal values which, more often than not, are nothing but the European cultural imperialists' salesmanese for Western values'.[53]

For both postcolonial criticism and theory, the critique of the West's universals is centred on the cultural domain since this has traditionally been considered the repository of the finest liberal, indeed 'universal', values. In both branches of analysis, it begins in a shared challenge to the humanist assumption that culture is an autonomous sphere which transcends questions of political or institutional affiliation. Both branches of analysis, moreover, insist upon the fact that artistic representations have powerful effects on the worlds in which they circulate. No less so than postcolonial theory, then, African criticism – to take just one example – has long recognized the role played by 'primary' forms of Western culture in securing its hegemony over the rest of the world. As Ngugi puts it, with typical trenchancy, in *Writers and Politics* (1981): 'Cultural imperialism was then part and parcel of the thorough system of economic exploitation and political oppression of the colonized peoples and [Western] literature was an integral part of that system of oppression and genocide.'[54] No less so than postcolonial theory, moreover (and in contradiction of some of those who criticize its focus on the semiotic domain), the African tradition proposes that criticism is a practice which can play an important role in the ongoing struggle for the political and economic, as well as cultural liberation of the Third World.

These practices of cultural resistance take a number of forms, many of which have their analogue in postcolonial theory. To begin with, there is a long tradition of what has now come to be known as colonial discourse analysis in African criticism. Achebe's essay 'An Image of Africa: Racism in Conrad's *Heart of Darkness*', published two years prior to *Orientalism* in 1976, remains one of the most sustained expositions in the whole postcolonial field of the cultural politics of a canonical metropolitan 'masterpiece', and is worth spending some time on insofar as it shows the degree to which certain ideas and approaches which have become closely identified with postcolonial theory have, in fact, been anticipated in earlier postcolonial criticism. Achebe provides a valuation of Conrad's text which is in marked contrast to its canonical status in the West (and, it must be said, its elevated place in Said's *Culture and Imperialism*). According to Achebe, *Heart of Darkness* proves Conrad to be a 'thoroughgoing racist. That this simple truth is glossed over in Western criticism of his work is due to the fact that white racism against Africa is such a normal way of thinking that its manifestations go completely unremarked.'[55] In direct contradiction of F. R. Leavis's reading of the text in *The Great Tradition* (1948) which did more, perhaps, than any other to canonize it, Achebe argues that what Leavis calls Marlow's 'adjectival insistence' works to reinforce conceptions of Africa as the mysterious Other and, indeed, the place of darkness and home of the irrational. Achebe further suggests that the regime of stereotype in Conrad's text organizes a hierarchical system of binary oppositions so that, for instance, Kurtz's noticeably taciturn African mistress is 'a savage counterpart to the refined, European woman who will step forth to end the story'.[56] For Achebe, the most pernicious example of such binarism is the contrast between Marlow's eloquence and the 'language' of the local Africans, some of whom, almost inevitably, are represented as cannibals. Achebe points out that for most of their time on stage, the black passengers on Marlow's boat tend to communicate only by grunts – except, notably, for the moment when they betray their identity as cannibals: 'Weighing the necessity for consistency in the portrayal of the dumb brutes against the sensational advantages of securing their conviction by clear, unambiguous evidence issuing out of their own mouths, Conrad chose the latter.'[57] All this anticipates the general emphasis of *Orientalism* on the dichotomous regime of Western representations of the non-West and, more specifically, Said's attention to the way that colonial discourse constructed the subject peoples as the 'the silent Other' (or in the case of Conrad, the inarticulate counterpart) of the West.

Achebe also suggests that while Marlow does come to recognize some degree of common humanity with the Africans, this is generally the case only insofar as, like the cannibals, they remain in their 'proper' place; thus, despite his important services to Marlow, the partially Westernized helmsman is treated parodically precisely because he displays signs of losing his aboriginal identity. In this respect, Achebe anticipates Spivak's argument that 'authenticity' is all too often something which the West demands of the non-Western subject at the same time as it also demands its 'entrance into history'. As Bhabha later reminds one, albeit in a different idiom to Achebe's, this is a situation of ideological and representational double-bind in which the subject peoples are all too often enmeshed, historically, in metropolitan representations of the Other. Colonial discourse excoriates the 'savagery' of the subject peoples and demands their 'reformation' through mimicry of the West. However, while demanding that this process is not carried to the point where they become indistinguishable from the dominant order, colonial discourse often parodies or mocks precisely those signs of difference which are required of the subaltern. In identifying an 'ambivalence' in Marlow's troubled part recognition, part disavowal, of the 'transitional' helmsman, Achebe also anticipates Bhabha's conception of the destabilizing effects of mimicry on the colonizer's psyche.

Such brief appearances of African characters aside, Achebe argues that Africa exists in Conrad's text primarily as a backdrop, with its inhabitants more or less discursively effaced in order to clear centre stage for white protagonists. This act of aesthetic repression (one is reminded here of Spivak's discussion of the 'disappearance' of Christophine from *Wide Sargasso Sea* in 'Three Women's Texts and a Critique of Imperialism'), Achebe implies, is the artistic analogue of the political suppression of Africans being enacted at the time and provides a clear instance of the complicity of even the 'benevolent' Western critic of the system – despite his best intentions – in the underlying vision of colonialism. The major irony which Achebe stresses is the fact that at the same moment that Conrad is writing about/out Africans in this demeaning way, African art was on the point of providing a crucial stimulus for the sea-change in the European visual arts and for the emergence of Modernism more generally. Thus the mask sold by Vlaminck to Derain, and subsequently shown to Picasso and Matisse with such enormous consequences, Achebe reminds his reader, 'was made by other savages living just north of Conrad's River Congo'.[58]

Achebe is at pains to argue that the defects of Conrad's depiction of Africa are not to be explained away simply in terms of the psychopathology of a particular individual (though he supplies an extraordinary passage from Conrad's *A Personal Record* which suggests how far the writer was infatuated with all things English, including the lower extremities of the male English physique). Rather, they are symptomatic of a whole cultural system of representation of the Other at the historical moment that *Heart of Darkness* appeared. As Said was to argue in a more theorized way later on, Achebe implies that Conrad exists in an 'archive' which characteristically overdetermines the ways that the colonized are represented by any individual Western writer. Anticipating another of the principal arguments of Said's *Orientalism*, Achebe also suggests that this archive of cultural descriptions is organized around a consistent attempt 'to set Africa up as a foil to Europe, as a place of negations ... in comparison with which Europe's own state of spiritual grace will be manifest'.[59] In a striking analogy, he argues that the traditional discursive relationship of West to non-West is akin to Dorian Gray's with his portrait, which is used to offload all its owner's inner guilt and horror through a process of symbolic projection. In identifying this system of representation as something which is rooted in 'the desire – one might indeed say the need'[60] of the Western psyche, Achebe offers insights into the cultural psychopathology of domination which Bhabha subsequently develops in greater detail.

As Achebe's riposte to Leavis in this essay suggests, such work anticipates the argument of postcolonial theory that traditional Western critical values can no more necessarily be taken to apply 'universally' than its literature. Thus, while Ashcroft, Griffiths and Tiffin argue in *The Empire Writes Back* that postcolonial theory primarily 'emerges from the inability of European theory to deal adequately with the complexities and varied cultural provenance of post-colonial writing',[61] comparable views had long been expressed about earlier kinds of Western criticism. While there is a general continuity with postcolonial theory in this respect, there is less emphasis in African criticism, at least, on an 'internal' or deconstructive critique of such forms of analysis. Instead, the impetus derives in the first instance from an insistence on the fundamental differences in social organization and cultural values between the centre and periphery which in turn engender quite different conceptions not only of what art is, but of its social functions. For Achebe, for instance, the *mbari* festivals of the Owerri Igbo on the one hand typify the emphasis placed by African cultures in general on art as a shared social praxis; and on the other constitute 'a profound affirmation of the people's belief in the indivisibility of art and society'.[62] (Having said this, one must not exaggerate the differences; in her approach to Mahasweta Devi's fiction, for instance, Spivak is just as concerned as Achebe – whose work is in fact cited as a point of comparison in her essay 'A Literary Representation of the Subaltern' – with the lack of easy fit between a number of branches of Western criticism and such 'subaltern material', on account of deep differences in the contexts in which, and for which, it is produced compared with fiction in the West.)

The rejection of traditional Western systems of cultural analysis and critical values is most polemically expressed in the work of cultural nationalists (or so-called 'nativists'), like Chinweizu, Onuchekwa Jemie and Inechukwu Madubuike, whose *Towards the Decolonisation of African Literature* (1980) decries the Eurocentric prejudices of metropolitan criticism of African culture, and seeks to release it 'from the death-grip of the West'.[63] While the more ecumenically minded Soyinka rejects what he sees as cultural nationalism's essentialist model of black cultural identity and himself adopts, or adapts, some strands of metropolitan criticism, he also expresses frustration with the way that it has at times been brought to bear unreflectingly on African writing. Consequently he argues that it is 'a serious academic lapse to transfer the entirety of that language of criticism to any literature which, while undeniably cognizant of other world literatures, nevertheless consciously explores the world-view of its own societies'.[64] Somewhat ironically, given the often bitter exchanges between them, Soyinka, as much as the Chinweizu 'troika', reserves his strongest rebukes for 'undiscriminating African critics [who] have been trapped into transposing the petit-bourgeois signs and iconography of their mentor cultures into a universal culture'.[65] (Soyinka would include the 'troika' in this category – and vice versa.)

Achebe's position is similar, if more kindly expressed. Observing that 'our own critics have been somewhat hesitant in taking control of our literary criticism',[66] he calls for renewed attention to African aesthetics, as a means to circumvent problems in Western criticism identified as early as 'Where Angels Fear to Tread' (1962). Here Achebe reviewed and rejected three principal strands in Western criticism of the new African novel. The first was 'peevishly hostile' to the very notion of the African novel; the second resented the appropriation of such 'Western' forms by the periphery. The third, most insidiously, presumed to judge African fiction against Western models. Rejecting the supposition that the novel form was to be approached as a more or less self-contained aesthetic artefact (the Commonwealth literary critic William Walsh, for example, had complained that the fiction of Mulk Raj Anand 'has to be severely sieved' to remove 'the dross of propaganda'[67]), Achebe's 'The Novelist as Teacher' (1965) defends the 'earnestness' (or commitment) of the African writer, whose work is conceived of in instrumental terms as an 'applied art', which acts as both the voice of his people and as its conscience. 'Africa and her Writers' (1972) took up this argument more polemically: 'Words like *use, purpose, value* are [according to normative Western critical assumptions] beneath the divine concerns of this Art, and so are we the vulgarians craving the message and the morality.'[68]

Given its dissatisfaction with both metropolitan representations of Africa, and traditional metropolitan criticism of African literature, it is no surprise that African criticism anticipates the agitation of Spivak in particular for curricular reform (with the difference, of course, that the context addressed is not the metropolitan academy but the non-Western university). As many critics have observed, the neo-colonial dispensation in Africa was to be secured partly by means of Western 'aid' in the area of education, in which the humanities, including the study of English literature, were to play their part. G. D. Killam has recently recalled the ethos surrounding the recruitment of literature lecturers for service in the new post-independence African universities, describing his 'passage on the M. V. Accra from Liverpool on January 14th, 1963, reliving, to the strains of "Pomp and Circumstance", the departure of generations of schoolboy masters, off to the dark places of the world to serve the Empire'.[69] The smooth transition from a colonial to a neo-colonial system of control in Africa, and the role of English literature in securing the new dispensation in the ideological sphere, is neatly symbolized by the fact that the English department to which Killam was sent out was housed in a complex of buildings built originally for British troops engaged in the last Ashanti war. Unsurprisingly, there was increasing opposition to this conception of the humanities as the problems facing independent Africa became more acute. Chinweizu's *The West and the Rest of Us* (1975) contains a chapter entitled 'Africa's Universities: Roadblocks to Cultural Renaissance' in which he argues that the African university was operating primarily to produce skills and human resources to service neo-colonial interests. In humanities departments especially, 'university culture . . . spreads its blanket of sterility and its assimilationist tendencies wherever it can.'[70] Such disaffection was widely echoed in the former colonies. At the University of Nairobi in Kenya, for example, there was agitation at the end of the 1960s for the decentring of the English department within the Faculty of Arts in order to free resources for the creation of a department of African Languages and Literature, an account of which is provided by Ngugi wa Thiongo in 'On the Abolition of the English Department' (1972). For the reformers there was one key question in this debate: 'If there is need for a "study of the historic continuity of a single culture" [the argument proposed by defenders of the status quo], why can't this be African? Why can't African literature be at the centre so that we can view other cultures in relationship to it?'[71]

Conviction of the West's oppressive 'universalism' was not, however, restricted to the case of liberal humanism. Earlier African criticism again anticipates some postcolonial theory insofar as it also attacks the pretensions of various supposedly 'radical' forms of Western cultural and political analysis to be able adequately to address the heterogeneous realities of the non-Western world. As has been seen, Fanon's *Black Skin, White Masks* (1952) attacks Sartre's 1948 preface to a new literary anthology edited by Senghor for attempting to subsume *négritude* into a class struggle which was defined in terms of Western experience.[72] Fanon's objections were twofold. Firstly, that in defining the identity of black resistance on behalf of those actually involved in the struggle, Sartre was repeating the archetypal imperial gesture of assimilating the 'Other' to itself. Thus 'at the very moment when I was trying to grasp my own being, Sartre, who remained The Other, gave me a name and thus shattered my last illusion'.[73] Secondly, Sartre not only reduced the struggle for decolonization to a minor part in a more important (allegedly universal) struggle, but he further denied the non-Western liberation movements any choice or existential self-awareness about their participation in this dynamic. Consequently, Sartre's historiographical determinism in the end constructed the anti-colonial struggle as simply a movement called forth by (Western) History in a manner analogous to the conception in mainstream colonial discourse of the West 'leading' the non-Western world 'into History'.

For two decades after Fanon's death, Marxism remained the 'radical' Western theory most often decried by African critics (though it has continued to have influential adherents, such as Ngugi). Soyinka's analysis of the African intellectual leftocracy in *Myth, Literature and the African World* sees African Marxism as reversing, but not displacing, many of the arguments of the *négritudinist* critics to whom it was, in general, manifestly hostile. In Soyinka's view, what he calls the 'new black ideologues' are equally involved in an act of self-negation by generating 'fantasies of redemptive transformation in the image of alien masters'.[74] In the early 1980s, he turned his attention to Barthes, whom he located squarely within the Marxist tradition. While 'The Critic and Society' recognizes Barthes as an effective scourge of Western bourgeois values, he is also criticized severely for complicity in the domestication of 'Third World' material struggles (an argument which of course, anticipates Said's 'Traveling Theory' in *The World, the Text, and the Critic* and Ahmad's *In Theory*). Citing the essay in *Mythologies* entitled 'Wine and Milk', Soyinka suggests that it consists of a double appropriation of the labour of the Algerian worker who produces the wine to which Barthes's title alludes, by 'first converting his labour into the language exchange of the intellectual class, then crediting this act with a basic political consciousness. Neither achieves anything concrete for the expropriated Algerian worker.'[75]

As all this evidence suggests, then, the West has long been assailed for universalizing what are in reality historically, culturally and geographically specific systems of analysis and representation, as part of its attempt to secure its dominance over the rest of the world. What is perhaps more surprising than these strategic continuities is the degree to which some of the apparently distinguishing tactical procedures and concept-metaphors of postcolonial theory are also anticipated by earlier critics in the field. For instance, Spivak's notion of 'strategic essentialism' (discussed in chapter 3), which has excited so much subsequent debate, is prefigured in Fanon's defence of *négritude* in *Black Skin, White Masks* and *The Wretched of the Earth*.[76] Both texts insist that the construction of essentialist forms of 'native' identity is a legitimate, indeed necessary, stage in the emergence from the process of 'assimilation' imposed by colonial regimes to a fully decolonized national culture. A related version of this argument recurs in Achebe's attempt to negotiate a way between the essentialism of *négritude* and the simultaneously abstract yet highly context-specific, indeed often blatantly ethnocentric, conception of the human in Western liberalism. In 'The African Writer and the English Language' (1962), Achebe decries attempts to fix absolutely the characteristics of African literature and, by implication, African identity, through an insistence on the irreducibly heterogeneous nature of both. Three years later in 'The Novelist as Teacher', by comparison, he is more alert to the tactical advantages of a recourse to the kind of vision which is embodied in *négritude*:

> You have all heard of the African personality; of African democracy, of the African way to socialism, of negritude, and so on. They are all props we have fashioned at different times to help us get on our feet again. Once we are up we shall not need any of them any more. But for the moment it is in the nature of things that we may need to counter racism with what Jean-Paul Sartre has called an anti-racist racism, to announce not just that we are as good as the next man but that we are better.[77]

A second example concerns Said's concept of 'counterpoint', which is theorized in *Culture and Imperialism* as a means to overcome what he sees as the disabling binary division constructed in some quarters between (neo-)colonial and postcolonial cultures and their societies of origin. As has been suggested already, whereas Ferial Ghazoul traces this method back to Arab-Islamic critical sources, a perhaps more immediate precedent is to be found in the tradition of Commonwealth literary criticism. This has always stressed the importance of comparison between both Western and postcolonial literatures and, from the mid-1970s at least, between different postcolonial literatures themselves. In Goodwin's *National Identity* (1970), to take just one example, certain contributors variously compared Nina Bawden with David Rubadiri, Maori and *pakeha* poetry in New Zealand and vernacular Bengali with British literature. Perhaps the most specific precedent for *Culture and Imperialism* in Goodwin's collection, however, is provided by Wilson Harris's 'Interior of the Novel: Amerindian/European/African Relations' (the title typifies Harris's characteristic commitment to the comparative method). This predates by two decades Said's recently developed approach to texts such as Conrad's *Heart of Darkness*. Like Said (but unlike Achebe's 'An Image of Africa', which was almost exactly contemporary with his own essay), Harris seeks to consider it in 'a new dimension . . . within which the losses and the gains on both sides are beginning to cross-fertilize the imagination of our times'.[78] Crucial to Harris's conception of counter-point is the desire, as in Said, to circumvent the 'politics of blame' identified with cultural nationalism. Parallels could also be drawn in this respect with the work of the Nobel laureate Derek Walcott, who in his critical and creative work alike seeks to draw on both African-Caribbean and Euro-American traditions and for whom, too, there can be no legitimacy in a cultural politics based on a 'vision of revenge'.[79]

As suggested earlier in this section, the postcolonial theorist whose work is perhaps most consistently comparable to earlier forms of postcolonial criticism is Homi Bhabha. The convergences are clearest in the context not of the African tradition on which I have thus far largely concentrated, but of Caribbean criticism. (Despite abundant common interests and many comparable concept-metaphors, these Caribbean critics should not be seen as a homogeneous unit or school. At times, the disagreements between them are as sharp as those between Soyinka and the Chinweizu 'troika'. Walcott's stinging criticism of 'the black critic who accuses poets of betraying dialect'[80] might be understood as an attack on the kind of revaluation which Brathwaite effects in respect of Claude McKay and George Campbell in *History of the Voice*, where they are upbraided for adopting the dominant stylistic conventions and linguistic norms of their respective host-cultures.) Certain figures in Commonwealth literary studies have already suggested, albeit in quite general terms, possible points of comparison between such work and Bhabha's theory at the tactical level. Thus Graham Huggan explores the importance of Wilson Harris's conception of 'hybridization' in a piece which cites the collection *Europe and Its Others* (to which Bhabha contributed the essay 'Signs Taken for Wonders') without, however, offering a specific comparison with Bhabha's definitions of the term.[81] Stephen Slemon perhaps misses a similar opportunity in his important discussion of 'ambivalence' in Wilson Harris in an essay which cites Bhabha's 'Representation and the Colonial Text' but not those of his early works which explicitly theorize the term, like 'The Other Question'. Instead Slemon focuses on Harris as a critic who prefigures the deconstructive work of Paul de Man[82] (on whom, of course, Spivak draws heavily in her own criticism).

While I now want to pursue such hints, it is worth remembering Parry's cautions in 'Signs of Our Times', so that one must not assume that Bhabha's definition(s) of hybridity, for example, can necessarily be mapped precisely onto 'equivalent' ideas in his predecessors. She is right to suggest that Brathwaite's concept of 'creolization' involves a recognition that loss, or what Derek Walcott calls the 'anguish of the race',[83] is an inextricable part of this process. For Harris, Brathwaite and Walcott alike, 'mimicry' has negative characteristics insofar as it at times connotes simple imitation/assimilation of the colonizer's culture and not, as at other times, a process of hybridization/indigenization of the hegemonic order. As Harris puts it, from this perspective mimicry always to some extent involves the postcolonial subject's deployment of his/her 'self-mutilating and self-critical faculties'.[84] Bhabha does not really consider these implications, a shortcoming which – as has been seen – is related to his insufficient recognition of the effectiveness of mimicry as a strategy of colonial control; instead he characteristically presents mimicry as a site of successful resistance by the colonized subject to the the dominant. Equally, there is at times (but not always, as will shortly be seen) a synthesizing, dialectical and 'progessivist' (in both senses) teleology in some Caribbean versions of 'hybridity', which contrasts with Bhabha's emphasis on preventing sublation of subordinate cultures by the dominant, by insisting on the incommensurable aspects of cultural differences.

Notwithstanding these caveats, it seems to me that there are many areas in which the criticism of Bhabha and his Caribbean colleagues do, in fact, converge. For instance, E. K. Brathwaite's theory of 'creolization', elaborated most fully in *The Development of Creole Society in Jamaica* (1971), sees this process in a similar way to Bhabha's conception of 'hybridization', insofar as it can be a defence against the oppressions of the dominant order, notably through cultural forms like carnival and, especially, the construction of 'nation language'. This concept is described in *The History of the Voice* in Bhabhalian terms as 'a *strategy*: the slave is forced to use a certain kind of language in order to disguise himself . . . and to retain his culture'.[85] As suggested in the first section of this chapter, however, according to Brathwaite, 'nation language' is also the domain in which the most effective subversion of the dominant culture takes place. Such forms of resistance operate through the same strategies of mobility, elusiveness and indeterminacy as processes like 'mimicry' in Bhabha's work.

These structures of creolization and hybridization are accompanied, in the eyes of some Caribbean critics, by the same kind of 'ambivalence' which is theorized in Bhabha's work. As Stephen Slemon points out in A Shaping of Connections, the concept was already well developed in Wilson Harris's critical work of the 1960s. Of particular relevance to a comparison with Bhabha is that Harris sees ambivalence as an affective response which binds together the different parties involved, even when their basic relationship is highly conflictual. This aspect of Harris's conception of ambivalence is most strikingly illustrated in the disturbing symbol of the 'bone flute' which recurs in his critical and creative writing alike. (This motif is drawn from the Amerindian custom of eating part of the flesh of the thighbone of an enemy and using the bone itself to fashion a musical instrument.) As Harris comments, such practices 'relate to protagonist and antagonist, they relate to a mutual psyche. How can one know what the enemy is planning, if one does not in a sense share the biases of the enemy? One cannot know the enemy unless the enemy has something in common with oneself.'[86] Comparable ideas are evident in Brathwaite's Contradictory Omens (1974), which includes a chapter entitled 'Creative Ambivalence'. In this section of the book, Brathwaite takes issue with Sylvia Winter for dividing the concept of creolization into two aspects, an imitative process which corresponds to assimilation by the dominant and the subversive, resistant strategy of indigenization. For Brathwaite, the force of the idea of creolization is that it embodies both processes simultaneously, reflecting (or producing) the characteristically complex affective economy of the (post)colonial subject: 'For me, the problem and reality of Caribbean culturation lies in its ambivalent acceptance–rejection syndrome, its psycho-cultural plurality.'[87]

As in Bhabha's essays, moreover, the corollary of such forms of 'negotiation' with the dominant is that essentialist ideas of identity become inadmissible. For Brathwaite, creolization involves 'many possibilities . . . and many ways of asserting identity'.[88] For Wilson Harris as well, 'the inescapable partiality' of postcolonial identity is empowering, enabling the postcolonial subject 'to speak through a variety of masquerades'.[89] As long ago as 1972, the Nobel laureate Derek Walcott was advancing a model of identity based on the principle of facing the world 'with black skins and blue eyes'.[90] What Harris and Walcott both describe as the predicament of 'cultural schizophrenia' characteristic of the postcolonial condition allows circumvention of what Walcott calls 'the most conservative and prejudiced redoubts of imperialism' without falling into the equally monolithic reverse ethnocentrism represented by the 'reactionaries in dashikis'.[91] As in Bhabha's work, such Caribbean critics also at times make strenuous efforts to distinguish these kinds of 'plural identity' from the narratives of multi-culturalism characteristic of Western society. For Brathwaite, for example, 'the concept of a "plural society" would appear to be a colonial rather than a creole contribution.'[92] While Harris at times seems to propose a teleologically based principle of synthesis as a means to overcome what *The Womb of Space* (1983) describes as the 'conquistadorial legacies of civilisation',[93] more characteristically he offers a vision which respects the principle of cultural difference in the way that Bhabha does. This is symbolized by his recurrent interest in narrative figures like Tiresias, who crops up in both Harris's fiction and non-fiction through the 1970s and 1980s. For Harris, the appeal of the Tiresias figure is that the contrary but mutually necessary and inextricably linked principles of male and female, natural and supernatural, life and death are held in productive tension and do not resolve into a stable final synthesis.

Of these three Caribbean critics, it is with Wilson Harris that Bhabha perhaps has most affinities and it may be as well to conclude this chapter by identifying some further points of connection between the two figures. To begin with, Bhabha's style of critical writing bears comparison with Harris's. The description in Riach and Williams's *The Radical Imagination* of 'the intricate spiralling of Harris's thought and the interconnecting nature of his logic, which continually reiterates and revises itself'[94] could be adapted with little difficulty to Bhabha's work. The elusive style which both share can, moreover, be related to a common suspicion of realism as a fictional mode and its empiricist, positivist analogues in criticism. For Harris as for Bhabha, 'realism is authoritarian'[95] and embodies all the unattractive characteristics of what Bhabha would call the 'pedagogical', above all fixity. Harris's model of an experimental style characterized by the play of 'infinite rehearsal' (whether in fiction or criticism), by comparison, is akin to Bhabha's conception of the 'performative', whereby the tendency of what he would call the 'symbol' (this term at times has significantly different meanings for the two writers) towards closure is interrupted by the liberating instability of the 'sign'. In Harris's criticism, the concept of 're(-)vision' (the same word is sometimes used by Bhabha, too, in similar senses), is broadly cognate with Bhabha's liberatory conception of 'catchresis'. For example, Harris alludes to the way that the 'revisionary cycle' empowers the writer or critic 'with ways of reversing certain structures, certain expectations'.[96]

Most importantly of all, perhaps, Harris's work seems to provide a crucial stimulus to the emergence and development of the concept of the 'third space' in Bhabha's writing, from 'The Commitment to Theory' (which, as has been seen, cites *Tradition, the Writer and Society* for the first time) onwards. The concept has its analogues in the work of other Caribbean critics. Brathwaite, for instance, offers the neologism of 'the in-between'[97] (the same phrase recurs in Bhabha's writing) as a means to figure a positioning between cultures which corresponds to one version of the 'third space'). However, it is Harris's elaboration of what he calls 'a certain "void" or misgiving attending every assimilation of contraries'[98] which comes closest to Bhabha's characteristically metaphorical and often psychological conception of the 'third space'. In particular, the idea of the 'void' prevents the cultures or cultural forms which are being negotiated from ever reaching full equivalence or synthesis and therefore closure. In Harris's definition, the 'void' connotes that element which in Bhabha prevents full 'translation' (the concept of 'translation' is one which Harris also recurrently employs in discussing cross-cultural trans-actions). However, like Derrida's figure of the hymen or the *entre*, or the 'non-space' of the border-line, or Bhabha's 'third space', Harris's 'void' is also a place which allows cultures to come together. As *The Radical Imagination* puts it, the genuinely cross-cultural imagination 'does not erase difference between cultures'; rather, it is a question of 'endorsing differences yet creatively undermining biases'.[99] As the Conclusion will now attempt to show, this formulation of the dynamics of cross-cultural exchange does not just prefigure some key arguments in Bhabha's work, but foreshadows some of the most intractable problems now facing the whole postcolonial field.

Conclusion

Postcolonial futures:

things fall apart?

The first part of chapter 5 argued that some of the objections to postcolonial theory which were discussed in chapter 1 of this text can be discounted and that many of the others need careful reconsideration and, more often than not, at least some modification. The second part suggested that the growing divide which emerged in the late 1980s between what I have been calling (for the sake of convenience) postcolonial theory and postcolonial criticism, is by no means a necessary or intrinsically legitimate one. As I have tried to show, there are substantial and important links and areas of overlap between the two sub-fields at both strategic and tactical levels.

My conviction of their complementarity is further reinforced by my sense that the most significant problems each sub-field now faces are to a large extent shared by the other. For example, the assaults on postcolonial theory which have come from outside the domain of English studies, from a number of disciplinary fields into which such forms of analysis have 'intruded', often implicitly delegitimize postcolonial criticism, too. And what Spivak would call the 'sanctioned ignorance' about postcolonial theory which is still widespread within contemporary English studies is equally evident in respect of postcolonial criticism. More significantly, perhaps, there must be a suspicion that the postcolonial 'moment' has been and gone or at least that the erstwhile impetus of postcolonial studies has been dissipated. As early as *Orientalism*, Said warned that colonial discourse analysis risked falling into a premature 'slumber' if it did not continue to develop.[1] In *Colonial Desire* (1995), Robert Young suggests that the danger which Said foresaw has now been realized. He argues that 'colonial-discourse analysis as a general method and practice has reached a stage where it is itself in danger of becoming oddly stagnated, and as reified in its approach . . . as the colonial discourse that it studies'.[2] Stuart Hall's 'When Was "The Post-Colonial"?'

(note past tense), by comparison, argues that the impasse which now besets the field derives from the failure of its practitioners to be sufficiently interdisciplinary, to move out from a focus on essentially literary concerns to engage with disciplines like economics and sociology, in particular, which are addressing the material operations and cultural consequences of globalization, in a quite different manner to what is habitual in the arena of postcolonial studies.[3]

To some extent, perhaps, the somewhat downbeat tone of the debate over the current state of postcolonial studies may reflect a more widespread atmosphere of disillusion in contemporary cultural criticism. In the first place, there are many signs of an increasing disenchantment with 'high' theory, and not just in the domain of literary studies. This has been reflected in a number of ways, including the retraction or serious modification of earlier enthusiasms by some of its exponents and advocates, a notable example being Christopher Norris's *Uncritical Theory* (1992). Since the early 1990s, there has also been something of a reaction against the new forms of political criticism which emerged in the late 1970s and early 1980s and, more particularly, a weariness with the issues of gender, class and race which these brought to the fore, a case in point being Frank Lentriccia's 'The Last Will and Testament of an Ex-Literary Critic' (1996). One symptom of this in literary studies is that traditional literary history is enjoying something of a vogue, and there has been an increasing engagement with less overtly politicized (but nonetheless important) issues such as values and ethics.

Such factors aside, there is certainly some evidence that postcolonial theory, in particular, seems to have suffered a certain loss of its former radicalism and energy. As has been seen, Said has retracted much of what made *Orientalism* such a decisive departure from traditional modes of study of the cultures of (neo-)colonialism within the Western academy. *Culture and Imperialism* at times seems to wish to refurbish elements of the methodology which shaped these older forms of analysis (and the values underlying them). What is most striking in this respect is Said's return to the criticism of Eliot and Arnold as a means to organize the study of the new global 'common culture' which he wishes to promote. Some of the recent work of Spivak may also seem disappointing in comparison with her work up to 1990. She, too, is in the process of modifying or retracting some of her most celebrated interventions, such as 'Can the Subaltern Speak?'. Several of her other recent essays seem to supplement rather than really develop and extend earlier positions. Meanwhile some might argue that Bhabha seems to have been treading a fine line between what Wilson Harris would call 're-vision' of his arguments and straightforward recycling. 'The Postcolonial and the Postmodern', which I suggested was the most important essay in the second phase of his work, was published in almost identical form, under three different titles, in a period of eighteen months between 1992 and 1994. (This seems somewhat ironic given that one of the principal arguments of the essay is that 'repetition' is a cultural marker of the 'symbolic' regimes of Western culture specifically.) At the 1995 Fanon conference at the Institute of Contemporary Arts, Bhabha appeared to have little to add to his earlier analyses of Fanon (and little to retract either) and the title of another recent essay, 'Unpacking my Library ... Again' (1996), perhaps expresses a weariness in Bhabha's work which is symptomatic of the sub-field as a whole.[4]

This diagnosis may, however, be unnecessarily pessimistic. (I'm conscious that I may be projecting my own sense of exhaustion, as this text nears completion, onto the 'Holy Trinity'.) For one thing, all three critics have signalled that substantial new work is on the way. Moreover, one could argue that postcolonial theory has helped to establish areas of inquiry, conceptual frameworks and tactical procedures which are now in fact being variously extended, challenged or modified by a new generation of critics which is still in the process of emergence. By comparison, the broader field of postcolonial criticism seems as lively as it has always been since the 1960s, even in areas which one might consider to have come under considerable pressure from subsequent developments both within and outside the field. Thus G. D. Killam commented in 1989 of Commonwealth literary studies that they 'are in good shape and moving forward'. One could also certainly argue that much remains to be done in the postcolonial field. There is room to extend what has already been achieved in terms of the analysis of the role of Western culture, and metropolitan canons more specifically, in the histories of (neo-)colonialism. As I have suggested, the area of class has been insufficiently considered, even in colonial discourse analysis, and the same is true of the broader postcolonial field in respect of 'popular' culture. Much more work could also be undertaken in terms of comparisons between the Anglophone and non-Anglophone worlds, and between work in metropolitan and vernacular languages. And, as Stuart Hall has suggested, there is scope for more interdisciplinary work – despite the hostility from some of those in fields adjacent to literary studies of the kind discussed in chapter 1. From these perspectives, it might be argued that postcolonial studies have only just got going or, at worst, have simply completed the initial stages of their development and are now gathering their energies for fresh endeavours. Finally, whatever the problems which the field now faces, one should not discount the considerable successes which postcolonial studies have enjoyed. As suggested in chapter 1, they have played an important role in transforming the ways in which cultural production was traditionally studied in the West since the 1970s. In particular, they have been decisive in making the interconnections between cultural production and issues of race, empire and ethnicity far more visible than they were as recently as the mid-1970s.

For these reasons, it seems to me that the most pressing problems which face postcolonial studies are not so much a loss of their initial impetus, or the emergence of a more critical audience than they once enjoyed, but issues which arise from the multiplicity of historical and social contexts out of which 'the postcolonial' has emerged and the diverse cultural forms and modes of critical engagement which, consequently, it now inhabits. As has been noted, there is a considerable degree of contestation over what is, and is not, 'properly' postcolonial in terms of identities, geographies, histories, political positionings, cultural affiliations, disciplinary formations and critical practices. While much of this debate is perfectly legitimate and, indeed, necessary, in their less edifying manifestations such taxonomies (they are usually performed by white critics based in the West) have uncomfortable echoes of the colonial systems of classification of the formerly colonized, setting up new hierarchies of 'good' subjects and substituting new kinds of inclusion/exclusion for old. For the reasons set out in chapter 1, it seems to me imperative to maintain as broad and flexible a conception of the cultures of (neo-)colonialism as is possible. From this it follows that what is now perhaps most pressingly at stake as far as postcolonial studies are concerned is how to conceptualize the relationship between these plural kinds of postcolonial identity, and the wide variety of cultural forms and modes of cultural analysis to which they give rise. This problem is also bound up with the issue of how to theorize the relationship between the complex varieties of postcolonial identity and modes of cultural/critical production on the one hand and, on the other, groupings and cultural/critical forms which are organized in reference to often quite different forms of social and historical experience, more particularly the areas of gender, class and sexuality.

A principal theme of this text has been that while there are important continuities, at both the strategic and tactical levels, between the criticism of figures such as Achebe, Soyinka and Harris on the one hand, and Said, Spivak and Bhabha on the other, nuance and difference must always be recognized in terms of their understanding, formulation and deployment of some of the thematic preoccupations, strategies, tactical procedures and analytic concepts which they share. Despite their problems in some areas, the merit of texts such as *In Theory* and *After Europe* is to foreground the extent and vigour of the debate within the field over issues as diverse as its cultural-political affiliations and what is most appropriate to it in terms of its objects of study, methodologies, sites of production and intended audiences. The differences between Said and Achebe over the status of Conrad, or the mutual hostility which has sometimes been evident between Spivak and Bhabha on the one hand and certain Commonwealth literary critics on the other, are salutary reminders of the dangers of prematurely collapsing the two sub-fields into one. Within each particular sub-field, moreover, the same sort of warning applies. From this perspective, what is perhaps most surprising about the postcolonial theory which I have considered in this text is how little mutual cross-referencing there is between the work of Said, Spivak and Bhabha. While the two latter figures recognize Said as the founding figure in their field, the directions they subsequently take are often radically at odds with the assumptions and methods of both Said and each other. This is strikingly true of the 'high' theory which each of the trio favours. Thus Said and Spivak take very different views, during the 1980s particularly, on the value of Foucault and Derrida respectively; by comparison, Spivak and Bhabha disagree equally strongly over the applicability of Lacan, Marx and Kristeva to postcolonial concerns. (This also usefully reminds one that 'high' theory is itself often quite radically heterogeneous in its preoccupations, assumptions and procedures, and cannot, as some of those who decry its influence on postcolonial theory seem to assume, be seen as a monolithic and unified body of work.) Similar differences are evident in postcolonial criticism. The polemics between Soyinka and the Chinweizu 'troika', of Fanon against *négritude* or the disagreements between Walcott and Brathwaite over the import-ance of 'nation language', provide evidence of the conflict which can exist even within the same national or regional tradition at a given historical moment.

The difficulty of reconciling respect for such differences with the equally pressing need for solidarity against the obstacles confronting cultural (and political) decolonization is exacerbated by the character-istic dynamic which accompanies what, adapting Henry Louis Gates, I have called the 'multiplication of the margins'. As Gates suggests in 'African American Criticism' (1992), each new 'margin' comes to voice in the first instance through a double process which involves defining itself not just against an oppressive centre, but against the 'margins' immediately adjacent to it. These in the process can become essentialized and reified, even at times identified as a new kind of centre. In the context which Gates addresses, African-American women's criticism has mobilized just as fiercely against what it sees as the patriarchal assump-tions of male African-American critics like Gates himself[6] as against either white feminism or white patriarchy. Lesbian African-American criticism in turn begins by defining itself in the first instance against the heterosexist assumptions of many of those feminist critics who attacked Gates. This same process is observable in almost every development in the postcolonial field that I can think of. For example, in the 1970s, a new paradigm of Commonwealth literary studies emerged through excis-ing Britain as the central point of reference from the new comparative method being developed; British exponents of Commonwealth literary studies were increasingly excluded from the new dispensation – implicitly or explicitly – insofar as they were now deemed to represent the oppressive values and ethnocentric methods of the traditional 'centres' of literary study (against the indifference of which such figures had in fact themselves initially defined the new sub-field). In due course, this new paradigm of Commonwealth studies was attacked by those who interpreted its emphasis on comparison between different literatures as an obstacle which prevented due attention to the newly developing individual national traditions in themselves. Indeed, the divide which has been constructed (on both sides at different moments) between postcolonial theory and postcolonial criticism can also be broadly understood as a symptom of this same process.

The dilemma between respect for difference and the desire to stress points of connection and to make common cause is reflected in the existence of two apparently incompatible models of cultural identity and political positioning in postcolonial studies, which lead to conflicts and contradictions which are evident in the work of each of the three postcolonial theorists addressed in this text and, equally strikingly, in some of their critics. Thus on the one hand, Ahmad seeks to locate *Orientalism* within the project of cultural nationalism with its attendant 'foundationalist' conceptions of identity. For instance, *In Theory* claims that Said's text gained its status 'from the way it panders to the most sentimental, the most extreme forms of Third-Worldist nationalism'.[7] By essentializing differences between East and West, and by denying that any Western observer was capable of a truthful representation of the Orient, Said, in Ahmad's view, is at best reversing the hierarchical binary oppositions upon which the epistemology of imperialism depended while keeping its pernicious logic in place. At the same time, however, Ahmad's hostility to what he sees as a naive espousal of theories of the decentred subject underlies his general suspicion of the (migrant) postcolonial intellectual, whether artist or critic, who – Ahmad argues – loses a key point of purchase in resistance to the hegemonic order by prematurely severing links with his culture of origin. In Ahmad's eyes, the failure of Rushdie's vision of the Third World, for example, is traceable to an 'aesthetic of despair that issues from his overvalorisation of unbelonging'.[8] This prevents Rushdie from giving sufficient recognition to the kind of regenerative communal projects available in movements of national liberation or cross-national co-operation on class lines. Ahmad accuses Said, too, of a failure sufficiently to recognize nationalism as a legitimate site of collective resistance to domination.[9] This, as much as his conviction of its allegedly self-reflexive concern with the nature of discourse, underwrites Ahmad's reading of *Orientalism* as a quintessentially post-structuralist text.

While an apparently unsustainably contradictory reading, Ahmad's critique does in fact reflect a fault-line in Said's own thinking. On the one hand, as an engaged supporter of the Palestinian cause, Said is clearly committed to a politics of resistance based primarily on aspirations to a separate and distinct national identity. In essays like 'American Intellectuals and Middle East Politics' or 'C. L. R. James: The Artist as Revolutionary', Said recognizes the need for oppressed groups to be able to organize around communitarian politics of identity and to embrace national liberation as a master-narrative. On the other hand, particularly in more recent years, he severely criticizes essentialist models of identity for leading to the reification of differences between people and cultures. Essays like 'An Ideology of Difference' and 'Representing the Colonized: Anthropology's Interlocutors' see such ways of thinking as purely reactive, interpellated by, and ultimately reinforcing, the assumptions of (neo-)colonial discourse – in the same way, ironically, that Ahmad accuses *Orientalism* of doing. In his 1989 interview with Michael Sprinker, Said is forthright on this point: 'All that entire ideology of separation and exclusion and difference etc. – the task is to fight it.'[10] Nubar Hovsepian usefully reminds one of the hostility expressed by certain Palestinian factions to Said's apparent readiness to come to an understanding with Israel and argues that *The Question of Palestine* 'could also be interpreted as "An Essay in Reconciliation"'.[11] Thus there is some justice in Benita Parry's perception of a fundamental conflict in Said's argument:

> Said's work commutes between a position conserving specific structures of communal subjectivity invented by dominated peoples, and that which conceptualises the subject as split, unfixed and disseminated and is implacably hostile to what is perceived as essentialist claims to perpetuate holistic cultural tradition and a transcendent native self.[12]

The same kind of conflict recurs in the work of both Bhabha and Spivak. On the one hand, Bhabha insists on the principle of respect for cultural difference and the 'untranslatable' element of identity. As he puts it in a formulation which once more owes a great deal to Lacan, not least in its baroque style, this involves a recognition 'of the problem of the not-one, the minus in the origin and repetition of cultural signs in a doubling that will not be sublated into a similitude'; this is what distinguishes cultural difference from cultural pluralism 'with its spurious egalitarianism – different cultures in the same time' or the vision underlying cultural relativism, which conceives of 'different cultural temporalities in the same "universal" space'.[13] On the other hand, Bhabha's work is notable for its persistent critique of the epistemology and politics of cultural nationalism or separatism, which is what gives rise to his consistent elaboration of concept-metaphors such as the 'in-between', the 'hybrid' and the 'third space'. By comparison, especially in her 1980s work, Spivak characteristically seems to place greater emphasis on the persistent recognition of heterogeneity and, in support of this, advances the problematic concept-metaphor of the *'tout-autre'* as a means to prevent premature sublation of social categories like the subaltern into dominant conceptions of class formation and social identity. Such radical heterogeneity is compounded once the issue of gender, for example, is brought into the equation, as Spivak argues forcefully. On the other hand, one could argue that the very term 'subaltern' is, in fact, itself homogenizing. There are surely differences too large to be negotiated within this single term between the 'tribal', the urban homeworker and the unorganized rural peasant. Yet when Spivak equates the experience of a middle-class female like Bhaduri with that of the subaltern, as happens at the end of 'Can the Subaltern Speak?', it is clear that the principle of heterogeneity is negotiable, and may be legitimately displaced (in Spivak's view) in the cause of promoting a common alliance between differentially marginalized groups. In Spivak's more recent work, the tension between these two approaches is even more visible, with *Outside in the Teaching Machine* warning against the dangers of multiplying differences and *The Spivak Reader* calling for even greater attention to the heterogeneity of the postcolonial formation.[14]

These different conceptions of identity in fact run through postcolonial cultural history, and each has different corollaries for the question of how to formulate the relations between different postcolonial formations and cultural/critical practices on the one hand, and between other social groupings with their respective cultural/critical practices on the other. The model which has been most influential since 1990 at least has stressed the plurality and differentiality of identity and, through various versions of the concept of hybridity, it has emphasized the complementarities which exist between the different aspects of the postcolonial formation – and other groupings outside – and tries to build upon them. Not only is this the favoured approach in a wide variety of other postcolonial criticism, in particular the Caribbean tradition analysed in the last chapter and in the comparative method of Commonwealth literary studies, it is also the vision which predominates in postcolonial theory. Said, for example, has had persistent recourse, even in certain passages of *Orientalism*, to a pluralistic vision of social identity which is derived, in the first instance, from the Western liberal model of the 'family of Man' as a way forward beyond the 'politics of blame'. However, *Culture and Imperialism* makes clear that there can be no return to the false universalism and pluralism of the old tradition of Western academic liberalism. Counterpoint is not only linked to a politics of liberation which is antagonistic to the current geo-political settlement represented by 'the New World Order', but it also seeks to recognize and accept cultural difference, not abolish it or sublate it under the over-arching sign of the white Western middle-class male. In a telling image, which is worth citing again, Said suggests that 'contrapuntal analysis should be modelled not (as earlier notions of comparative literature were) on a symphony but rather on an atonal ensemble'.[15] Said's interest in a reconstituted 'humanism' as a way forward from binary oppositions and confrontation between the West and the non-West is also a feature of a lot of earlier postcolonial analysis; for instance, Senghor, Césaire, Fanon – whom Said acknowledges as a source in this respect in *Culture and Imperialism*[16] – and Achebe in turn travel to the same conceptual destination. As Wilson Harris argues, despite its historical complicity in colonial history, humanism is 'susceptible to new eruptions' and a process of 'transubstantiation'.[17] What such work suggests is that what is now needed is not so much a refurbished version of an abstract, idealist model of 'Universal Man' but a sense of the concrete and multiple identities which might be represented in a concept like 'the global(ized) human' which, however clumsily, would register the fact that the category is constructed by the processes of history and has not sprung directly from the fingertip of God.

However, while it has proved a seductive path for many in the field, and has informed the approach that I myself have taken in this text, the emphasis on hybridity and plural identity has generated significant problems. Indeed, Said's reconstituted version of this older vision has excited considerable criticism from critics like Robert Young and Benita Parry, who complains of his 'tendency to lapse into a sentimental humanism'.[18] While Said is evidently appropriating or 'catachretizing' the concept from its habitual usage and traditional political/cultural meanings, such redefinitions are certainly vulnerable, especially from a gendered perspective (as is the case with Fanon's more muscular redefinition of the term towards the end of *The Wretched of the Earth*). What gets lost in Said's benevolent vision is the difficulty of creating global solidarities through reference to a cultural ensemble which is so largely based around the Western canon. This, as he is at such pains to point out, has been complicit in the long history of oppression of those same social formations who are now invited in *Culture and Imperialism* to consider this same canon as a constituent element of their 'common culture'.

A second problem is that, as noted in chapter 4, the term 'hybridity' only has conceptual force by virtue of the assumption that there are such things as 'non-hybrid' cultures, which no one has yet been able to demonstrate. Inevitably, some such accounts tend to homogenize the centre (and the Third World, to a lesser extent) more or less implicitly and make it monolithic in a way which simply does not do justice to the realities (as in Said's insufficient discrimination between the varied national traditions of Orientalism, or Bhabha's construction of the colonizer's identity and psychic economy as invariant across gender and class). In fact, some cultures of the centre have historically prided themselves on their hybridity, as is suggested in the US motto of *e pluribus unum*. As Robert Young cogently demonstrates in *Colonial Desire*, Matthew Arnold – as much as anyone in the contemporary period – advocated hybridity and, indeed, proposed that this was the peculiarly distinctive feature of English culture. At the same time, the conception of the centre which often accompanies contemporary theories of hybridity seems inappropriate insofar as the power of the current economic dispensation associated with the international division of labour arises precisely from the fact that the 'centre' has been to a considerable degree decentred. Ahmad is right to insist that capital and its operations have been globalized and that the old centre/periphery model, on which some theories of hybridity continue to rely in theorizing the 'in-between', has consequently ceased to have the conceptual force that it once did. Insofar as the 'centre' is just as heterogeneous and unstable, in terms of its class, gender and even (now) ethnic identities, as the 'periphery', the matrices of oppositional alliance have become potentially almost infinitely complex, so that various groups can at one time be part of the 'centre', at other times of the 'periphery' and, at moments, of both simultaneously. (The shifting positions of centre and margin are strikingly illustrated in 'single-issue' campaigns. For example, opposition to the building of the Newbury bypass generated an ostensibly unlikely alliance of 'crusties' and tweed-skirted 'county' women against the bulldozers).

Moreover, the celebration of cultural hybridity can all too easily mask a new system of hierarchies – or rather the continuation of the old system in a new guise. Dirlik is right to caution that one of the most enthusiastic advocates of global hybridization is *The Harvard Business Review*. Some current theorizations have perhaps not taken sufficient account of the way hybridity has been historically deployed on behalf of the dominant. In this sense there may be a direct continuity between some conceptions of hybridity employed in colonial discourse and in the current (neo-) colonial dispensation. In the colonial period, the discourse of hybridity operated in two principal ways. Firstly, the hybrid and multiple nature of the subject social formations was used to legitimate the imposition of central power as a 'unifying' force, a discourse which operates clearly in the Indian context, for example, in literary texts as diverse as Meadows Taylor's *Confessions of a Thug* (1839) and Kipling's *Kim* (1901). (Compare the 'necessity' for US 'leadership' in the New World Order.) Secondly, through the programmes of acculturation, represented most notoriously by Macaulay's 'filtration' theory, cultural hybridity became a means of securing colonial control through the production of complicit 'mimic men'. This reminds one that the most hybridized portion of the subject culture, the national bourgeoisie, was the one to which control was relinquished at the beginning of the (neo-)colonial period, and serves as another warning that 'hybridity' in itself can be as oppressive as the supposedly monocultural systems it opposes. One illustration of this problem can be found in the criticism of E. K. Brathwaite, more particularly in his concept of creolization. While Brathwaite recognizes that Caribbean identity and culture have been constructed by a multiplicity of cultural exchanges, the clear implication of his writing is that the contributions of Indian and Chinese cultures, as more recent arrivals, are secondary in importance to the creolization effected as a result of contact between black and white cultures.[19] And, as Bev Brown has complained, Brathwaite's 'sun-aesthetics' show little awareness of the specific problems of women in the decolonized world – indeed, they may exacerbate them.[20] (The same kind of problem in respect of a flattening of the gender – and class – identities of the subordinate is evident in Bhabha's work on hybridization, as chapter 4 suggested.)

The appeal to anti-essentialist models of postcolonial identity involves other difficulties. For one thing, doctrines of hybridity perhaps do not take sufficient cognizance of those who resist the vision it inscribes. Are all 'fundamentalists' or 'separatists' to be stripped of their rights in the new dispensation which some theories of hybridity anticipate? Perhaps such theories also give insufficient recognition to some of problems involved in respecting the principle of cultural difference. How does a Western-based 'liberal' 'negotiate with' issues like child marriage, polygyny or clitoridectomy in non-Western societies? By contrast, how are non-Westerners to 'negotiate with' hysterectomy as a treatment for depression, the neglect of the old or (child) pornography in the West? There has also perhaps been a tendency to underestimate the difficulties in constructing the kind of plural alliances proposed in the discourse of hybridity. Said has recently acknowledged the practical difficulty of constructing the desired kinds of 'intertwined and interdependent, and above all, overlapping' alliances he desires; he suggests that

> few of these movements seem (to me at least) to be interested in, or have the capacity and freedom to generalize beyond their own regionally local circumstances. If you are part of the Philippine, or Palestinian, or Brazilian oppositional movement you are necessarily circumscribed by the tactical and logistical requirements of the daily struggle.[21]

It may also be that that some theories of hybridity risk underestimating the separatist tendencies which, paradoxically, accompany the contemporary process of globalization. Many observers of recent history have detected a drift, not towards reconciliation, but greater social and cultural division, not least within the metropolitan West. The comments of Shahid, the narrator of Hanif Kureishi's *The Black Album* (1995), typify this perception:

> He had noticed, during the days that he'd walked around the area, that the races were divided. The black kids stuck with each other, the Pakistanis went to one another's houses, the Bengalis knew each other from way back, and the whites too. Even if there was no hostility between groups – and there was plenty . . . there was little mixing. And would things change? Why should they? A few individuals would make the effort, but wasn't the world breaking up into political and religious tribes? The divisions were taken for granted, each to his own.[22]

This attests to the appeal of a second, essentialist, conception of identity which recurs in postcolonial culture and criticism. While perhaps more influential in previous periods, it still flourishes today, in contradiction of Bhabha's claim that it has ceased to have any real purchase on current debates. The kind of separatist vision which underlies Houston A. Baker's *Blues, Ideology, and African-American Literature: A Vernacular Theory* (1984) and which recurs in Clinton M. Jean's *Behind the Eurocentric Veils: The Search for African Realities* (1992) suggests that the line of criticism associated with the Chinweizu 'troika' (and a generation further back again, with some of the *négritudinists*), continues to have influential adherents. Traces of such 'reverse ethnocentric' particularism are evident in the work of even characteristically more ecumenically minded critics like Henry Louis Gates. In contrast to the generally synthesizing tendencies of his earlier critical texts like *Figures in Black* (1987) or *The Signifying Monkey* (1988), in his contribution to JanMohamed and Lloyd's *The Nature and Context of Minority Discourse* (1990), Gates argues that 'we must, at last, don the empowering mask of blackness and talk *that* talk, the language of black difference':

> As deconstruction and other post-structuralisms, or even an aracial Marxism and other 'articles of faith in Euro-Judaic thought,' exhaust themselves in a self-willed racial never-never land in which we see no true reflections of our black faces and hear no echoes of our black voices, let us – at long last – master the canon of critical traditions and languages of Africa and Afro-America.[23]

One certainly has to recognize the reasons for the continuing appeal of the discourses and politics of cultural nationalism. In the first place, cultural nationalism proved extremely effective in helping to end the era of formal colonialism. In situations where comparable forms of oppression are still being experienced, whether in the Western or non-Western worlds, it should come as no surprise that the discourse resurfaces. Thus it can hardly require explanation that the Black Arts Movement of the 1960s, for example, was by and large culturally nationalist in the face of such strong resistance, on the part of large swathes of mainstream American society, to the emergence of Black America into something like citizenship. (Equally, while the West rushes to condemn contemporary separatist figures like Louis Farrakhan, or the 'fundamentalism' of the Iranian clergy, it all too easily forgets its own responsibility for creating the contexts of extreme exploitation and discrimination which produce the anger and despair out of which such 'rejectionism' emerges.) Moreover, while capital may well be dispersed in the neo-colonial era, the centre still tends to operate politically through the medium of the nation state, or nation-state alliance. To this extent cultural nationalism can still play an effective part in resistance to the dominant global orders.

But the particularist approach runs several obvious dangers. Firstly, the 'centre' is likely to be left largely untroubled by oppositional movements which – in respecting (or deriding) each other's cultural differences – remain radically divided. Divide and rule was, after all, a key strategy in colonial management. This policy was, of course, premised on the supposedly irreconcilable Otherness of subordinate peoples, not just in respect of the dominant but of each other (as was made clear in the 'logic' of separate development in apartheid). The way that particularism can play into the hands of the dominant is also evident in the way that 'authenticity' has become such a commodity in the neo-colonial era, insofar as the Western consumer often demands (rather as Marlow unconsciously does in *Heart of Darkness*) that Third World culture, peoples and places be as 'original' and 'unspoiled' as possible, a discourse particularly apparent in the domain of tourism. The father of Shahid in Hanif Kureishi's *The Black Album*, a travel agent based in Kent, makes his living out of precisely this sort of neo-primitivist longing in his customers. The same sentimental but coercive demand for the authenticity of the Other is evident even in Shahid's supposedly 'alternative' and 'benevolent' friend, Strapper:

'I thought you loved the Asian people.'
  'Not when they get too fucking Westernized. You all wanna be just like us now. It's the wrong turnin'.'[24]

Moreover, one of the paradoxes of cultural nationalism is that it implicitly depends for its success on the continuing authority of the centre. As Derrida cautions, directly oppositional or confrontational modes of decentring the centre can simultaneously recentre it.[25] And, as

Shahid observes, there is even a danger that in certain instances the 'marginal' will become part of the 'centre'; in some circles of the neo-colonial metropolis, he comments, 'there's nothing more fashionable than outsiders'.[26]

Furthermore, the corollary of the particularist approach is to accept as inevitable – or even desirable – the fragmentation of the postcolonial or minoritarian terrain into a series of competing or even hostile social and cultural formations. There are similar implications in the particularist position for relations between these various fragments and other cultural, social and political groupings. If the differences between these different constituencies are, indeed, essentially grounded, there can be little possibility of combination with other groupings which organize on the basis of class, gender or religion, for example. In practice, the 'ideology of difference', as Said calls it, discounts the abundant evidence of continuity between the various postcolonial and minoritarian formations and their cultural/critical practices, of the kind that this book has attempted to foreground. For instance, H. L. Gates is, at times, led into making excessive claims on behalf of the distinctiveness of black poetics. Many of the features he identifies, such as 'signifying' and 'troping', have clear analogues in both feminist and postcolonial criticism and creative writing more broadly understood.[27]

Such factors have led some critics, from Fanon and Achebe to Spivak, to propose an 'intermediate' model of postcolonial identity which Spivak has conceptualised as 'strategic essentialism'. This has many advantages compared with some versions of both cultural nationalism and hybridity. In the first place, it allows a conception of essentialism as – at the very least – a stage which must be passed through in the process of cultural decolonization. As Terry Eagleton notes, in terms which have resonance with some of the arguments of the figures identified above: 'To wish class or nation away, to seek to live in sheer irreducible difference *now* . . . is to play straight into the hands of the oppressor':

> Sexual politics, like class or nationalist struggle, will thus necessarily be caught up in the very metaphysical categories it hopes finally to abolish; and any such movement will demand a difficult, perhaps ultimately impossible double optic, at once fighting on a terrain already mapped out by its antagonists and seeking even now to prefigure within that mundane strategy styles of being and identity for which we have as yet no proper names.[28]

Without such a strategic commitment to its own kind of 'master-narrative', paradoxically provisional as this may be, of the kind that the essentialist model can offer, emerging postcolonial cultural formations can easily face either co-option by the centre into a larger, official multi-culturalism, or an equally damaging dissipation into what Eagleton, like

Spivak, calls 'premature Utopianism'.[29] Some Western critics, too, have now begun to reassess cultural nationalism, and its modes of critical engagement, in a positive light, both as a corrective to some of the more sloppy versions of cultural pluralism and in terms of the advantages it offers for a coherent politics of resistance.[30]

Equally, 'strategic essentialism' seems to offer a way of conceptualizing the relations between postcolonial and other forms of social mobilization and cultural/critical production which avoids the dangers which are identifiable in some recent theorizations from outside the field of the possibility of solidarity between different kinds of 'margin'. Ernesto Laclau and Chantal Mouffe, for example, have argued that:

> The strengthening of specific democratic struggles requires, therefore, the expansion of chains of equivalence which extend to other struggles. The equiv-alential articulation between anti-racism, anti-sexism and anti-capitalism, for example, requires a ... logic of equivalence ... [which] taken to its ultimate consequences, would imply the dissolution of the autonomy of the spaces in which each one of the struggles is constituted; not necessarily because any of them have become subordinated to others, but because they have all become, strictly speaking, equivalent symbols of a unique and indivisible struggle.[31]

From a postcolonial perspective, there are uncomfortable echoes of colonial discourse in this proposal, insofar as at certain moments colonial discourse itself does not recognize the significant differences of the subject peoples, insisting instead that the 'natives are all the same', and, by implication, 'equivalential' or interchangeable. This vision has its analogue in the neo-colonial period in the discourse of 'cultural relativ-ism', which recognizes difference 'equally' but, again, only in relation to the assumed centrality of the dominant culture. Moreover, a sceptic might argue that such a model does not take sufficient account of what happens after the centre gets overthrown (if it does). The tensions within alliances of marginals which are based on this kind of paradigm usually derive from an insufficient recognition of internal differences at the outset. The consequences to which this can lead are all too evident in far too many decolonized countries, from Angola to Cambodia (admittedly the West usually plays its part by siding with one of the factions). This historical lesson more than any other must make one cautious about the efficacy of combining on the basis of common differences as has been proposed at different times by figures as diverse as Homi Bhabha, Stuart Hall and Chandra Talpade Mohanty.

In practice, the stress on the interchangeability of different marginal constituencies and cultural formations has often, in fact, led to the subordination of one of these 'allied' terms by another. The most striking example of this in the field under consideration, perhaps, is Ahmad's *In*

Theory, which seeks to sublate 'the postcolonial' within class-based forms of analysis. Perhaps the most important advantage of a recourse to Marxism, according to Ahmad, is that it can provide a more accurate and differentiated model of current political and cultural geographies, by challenging the 'Three Worlds' theory which makes nationalism the privileged form of political resistance to Western power in the modern era. Ahmad argues (like Spivak) that this discourse homogenizes states at different stages of development, with very different social, economic and cultural formations and varied modes of insertion in the international division of labour. Equally the 'Three Worlds' model clearly undervalues modes of resistance based on class, gender or religion, which may not exist in a coherent matrix of opposition with nationalism against the metropolis. Since most Third World states were – politically speaking – the creation of imperial powers, which characteristically installed regimes drawn from a compliant local bourgeoisie at the end of the era of formal imperialism, and given the development of a global economy dominated by multinationals, Ahmad argues cogently that nationalism can no longer be seen in any straightforward way as the privileged narrative of liberation movements. Instead he advances a 'One World' theory, in which the primary struggle is neither between West and East, or North and South, nor even between former metropolitan imperial powers and newly independent states, but between globally allied classes. Since capital now reproduces world-wide and the bourgeoisie is equally dispersed, so resistance to it must be global and organized principally round a transnational alliance of interest amongst the world's working classes.

This, however, merely displaces rather than solves the problem posed by Laclau and Mouffe's strategy. While Ahmad provides a substantial and powerful argument for the restoration of class as a means of understanding the cultural problematics of the contemporary neocolonial period, he achieves this at a considerable price. In making class the determining point of reference of his critique, arguably Ahmad in turn himself represses other kinds of difference – ethnic, religious, gender and cultural – which seem at least as deserving of attention as class-based forms of resistance. Equally, his insistence on a 'One World' paradigm of political economy itself tends to homogenize groups which are, as he himself acknowledges, in fact differentially inserted in the international division of labour. The industrial workers of Detroit are by no means identical in terms of class identity even with those of Gdansk or Seoul, let alone with the subsistence peasantry of Zimbabwe, the homeless unemployed of Calcutta, or the hunter-gatherers of the Brazilian rainforest – unless the term 'class' is so stretched as to become almost meaningless. Indeed, the interests – political and economic – of such groups may be in competition or conflict with each other. While many of these conflicts are caused, or exacerbated, by the international division of labour, others are quite clearly not. The caste system in India predates and survives the period of British domination, as does a phenomenon like the oppression of the Khoi people by the majority Tswana in Botswana.

Similar problems attend Lisa Lowe's implication that 'the postcolonial' might be profitably subsumed within a feminist politics and associated modes of cultural analysis. At the end of her excellent study of colonial discourse in *Critical Terrains*, she asserts that 'feminist theory is the least restrictive, and perhaps the most capable – among other paradigms of analysis . . . of accounting for and theorizing heterogeneity'.[32] This, once again, simply displaces the essential problem. Chapter 3 explored in some detail Spivak's conviction of the difficulties of building alliances between Western and Third World women, problems which have showed no sign of abating. Thus Laura Donaldson's 'The Miranda Complex: Colonialism and the Question of Feminist Reading' (1988) blames Caliban for contributing to Miranda's disadvantages under patriarchy in *The Tempest* in a way which implicitly valorizes the importance of (attention to) Western woman's oppression over that of the colonized subject.[33] One of the most celebrated recent white feminist critics, Donna Haraway, once more reveals the difficulty of establishing common cause on an 'equivalential' basis with her postcolonial peers. In *Simians, Cyborgs and Women* (1991), she attempts to 'resolve' an argument between the Nigerian critic Chikwenye Ogunyemi and Barbara Christian, the Caribbean critic working in the United States, over the meanings of the model of black femininity provided in Buchi Emecheta's fiction in a way which inescapably reminds one of the problematic 'benevolence' of earlier phases of feminism.[34] (Neo-) colonial history has for so long played its part in the development of Western feminism (from its exploitation of the rhetoric of the abolition movement to facilitate its own emergence in the modern period, through the material contribution of the Bombay-based aunt to the achievement of the 'room of one's own' advocated by Virginia Woolf as one feminist goal, and on to Kristeva's 'appropriation' of Chinese women to constitute contemporary Western feminism), that Lowe's strategy can only be a hazardous one to pursue.[35] As Bronwen Levy has commented in respect of the more limited arena of the women's movement within the West:

> the varying circumstances of women from different backgrounds may thus make the forming of alliances, of a community of women, unlikely or even imposible (even if French theorists like Cixous or Julia Kristeva have suggested, each in their own way, that the women's struggle can be a model for other struggles also).[36]

This eloquently suggests the difficulties of broadening such attempted alliances to include the postcolonial field.

In each of these cases, the postcolonial is made – explicitly in Ahmad's case, implicitly in Lowe's – subordinate to discourses or social formations which have played their part in certain instances, and in different measures, in the oppressions of the postcolonial subject. The reverse is also true, as a consideration of the secondary and often subordinate role of women in liberation struggles and nationalist discourse (like Fanon's, for instance) indicates. (As has been suggested, class differentials have also been too little considered in the postcolonial arena.) 'Strategic essentialism' offers a way of avoiding the danger that different kinds, and histories, of oppression may be collapsed together artificially by discounting the importance or legitimacy of specific case histories. At the same time it offers the possibility of alliances in a 'war of position' in a way that cultural particularism is reluctant to do. Nonetheless, there must be some doubts about the political effectiveness of doctrines of 'strategic essentialism'. The problem with the kind of voluntaristic position-taking that this involves, is that it has historically proved singularly ineffective, as attempts to build rainbow coalitions in Britain and the United States since the 1960s have demonstrated. In Britain, for example, such a politics has been on the agenda at least since *The May Day Manifesto* of 1968; yet other than in the realm of single issues, it has only very modestly disturbed the traditional configurations of British politics and the power bases to which they correspond, as almost a generation of unbroken Tory rule suggests. What is sometimes over-looked by the advocates of the 'the war of position' is that the multiple identities and alliances which such a strategy allows also offer the dominant a greater range of targets. As is obvious, discrimination operates across a whole range of domains, from class and gender to sexuality, ethnic identity, age and so on. This suggests that the dominant order can respond in the same flexible patterns as those who seek to evade it by their own multiple positionings.

I am painfully aware that by entering this complex debate, I am in danger of writing a text which, by proposing a choice between, or synthesis of, these different paradigms of postcolonial cultural identity and positioning, and their respective conceptions of the relationship between different formations within the field on the one hand, and other forms of cultural mobilization on the other, might be satirically described, after the title of the District Officer's text in Achebe's *Things Fall Apart*, as *The Pacification of the Warring Tribes of the Postcolonial*. It is certainly not for me as a white, male, middle-class, erstwhile colonial child to decide what is and is not a 'properly' postcolonial conception of identity or positioning, (nor to adjudicate on the narrower issue of the most appropriate methods of cultural analysis for the field). But in any case it seems to me that a choice between the predominant paradigms, or an attempted synthesis of them, is perhaps equally unnecessary if one applies an historical and differential perspective to the question of the heterogeneity of 'the postcolonial'. This provides the salutary reminder that postcolonial societies, cultural formations and movements emerge at different times, in different forms and in different places around the globe. Because colonialism has taken many forms and has many histories, and is accompanied by a plethora of at times internally and mutually contradictory discourses, decolonization has been similarly multiform and complex – and its discourses may therefore at times be incommensurable with each other – as well as complementary. As Brathwaite argues in *Contradictory Omens*, the forms – and pace – of creolization vary from island to island in the Caribbean because no two islands have identical histories. It seems perfectly legitimate for one postcolonial formation to be insisting first and foremost on the principle of cultural difference while an adjacent or related formation, with somewhat different historical experiences, may at the same moment be espousing the virtues of cultural hybridity, in conformity with the particular circumstances of its own development. As such circumstances change, moreover, the same culture (or sub-cultures within it) may move from one emphasis to the other (and back again, if necessary, as has happened in many decolonized countries around the world). Because postcolonial histories, and their presents, are so varied, no one definition of the 'postcolonial' can claim to be correct at the expense of all others, and consequently a variety of interrelated models of identity, positionality and cultural/critical practice are both possible and necessary. For this reason, more than any other, I will conclude by strongly endorsing – and generalizing it to apply to the engagement of the whole postcolonial field with the cultural legacy of imperialism – the position espoused by Ranajit Guha in the debate over what is, or is not, an appropriate or 'proper' mode of analysis of the colonial history of India: 'There is no one way of investigating this problematic. Let a hundred flowers blossom and we don't mind even the weeds.'[37]

Notes

PREFACE

1. Robert Young, *White Mythologies: Writing History and the West* (London: Routledge, 1990), p. 175.

2. Derek Walcott, 'Caligula's Horse' in Stephen Slemon and Helen Tiffin eds., *After Europe: Critical Theory and Post-Colonial Writing* (Mundelstrup: Dangaroo, 1989), p. 141.

3. Barbara Christian, 'The Race for Theory' in Abdul R. JanMohamed and David Lloyd eds., *The Nature and Context of Minority Discourse* (New York: Oxford University Press, 1990), p. 38. As will be seen in chapter 5, a case has been made for seeing a lot of 'primary' postcolonial culture as implicitly theoretical.

4. For more on this topic, see Cedric Robinson, *Black Marxism: The Making of a Radical Tradition* (London: Zed, 1983).

5. See Jacques Derrida, *Of Grammatology*, trans. Gayatri Spivak (1967; Baltimore: Johns Hopkins University Press, 1976), p. 24.

1: POSTCOLONIAL CRITICISM OR POSTCOLONIAL THEORY?

1. On the history of the term, see Vijay Mishra and Bob Hodge, 'What is Post(-) Colonialism?', *Textual Practice*, 5.3, 1991, pp. 399–414; compare Aijaz Ahmad, 'The Politics of Literary Postcoloniality', *Race and Class*, 36.3, 1995, pp. 1–20.

2. See, for example, Martin J. Evans, *Milton's Imperial Epic: 'Paradise Lost' and the Discourse of Colonialism* (Ithaca: Cornell University Press, 1996); Laura Brown, *Alexander Pope* (Oxford: Basil Blackwell, 1985); Edward Said, 'Jane Austen and Empire' in *Culture and Imperialism* (London: Chatto & Windus, 1993), pp. 95–116; Moira Ferguson, 'Mansfield Park: Slavery, Colonialism and Gender', *Oxford Literary Review*, 13, 1991, pp. 118–39; Gayatri Spivak, 'Three Women's Texts and a Critique of Imperialism' in Henry Louis Gates jr. ed., *'Race', Writing and Difference* (Chicago: University of Chicago Press, 1986), pp. 262–80.

3. See, for example, Stephen Greenblatt, *Marvelous Possessions: The Wonder of the New World* (New York and Oxford: Clarendon Press, 1991); Ania Loomba, *Gender, Race, Renaissance Drama* (Manchester: Manchester University Press, 1989); Margo Hendricks and Patricia Parker eds., *Women, 'Race' and Writing in the Early Modern Period* (London: Routledge, 1994); Peter Hulme, *Colonial Encounters: Europe and the Native Caribbean 1492–1797* (London: Methuen, 1986); Emily C. Bartels, *Spectacles of Strange-*

ness: Imperialism, Alienation, and Marlow (Philadelphia: University of Pennsylvania Press, 1993); Kim F. Hall, *Things of Darkness: Economies of Race and Gender in Early Modern England* (London: Cornell University Press, 1996).

4. See, for example, John Barrell, *The Infection of Thomas de Quincey: A Psychopathology of Imperialism* (New Haven: Yale University Press, 1991); Javed Majeed, *Ungoverned Imaginings: James Mill's 'History of British India' and Orientalism* (Oxford: Clarendon Press, 1992); Nigel Leask, *British Romantic Writers and the East: Anxieties of Empire* (Cambridge: Cambridge University Press, 1993).

5. Cited in Patrick Brantlinger, *Rule of Darkness: British Literature and Imperialism 1830–1914* (Ithaca: Cornell University Press, 1988), p. 3.

6. See, for example, Brantlinger, *Rule of Darkness*; Said, *Culture and Imperialism*, *passim*; Jonathon Arac and Harriet Ritvo eds., *Macropolitics of Nineteenth Century Literature: Nationalism, Exoticism, Imperialism* (Philadelphia: University of Pennsylvania Press, 1991); Deborah Thomas, *Thackeray and Slavery* (Athens: Ohio University Press, 1993); Spivak, 'Three Women's Texts and a Critique of Imperialism'; Firdous Azim, *The Colonial Rise of the Novel* (London: Routledge, 1993); Katherine Bailey Lineham, 'Mixed Politics: the Critique of Imperialism in *Daniel Deronda*', *Texas Studies in Literature and Language*, 34.3, Fall 1992, pp. 322–46; Daniel Bivona, *Desire and Contradiction: Imperial Visions and Domestic Debates in Victorian Literature* (Manchester: Manchester University Press, 1990); Susan Meyer, *Imperialism at Home: Race and Victorian Women's Fiction* (London: Cornell University Press, 1996); V. G. Kiernan, 'Tennyson, King Arthur and Imperialism' in V. G. Kiernan, *Poets, Politics, and the People* (London: Verso, 1989), pp. 129–51.

7. See, for example, David Trotter, 'Modernism and Empire: Reading *The Waste Land*', *Critical Quarterly*, 28.1–2, 1986, pp. 143–5; Terry Eagleton, Fredric Jameson and Edward Said, *Nationalism, Colonialism, and Literature* (Minneapolis: University of Minnesota Press, 1990); Jane Marcus, 'Britannia rules *The Waves*' in Karen Lawrence ed., *Decolonizing Tradition: New Views of Twentieth Century 'British' Literary Canons* (Urbana: University of Illinois Press, 1992), pp. 136–61; Zhaoming Qian, *Orientalism and Modernism: The Legacy of China in Pound and Williams* (Durham: Duke University Press, 1995); Vincent Cheng, *Joyce, Race and Empire* (Cambridge: Cambridge University Press, 1995); Kathy J. Phillips, *Virginia Woolf Against Empire* (Knoxville: Tennessee University Press, 1996).

8. See, for example, Dennis Porter, *Haunted Journeys: Desire and Transgression in European Travel Writing* (Princeton: Princeton University Press, 1991); Billie Melman, *Women's Orients: English Women and the Middle East, 1718–1918: Sexuality, Religion and Work* (London: Macmillan, 1992); Mary Louise Pratt, *Imperial Eyes: Travel Writing and Transculturation* (London: Routledge, 1992); Sara Mills, *Discourses of Difference: An Analysis of Women's Travel Writing and Colonialism* (London: Routledge, 1993); David Spurr, *The Rhetoric of Empire: Colonial Discourse in Journalism, Travel Writing and Imperial Administration* (Durham: Duke University Press, 1993).

9. Edward Said, *Orientalism* (1978; reprinted London: Penguin, 1991), p. 13.

10. Ahmad, 'The Politics of Literary Postcoloniality', pp. 5–7.

11. Bill Ashcroft, Gareth Griffiths and Helen Tiffin, *The Empire Writes Back: Theory and Practice in Post-Colonial Literatures* (London: Routledge, 1989), p. 2.

12. See, respectively, Lata Mani, 'The Production of an Official Discourse on *Sati* in Early Nineteenth-Century Bengal' in Francis Barker, Peter Hulme, Margaret Iverson and Diana Loxley eds., *Europe and Its Others* vol. 1 (Colchester: University of Essex, 1985), pp. 107–27; Gayatri Spivak, 'The Rani of Sirmur' in Barker *et al.*, *Europe and Its Others* vol. 1, pp. 128–51; Edward Said, 'Representing the Colonized: Anthropology's Interlocutors', *Critical Inquiry*, 15.2, 1989, pp. 205–25; James Clifford, *The Predicament of Culture: Twentieth-Century Ethnography, Literature and Art* (Cambridge, Mass.: Harvard

University Press, 1988); Majeed, *Ungoverned Imaginings*; Partha Chatterjee, *The Nation and Its Fragments: Colonial and Post-Colonial Histories* (Princeton: Princeton University Press, 1993); Aijaz Ahmad, *In Theory: Classes, Nations, Literatures* (London: Verso, 1992); Aimé Césaire, *Discourse on Colonialism* trans. Joan Pinkham (1955; New York: Monthly Review Press, 1972); Léopold Senghor, *Ce que je crois: Négritude, francité et civilisation de l'universel* (Paris: Grasset, 1988); V. Y. Mudimbe, *The Invention of Africa: Gnosis, Philosophy and the Order of Knowledge* (London: James Currey, 1988); Ranajit Guha and Gayatri Spivak eds., *Selected Subaltern Studies* (Oxford: Oxford University Press, 1988); Young, *White Mythologies*; Rana Kabbani, *Europe's Myths of Orient: Devise and Rule* (London: Macmillan, 1986); Linda Nochlin, *The Politics of Vision: Essays on Nineteenth-Century Art and Society* (1989; London: Thames & Hudson, 1991); Griselda Pollock, *Avant-Garde Gambits 1888–1893: Gender and the Colour of Art Theory* (London: Thames & Hudson, 1993); Partha Mitter, *Art and Nationalism in Colonial India 1850–1922: Occidental Orientations* (Cambridge: Cambridge University Press, 1994); Reina Lewis, *Gendering Orientalism: Race, Femininity and Representation* (London: Routledge, 1995); Frantz Fanon, *Black Skin, White Masks* trans. C. L. Markmann (1952; London: Pluto, 1986); Wole Soyinka, *Myth, Literature and the African World* (Cambridge: Cambridge University Press, 1976); Anne McClintock, 'The Return of Female Fetishism and the Fiction of the Phallus', *New Formations*, 19, Spring 1993, pp. 1–22.

13. See, for example, David Cairns and Shaun Richards, *Writing Ireland: Colonialism, Nationalism and Culture* (Manchester: Manchester University Press); David Lloyd, *Anomalous States: Irish Writing and the Post-colonial Moment* (Dublin: Lilliput, 1993); Declan Kiberd, *Inventing Ireland: The Literature of the Modern Nation* (London: Cape, 1996). Much of the Derry Field Day group's work can also be considered in the same light. There is, however, considerable controversy over the use of postcolonial perspectives in the study of Irish culture. See the *Irish Studies Review*, 15 and 16, 1996, for more on this debate. In focusing so much on 'mainstream' metropolitan culture, I would not want it to be thought that I am forgetting about the valuable archaeologies of migrant cultural production in the metropolis which have been produced by figures as diverse as Henry Louis Gates and John Blassinghame in the USA, or Paul Edwards, David Dabydeen, Prabhu Guptara and Lauretta Ngcobo in Britain. As a result of their work much more is now known about the place of non-Western writers in metropolitan cultural history and much valuable material has been republished. Since it is not, however, part of the controversies under discussion, I will not be dealing with it.

14. The paradigm shift within 'Commonwealth' literary studies has been described in the following terms: '[The] Commonwealth project of the Sixties and Seventies has become the terrain of post-colonial criticism, a practice which foregrounds the tension between the imperial centre and colonial space in a way that Commonwealth criticism did not.' See Gillian Whitlock, 'Exiles from Tradition: Women's Life Writing' in Gillian Whitlock and Helen Tiffin eds., *Re-Siting Queen's English: Text and Tradition in Post-Colonial Literatures: Essays Presented to John Pengwerne Matthews* (Amsterdam: Rodopi, 1992), p. 11. Contemporary critics like the Canadian Stephen Slemon use 'Commonwealth' and 'post(-)colonial' pretty much interchangeably. See Slemon and Tiffin, *After Europe*, p. 113. Some distinguished non-western critics like Wilson Harris continue to honour the term. See Alan Riach and Mark Williams eds., *The Radical Imagination: Lectures and Talks by Wilson Harris* (Liège: Département d'Anglais, Université de Liège, 1992), p. 127.

15. Pratt, *Imperial Eyes*, p. 1.

16. R. D. Mathews, 'The Canadian Problem' in John Press ed., *Commonwealth Literature: Unity and Diversity in a Common Culture* (London: Heinemann, 1965), pp. 157–67. This is not to discount the difficulties which are involved in claiming the culture of the old 'white Dominions', or their current predicament, as postcolonial. One

problem with the attacks made on the supposedly hegemonic status of postcolonial theory in some modern variants of Commonwealth literary criticism is the often unquestioning assumption that places like Canada are not also part of the dominant formation in the current neo-colonial dispensation. While some such critics blithely compare West Indian literatures with their own, what is rarely mentioned in such analyses is the hegemonic role (both historically and in the contemporary period) which nations like Canada have played in regions such as the Caribbean (let alone in the context of their own indigenous populations), a history of sometimes direct oppression which is amply documented in texts like B. D. Tennyson's *Canada and the Commonwealth Caribbean* (Lanham, Maryland: University Press of America, 1988). Thus when Diana Brydon, for example, demands that if 'contemporary "mainstream" critics [she is referring to those dealing with postcolonial problematics who are influenced by "high" theory] are truly interested in post-colonial literatures and perspectives, they will come to us', one must ask in what ways critics in Canadian universities are not also 'mainstream' and who exactly the 'us' refers to. See Diana Brydon, 'New Approaches to the New Literatures in English' in Hena Maes-Jelinek, Kirsten Holst Petersen and Anna Rutherford eds., *A Shaping of Connections: Commonwealth Literature Studies – Then and Now: Essays in Honour of A. N. Jeffares* (Mundelstrup: Dangaroo, 1989), p. 95.

17. Some indication of the current contestation over the definition and application of the term 'post(-)colonial' is given by Anne McClintock in 'The Angel of Progress: Pitfalls of the Term "Post-Colonialism"', *Social Text*, 31/32, Spring 1992, pp. 1–15; compare Ella Shohat, 'Notes on the "Post-Colonial"' in the same issue, pp. 99–113; Misao Miyoshi, 'A Borderless World? From Colonialism to Transnationalism and the Decline of the Nation State', *Critical Inquiry*, 19, Summer 1993, pp. 726–50; Stephen Slemon, 'The Scramble for Post-Colonialism' in Chris Tiffin and Alan Lawson eds., *De-Scribing Empire: Post-Colonialism and Textuality* (London: Routledge, 1994), pp. 15–32; Arif Dirlik, 'The Postcolonial Aura: Third World Criticism in the Age of Global Capitalism', *Critical Inquiry*, 20, Winter 1994, pp. 329–56; and Deepika Bahri, 'Once More with Feeling: What is Postcolonialism?', *Ariel*, 26.1, January 1995, pp. 51–82. Much of the discussion in these articles centres on the political implications of the term 'postcolonial'. Stuart Hall conveniently reviews much of this material in 'When was "the Post-colonial"? Thinking at the Limit' in Iain Chambers and Lidia Curti eds., *The Post-Colonial Question: Common Skies, Divided Horizons* (London: Routledge, 1996), pp. 242–60.

18. Henry Louis Gates jr., 'African American Criticism' in Stephen Greenblatt and Giles Gunn eds., *Redrawing the Boundaries: The Transformation of English and American Literary Studies* (New York: MLA, 1992), p. 315.

19. Bahri, 'Once More with Feeling', p. 56.

20. Peter Conrad, 'Empires of the Senseless', *Observer*, 7 February 1993, p. 55. The traditionalists have remained powerful enough to stymie many of the initiatives of postcolonial criticism abroad as well. For a gloomy assessment of the situation in Australia, see Helen Tiffin, '"Lie Back and Think of England": Post-Colonial Literature and the Academy', in Maes-Jelinek *et al.*, *A Shaping of Connections*, pp. 116–26. For the situation in the Indian sub-continent, see Sunti Joshi ed., *Re-Thinking English: Culture, Literature, Pedagogy* (New Delhi: Trianka, 1991); Zakia Pathak, Sawati Sengupta and Sharmila Purkayastha, 'The Prisonhouse of Orientalism', *Textual Practice*, 5.2, Summer 1991, pp. 195–218; R. S. Rajan ed., *The Lie of the Land: English Literary Studies in India* (Delhi: Oxford University Press, 1992); Ahmad, *In Theory*; Azim, *The Colonial Rise of the Novel*.

21. Sara Danius and Stefan Jonsson, 'An Interview with Gayatri Chakravorty Spivak', *boundary 2*, 20.2, 1993, p. 40. See Hilton Kramer, 'Notes and Comments', *The New Criterion*, 9.7, March 1991, pp. 1–2.

22. *Times Literary Supplement*, 9 April 1993, p. 15. Compare the occasionally

scathing comments about postcolonial theory in the work of another anthropologist, T. M. Luhrmann, in *The Good Parsi: The Fate of a Colonial Elite in a Postcolonial Society* (London: Harvard University Press). See p. 187, for example.

23. Russell Jacoby, 'Marginal Returns: The Trouble with Post-Colonial Theory', *Lingua Franca*, September/October 1995, p. 32. Stuart Hall, by comparison, locates the current stasis, as he sees it, in postcolonial analysis, in a failure on the part of literary critics, who he thinks of as the chief exponents of 'the postcolonial', to be sufficiently ambitious in terms of their interdisciplinary interests. See 'When Was "the Post-colonial"?', p. 258.

24. John MacKenzie, *Orientalism: History, Theory and the Arts* (Manchester: Manchester University Press, 1995), p. 36.

25. Given his powerful attempt to incorporate this kind of cultural analysis within a Marxist framework, it is unsurprising that Ahmad strongly objects to being described as a postcolonial critic. See Ahmad, 'The Politics of Literary Postcoloniality', p. 10. However, his interests are consistent with those of postcolonial criticism as defined in this introduction, and elsewhere he describes himself as occupying the same critical field as Said. See Ahmad, '*Orientalism* and After: Ambivalence and Metropolitan Location in the Work of Edward Said', *In Theory*, p. 159.

26. ibid., p. 174; compare Benita Parry, 'Problems in Current Theories of Colonial Discourse', *Oxford Literary Review*, 9.1–2, 1987, pp. 27 and 34.

27. Edward Said, 'Orientalism Reconsidered' in Barker *et al.*, *Europe and Its Others* vol. 1, p. 17.

28. Homi Bhabha, 'Representation and the Colonial Text' in Frank Gloversmith ed., *The Theory of Reading* (Brighton: Harvester, 1984), p. 95; Bhabha, 'Signs Taken for Wonders: Questions of Ambivalence and Authority Under a Tree Outside Delhi, May 1817', *The Location of Culture* (London: Routledge, 1994), p. 105.

29. Gayatri Chakravorty Spivak, 'Criticism, Feminism and the Institution', 'Post-marked Calcutta, India', 'The *Intervention* Interview', *The Post-Colonial Critic: Interviews, Strategies, Dialogues*, ed. Sarah Harasym (London: Routledge, 1990), pp. 15–16, 79, 126–9.

30. Patrick Williams and Laura Chrisman eds., *Colonial Discourse and Postcolonial Theory: A Reader* (Hemel Hempstead: Harvester Wheatsheaf, 1993), p. 5.

31. Young, *White Mythologies*, p. 175.

32. For analysis of Barthes' complicity in the perspectives of colonial discourse, see Wole Soyinka, 'The Critic and Society: Barthes, Leftocracy and Other Mythologies' in Henry Louis Gates jr. ed., *Black Literature and Literary Theory* (London: Methuen, 1984), pp. 27–57; compare Lisa Lowe, *Critical Terrains: French and British Orientalisms* (Ithaca: Cornell University Press, 1991), chapter 5; and chapter 4 of my own text.

33. Bryan Cheyette, 'Struggle as a Campus Commodity', *The Times Higher*, 29 January, 1993, p. 22.

34. Ahmad, 'Introduction: Literature Among the Signs of Our Times', *In Theory*, p. 7.

35. Compare Dirlik, 'The Postcolonial Aura', pp. 354ff.; and Shohat, 'Notes on the "Post-Colonial"', pp. 99ff.

36. *In Theory* makes an eloquent case against the use of this term. See pp. 99–110 especially. However, alternative terms are also plagued with problems and I will follow the precedent of a number of critics who have decided to stick with 'Third World', like Chandra Talpade Mohanty in Chandra Talpade Mohanty, Ann Russo and Lourdes Torres eds., *Third World Women and the Politics of Feminism* (Bloomington: Indiana University Press, 1991), p. ix; compare Amin Malak in 'From Margin to Main: Minority Discourse and "Third World" Fiction Writers in Canada' in Anna Rutherford ed., *From Commonwealth to Post-Colonial* (Mundelstrup: Dangaroo, 1992), p. 44. Shohat argues that the term still has heuristic value ('Notes on the "post-Colonial"', p. 111), a stance

endorsed by Spivak in 'Subaltern Talk: Interview with the Editors', in Donna Landry and Gerald MacLean eds, *The Spivak Reader*, (London: Routledge, 1996), p. 295. By comparison, she finds the term 'postcolonial' to be 'totally bogus'. See 'Neocolonialism and the Secret Agent of Knowledge', *Oxford Literary Review*, 13.1–2, 1991, p. 224. (This does not, of course, prevent her from using it widely, even in the title of one of her books.)

37. Ahmad, 'Languages of Class, Ideologies of Immigration', *In Theory*, p. 94.

38. ibid., p. 211.

39. Stephen Slemon and Helen Tiffin, 'Introduction' to Slemon and Tiffin eds., *After Europe*, p. xviii; compare Parry, 'Problems in Current Theories' *passim*.

40. Ahmad, 'Languages of Class', *In Theory*, p. 76. G. N. Devi complained in 1989 in much the same terms of the excessive attention being paid to the Indian literatures in English. See 'The Commonwealth Literature Period: A Note Towards the History of Indian English Literature' in Maes-Jelinek *et al.*, *A Shaping of Connections*, p. 60.

41. Diana Brydon, 'New Approaches to the New Literatures in English' in Maes-Jelinek *et al.*, *A Shaping of Connections*, p. 93.

42. Diana Brydon, 'Commonwealth or Common Poverty?' in Slemon and Tiffin, *After Europe*, p. 12.

43. Ahmad, 'Salman Rushdie's *Shame*: Postmodern Migrancy and the Representation of Women', *In Theory*, p. 142.

44. 'Introduction', ibid., p. 3.

45. '*Orientalism* and After', ibid., p. 178.

46. Slemon and Tiffin, 'Introduction' to *After Europe*, p. xi.

47. Helen Tiffin, 'Transformative Imageries' in Rutherford, *From Commonwealth to Post-Colonial*, pp. 429–30.

48. Ahmad, 'Introduction', *In Theory*, p. 38.

49. ibid., p. 69. Compare Dirlik on Homi Bhabha, 'The Postcolonial Aura', p. 333; and on Spivak, Tzvetan Todorov, '"Race", Writing and Culture' in Gates, '*Race*', *Writing and Difference*, p. 377.

50. Graham Huggan, 'Opting Out of the (Critical) Common Market: Creolization and the Post-Colonial Text' in Slemon and Tiffin, *After Europe*, p. 38.

51. Ketu Katrak, 'Decolonizing Culture: Towards a Theory for Postcolonial Women's Texts', *Modern Fiction Studies*, 35.1, Spring 1989, p. 158.

52. Abdul JanMohamed, 'The Economy of Manichean Allegory: The Function of Racial Difference in Colonialist Literature', in Gates, '*Race*', *Writing and Difference*, p. 78.

53. Benita Parry, 'The Contents and Discontents of Kipling's Imperialism', *New Formations*, 6, Winter 1988, p. 51.

54. Compare Lisa Lowe's analysis of the tradition of Anglo-American Forster criticism in the period from 1945 to the 1970s, in *Critical Terrains*, chapter 4.

55. Alan Sandison, *The Wheel of Empire: A Study of the Imperial Idea in Some Late Nineteenth and Early Twentieth-Century Fiction* (London: Macmillan, 1967), p. 100.

56. Bonamy Dobree, 'Rudyard Kipling' in Elliot L. Gilbert ed., *Kipling and the Critics* (London: Peter Owen, 1965), pp. 51 and 43.

57. Gilbert, 'Introduction' to *Kipling and the Critics*, p. vi.

58. Robert Buchanan, 'The Voice of the Hooligan' in R. L. Green ed., *Kipling: The Critical Heritage* (London: Routledge, 1971), p. 241. As this volume suggests, early Kipling criticism often focused explicitly on Kipling's politics. Liberal critics, such as Robert Buchanan, deplored them, while nationalists like Walter Beasant or George Saintsbury lauded them.

59. J. M. S. Tompkins, *The Art of Rudyard Kipling* (London: Methuen, 1959), p. 8.

60. Rudyard Kipling, 'On the City Wall', *The Man Who Would Be King and Other Tales*, ed. Louis Cornell (Oxford: Oxford University Press, 1987), p. 203.

61. ibid., p. 238.

62. Rudyard Kipling, *Something of Myself: For My Friends Known and Unknown* (1937; reprinted Harmondsworth: Penguin, 1977), p. 38.

63. For a more detailed reading of Kipling's treatment of colonial violence, see my 'The Bhabhal of Tongues: Reading Kipling, Reading Bhabha' in Bart Moore-Gilbert ed., *Writing India 1757–1990: British Representations of India* (Manchester: Manchester University Press, 1996), pp. 111–38.

64. Martin Green, *Dreams of Adventure, Deeds of Empire* (London: Routledge, 1980), p. 340.

65. ibid., p. 24.

66. ibid., p. xii.

67. ibid., p. xiii. All of this makes Said's approval of Green in 'Consolidated Vision', *Culture and Imperialism*, rather puzzling. See pp. 71 and 76.

68. Salman Rushdie, 'Outside the Whale', *Imaginary Homelands: Essays and Criticism 1981–1991* (London: Granta, 1991), p. 87. For a better example of 'Raj revivalism' in this period than Rushdie's ill-judged (indeed Oedipal) attack on Paul Scott, see Anthony Burgess's foreword to a new edition of H. Yule and A. C. Burnell's *Hobson-Jobson: A Glossary of Colloquial Anglo-Indian Words and Phrases* (1886; reprinted London: Routledge, 1985).

69. For a critique of some of the problems associated with post-Saidian methods of colonial discourse analysis see my 'Writing India, Re-Orienting Colonial Discourse Analysis' in Moore-Gilbert, *Writing India*, pp. 1–29, and chapter 2 of this text.

70. 'Foreword' to Press, *Commonwealth Literature*, p. ix. While *Commonwealth Literature* was the first book in Britain to describe the field, it was anticipated by the US-based Australian critic A. L. McLeod's *The Commonwealth Pen: An Introduction to the Literature of the British Commonwealth* (Ithaca: Cornell University Press, 1961). McLeod provides a useful pre-history of the field in 'Commonwealth Studies in the United States' in Maes-Jelinek et al., *A Shaping of Connections*, pp. 8–13.

71. Press, *Commonwealth Literature*, p. v.

72. Norman Jeffares, 'Introduction' to Press, *Commonwealth Literature*, p. xvii.

73. ibid., p. xii.

74. B. Argyle, 'Problems in Studying Nineteenth-Century Australian Fiction', in Press, *Commonwealth Literature*, p. 61.

75. Jeffares, 'Introduction' to Press, *Commonwealth Literature*, p. xiv.

76. ibid., p. xvi.

77. Norman Jeffares, 'Introduction' to K. L. Goodwin ed., *National Identity: Papers Delivered at the Commonwealth Literature Conference, University of Queensland, Brisbane, 9–15 August, 1968* (London: Heinemann, 1970), p. xv.

78. William Walsh, *Commonwealth Literature* (London: Oxford University Press, 1973), p. 36.

79. S. Nagarajan, 'The Study of English Literature in India' in Press, *Commonwealth Literature*, p. 125.

80. D. E. S. Maxwell, 'Landscape and Theme' in Press, *Commonwealth Literature*, p. 82.

81. Helen Tiffin, 'Commonwealth Literature: Comparison and Judgement' in Dieter Riemenschneider ed., *The History and Historiography of Commonwealth Literature* (Tübingen: Gunter Narr Verlag, 1983), p. 23.

82. Hena Maes-Jelinek ed., *Commonwealth Literature and the Modern World* (Brussels: Didier, 1975), p. 7.

83. Tiffin, 'Commonwealth Literature' in Riemenschneider, *History and Historiography of Commonwealth Literature*, p. 19.

84. In *Colonial Discourse and Post-Colonial Theory*, for example, Williams and Chrisman deny the legitimacy of seeing the culture of the former white Dominions as

postcolonial (p. 4). See *The Post-Colonial Critic*, *passim*, for evidence of Spivak's ambivalence on this score.

85. Ahmad, 'Orientalism and After', *In Theory*, p. 211.

86. Brydon, 'Commonwealth or Common Poverty?' in Slemon and Tiffin, *After Europe*, p. 1. Compare her comments in this essay on H. L. Gates jr.'s attack on 'Commonwealth' literary studies, which she sees as articulated in terms as vague as Bhabha's.

87. Edward Said, 'Figures, Configurations, Transfigurations' in Rutherford, *From Commonwealth to Post-Colonial*, p. 16. Compare Ahmad's scathing comments on Said's accommodation with 'Commonwealth' literary studies in 'Orientalism and After', *In Theory*, pp. 211–13.

2   EDWARD SAID: *ORIENTALISM* AND BEYOND

1. Said, 'Orientalism Reconsidered', p. 15.

2. Young, *White Mythologies*, p. 126.

3. Joseph Bristow, *Empire Boys: Adventures in a Man's World* (London: Routledge), p. 3.

4. Bhabha, 'Postcolonial Criticism' in Greenblatt and Gunn, *Redrawing the Boundaries*, p. 465; Gayatri Chakravorty Spivak, 'Marginality in the Teaching Machine', *Outside in the Teaching Machine* (London: Routledge, 1993), p. 56.

5. Said, 'Orientalism Reconsidered', p. 22.

6. Ahmad uses other aspects of Said's arguments against him. It is Said and not Ahmad who first links the success of post-structuralism in the Western academy to the ascendancy of the New Right under Reagan and who complains of the Western academy's domestication of the material struggles of oppressed peoples as 'theory'. See Said's 'Secular Criticism', *The World, the Text, and the Critic* (1983; London: Vintage, 1991), p. 4, and the interview with Said in Imre Salusinszky's *Criticism in Society* (London: Methuen, 1987), p. 4, on the former point; and Said, 'Traveling Theory', *The World, the Text, and the Critic*, pp. 226–47, on the second.

7. Said, *Orientalism*, p. 5.

8. Michel Foucault, *The History of Sexuality* vol. 1, trans. Robert Hurley (1976; Harmondsworth: Penguin, 1981), p. 10.

9. ibid., p. 12.

10. Michel Foucault, *Discipline and Punish: The Birth of the Prison* trans. Alan Sheridan (1975; Harmondsworth: Peregrine, 1979, p. 194.

11. Said, *Orientalism*, p. 23; compare Michel Foucault, *Language, Counter-Memory, Practice* ed. and trans. Donald Bouchard (Ithaca: Cornell University Press, 1977), pp. 137–42.

12. Antonio Gramsci, *Selections from the Prison Notebooks of Antonio Gramsci* ed. and trans. Quintin Hoare and Geoffrey Nowell-Smith (London: Lawrence & Wishart, 1971), p. 59.

13. ibid., p. 207.

14. Said, *Orientalism*, p. 7. The debt to Gramsci is acknowledged again in 'Connecting Empire to Secular Interpretation', *Culture and Imperialism*, pp. 56–7.

15. For an excellent account of this historical context, see Gauri Viswanathan, *Masks of Conquest: Literary Study and British Rule in India* (New York: Columbia University Press, 1989).

16. For a more sympathetic view of the Orientalists, see David Kopf, *British Orientalism and the Bengal Renaissance: The Dynamics of Indian Modernisation 1773–1835* (Berkeley: University of California Press, 1969).

17. Said, *Orientalism*, p. 12.

18. ibid., p. 224.

19. ibid., p. 23.

20. James Clifford, 'On *Orientalism*', *The Predicament of Culture*, p. 260. See also Robert Young, 'Disorienting Orientalism', *White Mythologies*, pp. 119–40, and Dennis Porter, 'Orientalism and Its Problems' (1983), reprinted in Williams and Chrisman, *Colonial Discourse and Post-Colonial Theory*, pp. 150–61.

21. Said, *Orientalism*, p. 15.

22. ibid., p. 254.

23. ibid., p. 15.

24. ibid., p. 20.

25. ibid., p. 3; compare Michel Foucault, *The Order of Things: An Archaeology of the Human Sciences* (1966: New York, Vintage, 1973), which declares that 'the Other . . . is at once interior and foreign' (p. xxiv).

26. Said, *Orientalism*, p. 8.

27. Young, *White Mythologies*, p. 135.

28. See also the distinctions drawn by Anthony Pagden in *Lords of All the World: Ideologies of Empire in Spain, Britain and France* (New Haven: Yale University Press, 1995).

29. C. F. Beckingham, 'Edward W. Said: *Orientalism*', *Bulletin of the School of Oriental and African Studies*, vol. xlii, part 3, 1979, p. 38; and Clifford, 'On *Orientalism*', p. 267.

30. Said, *Orientalism*, pp. 19 and 17.

31. ibid., p. 192.

32. ibid., p. 211.

33. ibid., p. 15.

34. ibid., p. 290.

35. ibid., p. 307.

36. ibid., p. 96.

37. Foucault, *History of Sexuality* vol. 1, p. 95; Foucault, *Discipline and Punish*, pp. 222–3.

38. Foucault, *Language, Counter-Memory, Practice*, p. 151. At the same time, the phenomenon of neo-colonialism might be used to corroborate Foucault's argument, insofar as the national(ist) bourgeoisie takes over the existing forms and institutions of colonial power and use them to exploit the Third World on behalf of the former masters. This also serves to remind one of the fact that Foucault was essentially hostile to Marxism, principally for its conception of the state as the locus of power, and to its key analytic instrument, the dialectic, which he saw as premised upon a linear teleology of synthesis and progression. See Michel Foucault, *Power/Knowledge* trans. C. Gordon (Brighton: Harvester Press, 1980), pp. 114–15 and 143–4. Moreover, he was particularly hostile to the concept of ideology (and the conception of the subject on which ideology is premised), which, of course, is central to the thought of Gramsci, like all Marxists, insofar as it is the primary medium through which social control is exercised. (See ibid., pp. 58 and 118–19.)

39. Antonio Gramsci, *Further Selections From the Prison Notebooks* ed. and trans. Derek Boothman (London: Lawrence & Wishart, 1995), p. 351. I will pass over, for the time being, Gramsci's stereotypical vision of the Oriental despot.

40. ibid., pp. 358–9.

41. Porter, 'Orientalism and Its Problems', p. 152.

42. Said, *Orientalism*, pp. 117–20.

43. ibid., p. 154.

44. ibid., p. 204.

45. ibid., p. 263.

46. On the effect of the 'Mutiny' in changing British perceptions of the Indian subject, see also Jenny Sharpe, *Allegories of Empire: The Figure of Woman in the Colonial Text* (Minneapolis: University of Minnesota Press, 1993). On the anxiety in colonial discourse, which Said characteristically ignores, see Sara Suleri, *The Rhetoric of English India* (Chicago: University of Chicago Press, 1992); Hulme, *Colonial Encounters*; Bart Moore-Gilbert, *Kipling and 'Orientalism'* (London: Croom Helm, 1986).

47. On the neo-Orientalist discourse generated by the current rising economic power of Asia, see Dave Morley and Kevin Robbins, 'Techno-Orientalism: Foreigners, Phobias and Futures', *New Formations*, 16, Spring 1992, pp. 136–56.

48. Said, *Orientalism*, p. 7.

49. ibid., p. 204.

50. ibid., p. 138.

51. Pathak *et al.*, 'The Prisonhouse of Orientalism', p. 215. For evidence of the ways in which colonial discourse itself provided the means to generate a counter-discourse, see Suleri, *The Rhetoric of English India*; Pratt, *Imperial Eyes*; and the work of Spivak and Bhabha, discussed in the next two chapters.

52. Said, 'Orientalism Reconsidered', p. 17.

53. Said, *Orientalism*, p. 205.

54. ibid., p. 248.

55. ibid., pp. 104 and 323.

56. ibid., p. 326.

57. ibid, p. 120.

58. ibid., p. 322.

59. ibid., pp. 48, 309–11 and 320 respectively.

60. Said certainly recognizes to some extent the gendered nature of colonial discourse. *Orientalism* argues that it encouraged a peculiarly (not to say invidiously) male conception of the world, especially insofar as Orientalism characteristically isolated the Oriental male for study (for obvious political imperatives). Secondly, Said observes that there is a consistent association between the Orient and sexual experience unobtainable in Europe. Insofar as the Oriental female was represented, she was constructed as passive, sensual, silent and 'willing'. Thirdly, Orientalism was itself a peculiarly male institutional practice. Finally, Said relates the *style* of Orientalism to its masculinist perspectives, as in the trope of 'surveying as if from a peculiarly suited vantage point the passive, seminal, feminine, even silent and supine East' (p. 208).

A number of feminist critics have nonetheless denounced his treatment of gender as inadequate. Thus Jane Miller's *Seductions: Studies in Reading and Culture* (London: Virago, 1990) complains that Said reproduces the very masculinism he decries in colonial discourse and that *Orientalism* can only work for a woman reader if she effaces, or suspends, her gender. Equally, Sara Mills's *Discourses of Difference* argues that it is impossible adequately to consider the general question of gender in colonialism within the frameworks established by Said.

Subsequent work on the gendering of colonial discourse has complicated Said's model in three principal ways. Firstly, it has challenged his assumption that the imperial encounter was figured quite so consistently in the masculinist terms that *Orientalism* suggests. According to Jenny Sharpe's *Allegories of Empire*, for instance, Said ignores not just the nuanced and variable nature of the ways in which the colonized formation is gendered female (the colonized is frequently figured as the resistant Amazon as well as the passive and helpless maiden), but the moments at which the colonizer is in turn feminized, usually at times when colonial authority is under pressure, as in the 1857 uprisings in India. Compare Kabbani's *Europe's Myths of Orient* on the change of gender register in T. E. Lawrence's account in *The Seven Pillars of Wisdom* of his time in Der'aa prison. Such reversals have a long history. See Peter Hulme, 'Polytropic Man: Tropes of

Sexuality and Mobility in Early Colonial Discourse' in Barker *et al.*, *Europe and Its Others* vol. 2, pp. 17–32.

Secondly, recent feminist work questions whether white women played as insignificant a part in the reproduction of imperialism as *Orientalism* implies. One initiative in recent women's historiography has been the attempt to recover this lost history of the involvement of Western women in the empire. Examples range from Helen Callaway's *Gender, Culture and Empire* (Urbana: University of Illinois Press, 1987) to Margaret Strobel's *European Women and the Second British Empire* (Bloomington: Indiana University Press, 1991) and Antoinette Burton's *The Burdens of History: British Feminists, Indian Women and Imperial Culture, 1865–1915* (Greensborough: University of North Carolina Press, 1995). Similarly, recent women literary critics have made considerable efforts to recover the lost canon of women's colonial discourse, a body of work which suggests that a further limitation of *Orientalism* is its lack of acknowledgement of Western women's part in the production of colonial textuality.

Thirdly, feminist criticism has challenged the implication of *Orientalism* that insofar as white women were present in the empire, they were simply complicit in the ideologies of imperialism and did not challenge them. Callaway, for example, argues that white women in colonial Nigeria posed a subtle challenge to the dominant discourse of masculinist imperialism by 'helping to build a reservoir of mutual understanding' (p. 240) between the races, which was to smooth the way to decolonization. For literary critics, the debate has centred on how far women's colonial discourse can be distinguished from its male equivalent. Mary Louise Pratt's argument in *Imperial Eyes* (1992), that women's travel writing about the non-Western world was markedly different from men's in form, thematic preoccupations and political positionality is corroborated by a number of other critics, including Sara Mills in *Discourses of Difference* and Lisa Lowe in *Critical Terrains*. Lowe demonstrates in the writing of Lady Mary Wortley Montagu, for example, 'an emergent feminist discourse that speaks of common experiences among women of different societies' (p. 32). This 'rhetoric of identification' problematizes the binary division between West and East, the 'natural' alliance of interest between Western men and women, and the superiority of both over Turkish women – which are all assumed to be self-evident truths in the work of earlier male travellers in Turkey.

A growing body of recent work also suggests that Said's unconscious masculinism is of a narrowly heterosexist kind. Suleri's *Rhetoric of English India* has demonstrated how old and persistent is the trope of 'the effeminate groom' in colonial discourse about the East. Other important work in this field includes Bristow, *Empire Boys*, and Christopher Lane, *The Ruling Passion: British Colonial Allegory and the Paradox of Homosexual Desire* (Durham: Duke University Press, 1995). Greater attention is now being paid from the perspective of 'queer studies' to individual writers like Forster and Scott. See, for example, some of the essays in Tony Davies and Nigel Woods eds., *A Passage to India* (Buckingham: Open University Press, 1994); and Danny Colwell, 'I am your Mother and your Father: Paul Scott and the Dissolution of Imperial Identity' in Moore-Gilbert, *Writing India*, pp. 213–35. In terms of the female 'homosocial' (or should it be 'gynosocial'?) sphere in colonial discourse, see Lisa Lowe's *Critical Terrains*, chapter 1 (on Lady Mary Wortley Montagu); and Nancy Paxton, 'Secrets of the Colonial Harem: Gender, Sexuality, and the Law in Kipling's Novels' in Moore-Gilbert, *Writing India*, pp. 139–62. The colonial arena is featuring more and more in the study of gender formation. See, for example, Mills, *Discourses of Difference*; Mrinalini Sinha, *Colonial Masculinity: The 'Manly Englishman' and the 'Effeminate Bengali' in the late Nineteenth Century* (Manchester: Manchester University Press, 1995); and Graham Dawson, *Soldier Heroes: British Adventure, Empire and the Imagining of Masculinities* (London: Routledge, 1994). For comments on the much more limited place of class in postcolonial criticism, see chapter 5.

61. Said, *Orientalism*, p. 240.

62. James Mill, *History of British India* 9 vols, 4th edition, ed. H. H. Wilson (London: Cox and Bentley, 1840–48), vol. ix, 1848, pp. 32–3. Wilson's comment is in vol. 1 (1840), p. viii.

63. Said, *Orientalism*, pp. 162 and 239.

64. ibid., p. 158.

65. ibid., pp. 168 and 184.

66. ibid., pp. 173 and 197.

67. Porter, 'Orientalism and Its Problems', p. 160.

68. Said, *Orientalism*, p. 15.

69. ibid., p. 291.

70. ibid., p. 70.

71. ibid., p. 328.

72. Ferial Ghazoul, 'The Resonance of the Arab-Islamic Heritage in the Work of Edward Said' in Michael Sprinker ed., *Edward Said: A Critical Reader* (Oxford: Blackwell, 1992), p. 158; Ahmad, 'Introduction', *In Theory*, p. 13.

73. Jacques Derrida, 'Limited Inc., a b c . . .', *glyph* 2, 1977, p. 209.

74. Said, *Orientalism*, p. 205. Kabbani argues that medieval Arab travellers' accounts of Europe reflected a sense of cultural superiority which accompanied their military superiority. At the same time, however, she claims that Said's interpretation of Orientalism can be applied to European representations of Islam in this period. See *Europe's Myths of Orient*, pp. 2, 14 and 20.

75. Dante, *The Divine Comedy*, trans. C. H. Sisson, ed. David Higgins (Oxford: Oxford University Press, 1993), p. 559.

76. Boccaccio, *The Decameron* trans. and ed. G. H. McWilliam (Harmondsworth: Penguin, 1995), p. 765.

77. *The Song of Roland* trans. and ed. Glyn Burgess (Harmondsworth: Penguin, 1990), pp. 89 and 129.

78. Wolfram von Eschenbach, *Parzifal* trans. and ed. A. T. Hatto (Harmondsworth: Penguin, 1980), p. 26.

79. ibid., p. 369.

80. ibid., p. 404.

81. Boccaccio, *Decameron*, p. lxii.

82. ibid., p. lix.

83. This is not, however, a completely new departure for Said. Tim Brennan usefully reminds one that Said was already writing about Arab authors in the mid-1970s. See 'Places of Mind, Occupied Lands: Edward Said and Philology' in Sprinker, *Edward Said*, p. 76.

84. Said, 'Secular Criticism', *The World, the Text, and the Critic*, p. 26.

85. ibid., p. 212.

86. While 'counterpoint' owes something to the comparative method long established in 'Commonwealth' literary studies, Ferial Ghazoul claims a specifically non-Western provenance for the concept in 'The Resonance of the Arab-Islamic Heritage' in Sprinker, *Edward Said*, pp. 161ff.

87. Said, 'Introduction', *Culture and Imperialism*, p. xxii.

88. ibid., p. xxvi.

89. ibid., pp. 297 and 302.

90. This seems very unfair to Guha, who collaborates in Subaltern Studies historiography with a number of Western critics, was himself based in Australia for much of the project, and seems (to me at least) exemplary in his negotiations between dominant and 'subaltern' models of historiography.

91. Jennifer Wicke and Michael Sprinker, 'Interview with Edward Said' in Sprinker, *Edward Said*, pp. 250 and 252.

92. Said, 'Introduction', *Culture and Imperialism*, p. xxiii.

93. 'The Cultural Integrity of Empire', ibid., p. 126.

94. 'Counnecting Empire to Secular Interpretation', ibid., p. 67.

95. 'Empire, Geography and Culture', ibid., p. 12

96. 'Jane Austen and Empire', ibid., p. 104. B. C. Southam challenges the legitimacy of Said's reading of Austen in 'The Silence of the Bertrams: Slavery and the Chronology of *Mansfield Park*', *Times Literary Supplement* 17 February 1995, pp. 13–14.

97. Said, 'The Cultural Integrity of Empire', *Culture and Imperialism*, p. 126.

98. Said, *Orientalism*, p. 94.

99. 'The Empire at Work: Verdi's *Aida*', ibid., p. 137.

100. Julian Budden, *Verdi* (London: Dent, 1985), p. 150. V. G. Kiernan corroborates Budden's argument about Verdi's hostility to imperialism in *Imperialism and its Contradictions* ed. Harvey J. Kaye (London: Routledge, 1995), p. 178.

101. Said, 'Narrative and Social Space', *Culture and Imperialism*, p. 82.

102. 'Jane Austen and Empire', ibid., p. 115.

103. 'Overlapping Territories, Intertwined Histories', ibid., p. 13.

104. 'Narrative and Social Space', ibid., pp. 83–4.

105. Compare Said's suggestive, but in the end simplistic, genealogy of Modernism; 'A Note on Modernism', ibid., pp. 225–9.

106. Abdul JanMohamed, 'Worldliness-without-World, Homelessness-as-Home: Toward a Definition of the Specular Border Intellectual' in Sprinker, *Edward Said*, p. 100.

107. Said, 'Collaboration, Independence and Liberation', *Culture and Imperialism*, p. 336.

108. Michael Sprinker, 'Introduction' to *Edward Said*, p. 2.

109. Said, *Orientalism*, p. 45.

3   GAYATRI SPIVAK: THE DECONSTRUCTIVE TWIST

1. Spivak, 'Scattered Speculations on the Question of Value', *The Spivak Reader*, p. 107.

2. Rey Chow, 'Ethics After Idealism', *Diacritics*, 23.1, Spring 1993, p. 7; Spivak, 'Feminism and Deconstruction, Again: Negotiations', *Outside in the Teaching Machine*, p. 122.

3. Spivak, 'French Feminism in an International Frame', *In Other Worlds: Essays in Cultural Politics* (London: Routledge, 1987), p. 135; Spivak's style may owe something to the unorthodox mode of some French feminist writing, which she characterizes as 'essay-cum-prose-poem'. See p. 141.

4. Robert Con Davis and David Gross, 'Gayatri Chakravorty Spivak and the *Ethos* of the Subaltern' in James S. Baumlin and T. F. Baumlin, eds., *Ethos: New Essays in Rhetorical and Critical Theory* (Dallas: Southern Methodist University Press, 1994), p. 70.

5. Spivak, 'In a Word: *Interview*', *Outside in the Teaching Machine*, p. 21.

6. Spivak, 'Subaltern Studies: Deconstructing Historiography', *In Other Worlds*, p. 211.

7. Spivak, 'Bonding in Difference: Interview with Alfred Arteaga', *The Spivak Reader*, p. 19.

8. Spivak, 'Feminism and Critical Theory', *In Other Worlds*, p. 90; Spivak, 'Negotiating the Structures of Violence', *Post-Colonial Critic*, p. 147.

9. Spivak, 'A Literary Representation of the Subaltern: A Woman's Text from the Third World', *In Other Worlds*, p. 241.

10. 'Feminism and Critical Theory', ibid., pp. 84–5; compare her comments on the politics of 'disinterested' reading in 'Three Women's Texts and a Critique of Imperialism', p. 276.

11. Spivak, 'Subaltern Studies', In Other Worlds, p. 210.

12. Spivak, 'Neocolonialism and the Secret Agent of Knowledge', p. 234.

13. Spivak, 'Subaltern Talk', The Spivak Reader, p. 308; Spivak, 'Strategy, Identity, Writing', Post-Colonial Critic, p. 45.

14. Danius and Jonsson, 'An Interview with Gayatri Chakravorty Spivak', p. 31; Spivak, 'Neocolonialism and the Secret Agent of Knowledge', p. 244.

15. Spivak, 'Neocolonialism and the Secret Agent of Knowledge', pp. 242–4; like Derrida, Spivak is interested in 'radicalizing' Marx and an 'open' Marxism.

16. Colin McCabe, 'Foreword', to Spivak, In Other Worlds, p. ix.

17. Spivak, 'French Feminism', ibid., p. 149.

18. Spivak, 'Foreword', Outside in the Teaching Machine, p. x.

19. Spivak, 'Subaltern Studies', In Other Worlds, p. 211.

20. Spivak, 'Can the Subaltern Speak?' (1988), reprinted in Williams and Chrisman, Colonial Discourse and Post-Colonial Theory, p. 84.

21. ibid., p. 67.

22. ibid., p. 69. As was suggested in Note 38 of the last chapter, Foucault was, of course, generally unsympathetic to Marxism, and particularly hostile to the concept of ideology.

23. ibid., pp. 69 and 71.

24. ibid., p. 104.

25. See, in particular, the attack on Derrida by Anne McClintock and Rob Nixon in 'No Names Apart: The Separation of Word and History in Derrida's "Le Dernier Mot du Racisme"', Gates, 'Race', Writing and Difference, pp. 339–53. Since Spivak herself contributed 'Three Women's Texts and a Critique of Imperialism' to this collection, there can be little doubt that she was aware of this debate, though it is not directly referred to in her writings. The gist of McClintock and Nixon's argument is that Derrida is inattentive to the real material conditions determining the emergence and evolution of apartheid, as is implied in the very title of their piece.

26. Said, 'Criticism Between Culture and System', The World, the Text, and the Critic, p. 214.

27. ibid., p. 189.

28. ibid., p. 183.

29. ibid., p. 214.

30. ibid., p. 216.

31. ibid., p. 220.

32. See, for instance, Derrida's 'Limited Inc., a b c . . .', p. 198, and 'Biodegradables: Seven Diary Fragments', Critical Inquiry, 15.4, 1989, p. 841. Moreover, Derrida is always at particular pains to deny the structuralist assumption that the critic can remain objectively detached from the object of analysis. See, for example, 'Structure, Sign, and Play in the Discourse of the Human Sciences', Writing and Difference, trans. Alan Bass (1967; London: Routledge & Kegan Paul, 1978), especially pp. 280–81.

33. Spivak, 'Can the Subaltern Speak?', p. 87. Derrida himself denies the charges made about his ahistoricism. See 'But Beyond . . . (Open Letter to Anne McClintock and Rob Nixon)', trans. Peggy Kamuf, in Gates, 'Race', Writing and Difference, pp. 339–53; in 'Biodegradables' he argues that deconstruction is, in fact, the most historical of methods. See p. 821 particularly. Nonetheless, the relevance of Derrida to postcolonial analysis remains hotly debated. For sceptical, even hostile, accounts, see R. Radhakrishnan, 'Ethnic Identity and Post-Structuralist Différance' in JanMohamed and Lloyd, The Nature and Context of Minority Discourse, pp. 50–71; and Rosemary Jolly,

'Rehearsals of Liberation: Contemporary Postcolonial Discourse and the New South Africa', *PMLA*, 110.1, January 1995, pp. 17–29.

34. Spivak, 'Can the Subaltern Speak?', p. 87.

35. Spivak, 'Subaltern Studies', *In Other Worlds*, p. 202.

36. 'A Literary Representation of the Subaltern', ibid., p. 241.

37. Spivak, 'Rani of Sirmur', p. 147; Spivak, 'Limits and Openings of Marx and Derrida', *Outside in the Teaching Machine*, p. 97.

38. Spivak, 'The Post-modern Condition: The End of Politics?', *Post-Colonial Critic*, p. 31; compare Derrida, 'Biodegradables', p. 821.

39. Spivak, 'A Literary Representation of the Subaltern', *In Other Worlds*, p. 250.

40. 'Subaltern Studies', ibid., p. 204.

41. Spivak, 'The Politics of Translation', *Outside in the Teaching Machine*, pp. 180 and 179.

42. 'Inscriptions: of Truth to Size', ibid., p. 211; for Spivak, moreover, the fetishization of such names as 'Indian' or 'Asian' as 'pure' essences collapses important class and gender distinctions and inequalities within the master-narrative of national or ethnic origin; too much emphasis on the latter conflicts with her demand for a persistent acknowledgement of the heterogeneity of 'individual' identity.

43. Gyan Prakash, 'Postcolonial Criticism and Indian Historiography', *Social Text*, 31.2, 1992, p. 8.

44. Spivak, 'The *Intervention* Interview', *Post-Colonial Critic*, p. 121.

45. Prakash, 'Postcolonial Criticism and Indian Historiography', p. 9. Such comments are not entirely fair. Guha does admit that while his focus is on subaltern experience as an 'autonomous sphere, as far as this is possible, there is also 'a great deal of overlap' between the elite and subaltern spheres. See 'Preface' to *Selected Subaltern Studies*, pp. 40–42.

46. Spivak, 'Subaltern Studies', *In Other Worlds*, p. 202.

47. Spivak, 'In a Word', *Outside in the Teaching Machine*, p. 10.

48. Spivak, 'Subaltern Studies', *In Other Worlds*, p. 202.

49. Spivak, 'Three Women's Texts and a Critique of Imperialism', p. 264.

50. Spivak, 'Can the Subaltern Speak?' p. 101.

51. ibid., p. 93.

52. ibid., p. 102.

53. ibid., p. 70.

54. ibid., p. 92.

55. ibid., p. 87; see *Of Grammatology*, pp. 74–81, for Derrida's discussion of the eighteenth-century project of a descriptive 'universal language'. One might argue that Derrida himself repeats the ethnocentrism of which he complains in European philosophy by seeing it as a specifically European problem.

56. Spivak, 'Can the Subaltern Speak?', p. 89.

57. Spivak, 'Subaltern Studies', *In Other Worlds*, p. 217.

58. 'French Feminism', ibid., p. 150.

59. ibid., p. 134.

60. ibid.

61. ibid., p. 137; compare Lowe, *Critical Terrains*, chapter 5, and Rey Chow, *Writing Diaspora: Tactics of Intervention in Contemporary Cultural Studies* (Bloomington: Indiana University Press, 1993), pp. 31–5 for other analyses of Kristeva's treatment of Chinese women.

62. Spivak, 'French Feminism', *In Other Worlds*, p. 140.

63. ibid., p. 135.

64. ibid., pp. 135–6.

65. ibid., p. 152.

66. ibid., p. 153; for a critique of Western Marxist-feminism conducted in much the same terms, see 'A Literary Representation of the Subaltern', In Other Worlds, pp. 251–8.

67. Said, 'Islam, Philology and French Culture', The World, the Text and the Critic, p. 273.

68. Spivak, 'Three Women's Texts and a Critique of Imperialism' in Gates, 'Race', Writing and Difference, p. 270.

69. ibid., p. 269.

70. ibid.

71. ibid., p. 270.

72. ibid., p. 272.

73. ibid., p. 273.

74. ibid., p. 274.

75. ibid., p. 277.

76. See Danius and Jonsson, 'An Interview with Gayatri Spivak', pp. 25–7.

77. Spivak, 'Translator's Preface and Afterword to Mahasweta Devi, Imaginary Maps', The Spivak Reader, p. 276. This text announces several forthcoming books in which one may expect Spivak's new interests to be more fully developed.

78. Spivak, 'Not Virgin Enough to say that [S]he Occupies the Place of the Other', Outside in the Teaching Machine, p. 155.

79. Spivak, 'Translator's Preface', The Spivak Reader, p. 281; see 'Subaltern Talk', ibid., pp. 287–93 for clues about Spivak's intended revisions.

80. Spivak, 'The Problem of Cultural Self-Representation', Post-Colonial Critic, p. 56.

81. 'The Intervention Interview', ibid., p. 127.

82. Spivak, 'Subaltern Studies', In Other Worlds, p. 201.

83. 'Explanation and Culture: Marginalia', ibid., p. 110.

84. Spivak, 'Can the Subaltern Speak?, p. 76.

85. Spivak, 'A Literary Representation', In Other Worlds, p. 242.

86. ibid., pp. 267 and 244.

87. Spivak, 'Can the Subaltern Speak?', p. 88.

88. Spivak, 'In a Word' and 'Not Virgin Enough', Outside in the Teaching Machine, pp. 17 and 177.

89. Spivak, 'Supplementing Marxism' in Bernd Magnus and S. Cullenberg eds., Whither Marxism? Global Crises in the International Context (London: Routledge, 1995), p. 115; compare Spivak, 'Reading The Satanic Verses', Outside in the Teaching Machine, p. 234.

90. Spivak, 'Negotiating the Structures of Violence', Post-Colonial Critic, p. 148.

91. Spivak, 'Subaltern Studies', In Other Worlds, pp. 208–9; compare 'Can the Subaltern Speak?', p. 80.

92. Spivak, 'Subaltern Studies', In Other Worlds, p. 210; Spivak, 'Neocolonialism and the Secret Agent of Knowledge', p. 227.

93. See Derrida, 'Of an Apocalyptic Tone Recently Adopted in Philosophy', trans. John P. Leavy, Semeia, 23, 1982, pp. 70–72. Moreover, the point of Derrida's critique of Foucault is precisely that the 'wholly-other' cannot 'in itself' be apprehended. 'Madness' cannot 'speak for itself' through a history (or archaeology) founded on principles of rationality. See Derrida, 'Cogito and the History of Madness' in Writing and Difference, pp. 31–63. It is worth remembering that by The Order of Things (1966), Foucault had decided that 'the Other . . . is at once interior and foreign' (p. xxiv).

94. Todorov, '"Race", Writing and Culture', in Gates, 'Race', Writing and Difference, p. 374.

95. Spivak, 'Marginality in the Teaching Machine' and 'Inscriptions: Of Truth to Size', Outside in the Teaching Machine, pp. 212 and 28 (my emphasis).

96. 'Women in Difference', ibid., p. 82.

97. Steven E. Cole, 'The Scrutable Subject: Davidson, Literary Theory, and the Claims of Knowledge' in R. W. Dasenbrock ed., *Literary Theory after Davidson* (Pennsylvania: Pennsylvania State University Press, 1993) p. 66.

98. Spivak, 'The Politics of Translation', *Outside in the Teaching Machine*, p. 183.

99. 'French Feminism Revisited', ibid., p. 157.

100. Bruce Robbins, 'The East is a Career: Edward Said and the Logics of Professionalism' in Sprinker, *Edward Said*, p. 50; see Parry, 'Problems in Current Theories of Colonial Discourse', p. 39, for a critique of Spivak's 'deafness' to the voice of the Other.

101. Spivak, 'Can the Subaltern Speak?', p. 104 (my emphasis).

102. Spivak, 'Subaltern Talk', *The Spivak Reader*, p. 289. A similar kind of slippage seems to happen with Devi's fiction. While Spivak argues on the one hand that no writer can be subaltern, Devi's writings are nonetheless described as 'subaltern material'. See Spivak, 'A Literary Representation of the Subaltern', *In Other Worlds*, p. 241.

103. Spivak, 'Three Women's Texts and a Critique of Imperialism', p. 272.

104. Spivak, 'Can the Subaltern Speak?', p. 103. Similar problems haunt 'Three Women's Texts and a Critique of Imperialism'. Spivak's conflation of the subject-position of the 'monster' in *Frankenstein* with that of the colonized subject implicitly reinscribes the humanist model of the colonized as 'intending subject of resistance'. While the 'monster', like the colonized subject, is on the one hand 'constructed' as a social being in the terms and image of the master, on the other, he clearly also comes to possess self-consciousness, voice, will and agency to a considerable degree (albeit that these are defined in relation to the dominant). These underwrite his 'heroic' and 'individual' resistance to Frankenstein and subsequent reversal of the master–slave model which initially characterizes their relationship. Other examples of Spivak's 'wishful use of history' include her simplistic claims about Israel's defeat by the Arabs in 1973, which would be news to many in Gaza and the Occupied West Bank (Spivak, 'Reading the World: Literary Studies in the Eighties', *In Other Worlds*, p. 99) and the equally unsupported allegations about the 'artificial' famine in India in 1942 (Spivak, 'More on Power/Knowledge', *Outside in the Teaching Machine*, p. 47).

105. 'Can the Subaltern Speak?', p. 104. Spivak's later defence against charges that she ventriloquizes, or speaks for, Bhaduri ('The Problem of Cultural Self-Representation', *Post-Colonial Critic*, p. 57) is not altogether convincing, since it relies on the position, long discredited by deconstruction itself, that the 'real' meaning of the essay must be understood in terms of Spivak's prior 'intention' not to speak for Bhaduri. Her more recent comments in *The Spivak Reader* are even more baffling, insofar as they seem to equate Bhaduri's menstruation with a 'text' which her family members 'ignore'. For Spivak, by comparison, it is a clear sign that 'illicit love' (i.e. an 'unwanted' pregnancy) is not the cause of the suicide: 'She *had* tried to represent herself, through self-representation of the body, but it had not come through' ('Subaltern Talk', p. 306) What Spivak describes as 'that incredible effort to speak did not fulfill itself in a speech act ... even when the subaltern [notice again how clearly Bhaduri represents the subaltern] makes an effort to the death to speak, she is not able to be heard'. (ibid., pp. 289 and 292). This conflates the impersonal processes of biology with the intentionality of human communication. It is 'true' that Bhaduri's menstruation may constitute a 'text' to be interpreted, but she can hardly be understood as the 'author' of that 'text' in any straightforward way.

106. See Silvia Tandeciarz, 'Reading Gayatri Spivak's "French Feminism in an International Frame": A Problem for Theory', *Genders*, 10, 1991, pp. 75–90, for an excellent account of Spivak's reinscription of other ideas and structures of thinking which she criticizes in Kristeva.

107. Spivak, 'French Feminism', *In Other Worlds*, p. 136.

108. ibid., p. 134.

109. ibid., p. 153.

110. Spivak, 'Can the Subaltern Speak?', p. 73.

111. ibid., p. 78.

112. Spivak, 'Neocolonialism and the Secret Agent of Knowledge', p. 238; a similar complaint about national-bourgeois historiography is made in 'A Literary Representation', In Other Worlds, p. 245.

113. See, for example, David Arnold's account of resistance to plague measures in India in the last century in 'Touching the Body' in Guha and Spivak, Selected Subaltern Studies, pp. 391–426; and the account of Egyptian peasant women's resistance to state programmes of contraception/sterilization today in Reza Hammami and Martina Reiker, 'Feminist Orientalism and Orientalist Marxism', New Left Review, 170, July/August 1988, pp. 105ff. There is 'massive evidence' of such resistance (as well as more direct forms of rebellion) in colonial records. See Veena Das, 'Subaltern as Perspective' in Ranajit Guha ed., Subaltern Studies VI: Writings on South Asian History and Society (Oxford: Oxford University Press, 1989), p. 315.

114. Spivak, 'Subaltern Studies', In Other Worlds, p. 207. This does not seem logical; how can this 'emergence' be registered, but not also be available for analysis? Where does this place the writing of figures like Phyllis Wheatley and Mary Prince?

115. Spivak, 'A Literary Representation', ibid., p. 253.

116. Spivak, 'The New Historicism: Political Commitment and the Postmodern Critic', Post-Colonial Critic, p. 158.

117. See Raymond Williams, Problems in Materialism and Culture (London: Verso, 1980), pp. 31–49; Gramsci, Selections from the Prison Notebooks, p. 388; Spivak seems to have taken this possibility more on board in The Spivak Reader. Here she acknowledges that there can be subaltern 'leaders' who conform to Gramsci's conception of the 'organic intellectual' without completely losing their subaltern identity. (See 'Translator's Preface', pp. 270–1.)

118. Spivak, 'More on Power/Knowledge' and 'Feminism and Deconstruction, Again', Outside in the Teaching Machine, pp. 48 and 137.

119. Spivak, 'Can the Subaltern Speak?', p. 84.

120. Spivak, 'More on Power/Knowledge' and 'French Feminism Revisited', Outside in the Teaching Machine, pp. 49 and 157.

121. Spivak, 'Post-marked Calcutta, India', Post-Colonial Critic, pp. 85 and 83.

122. ibid., p. 80.

123. Young, White Mythologies, p. 171.

124. Spivak, 'French Feminism', In Other Worlds, p. 135.

125. Spivak, 'Feminism and Deconstruction, Again', Outside in the Teaching Machine, p. 137.

126. 'Sammy and Rosie Get Laid', ibid., p. 244.

127. See Maria Koundoura, 'Naming Gayatri Spivak', Stanford Humanities Review, 1.1, 1989, p. 92; Parry, 'Problems in Current Theories of Colonial Discourse', pp. 34–9.

128. Spivak, 'Can the Subaltern Speak?', p. 108 note 54.

129. Spivak, 'Subaltern Studies', In Other Worlds, p. 197.

130. Spivak, 'Can the Subaltern Speak?', pp. 74–5; Spivak, 'French Feminism', In Other Worlds, p. 145.

131. Spivak, 'Can the Subaltern Speak', pp. 103 and 73.

132. Spivak, 'Strategy, Identity, Writing', Post-Colonial Critic, p. 47.

133. ibid., pp. 53 and 11.

134. Spivak, 'Explanation and Culture', In Other Worlds, p. 113.

135. Spivak, 'The Post-Colonial Critic', Post-Colonial Critic, p. 71; at the same time there is no shortage of testimony to the enabling impact of Spivak's criticism on 'real' social problems. See John Hutnyk, 'Articulation and Marginalia: Making Spaces for the

Other Voices in our Universities', *New Literatures Review*, 24, 1992, pp. 104–16; and the editors' introduction to *The Spivak Reader*, p. 3.

136. See Parry, 'Problems in Current Theories of Colonial Discourse', p. 43.

137. Spivak, 'French Feminism', *In Other Worlds*, p. 148.

138. ibid., p. 144.

139. Richard Freadman and Seamus Miller, 'Deconstruction and Critical Practice: Gayatri Spivak on *The Prelude*' in Richard Freadman and Lloyd Reinhardt eds., *On Literary Theory and Philosophy: A Cross-Disciplinary Encounter* (Basingstoke: Macmillan, 1991), p. 39. Compare Cole, 'The Scrutable Subject', p. 61.

140. Spivak, 'Bonding in Difference', *The Spivak Reader*, pp. 27–8.

141. Spivak, 'A Literary Representation', *In Other Worlds*, p. 258.

142. 'More on Power/Knowledge', *The Spivak Reader*, p. 150.

143. Spivak, 'Not Virgin Enough', *Outside in the Teaching Machine*, p. 177.

144. 'Marginality in the Teaching Machine', ibid., p. 28.

4 HOMI BHABHA: 'THE BABELIAN PERFORMANCE'

1. The phrase comes from Bhabha, 'Articulating the Archaic: Cultural Difference and Colonial Nonsense', *Location of Culture*, p. 135.

2. ibid., p. 128.

3. ibid., p. 275.

4. 'The Postcolonial and the Postmodern: The Question of Agency', ibid., p. 181.

5. 'DissemiNation: Time, Narrative and the Margins of the Modern Nation', ibid., p. 170.

6. 'The Post-colonial and the Postmodern', ibid., p. 188. Compare Bhabha's 'tendentious reconstruction' of Foucault in 'Articulating the Archaic', ibid., p. 131.

7. 'The Other Question: Stereotype, Discimination and the Discourse of Colonialism', ibid., p. 73.

8. ibid., p. 75

9. Bhabha, 'Remembering Fanon', Foreword to Fanon, *Black Skin, White Masks*, pp. xvii-xviii.

10. ibid., p. ix.

11. Bhabha, 'Representation and the Colonial Text' in Gloversmith, *The Theory of Reading*, pp. 93–122.

12. Bhabha, 'The Other Question', *Location of Culture*, p. 69.

13. ibid., p. 74.

14. ibid., p. 82.

15. Bhabha, 'Postcolonial Criticism', in Greenblatt and Gunn, *Redrawing the Boundaries*, p. 461. Compare the various critiques of Foucault in *The Location of Culture*, for example p. 91.

16. Bhabha, 'Signs Taken for Wonders', *Location of Culture*, p. 109.

17. 'The Commitment to Theory', ibid., p. 22.

18. For one version of Derrida's exposition of the effects of 'repetition', see 'Ellipsis' in *Writing and Difference*, pp. 294–300.

19. Bhabha, 'Sly Civility', *Location of Culture*, p. 97.

20. ibid., p. 96; compare 'Of Mimicry and Man. The Ambivalence of Colonial Discourse', p. 86. Bhabha's general thesis on the contradiction in Mill owes much to Eric Stokes's account, which he probably derives via Said's brief discussion of the topic in 'Secular Criticism', *The World, the Text and the Critic*, p. 13.

21. Macaulay quoted in Bhabha, 'Sly Civility', *Location of Culture*, p. 95.

22. ibid., p. 96–7.

23. 'Of Mimicry and Man', ibid., p. 85.

24. ibid., p. 86.

25. ibid., p. 91.

26. 'Signs Taken for Wonders', ibid., p. 113.

27. Simon During is fairly representative in his complaint that 'the concept postmodernity has been constructed in terms which more or less intentionally wipe out the possibility of post-colonial identity. Indeed, intention aside, the conceptual annihilation of the post-colonial condition is actually necessary to any argument which attempts to show that 'we' now live in postmodernity.' See Simon During, 'Postmodernism or Post-Colonialism Today?', 1987; reprinted in Thomas Docherty ed., *Postmodernism: A Reader* (Hemel Hempstead: Harvester Wheatsheaf, 1993), p. 449. For other sceptical accounts of postmodernism from a postcolonial or 'minoritarian' perspective, see bell hooks, *Yearning: Race, Gender, and Cultural Politics* (Boston: South End Press, 1991); Rey Chow, 'Rereading Mandarin Ducks and Butterflies: A Response to the "Postmodern" Condition', *Cultural Critique*, 5, 1986, pp. 69–93; Ahmad, *In Theory*, chapters 3–5; Kwame Anthony Appiah, 'Is the Post- in Postmodernism the same as the Post- in Postcolonial?', *Critical Inquiry*, 17, Winter 1991, pp. 336–57; Ian Adam and Helen Tiffin eds., *Past the Last Post: Theorizing Post-Colonialism and Post-Modernism* (Hemel Hempstead: Harvester Wheatsheaf, 1991); Kumkum Sangari, 'The Politics of the Possible', *Cultural Critique*, 7, 1987, pp. 157–86; Arun Mukherjee, 'Whose Post-Colonialism and Whose Post-Modernism?', *World Literature Written in English*, 30.2, 1990, pp. 1–9; Denis Ekpo, 'Towards a Post-Africanism: Contemporary African Thought and Postmodernism', *Textual Practice*, 9.1, Spring 1995, pp. 121–36; Neil Lazarus, 'Doubting the New World Order: Marxism, Realism, and the Claims of Postmodernist Social Theory', *differences: a Journal of Feminist Cultural Studies*, 3.3, 1991, pp. 94–138; Paul Gilroy, *The Black Atlantic: Modernity and Double Consciousness* (London: Verso, 1993), pp. 43–6. Compare Spivak's comments in 'Scattered Speculations on the Question of Value', *In Other Worlds*, pp. 171–2, 'The Post-modern Condition: The End of Politics', *The Post-Colonial Critic*, pp. 17–35, and 'Sammy and Rosie Get Laid', *Outside in the Teaching Machine*, p. 246. By comparison, Robert Young sees a far greater complementarity, if not equivalence, between the two discourses than the critics listed above: see *White Mythologies*, p. 119.

28. Bhabha, 'Conclusion: "Race", Time and the Revision of Modernity', *Location of Culture*, p. 240. Compare 'Signs Taken for Wonders', ibid., p. 111.

29. 'Conclusion', ibid.

30. 'The Postcolonial and the Postmodern', ibid., p. 175. Compare 'DissemiNation', p. 164.

31. 'Conclusion', ibid., p. 250.

32. ibid., p. 244.

33. ibid., p. 236.

34. ibid., p. 237.

35. 'DissemiNation', ibid., p. 170. This conception of 'ambivalent temporality' owes a lot to what 'DissemiNation' calls Kristeva's theory of 'parallel times', which Bhabha adapts from a feminist context to postcolonial problematics. See Julia Kristeva, 'Women's Time' in *The Kristeva Reader*, ed. Torril Moi (Oxford: Basil Blackwell, 1984), pp. 192ff. It also owes something to Fanon's conception of the ambivalent temporalities of the decolonized nation. See Bhabha, 'DissemiNation', *The Location of Culture*, p. 152. The distinction between temporalities also reminds one of Said's discrimination in *Orientalism* between synchronic vision and diachronic narrative, to which Bhabha alludes in 'Of Mimicry and Man', *Location of Culture*, p. 86.

36. Bhabha, 'Conclusion', *Location of Culture*, p. 252.

37. 'Articulating the Archaic', ibid., p. 125; for Bhabha's discussion of Benjamin's theories of translation, see 'DissemiNation' and 'How Newness Enters the World: Postmodern Space, Postcolonial Times and the Trials of Critical Translation', ibid., pp. 163–4 and 224–7 in particular.

38. 'Conclusion', ibid., p. 238.

39. 'How Newness Enters the World', ibid., p. 227; for the source of Bhabha's conception of the 'irreducible' element in identity, see Jacques Lacan, The Four Fundamental Concepts of Psycho-Analysis, trans. Alan Sheridan (1973; Harmondsworth: Penguin, 1977), pp. 249–52.

40. 'Conclusion', ibid., p. 238.

41. 'Articulating the Archaic', ibid., p. 127.

42. Roland Barthes, The Pleasure of the Text, trans. Richard Miller (1973; New York: Hill and Wang, 1975), p. 49. Barthes' general vision of Morocco reminds me irresistibly of Said's descriptions of Flaubert's attitude to Egypt. See Said, Orientalism, p. 187.

43. Bhabha, 'The Commitment to Theory', Location of Culture, p. 32.

44. 'The Postcolonial and the Postmodern', ibid., p. 172.

45. Lowe, Critical Terrains, p. 139. Oddly, Bhabha seemed to have recognized this problem with Barthes in 'The Commitment to Theory'; see Location of Culture, p. 31.

46. Barthes, The Pleasure of the Text, p. 50.

47. Bhabha, 'Conclusion', Location of Culture, p. 251.

48. Homi Bhabha, 'The Third Space' in Jonathon Rutherford ed., Identity: Community, Culture, Difference (London: Lawrence & Wishart, 1990), p. 211. Compare Bhabha, 'The Commitment to Theory', Location of Culture, pp. 35–6.

49. Bhabha, 'The Commitment to Theory', Location of Culture, p. 36.

50. 'Signs Taken for Wonders', ibid., p. 109. Compare Foucault's argument in The History of Sexuality that there is 'no binary and all-encompassing opposition between rulers and ruled' (p. 94).

51. Foucault, The History of Sexuality, p. 11. Compare p. 101 and Foucault, Power/ Knowledge, pp. 195–6. The History of Sexuality argues that the regime of domination can never be wholly stable: 'Discourse transmits and produces power; it reinforces it, but also undermines and exposes it, renders it fragile and makes it possible to thwart it' (p. 101).

52. Bhabha, 'Of Mimicry and Man', Location of Culture, p. 85.

53. 'Signs Taken for Wonders', ibid., p. 112.

54. ibid., p. 115.

55. ibid., p. 119.

56. 'Sly Civility', ibid., p. 98.

57. Young, White Mythologies, p. 152.

58. Bhabha, 'The Other Question', Location of Culture, p. 66. Compare ibid., p. 79, where the production of ambivalence also seems to be 'intended' and 'conscious'.

59. Compare Foucault, Discipline and Punish, pp. 219–21.

60. Bhabha, 'By Bread Alone: Signs of Violence in the Mid-nineteenth Century', Location of Culture, pp. 209 and 199.

61. On mimicry, see Lacan, The Four Fundamental Concepts of Psycho-Analysis, passim, especially pp. 98–100.

62. Bhabha, 'Of Mimicry and Man' and 'Sly Civility', Location of Culture, pp. 89 and 99.

63. In perhaps too hastily attempting to adapt his models of agency, resistance and politics in the colonial period to the postcolonial arena, Bhabha initially found himself facing identical problems to those outlined above. Thus if, as was argued in 'The Commitment to Theory' (1988), the 'Third Space', which is both produced by, and enables, hybridization in the contemporary era, is indeed 'an unconscious relation' ('The Commitment to Theory', Location of Culture, p. 36), how can it also provide the grounds

on which *consciously* to resist the hegemony of the West or as a means with which *programmatically* to propagate a new conception of relations between cultures, let alone more direct acts of solidarity against a putative 'New World Order'?

64. Sir Henry Maine, quoted in 'Articulating the Archaic', Bhabha, *Location of Culture*, p. 129.

65. 'By Bread Alone', ibid., p. 208.

66. It is crucial to the argument to understand that the catechist is Indian and not English, as Robert Young assumes; see Robert Young, *Colonial Desire: Hybridity in Theory, Culture and Race* (London: Routledge, 1995), p. 162.

67. E. M. Forster, *A Passage to India* (1924; Harmondsworth: Penguin, 1976), p. 39.

68. Kate Teltscher, *India Inscribed: European and British Writing on India 1600–1800* (Delhi: Oxford University Press, 1995), pp. 147–50.

69. Homi Bhabha, 'The Other Question: Difference, Discrimination, and the Discourse of Colonialism' in Francis Barker, Peter Hulme and Margaret Iverson eds., *The Politics of Theory* (Colchester: Colchester University, 1983), p. 205. For further discussion of such issues, see my 'The Bhabhal of Tongues: Reading Kipling, Reading Bhabha' in *Writing India*.

70. Bhabha, 'The Postcolonial and the Postmodern', *Location of Culture*, pp. 174–5.

71. ibid., p. 185; compare 'Interrogating Identity: Frantz Fanon and the Postcolonial Prerogative', ibid., p. 56. On the question of entry into the symbolic order, see Lacan, *Four Fundamental Concepts*, pp. 188, 204–5 and 246.

72. Bhabha, 'The Postcolonial and the Postmodern', *Location of Culture*, p. 187.

73. ibid., p. 190.

74. ibid., pp. 191–2.

75. ibid., p. 190.

76. 'Conclusion', ibid., p. 245.

77. 'The Postcolonial and the Postmodern', ibid., p. 190.

78. 'Conclusion' and 'The Postcolonial and the Postmodern', ibid., pp. 247 and 183.

79. Bhabha, 'Remembering Fanon', p. xxiv.

80. For a more extensive analysis of the consequences of reading Fanon backwards, see Neil Lazarus, 'Disavowing Decolonization: Fanon, Nationalism and the Problematic of Representation in Current Theories of Colonial Discourse', *Research in African Literatures*, 24.2, 1993, pp. 69–98. An equally hostile account of Bhabha's 'misreading' of Fanon is provided by Cedric Robinson, 'The Appropriation of Frantz Fanon', *Race and Class*, 35.1, 1993, pp. 79–91.

81. Parry, 'Problems in Current Theories of Colonial Discourse', pp. 31–46. Parry extends her critique of Bhabha (often in much the same terms as in the earlier article) in 'Signs of Our Times: Discussion of Homi Bhabha's *Location of Culture*', *Third Text*, 28–9, Autumn/Winter 1994, pp. 1–24; Ahmad, 'Literary Theory and "Third World Literature": Some Contexts', *In Theory*, pp. 68–9. Compare Ania Loomba, 'Overworlding the "Third World"' (1991; reprinted in Williams and Chrisman, *Colonial Discourse and Post-Colonial Theory*), in which she complains of Bhabha's 'too easy shift from semiotic to social' in cultural analysis (p. 309).

82. Young, *Colonial Desire*, p. 163.

83. Bhabha, 'DissemiNation', *Location of Culture* p. 145.

84. 'Signs Taken for Wonders', ibid., p. 110 (my emphasis).

85. Parry, 'Problems in Current Theories', p. 29.

86. Bhabha, 'The Third Space', p. 216.

87. Kristeva, 'Women's Time', p. 194.

88. ibid., p. 210.

89. Bhabha, 'The Postcolonial and the Postmodern', *Location of Culture*, p. 187.

90. Young, *White Mythologies*, p. 144. Further suggestive hints are offered in Young, *Colonial Desire*, p. 171.

91. Spivak, 'Negotiating the Structures of Violence', *Post-Colonial Critic*, p. 151.

92. Spivak, 'French Feminism', *In Other Worlds*, p. 149.

93. Spivak, 'Woman in Difference', *Outside in the Teaching Machine*, p. 91.

94. Spivak, 'Feminism and Critical Theory', *In Other Worlds*, p. 81. Compare Christine Holmlund, 'Displacing the Limits of Difference: Gender, Race, and Colonialism in Edward Said and Homi Bhabha's Theoretical Models and Marguerite Duras's Experimental Films', *Quarterly Review of Film and Video*, 13.1–3, 1991, p. 8; and Loomba, 'Overworlding the "Third World"', p. 307.

95. Spivak, 'French Feminism', *In Other Worlds*, p. 143.

96. Spivak, 'Can the Subaltern Speak?', p. 92.

97. Quoted in Bhabha, 'Of Mimicry and Man', *Location of Culture*, p. 89.

98. Sigmund Freud, 'Three Essays on Sexuality' (1905), *On Sexuality: Three Essays on Sexuality and Other Works*, trans. James Strachey, ed. Angela Richards (Harmondsworth: Pelican, 1983), p. 66. Space does not permit discussion of Freud's conception of woman as 'the dark continent', but it does reinforce the general argument I am making about the racialized categories of his thought.

99. Spivak, 'A Literary Representation', *In Other Worlds*, p. 262.

100. Sigmund Freud, 'The Taboo of Virginity' (1918) *On Sexuality*, p. 273.

101. Spivak, 'A Literary Representation', *In Other Worlds*, pp. 261–2.

102. McClintock, 'The Return of Female Fetishism', p. 15. Compare Spivak's reference to fetishism in 'Feminism and Critical Theory', *The Spivak Reader*, p. 72, and 'Unmaking and Making in *To the Lighthouse*', *In Other Worlds*, pp. 44–5; and Lowe, *Critical Terrains*, pp. 24–87, which draws on Marjorie Garber's work in the field (see *Vested Interests: Cross-Dressing and Cultural Anxiety* (London: Routledge, 1991)).

103. 'McClintock, 'The Return of Female Fetishism', p. 15.

104. Bhabha, 'Remembering Fanon', pp. xii-xiii.

105. Fanon, *Black Skin, White Masks*, pp. 12–13.

106. ibid., pp. 104–5.

107. ibid., p. 106.

108. ibid., pp. 151–2. Compare Soyinka's comments on Jung in 'Morality and Aesthetics in the Ritual Archetype', *Myth, Literature and the African World*, p. 34, and those of Wilson Harris in 'Judgement and Dream', in Riach and Williams, *The Radical Imagination*, p. 25.

109. Fanon, *Black Skin, White Masks*, p. 80.

110. ibid., pp. 109–10.

111. ibid., p. 161.

112. ibid., p. 223.

113. For a discussion of some of the problems in Fanon's treatment of the issue of gender, see my 'Frantz Fanon: En-Gendering Nationalist Discourse', *Woman: A Cultural Review*, 7.2, Autumn 1996, pp. 125–35. This builds on earlier work such as Marie Perinbam, 'The Parrot and the Phoenix: Frantz Fanon's View of the West Indian and Algerian Woman', *Savacou*, 13, 1977, pp. 7–15; and Winifred Woodhull, 'Unveiling Algeria', *Genders*, 10, 1991, pp. 112–31.

114. Fanon, *Black Skin, White Masks*, p. 211.

115. ibid., p. 186.

116. Bhabha, 'Remembering Fanon', p. xv.

117. ibid.

118. Bhabha, 'The Other Question', *Location of Culture*, p. 66.

119. 'Articulating the Archaic', ibid., p. 138. Compare p. 37.

120. 'The Other Question', ibid., pp. 76 and 75 (my emphasis).

121. 'Articulating the Archaic', ibid., p. 131.

122. JanMohamed, 'The Economy of Manichean Allegory', p. 79. Compare Robinson, 'The Appropriation of Frantz Fanon', p. 85, on Bhabha's erasure of the violence of the colonial arena.

123. Terry Eagleton, 'Goodbye to the Enlightenment', *Guardian*, 8 February 1994, p. 13. Bhabha is equally disobliging about Eagleton's failure to attend to the '"real" history of the "other"' in 'Conclusion', *The Location of Culture*, p. 240.

124. Fanon, *Black Skin, White Masks*, p. 220.

125. Bhabha, 'The Other Question', *Location of Culture*, p. 72.

126. Foucault, *History of Sexuality*, vol. 1, pp. 41 and 86ff.

127. Bhabha, 'The Other Question', *Location of Culture*, p. 76.

128. See my *Kipling and 'Orientalism'* for further discussion of this topic.

129. See Kiernan, *Imperialism and its Contradictions*, pp. 103ff.

130. McClintock, 'The Return of Female Fetishism', p. 2. Holmlund points out that Bhabha actually changes the gender of the child encountered by Fanon in the famous scene from *Black Skin, White Masks* from a boy to a girl, without either explaining why, or exploring the radical differences this might imply for his/Fanon's discussion of the process of psychic identification. See 'Displacing the Limits of Difference', pp. 5–8.

131. McClintock, 'The Return of Female Fetishism', p. 2.

132. ibid., p. 2.

133. Bhabha, 'By Bread Alone', *Location of Culture*, p. 199.

134. See Luhrmann's *The Good Parsi* for a fascinating account of one such 'assimilated' community in India.

135. Bhabha, 'Conclusion', *The Location of Culture*, p. 239.

5   POSTCOLONIAL CRITICISM *AND* POSTCOLONIAL THEORY

1. Of MacKenzie's earlier work as a historian of imperialism, Benita Parry has commented that it is 'dense in empirical research and thin on analysis'. See Parry, 'Problems in Current Theories of Colonial Discourse', p. 53. This judgement is even more pertinent in respect of MacKenzie's *Orientalism*. A more serious objection to such work is that it seems to corroborate the comment of the founding member of the Subaltern Studies group of Indian historians, Ranajit Guha, that some imperial historians in Britain continue to be immersed in 'the knowledges, techniques and attitudes which informed and sustained ... paramountcy [in India] for two hundred years'. See 'Dominance without Hegemony and Its Historiography' in Guha, *Subaltern Studies VI*, p. 305. While MacKenzie assumes that the methods of historians are uniformly the same (as his own), an increasing number of his colleagues have proved themselves open to many of the arguments of contemporary cultural theory. These would include the suggestions that facts themselves are constituted as such by interpretations, that history is a narrative which is no more inherently objective than any other form of cultural description and, most importantly, that culture and cultural analysis mediate relations of power and act in and on the world in powerful ways. See, for example, Hayden White, *Metahistory* (Baltimore: Johns Hopkins University Press, 1983); and Dominick LaCapra, *History and Criticism* (Ithaca: Cornell University Press, 1985). In the field of imperial history more specifically, several scholars are now drawing on French cultural theory in constructing their narratives. This is an especially notable feature of Subaltern Studies historiography. For instance Guha draws variously on Barthes, Benveniste, Jakobson and Lacan, Partha Chatterjee on Foucault and and Veena Das on Nietzsche and Baudrillard. See Guha, 'The Prose of Counter-Insurgency' in Guha and Spivak, *Selected Subaltern Studies*, pp. 45–88; Chatterjee, 'More on Modes of Power and the Peasantry' in Guha

and Spivak, *Selected Subaltern Studies*, pp. 351–90; Das, 'Subaltern as Perspective' in Guha, *Subaltern Studies VI*, pp. 310–29. See also David Arnold, 'Touching the Body: Perspectives on the Indian Plague, 1896–1900', in Guha, *Subaltern Studies VI*, pp. 391–426; and David Scott, 'Colonial Governmentality', *Social Text*, 43, 1995, pp. 191–220. At the same time, literary-critical exponents of colonial discourse analysis are increasingly learning the value of accurate historical contextualization both of themselves as critical observers and of the texts which they analyse. Such developments point to a continuing and healthy blurring of the boundaries between these disciplines as one productive way forward for the writing of the cultural history of colonial relations. This is not, of course, to propose that this kind of interdisciplinarity is without its problems or conflicts. Indeed, as Spivak suggests, the historian and the teacher of literature 'must critically "interrupt" each other, bring each other to crisis . . . especially when each seems to claim all for its own'. See Spivak, 'A Literary Representation', *In Other Worlds*, p. 241. C. A. Bayly's 'India and the British Imagination' gives a much more balanced account than MacKenzie's of the relations between literary critics and historians in respect of the colonial domain. This review by a distinguished imperial historian suggests that figures like MacKenzie and Jacoby may well be in the minority of his colleagues in terms of their methodological presuppositions. See *The Times Literary Supplement*, 12 July 1996, p. 29. Compare the different estimations of Said's work from Harvey Kaye and V. G. Kiernan in Kiernan's *Imperialism and Its Contradictions*, pp. 3–4 and 112 respectively. Spivak's comment on the nativist's resistance to theory when it is 'recognizably different from her or his own unacknowledged theoretical position' might be profitably adapted as a way of approaching the kind of attacks made by Jacoby and MacKenzie. See Spivak, 'A Literary Representation', *In Other Worlds*, p. 268.

2. Ahmad, 'Introduction', *In Theory*, p. 6.

3. ibid.

4. 'Jameson's Rhetoric of Otherness and the "National Allegory"', ibid., p. 122; compare 'Literary Theory and "Third World" Literature', ibid., pp. 43–5 on Ahmad's own ambiguous positioning.

5. One is sometimes irresistibly reminded, reading Ahmad, of C. L. R. James's comment: 'To talk about revolution and nationalization and the need to create a revolutionary party (on the discredited Stalinist model) is merely a senseless aping of the models of East and West'. See C. L. R. James, 'Introduction to Tradition and the West Indian Novel' in Wilson Harris, *Tradition, the Writer and Society: Critical Essays* (London: New Beacon Books, 1973), p. 74.

6. Parry, 'The Contents and Discontents of Kipling's Imperialism'; Laura Chrisman's 'The Imperial Unconscious? Representations of Imperial Discourse', *Critical Quarterly*, 32.3, 1990, pp. 38–58.

7. Ashcroft *et al.*, *The Empire Writes Back*, pp. 196–7.

8. Said, 'Connecting Empire to Secular Interpretation', *Culture and Imperialism*, p. 71. Despite the force of his strategic argument, it is hard to accept that Conrad has been considered a 'sport' by mainstream criticism – he is, after all, one of the principal actors in Leavis's *The Great Tradition*, where several of his 'imperial' novels receive close attention.

9. Foucault, *Discipline and Punish*, p. 29; compare the link made in *The History of Sexuality* between disciplinary power's 'concern with the body and sex to a type of "racism"' (p. 125).

10. Bernard Cohn, 'Representing Authority in Victorian India' in Eric Hobsbawm and Terence Ranger eds., *The Invention of Tradition* (Cambridge: Cambridge University Press, 1983), pp. 165–210.

11. Foucault, *Discipline and Punish*, p. 16. Indeed, Foucault's account begins with a description of the regicide Damiens in 1757 which is taken to mark the change of episteme.

12. Foucault, *History of Sexuality*, p. 41.

13. Das, 'Subaltern as Perspective' in Guha, *Subaltern Studies VI*, p. 319.

14. Cohn, 'Representing Authority in Victorian India', p. 166; compare Guha's argument that 'feudal practices, far from being abolished, or at least reduced, were in fact reinforced under the Raj'. See 'Dominance Without Hegemony' in Guha, *Subaltern Studies VI*, p. 236; for comparable arguments about Africa, see Terence Ranger, 'The Invention of Tradition in Colonial Africa' in Hobsbawm and Ranger, *The Invention of Tradition*, pp. 211–62.

15. David Scott, 'Colonial Governmentality', *Social Text*, 43, 1995, p. 214.

16. Gramsci, *Selections from the Prison Notebooks*, p. 416; compare p. 159.

17. Gramsci, *Further Selections from the Prison Notebooks*, p. 157. For an account of Gramsci as a means to understand colonial rule, which takes a different line to my own, see Kiernan, 'Antonio Gramsci and the Other Continents' in *Imperialism and Its Contradictions*, pp. 171–90.

18. Guha, 'Dominance Without Hegemony', in Guha, *Selected Subaltern Studies*, p. 228, his emphasis.

19. Bhabha, 'Articulating the Archaic', *The Location of Culture*, p. 129.

20. 'The Commitment of Theory', ibid., p. 21.

21. Paget Henry and Paul Buhle, *C. L. R. James's Caribbean* (Durham: Duke University Press, 1992), p. 140.

22. Stephen Slemon, 'Reading for Resistance in the Post-Colonial Literatures' in Maes-Jelinek *et al.*, *A Shaping of Connections*, p. 103.

23. Bhabha, 'The Commitment to Theory', *Location of Culture*, pp. 20–1.

24. ibid., p. 31.

25. Slemon, 'Reading for Resistance in the Post-Colonial Literatures', p. 101.

26. Even when Western theory is not addressing non-Western problematics, there are often interesting overlaps of focus. For example, as suggested earlier, Kristeva's discussion of dual temporalities in 'Women's Time' bears comparison with Fanon's discussion of the ambivalent temporalities of the newly decolonized nation in *The Wretched of the Earth*.

27. Tiffin, 'Transformative Imageries' in Rutherford, *From Commonwealth to Post-Colonial*, p. 430.

28. W. D. Ashcroft, 'Constitutive Graphonomy: A Post-Colonial Theory of Literary Writing' in Slemon and Tiffin, *After Europe*, pp. 61–4 especially.

29. Huggan, 'Opting Out of the (Critical) Common Market' in Slemon and Tiffin, *After Europe*, p. 38.

30. Derrida, *Of Grammatology*, p. 79; Jacques Derrida, *Margins of Philosophy* trans. Alan Bass (1972; Brighton: Harvester Press, 1982), p. 213.

31. Walsh, *Commonwealth Literature*, p. v; Jeffares, 'Commonwealth Literature in the Modern World', in Maes-Jelinek, *Commonwealth Literature and the Modern World*, pp. 12–13.

32. Said was, of course, for a while on the hit list of Meir Kahane's crypto-fascist Jewish Defence League and subject to disgraceful attacks made by sympathizers of Israel such as Edward Alexander in 'Professor of Terror', *Commentary*, 88.2, August 1989.

33. Jean Franco, 'Beyond Ethnocentrism: Gender, Power and the Third World Intelligentsia' (1988), reprinted in Williams and Chrisman, *Colonial Discourse and Post-Colonial Theory*, p. 359. Compare H. L. Gates jr.'s argument that theory is not the prerogative of the West in *The Signifying Monkey: A Theory of African-American Literary Criticism* (New York: Oxford University Press, 1988), pp. 78–9. In related fashion, a deconstructive approach may prevent the hostility to theory from reinscribing 'lived experience' or 'point of origin' as an intrinsically adequate, or even the sole legitimate,

basis on which to address postcolonial concerns. This all too often leads to the kind of essentialism which asumes that, for example, *only* a postcolonial subject can, or may, engage in postcolonial analysis.

34. Bhabha, 'The Commitment to Theory', *Location of Culture*, p. 19; compare Spivak, 'Limits and Openings of Marx in Derrida', *Outside in the Teaching Machine*, p. 98.

35. E. K. Brathwaite, *History of the Voice: The Development of Nation Language in Anglophone Caribbean Poetry* (London: New Beacon Books, 1984), p. 13; E. K. Brathwaite, *The Development of Creole Society in Jamaica 1770–1820* (Oxford: Clarendon, 1971), p. 237.

36. JanMohamed and Lloyd, *Nature and Context of Minority Discourse*, p. 12.

37. Said, 'Traveling Theory', *The World, the Text and the Critic*, p. 242.

38. On these points, see Spivak, 'The Politics of Interpretations' and 'Subaltern Studies', *In Other Worlds*, pp. 132 and 201, and 'Strategy, Identity, Writing', *Post-Colonial Critic*, pp. 44–5. Spivak's position can be contradictory; at times she argued that theory and practice must be kept apart; at others than both theory and practice are homologous even equivalent aspects of the same 'social text'. See 'Can the Subaltern Speak?' for versions of both positions.

39. Spivak, 'The Problem of Cultural Self-Representation', *The Post-Colonial Critic*, p. 56.

40. Spivak, 'Feminism and Deconstruction, Again', *Outside in the Teaching Machine*, p. 127.

41. MacKenzie, *Orientalism*, pp. 38–9.

42. Harris comments that: 'We live in a world where we fasten on the word clarity, where everything has to be clear. . . . In our blindness we mistake our clarity for sight, and we have to judge that clarity as partial.' See Harris, 'Judgement and Dream', in Riach and Williams, *The Radical Imagination*, p. 20.

43. Ian Saunders, 'On the Alien: Interpretation After Deconstruction' in Freadman and Miller, *On Literary Theory and Philosophy*, p. 43. Young mounts a defence of Bhabha in comparable terms: see *White Mythologies*, pp. 155–6, and *Colonial Desire*, p. 162. Parry, while hostile to the 'exorbitation of discourse' in Bhabha and Spivak recognizes that there is a price to be paid for using the 'ideologically coded' conventions of the dominant. See 'Problems in Current Theories of Colonial Discourse', p. 33.

44. Spivak, 'Subaltern Studies', *In Other Worlds*, pp. 215ff.

45. See, for example, the essays by Boehmer, Mann and Savory on postcolonial fiction in Michael Parker and Roger Starkey eds., *Postcolonial Literatures: Achebe, Ngugi, Desai, Walcott* (London: Macmillan, 1995).

46. Gates, *Black Literature and Literary Theory*, p. 16.

47. Tiffin, 'Commonwealth Literature' in Riemenschneider, *History and Historiography of Commonwealth Literature*, p. 19.

48. Helen Tiffin, 'Heartland, Heart of Darkness, and Post-Colonial Counter-Discourse' in Hena Maes-Jelinek ed., *Wilson Harris: The Uncompromising Imagination* (Mundelstrup: Dangaroo, 1991), p. 128. Mark McWatt makes similar claims for Wilson Harris in 'The Comic Vision in *Black Marsden*' in Maes-Jelinek, *Wilson Harris*, pp. 156–7. Compare Biodun Jefiyo in respect of Derek Walcott; see 'On Eurocentric Critical Theory' in Slemon and Tiffin, *After Europe*, p. 118. Compare the argument that in the critical field more specifically, C. L. R. James anticipated many of the procedures of deconstruction 'without resort to those of semio-linguistics'. See Paget Henry and Paul Buhle, 'Caliban as Deconstructionist: C. L. R. James and Post-Colonial Discourse' in Henry and Buhle, *C. L. R. James's Caribbean*, p. 136.

49. Parry, 'Signs of Our Times', pp. 13–15, and 'Problems in Current Theories of Colonial Discourse', p. 27; on the latter point, compare Gareth Griffiths, 'Post-colonial

Space and Time: Wilson Harris and Caribbean Criticism' in Maes-Jelinek, *Wilson Harris*, p. 69.

50. Dirlik, 'Postcolonial Aura', p. 352.

51. Harris, 'Reflection and Vision' in Maes-Jelinek, *Commonwealth Literature and the Modern World*, p. 19.

52. Chinua Achebe, 'Africa and her Writers', *Morning Yet on Creation Day* (London: Heinemann, 1975), p. 24.

53. Chinweizu, *The West and the Rest of Us: White Predators, Black Slavers and the African Elite* (New York: Vintage, 1975), p. 309.

54. Ngugi wa Thiongo, 'Literature and Society', *Writers in Politics: Essays* (London: Heinemann, 1981), p. 15.

55. Chinua Achebe, 'An Image of Africa: Racism in Conrad's *Heart of Darkness*', *Hopes and Impediments: Selected Essays* (New York: Doubleday, 1989), pp. 11–12.

56. ibid., p. 8.

57. ibid., p. 9.

58. ibid., p. 16.

59. ibid., p. 3.

60. ibid. pp. 2–3.

61. Ashcroft *et al.*, *The Empire Writes Back*, p. 11.

62. Achebe, 'Africa and her Writers', *Morning Yet on Creation Day*, p. 21; compare Soyinka, 'Ideology and the Social Vision', *Myth, Literature and the African World*, p. 62.

63. Chinweizu, Onuchekwa Jemie and Inechukwu Madubuike, *Towards the Decolonisation of African Literature: African Fiction and Poetry and Their Critics* (1980; London: KPI, 1985), p. 6.

64. Soyinka, 'The Critic and Society', in Gates, *Black Literature and Literary Theory*, p. 44.

65. ibid., p. 34.

66. Achebe, 'Colonialist Criticism', *Morning Yet on Creation Day*, pp. 17–18.

67. Walsh, *Commonwealth Literature*, p. 7; compare the comments on Katherine Prichard on p. 123.

68. Achebe, 'Africa and her Writers', *Morning Yet on Creation Day*, p. 19.

69. G. D. Killam, 'Something a Colonial Can Manage' in Maes-Jelinek *et al.*, *A Shaping of Conections*, p. 14.

70. Chinweizu, *The West and the Rest of Us*, p. 314.

71. Ngugi wa Thiongo, 'On the Abolition of the English Deartment', *Homecoming: Essays on African and Caribbean Literature, Culture and Politics* (London: Heinemann, 1972), p. 146. Compare the struggle for curricular reform in Uganda led by Okot p'Bitek (a former colleague of Ngugi's in Nairobi), an account of which is given by Bernth Lindfors in 'Okot's Last Blast: An Attempt at Curricular Reform after Idi Amin' in Maes-Jelinek *et al.*, *A Shaping of Connections*, pp. 164–70.

72. Such evidence is too conveniently forgotten by Ahmad in his enthusiasm for Marxism as the solution to the ills of the non-Western world. Fanon's quarrel with Sartre is replayed in Bhabha's polemics against Jameson in 'Conclusion', *The Location of Culture*.

73. Fanon, *Black Skin, White Masks*, p. 137.

74. Soyinka, Preface to *Myth, Literature and the African World*, p. xii.

75. Soyinka, 'The Critic and Society' in Gates, *Black Literature and Literary Theory*, p. 35.

76. Fanon, *Black Skin, White Masks*, pp. 133–8; *The Wretched of the Earth*, pp. 179ff.

77. Achebe, 'The Novelist as Teacher' in Press, *Commonwealth Literature*, p. 204.

78. Wilson Harris, 'Interior of the Novel: Amerindian/European/African Relations' in Goodwin, *National Identity*, p. 145.

79. Derek Walcott, 'What the Twilight Says: An Overture' (1970) in *Dream on Monkey Mountain and Other Plays* (London: Cape, 1972), p. 7.

80. ibid., p. 31.

81. Huggan, 'Opting Out of the (Critical) Common Market' in Slemon and Tiffin, *After Europe*, pp. 29ff.

82. Slemon, 'Reading for Resistance in the Post-Colonial Literatures' in Maes-Jelinek et al., *A Shaping of Connections*, pp. 111–12.

83. Benita Parry, 'Resistance Theory/Theorising Resistance, or Two Cheers for Nativism' in Francis Barker, Peter Hulme and Margaret Iverson eds., *Colonial Discourse/ Postcolonial Theory* (Manchester: Manchester University Press, 1994), p. 194; Walcott, 'What the Twilight Says', in *Dream on Monkey Mountain*, p. 5.

84. Harris, *Tradition, the Writer and Society*, p. 67; compare E. K. Brathwaite, *Contradictory Omens: Cultural Diversity and Integration in the Caribbean* (Mona, Jamaica: Savacou, 1974), p. 6.

85. Brathwaite, *History of the Voice*, p. 16 (my emphasis).

86. Harris, 'Judgement and Dream', in Riach and Williams, *The Radical Imagination*, p. 23. According to Paul Gilroy, comparable models of ambivalence were also being elaborated by African-American thinkers in the 1940s and 1950s. See Paul Gilroy, *The Black Atlantic: Modernity and Double Consciousness* (London: Verso, 1993), pp. 157–63 and 170–80, especially. Harris wrote an essay on one of these figures, Ralph Ellison, in Wilson Harris, *The Womb of Space: The Cross-Cultural Imagination* (London: Greenwood Press, 1983), pp. 27–38. Fanon's *Black Skin, White Masks*, of course, cites a passage from Richard Wright's *Native Son* on p. 139. By comparison, Soyinka is much more sceptical about the productivity of ambivalence. See 'The External Encounter: Ambivalence in African Arts and Literature' in *Art, Dialogue and Outrage* (Cambridge: Cambridge University Press, 1988), pp. 221–46. On this, too, he is in agreement with the Chinweizu 'troika', though he was no doubt much disobliged to find himself identified as one of the 'ambivalents' whom they condemn. See *The West and the Rest of Us* p. 314. The text also contains a chapter entitled 'Schizophrenia in the Arts'.

87. Brathwaite, *Contradictory Omens*, p. 16.

88. Brathwaite, *Development of Creole Society in Jamaica*, p. 310; compare *Contradictory Omens*, p. 25.

89. Wilson Harris, *The Infinite Rehearsal* (London: Faber, 1987), pp. 12 and 50.

90. Walcott, *Dream on Monkey Mountain*, p. 9.

91. ibid., pp. 19 and 27.

92. Brathwaite, *Development of Creole Society in Jamaica*, p. 311.

93. Harris, *The Womb of Space*, p. xv.

94. Alan Riach and Mark Williams, 'Introduction' to Riach and Williams, *The Radical Imagination*, p. 15.

95. Harris, 'Judgement and Dream', in ibid., p. 26.

96. Quoted in Stephen Slemon, 'Wilson Harris and the "Subect" of Realism' in Maes-Jelinek, *Wilson Harris*, p. 81.

97. Brathwaite, *Development of Creole Society in Jamaica*, pp. 304–5.

98. Harris, *Tradition, the Writer and Society*, p. 62.

99. Harris, 'Judgement and Dream', in Riach and Williams, *The Radical Imagination*, p. 20.

CONCLUSION POSTCOLONIAL FUTURES:
THINGS FALL APART?

1. Said, *Orientalism*, p. 327.

2. Young, *Colonial Desire*, p. 164.

3. Stuart Hall 'When Was the "Post-Colonial"?' in Chambers and Curti, *The Postcolonial Question*, p. 258; exhaustion with, if not within, the field is also marked in Ronald Warwick's review of *The Spivak Reader*, 'Inarticulating the Inarticulate', *The Times Higher*, 12 July 1996, p. 21.

4. This is to be found in Chambers and Curti, *The Post-Colonial Question*, pp. 199–211.

5. Killam, 'Something a Colonial Can Manage', in Maes-Jelinek *et al.*, *A Shaping of Connections*, p. 17.

6. See the controversy between Gates and Joyce A. Joyce in *New Literary History*, 18.2, Winter 1987, for example.

7. Ahmad, '*Orientalism* and After', *In Theory*, p. 195.

8. 'Salman Rushdie's Shame', ibid., p. 142.

9. 'Introduction', ibid., p. 12.

10. Wicke and Sprinker, 'Interview with Edward Said', in Sprinker, *Edward Said*, p. 242.

11. Nubar Hovsepian, 'Connections with Palestine', in Sprinker, *Edward Said*, p. 11.

12. Benita Parry, 'Overlapping Territories and Intertwined Histories', in Sprinker, *Edward Said*, p. 30.

13. Bhabha, 'Conclusion', *Location of Culture*, p. 245; on the former point, compare Lacan, *Four Fundamental Concepts of Psycho-Analysis*, pp. 18 and 104–5.

14. Spivak, 'In a Word', *Outside in the Teaching Machine*, pp. 18–19; Spivak, 'Bonding in Difference', *The Spivak Reader*, p. 25.

15. Said, 'Challenging Orthodoxy and Authority', *Culture and Imperialism*, p. 386.

16. ibid., *passim*, especially, in this respect, p. 258; compare Fanon, *The Wretched of the Earth*, pp. 165 and 251ff.

17. 'Interview with Wilson Harris', in Riach and Williams, *The Radical Imagination*, pp. 40–1.

18. Parry, 'Overlapping Territories and Intertwined Histories', in Sprinker, *Edward Said*, p. 30; compare Young, *White Mythologies*, pp. 131–32.

19. See Brathwaite, *History of the Voice*, pp. 13 and 25ff.

20. Bev Brown, 'Mansong and Matrix: A Radical Experiment' in Kirsten Holst Petersen and Anna Rutherford, *A Double Colonization: Colonial and Post-Colonial Women's Writing* (Mundelstrup: Dangaroo, 1986), p. 68.

21. Said, 'Figures, Configurations, Transfigurations' in Rutherford, *From Commonwealth to Post-Colonial*, pp. 11–13.

22. Hanif Kureishi, *The Black Album* (London: Faber, 1995), p. 111; for a similar vision of the contemporary non-Western city, see Geok-Lin Lim, 'Social Protest and the Success Motif' in Rutherford, *From Commonwealth to Post-Colonial*, pp. 292–9.

23. H. L. Gates jr., 'Authority, (White Power), and the (Black) Critic: It's All Greek to Me' in JanMohamed and Lloyd, *Nature and Context of Minority Discourse*, p. 89.

24. Kureishi, *The Black Album*, p. 162.

25. Derrida, *Of Grammatology*, p. 302.

26. Kureishi *The Black Album*, p. 145.

27. For moments where Gates's claims are pushed too far, see *Black Literature and Literary Theory*, pp. 285 and 313; and *The Signifying Monkey*, p. 79.

28. Terry Eagleton, 'Nationalism: Irony and Commitment' in Eagleton *et al.*, *Nationalism, Colonialism, and Literature*, pp. 23–4; compare Fanon on the three (each equally necessary) stages of the decolonizing struggle in *The Wretched of the Earth*, pp. 175ff; and Brathwaite, *Contradictory Omens*, p. 61. Compare Gilroy, *The Black Atlantic*, on the associated strategy of 'the war of position' (pp. 27–31).

29. Eagleton, 'Nationalism, Irony and Commitment', p. 24.

30. See Benita Parry, 'Resistance Theory/Theorising Resistance, or Two Cheers for

Nativism' in Barker *et al. Colonial Discourse/Postcolonial Theory*, pp. 172–96; compare Neil Lazarus, 'National Consciousness and the Specificity of (Post)colonial Intellectualism', in Barker *et al., Colonial Discourse/Postcolonial Theory*, pp. 197–220.

31. Ernesto Laclau and Chantal Mouffe, *Hegemony and Socialist Strategy: Towards a Radical Democratic Politics* trans. W. Moore and P. Cammack (London: Verso, 1985), p. 182.

32. Lowe, *Critical Terrains*, p. 196.

33. Laura Donaldson 'The Miranda Complex: Colonialism and the Question of Feminist Reading', *Diacritics*, 18.3 (1988), pp. 65–77.

34. Donna Haraway, *Simians, Cyborgs and Women: The Reinvention of Nature* (London: Free Association, 1991), pp. 109–24. On the relations between feminism and colonial history, see Vron Ware, *Beyond the Pale: White Women, Racism and History* (London: Verso, 1992), and Anne McClintock, *Imperial Leather: Race, Gender and Sexuality in the Colonial Contest* (London: Routledge, 1995).

35. On the relationship between early feminism and the abolition movement, see Moira Ferguson, *Subject to Others: British Women Writers and Colonial Slavery, 1670–1834* (London: Routledge, 1992).

36. Bronwen Levy 'Women Experiment Down Under: Reading the Difference' in Petersen and Rutherford, *A Double Colonization: Colonial and Post-Colonial Women's Writing*, p. 176.

37. Ranajit Guha, 'On Some Aspects of the Historiography of Colonial India', in Guha and Spivak, *Selected Subaltern Studies*, p. 43.

Index